'This new edition not only updates a series of important contexts through which HRM must operate – but places creativity and innovation, change and corporate governance centre stage. It is a book for our times, but also one that capitalizes on history. Replete with case studies and informed by the latest research, it makes an excellent teaching resource be the audience researchers or practitioners.'

Paul Sparrow, Professor of International HRM, Lancaster University Management School, UK

'This book represents a welcome contribution at the intersection between the human resource management and change management literatures, and will be required reading for students, academics and practitioners working in and studying these fields. This new edition presents an unprecedented collection of contemporary challenges that organizations are facing on an international scale, combined with clear chapter structures, captivating cases, and useful exercises for educators.'

Dr Elaine Farndale, Associate Professor of Human Resource Management, The Pennsylvania State University, USA

'This book integrates the fields of organizational learning and human resources with considerable conceptual clarity and practical insight. Tackling issues of contemporary concern including engagement, creativity and responsibility the work is consistently balanced and thoughtful. As a concise and authoritative guide to managing people in a context of organizational change this book is unparalleled.'

Professor Thomas Clarke, Centre for Corporate Governance, UTS Business School, Australia

'This book provides an intellectually stimulating overview of people management in changing contexts. Too often, human resource management is treated as a static process with little consideration of the dynamic context in which it is operating. Focusing on a number of different aspects of contextual change, this book is a must read for students, academics and professionals who want to learn more about the evolution of people management.'

Emma Parry, Professor of Human Resource Management, Cranfield School of Management, UK

'This new edition not only digs more deeply into how to manage people more effectively in changing contexts, but also broadens its scope to consider other key issues in human resource management such as: corporate governance, CSR, creativity and innovation, in highly relevant theoretical and practical terms. I hope that readers will get as much out of this book as I have.'

Dr Hong Zhang, Independent Consultant and Visiting Professor, Nanchang University, China

D0321979

'This new edition provides a wealth of theories, concepts, frameworks and cases for managing people in different contexts across the globe. It is highly accessible and well presented, and I highly recommend it to MBA students and practitioners.'

Dr Julie Hodges, Director MBA Programmes,
Durham University Business School, UK

'The second edition of this key text retains the sound structure of its predecessor and develops the themes and issues within a thorough updating to encompass the latest research and scholarship. Comprehensive coverage of the subject matter is complemented by interactive exercises, practical examples and case studies in every chapter that enable the reader to consolidate their learning and understanding. Recognizing that the management of people involves a complex interaction of content, process and context, this book provides a balanced approach that will be valued by students, practitioners and researchers.'

Martin Dowling, Director of Teaching and Operations,
School of Management, St Andrews University, UK

Managing People and Organizations in Changing Contexts

Managing People and Organizations in Changing Contexts, Second Edition, addresses the contemporary problems faced by managers in dealing with people, organizations and change in a theoretically informed and practical way. This textbook approaches people management from the perspective of practising and aspiring managers, making it a valuable alternative to existing texts on organizational behaviour and human resource management.

This new edition considers new emerging organizational forms such as e-lancing and recent management concerns such as employee engagement, de-professionalization and the growing challenges of social media. Built around a chapter framework that connects different themes to managerial action and practices, this textbook covers a wide range of topics including:

- managing at the individual, group and organizational levels
- change management
- managing creativity and innovation, and
- corporate governance and corporate social responsibility.

There is an increased international flavour, reflected in the range of contemporary case studies and literature used throughout, which explore business and management problems in the private and public sectors.

This text will be relevant to practising and aspiring managers studying people management, organizational behaviour and change management.

Graeme Martin is Professor and Head of Management and Marketing in the School of Social Sciences, the University of Dundee, UK. He has published widely in management, HRM and organization studies, including six books, numerous refereed journal articles and book chapters, as well as having management and consulting experience internationally.

Sabina Siebert is Professor of Management in the Adam Smith Business School, University of Glasgow, UK. Her research interests include organizational trust, sociology of the professions and management in the creative industries. She is currently the Editor-in-Chief of the *European Management Journal*.

Managing People and Organizations in Changing Contexts

Second edition

Graeme Martin and Sabina Siebert

Routledge
Taylor & Francis Group

LONDON AND NEW YORK

First published 2006
by Elsevier Ltd

This edition published 2016
by Routledge
2 Park Square, Milton Park, Abingdon, Oxon OX14 4RN

and by Routledge
711 Third Avenue, New York, NY 10017

Routledge is an imprint of the Taylor & Francis Group, an informa business

© 2006 Graeme Martin

© 2016 Graeme Martin and Sabina Siebert

The right of Graeme Martin and Sabina Siebert to be identified as authors of this work has been asserted in accordance with sections 77 and 78 of the Copyright, Designs and Patents Act 1988.

All rights reserved. No part of this book may be reprinted or reproduced or utilised in any form or by any electronic, mechanical, or other means, now known or hereafter invented, including photocopying and recording, or in any information storage or retrieval system, without permission in writing from the publishers.

Every effort has been made to contact copyright holders for their permission to reprint material in this book. The publishers would be grateful to hear from any copyright holder who is not here acknowledged and will undertake to rectify any errors or omissions in future editions of this book.

Trademark notice: Product or corporate names may be trademarks or registered trademarks, and are used only for identification and explanation without intent to infringe.

British Library Cataloguing in Publication Data
A catalogue record for this book is available from the British Library

Library of Congress Cataloging-in-Publication Data
Martin, Graeme
    Managing people and organizations in changing contexts/Graeme Martin
    and Sabina Siebert. – Second Edition.
        pages cm
    Revised edition of Managing people and organizations in changing contexts, 2006.
    Includes bibliographical references and index.
    1. Personnel management. 2. Organizational change. 3. Management.
    I. Siebert, Sabina. II. Title.
    HF5549.M3266 2015
    658.3 – dc23
    2015031143

ISBN: 978-1-138-78665-3 (hbk)
ISBN: 978-1-138-78666-0 (pbk)
ISBN: 978-1-315-76717-8 (ebk)

Typeset in Berling and Futura
by Florence Production Ltd, Stoodleigh, Devon, UK

658.4
269755
S.19

Nottingham College
Library

From Graeme
For Rhiannon, Alayna, Roz, Chris,
Sarah and Shona

From Sabina
To Konrad and Gustav

Contents

Figures

Tables

Preface to second edition

Those readers familiar with the first edition will notice that there are now two authors rather than one, which has had the effect of bringing in new ideas and refreshing older ones to make the book more relevant to the world of practising managers and those of you who hope to embark on a managerial career. The two of us have worked together extensively over the last five years on joint projects, including research into organizational trust, corporate reputations and the banking crisis. We have also worked separately: Graeme has done research into healthcare management, employee engagement and social media, and Sabina's research focused on management of the professions and employment in the creative industries. The net effect of this work has been to create this new edition that is research-led and takes a more critical approach to current management theory and practice. The co-authorship has also produced a text that is less UK-centric, although we cannot deny our roots in British university business schools.

This second edition retains its use of case studies in all chapters. We have sought to bring in new cases and examples where appropriate, especially where the changing contexts of organizations have brought fresh problems and new ideas, for example, new forms of organizing and working, such as Uber and e-lancing, how social media have impacted on people management, and in the development of theories of employee engagement and talent management. However, we have also retained and updated some of the cases from the first edition rather than always seek to bring in new cases of so-called best practice. First, we wanted to keep what has worked in the classroom. Second, it was instructive for us to revisit some older cases to find out what has happened to the firms and/or managers over the last ten years. For us, this longitudinal approach to cases is much more revealing than using snapshots of organizational 'excellence' that have often proved to be temporary. This is why we eschew the notion of 'best practice', and frequently resort to historical commentary and illustrations in various chapters.

We hope we have strengthened two of the core concepts guiding the choice of material in the changing contexts and internationalization. However, some topics have deliberately been left out. For example, we have chosen to avoid contributing to the 'leadership industry', which has come to dominate Anglo-American management texts and business books. Firstly, leadership is well covered in an increasing number of texts, and secondly we are not convinced of the often-made distinction between management and leadership – managers have to lead, have to create a sense of purpose and have to manage change as well as stability.

Finally, we hope to have retained the practical import of the book for readers who are managers and those who hope to practise management. We make no apologies, however, for its theoretical, critical and, sometimes, historical approach, since the old aphorisms that there is 'nothing so practical as good theory' and 'you can't have a present and a future without understanding the past' work for us.

Acknowledgements

The authors and publishers would like to acknowledge the following reproduced and adapted material:

Figure 2.2 adapted from Mintzberg. Figure 3.1 based on Turnley and Feldman, 1998. Figure 3.2 based on CIPD, 2003; Guest and Conway, 2002; and Martin *et al.*, 1998. Figure 3.3 adapted from Lepak and Snell, 2002. Figure 3.4 adapted from Collings and Mellahi, 2009. Table 3.3 based on Thompson and Bunderson, 2003; Conway and Briner, 2005; and Rousseau, 1995. Table 3.4 adapted from Handfield-Jones *et al.*, 2001. Table 3.5 adapted from Finegold and Mohrman, 2001; and Sparrow and Cooper, 2003. Table 3.6 adapted from Pierce *et al.*, 2001; and Avey *et al.*, 2009. Table 3.7 OECD.SatExtracts Table 3.8 Ray and Schmitt, 2007. Figure 4.1 adapted from Galbraith, 2002. Figure 4.2 adapted from Galbraith, 2002. Figure 4.8 based on Child, 2015; Goold and Campbell, 2002; Fjeldstad *et al.*, 2012; and authors' own research. Table 4.3 adapted from Miles and Snow, 2003. Table 4.4 based on Aldrich, 2008; Child, 2015; Miles *et al.*, 2010; Goold and Campbell, 2002; Malone, 2004; and Roberts, 2004. Table 4.5 based on Child, 2015; Goold and Campbell, 2002; Fjeldstad *et al.*, 2012; and authors' own research. Figure 5.1 adapted from Schein, 1985. Figure 5.2 based on Schneider and Barsoux, 2003. Figure 5.4 adapted from Gooderham and Nordhaug, 2003. Table 5.3 adapted from Schneider *et al.*, 2014. Table 5.4 adapted from Schneider *et al.*, 2014. Table 5.5 based on Burgoyne *et al.*, 2004; Lawrence, 2000, 2002; and Thomson *et al.*, 2001. Figure 6.1 adapted from Balmer and Greyser, 2003. Figure 6.2 adapted from Kaplan and Norton, 2001. Figure 6.3 based on Davies *et al.*, 2003. Figure 6.4 adapted from Hatch and Schultz, 2001. Figure 6.5 adapted from Fombrun and Van Riel, 2003. Figure 6.6 adapted from Fombrun and Van Riel, 2003. Table 6.1 Reputation Institute (2015) Global Reptrak Study. Table 6.2 adapted from Balmer and Greyser, 2003. Table 6.3 Reputation Institute. Figure 7.1 based on Choo and Bontis, 2002. Figure 7.2 based on Zahra and George, 2003; and Martin *et al.*, 2003. Figure 7.4 based on Leonard and Sensiper, 2002. Figure 7.5 based on Nonaka and Takeuchi, 1995. Figure 7.6 based on Blackler, 2002. Figure 7.8 adapted from Bontis, 2001. Table 7.1 based on Nonaka and Takeuchi, 1995. Table 7.2 adapted from CIMA/Cranfield, 2004 and Marr, 2008. Figure 10.3 based on Martin and Beaumont, 2001. Figure 9.4 based on Goffee and Jones, 1998. Chapter 9 Case Study: Linklaters – Arts Council England. Figure 10.2 adapted from Hatch, 1997. Figure 10.3 based on Martin and Beaumont, 2001. Figure 10.4 based on Goffee and Jones, 1998. Table 10.1 Pettigrew, 1990; Schoenberger, 1997; Goffee and Jones, 2006; Hatch, 1997, Kotter and Schlesinger, 2008; and McCalman, Paton and Siebert, 2015. Figure 11.1 based on Aguinis and Glavas, 2012.

Chapter 1

An introduction to managing people in changing contexts

LEARNING OBJECTIVES

By the end of this chapter you should be able to:

- describe and critically evaluate some of the key ideas underlying the management of people in changing contexts;

- apply the notions of universalism and relativism to the key ideas and practice of modern management, especially to our understanding of 'best practice';

- understand the importance of frames of reference and mindsets in management and how these influence managerial practice;

- understand how ideas about management change, and how the institutional environment and the influence of management thinkers can cause changes in our understanding of good practice in management;

- critically evaluate the role of management thinkers in producing useful knowledge for managers.

UNDERSTANDING MANAGEMENT

Introduction

According to Peter Drucker (1909–2005), who was one of the most prominent and most quoted business gurus of recent times, management is a timeless, human discipline. It has been used to build the Great Wall of China, to run empires and armies throughout history and to guide the development of the joint stock company, which has been the key institution in the development of modern capitalism. During the later part of the twentieth century and the early part of the twenty-first century, management became one of the fastest growing occupations, because managers are usually (but not always) seen to be essential to organizational success (Bloom *et al.*, 2005). Moreover, whether we work in the private, public or voluntary sectors of the economy, managers and their work touch virtually every aspect of our economic, social and, increasingly, political lives. Those of you who aren't yet a manager but aspire to become one most likely will have had direct experience of being managed by others. Sometimes this experience will have been positive, helping you achieve excellent results, and sometimes it will have been negative, perhaps causing you to underperform, experience undue levels of stress, lack of esteem or lack of job satisfaction. Those of you who are experienced managers will also understand that the people you manage don't always respond in the ways in which you expect or want them to react to your ideas, actions and/or evaluations of them. So all of us need to be *critically reflexive* of our managerial potential, capabilities and the roles we play in organizations, industries and societies. By critical reflexivity, we mean a constant need to query the relationships among ourselves as managers and those people we manage: how we construct the world, our assumptions and our impact on individuals, organizations and society (Cunliffe, 2014). For many managers, however, who are naturally oriented to action rather than reflection, this is an extremely difficult task (King and Learmonth, 2015).

With these points in mind, our revised text is aimed at helping both aspiring and experienced managers explore and be critically reflexive of the *nature of management* and some of the key *processes of management*, specifically the key problems associated with *managing people and organizations*. To this end, our book has also been written from the perspective that the theory and practice of managing people and organizations are heavily influenced by the *context* in which ideas occur and how management is performed, and that these contexts often *change* considerably over time.

Key questions on management knowledge

When we embark on any management education program, it is important for us to understand the relationship between theory and practice, not least because we are usually taught theories we rightly expect to be able to put into action. However, the gap between theory and practice seems extensive, with managers typically seeking simple guides to practice and academics often reluctant to provide them. With more than 40 years of experience of teaching management students and executives between us in many different countries, this gap is sometimes questioned by course participants. We can articulate their questions as follows:

1   Is there a one-best-way or set of best practices in management? Or, to put this question in slightly more formal terms: (a) is there a single set of truths about management that represents its core body of knowledge and (b) if so, can this body of knowledge be applied in most, if not all, contexts?
2   Why is it that ideas about business and management seem to be a bit like the fashion industry, with new ideas and new jargon appearing almost every week?
3   Have managers, especially senior managers, become disconnected from organizations and societies they purport to serve and become literally self-serving?

Increasingly, we believe that these three questions should be raised when studying management, or when contemplating ideas from consultants, conferences or the increasing volume of business books found in airport bookstores and on the Internet. Such questions are particularly relevant because managers generally seek knowledge that helps them simplify the world they must confront, especially given the increasingly complex nature of the environment in which they work. To be told there is the possibility of a 'magic bullet' or 'one-best-way' is an attractive proposition, because it means they don't have to think too much about what they are doing. And, as Henry Mintzberg (2011), one of the most insightful commentators on management, has pointed out, managers are very much focused on 'doing' rather than reflecting on academic theories concocted by people who have very little experience of practising management. However, the prospect of a magic bullet, contained in the nostrums of a single management book or PowerPoint presentation, is not something that usually accords with their experience of just how complex their world is. This disconnect is especially true when nearly all new books, courses or consultants tell them there is a better way of doing things, which is usually *the* way advocated by the author, teacher or adviser. Managers usually get little more from new 'guru-speak' than a recycling of even older ideas, often originating in the early 1900s, but dressed up in new clothing or new 'spin'. A good example is the prescriptions of the 'happiness' industry and the focus on well-being at work, heavily promoted by governments and business (Davies, 2015), which stems from early (and, some say, poor) research in the 1930s on human relations (see Case 1.1 on the development of human relations at the end of this chapter). As a result, many managers and those on the receiving end of some of these practices become sceptical or even cynical about any new business program or form of management education. If such a process sounds familiar, then you are in tune with many of the critics of business education and the management consulting industry. For example, Khurana and Spender (2012) have forcefully argued that American business schools and their 'products' (typically students who follow careers in management consulting) have fashioned an intellectual inertia in management education, which has promoted a disconnected managerialism that failed to serve practice and, more consequentially, was one of the principal causes of the Global Financial Crisis of 2007–8. Paradoxically, however, regardless of the extent to which the management education and consulting industries are challenged to explain their relevance by business leaders and politicians, their influence has become ever more widespread. The demand for management education is showing few signs of abating, fuelled by the growth of corporate universities which hire business school staff and by executives willing to self-fund their development (*The Economist*, 15 May 2015).

So in this chapter, and in the rest of the book, we shall address the three questions raised at the beginning of this section. We do so because it is in everyone's interests – teachers, students of management and examiners alike – to avoid the reputation for lack of relevance management knowledge enjoys with many practitioners (Rynes *et al.*, 2007) and for promoting a disconnected and self-serving managerialism. With respect to lack of relevance, this has largely come about because dominant sections of the producer community of management knowledge – the producers of business guru books and the management consulting industry – have oversold the idea of the one-best-way, in wave after wave of management fads (Pascale, 1999). Francis Wheen (2004), rather amusingly, has labelled much of this material, especially the self-help books by ex-business leaders, as 'old snake oil in new bottles', pointing to the often messianic salesmanship of banal aphorisms dressed up in jargon and pseudo-scientific phrases, such as 're-engineering, benchmarking and downsizing'. Moreover, since we live in an increasingly changeable and arguably unknowable world, what we can usefully teach about management often has a short 'shelf-life'.

If the guru industry has not helped the relevance cause, neither have some management academics who claim to pursue a practical agenda. Critical management scholars, a diverse group of academics who question the politics and values of managerialism (a set of ideas and practices that are tied to promoting the interests of managers), argue that many, ostensibly relevant, management academics and most consultants fail to engage in reflexive thinking over dominant business discourses (Cunliffe, 2014). Two examples of such discourses are shareholder value, the belief that businesses exist to create value for shareholders only, and transformational leadership, which places managers at the centre of change programs. Both are often expounded uncritically by those who benefit most from having such ideas accepted as truths – including, among others, highly paid leaders who benefit from share ownership, universities that benefit from running leadership courses and the business press that promotes and feeds off celebrity leaders (Clegg *et al.*, 2011).

It is not only critical management scholars, however, that question the relevance agenda. Even 'mainstream' management academics and some practicing managers are beginning to acknowledge the limitations of their craft and the problems of becoming disconnected from the organizations they are employed to serve. This was evident in a major soul-searching exercise run at Half-Moon Bay in California in May 2008 in the aftermath of the Global Financial Crisis, which brought together well-known academics and senior executives to redefine a more ethically based notion of leadership. Take a few minutes to think about the outcomes of this exercise.

TIME OUT Ethical leadership and management's grand challenges (based on Hamel, 2009)

Well-known management scholar and consultant, Gary Hamel, brought together a number of prominent business school academics in 2008, including Henry Mintzberg and Jeff Pfeffer, and business leaders to develop a list of challenges that leaders would have to address following the growing criticism of businesses during the period leading up to and after the GFC. These challenges included:

1 Ensuring that managers serve a higher purpose to achieve socially significant goals.
2 Embedding notions of community and citizenship in their values and practices.
3 Modernizing management's philosophical foundations and thinking to move beyond efficiency and focus on innovation.
4 Eliminating the focus on formal hierarchy as a solution to organization.
5 Reducing fear and building trust in management systems to create innovative cultures.
6 Recreating control systems to embed the notion of control from within rather than external control as being the most appropriate to innovation.
7 Redefining the current idea of leaders as heroic decision-makers to become architects and builders of systems.
8 Embracing diversity and pluralism as well as consensus.
9 Seeing strategy as emergent rather than planned and top-down.
10 Restructuring or de-constructing organizations into smaller, more flexible units.

11 Challenging the pull of the past and institutions that prevent change.
12 Distributing goal setting and leadership so that voice in the organization reflects insight, not power.

Questions

Reflect on your own organization or one with which you are familiar: to what extent does it mirror these ideas? Do you see evidence of organizations in general following these principles? If not, why is this so?

The above time-out exercise may have helped provide an answer to the third of our three questions raised in the early part of the chapter concerning the disconnection of senior managers from their organizations and society. While there are a small number of high-profile organizations pursuing socially responsible and sustainable agendas, such ideas are not part of mainstream thinking (Mayer, 2013).

To address the first two questions we raised in this chapter, however, we have to go back in time to examine two concepts in management that go straight to the heart of the rigour-relevance debate. These concepts are *universalism* and *change*.

MANAGEMENT AS A SET OF UNIVERSAL TRUTHS

Universalism and relativism in management

There have been many books aimed at helping managers understand and improve their management skills, not just in the area of people management but in other managerial functions such as managing information, budgets and finances, and operations. Many of these books take a *universalist* perspective on management.

KEY CONCEPT The universalist perspective on management

The proposition is that it is possible to discover a set of universal truths concerning principles, values and morals that can be equally applied in all business and management contexts. These truths can be established either by reasoning from first principles or by empirical observation. The fundamental points of this perspective are its universal application and its relative permanence, though most universalists acknowledge that the gradual accumulation of new knowledge can improve our thinking. Such a perspective is associated with attempts to establish a science of management, and to establish universal codes of ethics for business behaviour that transcend national boundaries (Crane and Matten, 2010).

Such a view dates back to before the end of the nineteenth century and is best exemplified by the works of Frederick Taylor in the USA, the so-called father of scientific management, and by the French businessman-theorist Henry Fayol. Both of these writers developed a set of principles of good management that have formed the basis for much management education (Clegg *et al.*, 2011), and their works are still discussed today in undergraduate and graduate classes in business and management all over the world. We shall return to their ideas later in this chapter.

Perhaps more controversially, the universalistic perspective contends that most of these management principles can apply regardless of national cultural and institutional context. Jack Welsh, the former CEO of General Electric, best exemplified this view when he once opined that what was good for his company was good for the rest of the world. Welsh's view reflected the dominance of the American management model, which has influenced thinking and practice in many countries. There are at least three possible explanations for such dominance. These are: (i) the influence of US multinationals on global economic development (Davis, 2009); (ii) the influence of management education programmes such as the MBA – an American invention in the late nineteenth century (Khurana and Spender, 2012); and (iii) the influence of the global, but mainly US, management consulting and management guru industries (Armbruster, 2006).

There is undoubtedly something in the claims of universalists, given the history of post-Second World War reconstruction and the reliance on US finance and ideas to rebuild the economies of Europe and Japan. The UK, Germany and Japan adopted many American ideas and accepted aid that, in turn, was dependent on their acceptance of American ways of managing (Locke and Spender, 2011). However, the adoption of American ideas did not, as some people claim, result in the 'Americanization' of business and management in these countries. For example, in the 1970s and 1980s, Japanese companies came to dominate world markets in industries that the USA had traditionally owned (Pascale and Athos, 1981) by using techniques of quality management and production management that have since become popular in many Western organizations. Similarly, German companies developed their own way of managing and running businesses, based on their historical veneration of engineering specialists and the adoption of 'co-determination' before and after 1945, a practice that gave employees a much greater say in the running of companies (much to the distaste of some US occupying generals and CEOs). Consequently, there were severe limitations placed on the forces for convergence on and around the American model of management. This limitation of universalist principles is one of the key themes of this book.

TIME OUT   **Think about this: the history of co-determination in Germany**

Historically, German business managers have had much less faith than the Americans or British in the powers of markets to regulate business and competition, and have placed greater store in the power of the national and state governments. Thus, co-determination in Germany has its origins in legislation passed in the early 1800s to give workers rights to social insurance and, later, in 1891, to rights to participate in management decision-making, involving joint consultation on social matters at work. Following the First World War, in 1918,

German employers, rather reluctantly, succumbed to pressure to give 'employees rights to co-determination with management in social policy and to be consulted in personnel and economic decisions' (Locke, 1996, p. 58). Subsequent legislation in 1920 allowed for the creation of works councils in firms employing more than 20 employees to act on social, personnel and economic matters. Hitler and the Nazis dissolved works councils when they came to power in the 1930s, but, following pressure from the Christian churches and trade unions after the Second World War, co-determination was re-established to give workers even greater rights to co-decisions in the running of firms on economic issues, including 'expansion, consolidations and shutdowns', and to joint consultation in the purchase and sale of equipment, changes in production methods, accounting procedures, etc.

The passing of such legislation was done when Germany was in the hands of occupying forces, most notably the Americans. This was surprising in some respects, because without US approval German discretion to pass legislation was severely limited. The American attitude to co-determination during the period varied between early acceptance – it wouldn't work in America, but was perhaps good for Germany – to outright opposition. However, what became the official American line was that German business would lose control of its affairs, and thus the essential and inalienable rights of stockholders would be violated. Such opposition by the US to German attempts to reintroduce co-determination was exemplified by the role played by General Lucius Clay, leader of the occupying US administration, who obstructed and vetoed the rights of individual German states (the *Länder*) to pass such legislation for as long as he was able. Though, over time, American opposition to the rights of the German government to establish co-determination diminished, the business press and major figures in the US business community continued to see such legislation as an attempt to establish socialism in capitalist industry. To the extent that these people had influence over American aid through the Marshall plan to German industry, German managers were perceived to be playing a dangerous game, but continued to do so nevertheless. In this important sense, US attempts to impose on Germany a US-style 'best practice' and a way of managing failed: 'German entrepreneurs rejected American managerialism' (Locke, 1996, p. 64).

Source: based on Locke, 1996.

We can see from this above example that the universalistic view on best practice in management has not always struck a chord with managers outside the USA, especially following events such as the Global Financial Crisis, which has had an acknowledged negative effect on the universal and enduring relevance of the American Business Model (Whitley, 2009). Moreover, the rise of the BRIC economies (Brazil, Russia, India and China) and other smaller ones during the first decade of the millennium have provided alternative models of growth. Similarly, many people working in the public or voluntary sectors of modern economies disagree that best practice developed in the private sector is superior or transferable to contexts that are not subject to the overarching goal of increasing the value of shareholders in the business. Consequently, we are witnessing a significant debate over the relevance of shareholder value as a dominant model of governing corporations in the Western developed economies and as a theory on which to base management principles (Mintzberg, 2015) and a more influential *relativist* view among management academics and practitioners (Whittington, 2000).

KEY CONCEPT Relativism in management

Relativism expresses the idea that it is not possible to establish a set of universal truths concerning principles, values and morals about management that will not at some later time be abandoned and replaced by another set of truths. Relativism in management is often associated with the idea that management practices and values cannot be abstracted from the context in which they were produced and easily transferred to other contexts. Extreme versions of relativism in management hold that there is no such thing as reality, certainty or 'social facts', and that all views about management are essentially value judgements. The principal aim of relativists in management is to give less-powerful people and groups a greater voice in public discourse about how they should be managed.

For example, the practice of management in France is sometimes quite different from the practice of management in the USA because of the relatively unique nature of the French business sector, its history, its national cultural characteristics and institutional (legal, social, educational and political) norms (Lawrence, 2002). Thus, managers brought up in the French business system literally see through different eyes and ears to American managers, and are sometimes not able to understand each other, even if they both use a version of American English. French business management is reputed to be hierarchical and individualist in nature, and was unable to accommodate the bottom-up, group decision-making of quality circles, one of the fashionable techniques adopted by many global companies in the 1980s. Another example of a relativist perspective that is influential in management is the so-called *constructivist approach to learning*, which we shall discuss more fully in a later chapter in this book (Petit and Huault, 2008). The constructivist approach to learning is often contrasted with a cognitive or 'schooled' learning approach, in which abstract principles are taught to students in a classroom, as is often the case in many management courses. Constructivists argue that we learn most effectively through active participation rather than as a passive recipient in which knowledge is 'poured' into our heads through instruction in a classroom. However, when we engage in active learning, all such knowledge becomes personal to us. So, for example, our knowledge and understanding of what were are writing will be different from yours as an individual reader of this text, and it will also be different from that of others who read the same text. But, since all knowledge is personal and subjective, and not something that is literally 'out there' and ready to be grabbed like an apple on a tree, it is mainly tacit (in people's heads and hands) and highly specific to the context in which it is produced. Seen in this way, management is best viewed as a craft learned in context rather than as an abstract science (Mintzberg, 2011). So, learning to become a manager is most effectively undertaken by serving a long, on-the-job 'apprenticeship', often as part of a 'community of practitioners' in a particular industry, such as healthcare (Spilg *et al.*, 2012), or company (Wenger *et al.*, 2002).

Our position on this debate between extreme versions of universalism and relativism is somewhere in between the two, often depending on the context of application. Clearly, ideas about management developed in one situation can take root in other contexts. For example, the popularity of the MBA as a global form of management education would be unsustainable if this were not possible. Moreover, the success of multinational companies rests, in part, on their ability to transfer learning in one part of the world to another, often in the form of model practices and values. However, the perspective taken in this book is more relativist in the sense that context and individual interpretation of ideas are seen as very important in influencing action. Perhaps this is best explained by an organic, gardening metaphor. According to John Seely Brown (2000), an eminent American academic, transferring so-called best practices from one context to another is like uprooting a tree from the fertile soil that gave it life and its particular form or shape and attempting to replant it into a different kind of soil, the properties of which are unknown or at least partially uncertain. It is unlikely that one can know with any certainty in advance the kind of tree, or anything resembling the original tree, that the soil and microclimate will produce. Thus, at best, the status of such best practices can be described as 'promising' (Leseure *et al.*, 2004), but they are burdened by being deeply embedded into historically, culturally and institutionally different contexts (Thornton *et al.*, 2012), as one of us has found in previous research into Sino-foreign joint ventures in China (Zhang and Martin, 2003). This transfer problem applies equally to industrial contexts, such as the transfer of private sector practices to the highly politicized public sectors of healthcare, education and local government.

To return to the first of our three questions, concerning the possibility of a one-best-way of doing things or set of best practices in management, our answer is a qualified yes and no. A 'yes' relates to the contention that there is a body of knowledge about management that we can legitimately teach and use in many different contexts, even though that body of knowledge has been developed for the most part in the USA and was founded on a private sector, market-driven, shareholder value model (Davis, 2009). 'No' is an answer because there are no 'magic bullets' nor a 'one-best-way'. Our knowledge and practices should enjoy the status of no more than 'promising', and we have to think deeply and sensitively when applying these in different contexts, whether these are national cultural, industrial or company settings.

STABILITY AND CHANGE IN MODELS OF MANAGEMENT

Key features of models of management

If context is an important theme in recent management literature, a second key theme concerns the nature of *change and stability* in models and theories of management and their acceptance by managers. Like many relatively immature bodies of knowledge, the study and practice of management is no exception to the influence of fashionable or faddish ideas, with change being a recurrent theme in the literature, and the new 'big' idea being promoted every few years.

However, as some writers have pointed out, the debates over what constitutes the best way to manage show a remarkable stability over time, especially with regard to the choices among available models and theories. These models are often said to resemble paradigms, a scientific word referring to the existence of particular kinds of worldview, which comprise a relatively coherent set of theories, metaphors and practices. Paradigms are also notable for being stable in a particular scientific community for many years until the next 'big idea' is developed around which a competing paradigm forms.

In business and management, the term 'paradigm' tends to be used a little more loosely (Clegg *et al.*, 2011), often describing a set of assumptions and values about how the organizational world works and how it should work. This is probably better described as a *frame of reference* (Fox, 1974), a notion that we have explored in some detail when examining trust in organizations (Siebert *et al.*, 2015). Most managers operate and adhere to particular frames of reference that reflect their own career interests and identities, even though they are unable to articulate the assumptions and theories underlying them.

There are at least three important points about frames of reference. First, they are simultaneously useful and limiting, since a way of seeing is also a way of not seeing. Second, seeing the world through particular frames of reference may lock us into our own 'psychic prison' (Morgan, 1997) and result in the self-perpetuation of tired and sometimes dysfunctional ideas. So, for example, Pierce and Aguinis (2013) have argued that managers are often guilty of implementing 'Too Much of a Good Thing', which results in an apparent paradox in organizational life that ordinarily beneficial leadership and management interventions, such as empowering people, delegation and communications, can actually cause harm to organizations when taken too far. Richard Pascale (1999) followed a similar line of reasoning when his research on business failure pointed to the conclusion that 'nothing fails like success'. Success, he argued, was based on becoming highly attuned to, and skilled in, managing and organizing in one set of competitive circumstances. However, if and when these circumstances change, we are often unable to change our mindsets rapidly enough to produce the appropriate responses. In effect, what were previously held as core capabilities became core rigidities, leading Jeff Pfeffer and Robert Sutton (2006) to claim that being locked into a frame of reference explained why otherwise 'smart managers did dumb things'. This lack of ability to see the world from different angles leads us to a third important point about frames of reference, which is that managers usually need to reflect critically on their assumptions, values and short-term interests to produce the kind of change that may be needed in creating sustainable organizations. Much of the criticism of companies since the Global Financial Crisis, especially in the financial services sector, has been directed at managers' unswerving assumptions of shareholder value as the guiding principle for running companies since the early 1980s (Martin *et al.*, 2012; Mayer, 2013), a critique we take up in Chapter 11.

These three points have given rise to what is probably one of *the* major debates in management theory over the last century between mechanistic forms of organization, characterized by 'top-down' modes of control, and organic forms of organization, characterized by 'bottom-up' modes of control, human relations principles and the attempts to engineer strong organizational cultures (Hoopes, 2003), issues to which we shall return in this book.

The mechanistic mindset

Many managers see their ideal organization as a well-oiled machine, in which everyone and everything is treated as a replaceable part. In such 'machines', predictability and control are the most important design features and are frequently accompanied by hierarchical organization structures. Not unnaturally, this view serves the interests of managers who advocate such a perspective, since the people who are most important in machine-like organizations are the designers and planners (i.e. the managers). Thus, managers who benefit from the machine view of organizations by running a 'smooth operation' tend to keep things that way. They do so by imposing their mindsets on others and by the kind of actions they take, such as recruiting, developing and promoting people with similar mindsets. Many years ago, Henry Mintzberg (1983) labelled these managers as the 'technostructure', a term still used to capture their rational design and planning mindsets and characteristics.

This machine view of organizations is not in and of itself a problem, since classical machine-like organizations, such as public sector bureaucracies and armies, usually work well in stable and predictable circumstances – for example, in state-run, planned economies or when fighting conventional warfare. However, if the circumstances change – for example, if economies suddenly become open to market circumstances, as happened in the former Soviet bloc and more recently in China, or if warfare becomes unconventional, as is the case with the current 'war against terror' being fought by drones and possibly robots in the future – machine-like organizations often lack the intelligent capacity to take action themselves to adapt to these changing environments. This inability to adapt is a direct consequence of the frames of reference and actions of machine-like minds, and of the vested interests of those who are in control. However, some organizations, such as those in the energy and extractive industries, often feel they have no other option than to be machine-like. This is because they operate in an 'unforgiving' social and political environment in which they are unable to learn because the financial and reputational costs of 'getting it wrong', even once, are extraordinarily high. Thus such organizations tend to centralize key management processes and exercise tight controls to ensure 'high reliability'. Good examples of organizations claiming to be high on reliability would be nuclear power plants, mining companies and drilling companies working in oil and gas extraction (Weick and Sutcliffe, 2007). However, this mechanistic mindset may not be enough to manage risk effectively, as evidenced by disasters such as the Deepwater Horizon oil spill in 2010, which led to wholesale changes in how BP operates.

Beyond the mechanistic mindset

This machine view of organizations dominated much managerial thinking and action until the 1970s, and continues to do so where risk management has had to be prioritized over innovation and creativity. However, with the changes that occurred during the last few decades of the last century, it became increasingly obvious that old ways of seeing had to give way to new paradigms, based on the notion of open systems and the need for organizations to take into account their external environments. Thus, we began to see a mindset developing among managers of organizations as adaptive systems, in which they had to take into account what happened outside the organization, e.g. changes in market structure and customer preferences, and be able to respond quickly and flexibly to these changes. Such a mindset or metaphor is often described as the *organic view*, reflecting the biological origins of open systems thinking and the relationship between living systems and their environments. This organic metaphor has dominated in current managerial thinking and practice, especially in the economies of the developed countries, in which uncertainty and, often fundamental, change are the key characteristics. These changes include the effects of disruptive technologies (Christensen and Raynor, 2003) that have essentially changed the rules of doing business in many industries, examples being the expansion of the Internet in retailing, social media in HRM (Martin *et al.*, 2015) and what Czarniawska (2011) calls 'cybernization' or the growing computerization and automation of news production. In the field of strategic management, the organic metaphor has become popular through the notion of dynamic capabilities (Teece, 2007). This theory is based on the idea that the sources of a firm's competitive advantage lie in its internal capabilities to:

(a) sense opportunities and threats in existing and developing markets and technologies;
(b) seize appropriate opportunities by making high-quality investment decisions in particular business models, product and service architectures;
(c) constantly reconfigure its assets and structures, including its human resources, organizational structures and culture, in response to market and technological changes.

Apple is one of the best examples of a company that has built its success on dynamic capabilities in developing the iPhone, iPad and Apple Watch.

In the energy and extractive industries, and others such as air traffic control and shipping, Weick and Sutcliffe (2007) have argued that traditional views of high reliability may not be good enough to prevent problems occurring such as major oil spills and airplane crashes. Instead, they suggest that the lessons learned from truly effective high reliability organizations are that they are pre-occupied with failure, seek complex rather than simple analysis and solutions, are continuously sensitive to all operations in the field, are resilient enough to deal with emergencies and open up their normally closed hierarchical structures of control to inputs from those 'in the know' by sharing leadership and responsibility throughout the organization. These processes can reduce the 'blindspots' that cause catastrophic failures.

The key problem of managing human resources from both a dynamic capabilities and a high reliability perspective lies in assisting managers to attend to the emotional and intuitive aspects of their work as well as the rational aspects. The solution in part involves creating supportive learning environments to avoid blindspots and help managers unlock their fixations by creating opportunities for safe reflection (Hodgkinson and Healey, 2011).

EXPLAINING CHANGING MINDSETS

The key questions

There are two key questions concerning the relationship between ideas and action that make it important for us to have some answers so that we can become more effective managers. The first question is: Why does a particular mindset, such as the mechanistic or the organic one discussed previously, come to dominate managers' thinking at particular points in time? Though you may think that much of what you read in management texts is new, most of the 'new' ideas have their origins in much earlier theories, and those of us who have been around for a long time often get a sense of 'old wine (or even old snake oil) in new bottles'. The second question arises from the first one and concerns the idea of progress in our thinking and practice. Much of what we read in management textbooks implies progress, involving a change from one mindset or model to another. This is particularly evident in the example of the mechanistic and organic mindsets, where we have come to believe that organizations (and their managers) that are 'fast, flexible and friendly' are inevitably superior to those of more traditionally mechanistic styles. Having an understanding of these questions is useful not merely to academics but also to practitioners because, as the famous British economist John Maynard Keynes once pointed out, everyone who claims to be practical is 'a slave of some usually defunct theory'. So, to provide answers to these questions on changing mindsets, we can briefly examine two sources of explanation. These explanations invoke changing models of national economic success and sources of institutional pressure to imitate new ideas and practice, such as 'guru' theory and international management consulting organizations that diffuse so-called best practice.

National economic success and business

As has already been pointed out, for most of the last century and certainly since the end of the First World War, models of business and management have been drawn from the success of the American economy and from the teachings of the US business gurus and business schools. American models of management, based on mass production, financial control and the M-form or multidivisional organizational structure, came to dominate (Goold and Campbell, 2002). As we have seen, their principles were exported overseas by the US government as a condition of aid for reconstruction, by US multinational companies and by the growing number of business schools, academic research and business gurus that began to influence European and Asian economies (Hoopes, 2003).

Interestingly, however, for a short period during the 1960s and 1970s, managers also began to look to Germany and Sweden for inspiration, following the economic success of these two countries during the same period. This was best exemplified by the interest shown in newer forms of work reorganization developed in companies such as Volvo and Saab, which adopted autonomous group working and job satisfaction as guiding principles to produce their automobiles. These ideas of autonomous group working and more democratic forms of decision-making were offered as a contrast to the more top-down models of low-skilled mass production associated with the US automobile industry.

The best example, however, of just how powerful national economic success is in explaining the acceptance of ideas about management is the case of Japan in the 1980s and 1990s. During that period, Japanese organizations came to dominate in industries that the USA had once 'owned', including automobiles, consumer electronics and business machines, such as electronic cash registers and photocopiers. They also became major players in other forms of manufacturing, including shipbuilding, heavy engineering, construction and financial services. This was often explained by the quality 'revolution' initiated in Japan by Edward Deming, a US civil servant and academic who was neglected by senior US business leaders but idealized by Japanese senior managers after his lengthy visit following the Second World War. Japan was also noticeable for exporting ideas in labour relations, group working and new forms of organization to the USA and Europe, most noticeably the 'lean production' system, during the 1980s and 1990s.

However, during the 1990s, America experienced eight years of unprecedented economic success under the Clinton administration, which, coupled with the relative decline of Japan and Germany during that same period, left the USA as the dominant world economic superpower. By the beginning of the current century the wheel had turned full circle, with the American model of business being the only one to show sustained success, apart from the developing economies such as China and India. As a consequence, there have been many attempts to attribute such exceptional US economic and industrial success to the American way of managing and to American values and institutions (Collins and Porras, 1994; Collins, 2001), which, in turn, has pressured countries such as Germany and Japan to accept US ideas, especially in respect of the virtues of flexible labour markets and freedom from government intervention. During this same period, the influence of US business gurus and the major US business schools has also been exceptional (Mintzberg, 2004), with the Master of Business Administration degree (MBA) becoming one of the world's major educational brands, especially when gained from prestigious universities in the developed world.

Just as in the 1960s, however, there have been limits to US dominance over ideas on effective business and management, especially following the problems of the collapse of major international companies such as Enron, WorldCom and Tyco in the early part of this decade and the 'fall-out' from the Iraq war in 2003. For example, during that year a major study by DDB, a US consulting company, was initiated to examine the brand image of America and American companies among 17 countries. This work showed that America and American business were 'viewed as arrogant and indifferent to others' cultures; exploitative, in the sense that it extracted more than it provided; corrupting, in that it valued materialism above all else; and willing to sacrifice almost anything to generate profits' (*Financial Times*, 29 December 2004). A further study was conducted one year later, showing little improvement in overseas perceptions of America's image. In the field of human resource management (HRM), this problem with the American model has been especially true for some considerable period of time. For example, many Europeans have questioned the appropriateness of much of US employee relations practice, with its focus on individualism and 'short-termism', its morality in laying off employees without warning and its appropriateness to social market economies that are based on employee participation in business decision-making (Pendleton and Gospel, 2013). As a result, there have been various attempts to develop an alternative European way of managing people (Sparrow *et al.*, 2004). Similarly, Australians have sought to develop their own models of leadership and management, and the rapidly growing Chinese economy and indigenous industry have attempted to embed mainly American ideas into their own culturally and institutionally specific ways of doing things (Zhang and Martin, 2003). Consequently, it is sometimes argued that we may be witnessing a fragmentation of models, with no single set of ideas dominating the management agenda (Clegg *et al.*, 2011). We also seem to be witnessing a major debate on the appropriateness of the appeal of the US business and management model to the rest of the world. Some writers have described this debate as being between the forces of global convergence (largely those of American multinational corporations and consultants) and those of divergence, with its emphasis on the importance of national mindsets (local cultural and institutional ways of seeing and working) (Harzing and Pinnington, 2014).

Dominant ideas and 'guru theory'

As we have noted, paradigms also appear to change because certain influential theorists or practitioners who make up the so-called management 'guru' industry develop new ways of working and thinking (Huczynski, 2006). Acceptance of these new ideas occurs not only because these ideas are in and of themselves somehow better than previous ones, but also because you need willing consumers as well as willing producers in the rapidly growing marketplace for knowledge. And, as many critics of management consultancy have noted, willing consumption is often associated with serving the career interests of particular groups of people in organizations or for non-rational institutional reasons such as the pressures to imitate other organizations because of what is expected by institutional shareholders or government officials, or to adopt practices to conform to social network pressures – the fear of being 'left out' (Wheen, 2004).

James Hoopes (2003) has described the role played by 'guru' academics, consultants and practitioners who have had a major influence on new ideas and examples of so-called best practice in management during the last 100 years. Hoopes analysed two recurrent 'big ideas' in management and showed how interest in these two ideas has ebbed and flowed in popularity over time. These two ideas are *top-down control* and *bottom-up management*. Top-down control is best exemplified by Frederick Taylor and his school of scientific management in the late 1800s and early 1900s, which emphasized the importance and power of a new managerial 'cadre' in convincing or forcing workers to do what these managers wanted them to do. Usually, this involved heavy doses of close and direct supervision, and payment-by-results systems to motivate workers. Taylor and his followers, including Henry Gantt and Frank and Lilian Gilbreth, were important in spreading the gospel of scientific management. However, it took Henry Ford, the founder of the Ford Motor Company, to apply Taylor's ideas by linking them to technological control embodied in the moving assembly line before they became practically important. As a result, Fordism became the dominant mode of organizing and managing during the twentieth century. It is usual in academic texts to trace some of the modern management techniques that we shall discuss during this course to Taylor and Ford's ideas of top-down control, including 'business process re-engineering' and 'lean production'.

By contrast, bottom-up management, according to Hoopes, is associated with a more humanistic or, some would argue, realistic belief that such top-down control is ultimately self-defeating. At least two arguments have been used to explain the negative side to top-down management. The first of these, the *alienation thesis*, became fashionable in the 1930s, and is still an important argument by many commentators on work and employment relations. It concerns the nature and scale of opposition by employees during the twentieth century to having their work 'Taylor-made'. Indeed, this kind of thinking was used to explain the rise of trade unionism during that period and much of the industrial unrest that characterized industrial and labour relations in many advanced economies. The second argument, the *changing nature of work thesis*, has two variants, according to which sector of advanced industrialized economies is being put under the spotlight. The slightly *older variant* has focused on the nature of work in the growing service sector of most developed and developing economies. Jobs in this sector, it is argued, are characterized by employees having greater control over how they perform their jobs than in the traditional manufacturing sectors, largely because of the difficulties in measuring employee output. Services are by definition more qualitative in nature because there is often no tangible output and, in the case of personal services, they are 'consumed' immediately. Think about the quality of service provided by checkout operators in a retail store and then think about the difficulties in measuring their output. High-performing retail organizations place great emphasis on the links between satisfied and engaged employees, high-quality service and strong brand performance (see Chapter 3). This link between engaged employees and the service–profit chain is the major element in Kaplan and Norton's (2008) 'theory of the business', to which we shall return.

The *newer variant* has developed because of the increased emphasis on knowledge work in modern economies, which became especially fashionable to emphasize following the 'dot-com' boom in the USA and Europe in the late 1990s. The argument here is that knowledge workers (and most skilled and professional employees can be labelled thus) enjoy genuine power *vis-à-vis* employers over the one scarce, non-substitutable resource that modern organizations use to compete, and that is knowledge and information (see Chapter 7). The old adage that 'knowledge is power' has never been more true, it is argued, and in organizations that rest on knowledge as their distinctive competence managing employees who have effective control over it has become a different proposition from managing large numbers of unskilled workers, whose prior knowledge has been effectively relocated into machines. So, for example, the models of top-down control that were employed in motor vehicle manufacture are not seen to be relevant in managing consulting firms, healthcare or science-based industries such as biotechnology. Getting the best from employees in these kinds of industry, where expertise is often located in unwritten, tacit know-how built up over years of experience, usually requires organizations to provide them with high levels of involvement in key decision-making rather than tell them what to do and how to do it, since managers often lack the expertise to do so. Think of the problems and conflicts that occur between hospital administrators and medical practitioners, or between managers who do not have a technical background and technologists, and you begin to get a sense of the need to manage differently.

There are two final points we wish to make in this section on dominant ideas and guru theory paradigms. The first is that our models of management do change over time, often in a cyclical fashion. In connection with the two big ideas of top-down control and bottom-up management, it is clear that they have ebbed in and out of fashion throughout the last 100 or so years. Often, this has been a reaction to the worst excesses of their application. This was the case of with scientific management because it failed to deliver what was promised in the form of business process re-engineering. It has also been evident in some human relations prescriptions, more of which will be discussed later. Change and changefulness are at the heart of business and management theory and practice because organizations are always in a process of 'becoming', especially given the, often turbulent, nature of their environments. Thus, any text and course on management has to reflect such change and make it a central feature of the analysis.

The second point is to warn you about some of the worst excesses of guru theory and the kinds of material that you can often pick up in airport bookstalls. Willing consumers of management knowledge, looking for quick fixes, are sometimes motivated by the search for 'newness'. As a consequence, we are witnessing the creation of a fads and fashion industry for management knowledge (Joyce *et al.*, 2003). Rosenzweig (2007) identified many such fads that, in their day, laid claim to paradigm status, most of which have been discredited or else have been countermanded by other fads and fashions. Because of this faddist nature of management, the whole discipline of management has been characterized as little more than an immature body of knowledge lacking a proper scientific basis and bedevilled by inconsistencies and contradictions that would not be tolerated in any other area of scientific life. This faddish nature of much of management knowledge has been seen as the cause of the low status of business schools within the university community and has raised severe question marks over the role and content of courses such as the MBA.

So, through this book we hope to help you avoid these pitfalls and help you learn useful, though often critical, ideas that have a longer shelf life than many of the guru books that dominate the market for management knowledge.

A FRAMEWORK FOR THE BOOK

Bearing in mind the issues previously raised in this chapter about the nature of management and change, our book focuses on the problems of managing people and organizations in changing contexts. To help guide you through the rest of the book, let's look at Figure 1.1.

Any book in management has to begin with an examination of the nature of what is being studied and practised, which is the subject of Chapter 2. In this chapter we have adapted and reworked some ideas by well-known management theorists to produce a model of a rounded manager who is capable of operating at different levels and in different contexts in modern economies. This model of management should help you to think more reflectively and, indeed, reflexively about your own job and others you may move into during your career.

The first premise of the model is that management is practised at different levels – managing on the inside, managing across the organization and managing on the outside, which we discuss in Chapter 2. Managers who are unable to deal effectively with people at these different levels are increasingly unlikely to deliver strategic goals. This is equally true for human resource managers and many line managers, who have traditionally defined their roles as managing on the inside, as well as marketing managers, whose roles have naturally inclined them to manage on the outside.

The second premise of the model is that managers are being asked to manage in changing contexts, which, in some respects, are qualitatively different from the experience of managing even a few decades ago. Let's take an example from a real life case of remote management we came across quite a few years ago. A senior sales manager, working for a leading international instrumentation company, was asked to take on the role of managing a global team of highly qualified, highly paid sales engineers, operating in ten countries. It made little sense to have these sales engineers relocate to head office, so the organizational structure had to be 'virtual' and the senior sales manager had to learn to manage at a distance and across time zones. This solution emerged because the company, Agilent Technologies, had grown rapidly through acquisition and had acquired these ten countries over a short period of time. His job was to instill a sense of corporate spirit into his engineers as well as support them in developing their own national markets. Thus, he faced the problems of managing a disparate group of people, from very different national and organizational cultures, to manage locally and integrate their efforts with each other.

This example throws up the problems of managing in multiple, changing contexts. Our senior sales engineer's initial problem required him to understand the different expectations, needs and attachments that engage individuals with organizations – their psychological contracts – and how best to exercise leadership in circumstances where people are likely to differ markedly in their

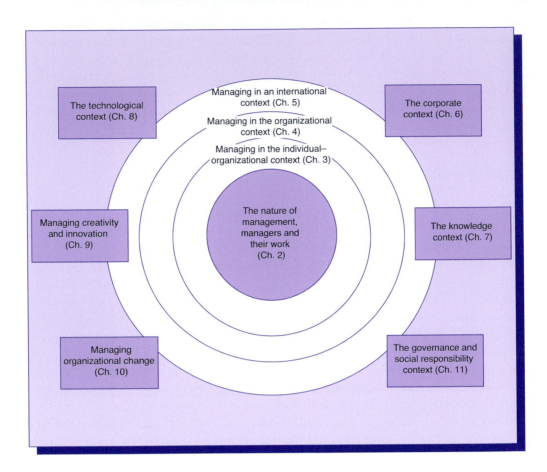

FIGURE 1.1 A framework for the book

expectations, needs and attachments. This is the subject of Chapter 3. Then he had to understand how organizational structures can influence individual and group behaviour, and how to design and operate in structures that were more complex and virtual than those he had previously experienced, which is the subject of Chapter 4. He also faced the problems of managing in an international context, which is sometimes defined in terms of overcoming the 'liability of foreignness': How should managers deal with the costs of doing business abroad, arising from unfamiliarity with the cultural and institutional environment and the needs for coordination across time and space? This is the subject of Chapter 5.

Moving on, the example raises problems of how to create a sense of 'corporateness' in a previously fragmented organization because the organization wishes to leverage its international brand for new markets. It also raises the problems of managing employees who are knowledge workers, many of whom are individualistic by nature and can exercise lots of power because of their understanding of local markets, and the issue of how technology might be used to achieve global integration of the sales team in a way that was close to impossible before the introduction of the Internet. So, in

Chapter 6 we shall look at the corporate context and examine the problems managers face in creating strong corporate reputations and corporate brands. In Chapter 7, we shall examine the changing nature of work, particularly the role of knowledge in creating value in organizations and the problems of managing so-called knowledge workers. In Chapter 8 we shall study the changing technological context, particularly the role of information and communications technologies and social media in being a positive, but sometimes negative, force for change. In a new Chapter 9, we examine the problems of managing creativity and innovation, a key problem for many organizations such as Agilent, asking the question: Can creativity and innovation be managed? While we touched on innovation and creativity in various chapters in the first edition of this book, it has become such an important context for firms in all countries as they strive to compete. Our senior sales engineer also faced the problems of managing the change process itself: How should he turn his plans for a globally integrated sales team into action? The old saying about the best-laid plans falling down in the implementation is even more appropriate in an increasingly unknowable world, which is the subject of Chapter 10.

Finally, we end with a new Chapter 11, which deals with the increasingly important context of corporate governance and the related agenda of corporate social responsibility (or corporate responsibility as it is increasingly being labelled). Our recent research into corporate governance and managing people has convinced us of the importance of different governance models and how they influence every aspect of what goes on in organizations, sectors and, indeed, national business systems. One only need consider the impact of the 2007–8 Global Financial Crisis on economies such as the USA and the UK. Such events have given even further impetus to the corporate (social) responsibility agenda and its concern to inject ethics into business. We hope by covering such a wide range of ground that you gain a greater understanding of the need to 'complexify', rather than simplify, the problems facing managers in an increasingly unknowable world, but at the same time find some ideas that you can put into practice. The old adage that there is 'nothing so practical as good theory' is one we commend to you, and we hope you find enough in this book that is sufficiently well-founded theoretically and practical to justify the time you devote to reading the rest of the chapters.

LEARNING SUMMARY

In this chapter we have learned about some of the key ideas underlying the management of people in changing contexts, including the relevance of universalism and relativism to management practice and the importance of mindsets in shaping how we view management problems and solutions.

First, we argued that the idea of 'best practice' is flawed because management practices are always 'context bound' in the sense that practices are developed in unique mixtures of organizational, industrial, cultural and historical 'soil'. Therefore, you cannot transfer practices easily from one situation to another without some adaptation and considerable time and effort to embed these practices in new fertile soil. Thus, practices can best be described as 'promising'; there is simply no 'one-best-way' to manage.

Second, we suggested that change is one of the few universals or constants of management. Therefore, understanding how contexts and ideas about management have changed and have often been recycled is important. However, such change is often cyclical, exemplified by *the* major debate in management theory and practice – top-down versus bottom-up management and organization. Management theory has been dominated at different points in history by the mechanistic mindset, which has resulted in bureaucratic organizations and control, and the organic mindset, which is revealed through a more bottom-up, humanistic and people-oriented mode of management. These cycles of interest reflect models of national economic and business success – for example, the Japanese model and organic management – and the role of management gurus in shaping dominant ideas. All managers are searching for something new; often, however, the latest fad is little more than 'old wine in new bottles', which usually turns into something quite disappointing. One good example is Case 1.1 on human relations, which is in the 'Review questions' section at the end of this chapter; the basis of modern human resource management rests on many of its assumptions and studies, which have continued to disappoint business leaders, judging by the lack of credibility of the HR function in most organizations.

Finally, we have set out a framework for the book. This framework is based on the ideas that management is practised at different levels and in changing contexts. Above all else, however, management has to produce change and innovation, for without these characteristics organizations are destined to go into a terminal decline. Given the importance of organizations to our economic success and social well-being, making effective managers is one of the key goals of advanced industrial societies; the remainder of this book is aimed at helping you in this regard.

REVIEW QUESTIONS

1 What is the difference between a universalist and relativist perspective on management and organizations?
2 Is it possible for managers to engage in reflexive thinking about their careers and organizations? What might help them to do so, and what might prevent them?

CASE 1.1 THE DEVELOPMENT OF HUMAN RELATIONS, ORGANIZATIONAL BEHAVIOUR AND THE ROLE OF ACADEMIC GURUS

Zhong and House (2012) summarized the feelings of many academics in our field, including ourselves, that few studies in management have had such a pervasive effect on organizational behaviour as the Hawthorne Studies. So it is only natural to begin a book like this by introducing you to this landmark study and problems it raised for the study and practice of management.

The conventional wisdom in many texts has been to attribute these studies to Elton Mayo, the founding father of what is now known as organizational behaviour but began as human relations. Mayo was of Scottish descent but grew up in Australia in the early 1900s. He attempted and failed a medical education in Adelaide, Edinburgh and London, but came to study economics and philosophy in Australia and was appointed to a lectureship in Queensland. How did this itinerant 'failure', with a rather conventional education, come to have such a huge influence on the study and practice of management for decades after his death in 1949?

Through a series of accidental meetings, Mayo became interested in the newly emerging discipline of psychology and psychotherapy and, following self-study, became Australia's first practising psychoanalyst. Because of previously formed interests in helping reduce conflict among workers and employers in Queensland, his adopted state, he wrote a book, published in 1919, entitled *Democracy and Freedom*, which warned against greedy employers and class-conscious workers and their unions pursuing their self-interests. Rather than see such a conflict of interests as a naturally occurring phenomenon during the early factory system, he described it in psychoanalytical terms as unconscious phobias. He proposed that the parties should act together to achieve a common social purpose through industrial cooperation and, in doing so, provide an alternative to political democracy. Intelligent managers, he argued, could, through therapeutic techniques and by allowing workers greater participation at work, promote social harmony, not only in industry but also in society at large. His message to the world became the importance of the human factor in an age that was dominated by the teachings of organizations as machines and the role of technology in transforming work and industrial enterprises.

Mayo decided to leave Australia in 1922 to return to London but, running out of money, ended up in California. Through personal charm, and an acute sense of opportunity, he managed to secure a research position with the influential Social Science Research Council, albeit aided by some rather dubious references he had created for himself. Through his heightened sense of networking as a way of getting career development, Mayo moved to the Wharton Business School and then to Harvard. By cultivating the attentions of its Dean, Walter Donham, Mayo managed to establish himself at Harvard Business School. Once there he introduced his ideas on psychotherapy into the curriculum and the notion that the manager's main mission was to produce social harmony in industry. While at Harvard he secured some grant funds, which he used to cultivate a group of gifted young researchers, who collectively became known as the 'Harvard human relations group'. He also made key connections with an anthropologist, W. Lloyd Warner, a statistician, T. N. Whitehead, and a biologist, Lawrence Henderson. This group would have an enormous influence on the progress of American industry and business education.

The most famous of their projects were the so-called Hawthorne experiments, begun in 1926–27 in the Western Electric subsidiary of AT&T, near Cicero, Illinois. This work began as a study of the effects of scientific management ideas on worker productivity and, in particular, the influence of natural or artificial lighting on worker output. However, manipulation of these variables seemed to have no effect. George Pennock, Hawthorne's technical superintendent who conducted these experiments, began to make other changes by introducing rest breaks, shorter hours and mid-morning meals. Eventually, Pennock decided to set up an experiment by isolating five women in the now famous Relay Assembly Test Room (RATR). Pennock asked them to work at a comfortable pace, and examined the effects of changes in work conditions on their output. At the same time, however, he also introduced a strong, group-based economic incentive. The five women were separated from the main hall, where 100 or so workers were employed and paid on a departmental-wide system; what individuals produced here didn't have much effect on individual earnings. Following a series of experimental changes to heating, lighting, length of working day, rest-breaks, etc., productivity rose in the RATR by approximately 10 per cent.

The women in the RATR had no supervisor, but Pennock introduced an observer called Homan Hilbarger, who initially became friendly with the women, but gradually began to annoy them by making advances and unwanted remarks. Later on, Hilbarger created further problems when he overheard two of the women discussing whether they would hold back their effort or go flat out. He told Pennock, who replaced them immediately. The result was record output levels. Pennock couldn't understand what the cause of the improvements were – the small group effect, lunches, rest periods or whatever. He chose to reject the explanation of higher output for higher pay for reasons we can only speculate on.

Meanwhile Mayo came across these experiments as the result of an invitation from the Personnel Director, following a talk Mayo had given in New York. He was asked to comment on what Pennock had found, and this he did with unbounded glee. Scarcely could he believe that he had come across a set of experiments that confirmed his thesis that men and women could use work as the basis for creating social harmony and quickly set about reinterpreting the 'data' to fit in with his prior ideas. Mayo originally analysed the conflict that emerged in the group through neurosis, but when he returned in 1928, Pennock had temporarily returned the improved working conditions of the RATR to their original state by removing all previous benefits. Productivity rose yet again, and Mayo, expecting the opposite to occur, was presented with the task of explaining this unwanted result.

Mayo turned to the now famous theory that the more sympathetic supervision and counseling in the RATR, aided by the observer Hilbarger, had helped the workgroup establish a group spirit, a sense of belonging and sense of working for each other that could not be easily demolished by removing external conditions. He also castigated scientific management explanations for being unable to explain these rises in output. He went on to train supervisors in social therapy techniques so that they could interview workers and use these interviews as a valve for emotional release. However, he soon lost interest in the actual experimental side and gave control of the programme to some of his junior colleagues, who set up another experiment, the Bank Wiring Test Room. This experiment used more rigorous techniques of observation and found evidence that totally contradicted Mayo's theses. However, Mayo chose not to report the Bank Wiring Test Room in the book he persuaded the Western Electric Company to sponsor, the 1933 edition of the *Human Problems of an Industrial Civilisation*. In this book Mayo devoted only 40 pages to Hawthorne, but described it in eulogizing terms – as a near-utopia in which the women were never under pressure. Therapeutic supervision had managed to create harmony among a group that subordinated its own self-interests in favour of the right to participate in the greater good of the group. To create such communities of practice was the job of the new breed of managers trained in psychotherapy. The result would be a form of industrial democracy in which unreasonable democratic conflict would be removed from the industrial landscape.

A subsequent, and much larger, account of the Hawthorne experiments by his acolytes, Roethlisberger and Dickson (1939), was written in such a manner as to confirm much of what Mayo had suggested, preserving the idea that human relations should be concerned with the explanation of group dynamics and output changes, and not the more obvious scientific management explanations of pay and rewards (though they did recognize pay as a contributory factor). From what has been described as the 'dullest book ever written', the 'scientific' study of human relations and organizational behaviour developed as a counter to Taylorism and the teachings of the day in American and European business schools.

Sources: Hoopes, 2003; Rose, 1975; Roethlisberger and Dickson, 1939; Zhong and House, 2012.

1 Why do you think Pennock chose not to report the possible explanation that output in the Relay Assembly Test Room rose because of the economic motivations of the workers, and why did Mayo also reject the explanation that money was at the root of output increases?
2 Why should the ideas of human relations become so widely popular, despite the rather obvious flaws in the 'experiments' and the reporting of them by Mayo?
3 How have these ideas that Mayo promoted been adopted and transformed in modern management techniques?
4 How does the concept of universalism apply to this case, and how universal are the ideas of human relations?

REFERENCES

Armbruster, T. (2006) *The Economics and Sociology of Management Consulting*. Cambridge, MA: Cambridge University Press.

Bloom, N., Dorgan, S., Dowdy, J., Van Reene, J. and Rippin, T. (2005) *Management Practices across Firms and Nations*. London School of Economics/McKinsey and Co/ESRC, available online at http://cep.lse.ac.uk/management/management.pdf.

Christensen, C. M. and Raynor, M. E. (2003) *The Innovator's Solution: Creating and sustaining successful growth*. Cambridge, MA: Harvard Business School Press.

Clegg, S. R., Kornberger, M. and Pitsis, T. (2011) *Managing and Organizations: An introduction to theory and practice*. London: Sage.

Collins, J. C. (2001) *Good to Great: Why some companies make the leap . . . and others don't*. New York: HarperCollins.

Collins, J. C. and Porras, J. I. (1994) *Built to Last: Successful habits of visionary companies*. New York: HarperCollins.

Crane, A. and Matten, D. (2010) *Business Ethics*, 3rd edn. Oxford: Oxford University Press.

Cunliffe, A. L. (2014) Reflexive inquiry in organizational research: Questions and possibilities. Reprinted in H. Willmott and E. Bell (eds), *Qualitative Research in Business and Management*. London: Sage.

Czarniawska, B. (2011) *Cyberfactories: How news agencies produce news*. Cheltenham: Edward Elgar.

Davies, W. (2015) *The Happiness Industry: How the government and big business sold us well-being*. London: Verso Books.

Davis, G. F. (2009) *Managed by Markets: How finance reshaped America*. Oxford: Oxford University Press.

The Economist (2015) *Keeping it on the company campus*. 15 May. London: Economist Newspapers.

Financial Times (2004) Is the world falling out of love with US brands? 29 December. Available online at http://www.ft.com/cms/s/1/502f6994-59d5-11d9-ba09-00000e2511c8.html#axzz3o44pRzJY.

Fox, A. (1974) *Beyond Contract: Work, trust and power relations*. London: Faber and Faber.

Goold, M. and Campbell, A. (2002) *Designing Effective Organizations: How to create structured networks*. San Francisco, CA: Jossey-Bass.

Hamel, G. (2009) Moonshots for managers. *Harvard Business Review*, February, pp. 1–21.

Harzing, A.–W. and Pinnington, A. (2014) *International Human Resource Management*, 4th edn. London: Sage.

Hodgkinson, G. P. and Healey, M. P. (2011) Psychological foundations of dynamic capabilities: reflexion and reflection in strategic management. *Strategic Management Journal*, 32 (13), 1500–1515.

Hoopes, J. (2003) *False Prophets: The gurus who created modern industry and why their ideas are bad for business*. Cambridge, MA: Perseus Publishing.

Huczynski, A. (2006) *Management Gurus*, revised edition. Oxford: Routledge.

Joyce, W., Nohria, N. and Robertson, B. (2003) *What Really Works: The 4+2 formula for sustained business success*. New York: Harper Business.

Kaplan, R. S. and Norton, D. P. (2008) *The Execution Premium: Linking strategy to operations for competitive advantage: How balanced scorecard companies thrive in the new business environment*. Cambridge, MA: Harvard Business School Press.

Khurana, R. and Spender, J. C. (2012) Herbert A. Simon on what ails business schools: more than a problem in organizational design. *Journal of Management Studies*, 49 (3), 619–639.

King, D. and Learmonth, M. (2015) Can critical management studies ever be 'practical'? A case study in engaged scholarship. *Human Relations*, 68 (3), 353–375.

Lawrence, P. (2002) *The Change Game: How today's global trends are shaping tomorrow's companies*. London: Kogan Page.

Leseure, M. J., Bauer, J., Birdi, K., Neely, A. and Denyer, D. (2004) Adoption of promising practices: a systematic review of the evidence. *International Journal of Management Reviews*, 5/6, 169–190.

Locke, R. R. (1996) *The Collapse of the American Management Mystique*. Oxford: Oxford University Press.

Locke, R. R. and Spender, J.-C. (2011) *Confronting managerialism*. London: Zed Books.

Martin, G. and Gollan, P. J. (2012) Corporate governance and strategic human resources management (SHRM) in the UK financial services sector: the case of the Royal Bank of Scotland. *International Journal of Human Resource Mangement*, 23 (16), 3295–3314.

Martin, G., Parry, E. and Flowers, P. (2015) Do social media enhance constructive employee voice all of the time or just some of the time? *Human Resource Management Journal*, doi: 10.1111/748-8583.12081

Mayer, C. (2013) *Firm Commitment: Why the corporation is failing us and how to restore trust in it*. Oxford: Oxford University Press.

Mintzberg, H. (1983) *Structure in Fives*. Englewood Cliffs, NJ: Prentice-Hall.

Mintzberg, H. (2004) *Managers not MBAs: A hard look at the soft practice of managing*. Harlow, UK: Financial Times/Prentice-Hall.

Mintzberg, H. (2011) *Managing*. New York: Berrett-Koehler.

Mintzberg, H. (2015) *Rebalancing Society: Radical renewal beyond left, right and center*. New York: Berrett-Koehler.

Morgan, G. (1997) *Images of Organization*. London: Sage.

Pascale, R. (1999) Surfing the edge of chaos. *Sloan Management Review*, 40 (3), 83–94.

Pascale, R. and Athos, A. (1981) *The Art of Japanese Management*. New York: Warner.

Pendleton, A. and Gospel, H. (2013) Corporate governance and human resource management. In: S. Bach and M. Edwards (eds), *Managing Human Resources*, 5th edn. Chichester: Sussex: Wiley, pp. 61–78.

Petit, S. C. and Huault, I. (2008) From practice-based knowledge to the practice research: Revisiting constructivist research works on knowledge. *Management Learning*, 39 (1), 73–91.

Pfeffer, J. and Sutton, R. I. (2006) *Hard Facts, Dangerous Half Truths, and Total Nonsense: Profiting from evidence-based management*. Cambridge, MA: Harvard Business School Press.

Pierce, J. R. and Aguinis, H. (2013) The too-much-of-a-good-thing effect in management. *Journal of Management*, 39 (2), 313–338.

Roethlisberger, F. J. and Dickson, W. J. (1939) *Management and the Worker*. Cambridge, MA: Harvard Business School Press.

Rose, M. (1975) *Industrial Behaviour: Theoretical developments since Taylor.* London: Allen Lane.

Rosenzweig, P. (2007) *The Halo Effect . . . and the Eight Other Business Delusions That Deceive Managers.* New York: Free Press.

Rynes, S. L., Giluk, T. L. and Brown, K. G. (2007) The very separate worlds of academic and practitioner periodicals in human resource management: implications for evidence-based management. *Academy of Management Journal,* 50 (5), 987–1008.

Seely Brown, J. (2000) *The Social Life of Information.* Cambridge, MA: Harvard Business School Press.

Siebert, S., Martin, G., Bozic, B. and Docherty, I. (2015) Looking 'beyond the factory gates': Towards more pluralist and radical approaches to intra-organizational trust research. *Organization Studies,* first published on 7 May 2015 as doi:10.1177/0170840615580010.

Sparrow, P. R., Brewster, C. and Harris, H. (2004) *Globalizing Human Resource Management.* London: Psychology Press.

Spilg, E., Siebert, S. and Martin, G. (2012) A social learning perspective on the development of doctors in the UK National Health Service, *Social Science and Medicine,* 75 (9), 1617–1624.

Teece, D. J. (2007) Explicating dynamic capabilities: the nature and microfoundations of (sustainable) enterprise performance. *Strategic Management Journal,* 28 (13), 1319–1350.

Thornton, P. H., Ocasio, W. and Lounsbury, M. (2012) *The Institutional Logics Perspective: A new approach to culture, structure and process.* Oxford: Oxford University Press.

Weick, K. E. and Sutcliffe, K. M. (2007) *Managing the Unexpected: Resilient performance in an age of uncertainty,* 2nd edn. New York: Jossey-Bass.

Wenger, E. C., McDermott, R. and Snyder, W. C. (2002) *Cultivating Communities of Practice: A guide to managing knowledge.* Cambridge, MA: Harvard Business School Press.

Wheen, F. (2004) *How Mumbo-Jumbo Conquered the World: A short history of modern delusions.* London: Perennial.

Whitley, R. (2009) U.S. capitalism: a tarnished model? *Academy of Management Perspectives,* 23 (2), 11–22.

Whittington, R. (2000) *What is Strategy? And Does Strategy Matter?* London: Thomson International.

Zhang, H. and Martin, G. (2003) *Managing Human Resources in Sino-Foreign Joint Ventures.* Jiangxi, China: Jiangxi Science and Technology Publishing.

Zhong, C.B. and House, J. (2012) Hawthorne revisited: Organizational implications of the physical work environment. *Research in Organizational Behavior,* 32, 3–22.

Chapter 2

The nature of management, managers and their work

LEARNING OBJECTIVES

By the end of this chapter you should be able to:

- understand the key roles and activities of a manager's job;
- apply these roles and activities to your own job and to those of your colleagues;
- understand the importance of different contexts in shaping the jobs of managers;
- understand how management competences relate to the different managerial roles and levels at which managers perform;
- distinguish between management as a form of control and management as a form of leadership;
- understand and recognize the components of wisdom and how it relates to sound judgement;
- apply sound judgement to your work;
- understand how the personal qualities of managers relate to effective managerial performance;
- self-assess your personal qualities for management.

A FRAMEWORK FOR UNDERSTANDING MANAGERS AND THEIR WORK

Introduction

In the previous chapter we examined some of the key ideas underlying the study of managing people in context, including universalism and relativism, the importance of changing contexts and their influence on managers' jobs, and the role of management thinkers in shaping our understanding of management. These ideas are further developed in this chapter, in which we also want to 'drill down' into the practicalities of management.

We shall develop a framework for thinking about a 'rounded' manager by drawing on the work of highly respected writers in this field. This framework integrates the personal qualities that managers bring to their jobs, the activities and contexts inherent in effective managerial work, and the different levels at which managers can take action. It also introduces you to the notions of wisdom and managerial decision-making, neglected areas in the literature on management but very important for you to understand and be able to apply to your career.

Because this is quite a complicated chapter, we have interspersed the text with four exercises that deal with specific aspects of the rounded manager framework, rather than having an integrative case at the end of the chapter. This should help break up the text and show how specific aspects of the framework can be applied to managers' jobs.

The background to the study of managerial work

To understand managers and the process of management, we can draw on a long tradition of research into the nature of managerial work, what managers do and what managers should be doing. Since the 1980s much of this research has focused on defining, measuring and developing managerial competences, especially in the USA and the UK. For example, the USA Office of Personnel has developed a set of standards for supervisors, and the UK government has sponsored research and development into producing new occupational standards for different levels and type of management, initially through the Management Charter Initiative during the 1990s, and more recently through the Management Standards Centre, which launched its new standards for management and leadership in 2004, further revised in 2008.

KEY CONCEPT **Management competence and standards**

Management competences are the functions and activities that individuals with management and leadership responsibilities are expected to be able to undertake in their organization. Sometimes a distinction is made between competence and competency. Competence usually refers to the functions or activities undertaken by managers, such as developing people, whereas competency usually refers to the personal qualities an individual may bring to a job, such as networking skills or creativity. There have been various attempts to turn these competence frameworks into management standards – responsibilities that managers are expected to be able to undertake regardless of their industry sector or type/size of organization. The National Standards for Management and Leadership in the UK is an excellent example (www.managementstandards.org.uk/). These standards describe the level of performance expected for a range of management and leadership functions and activities, including managing and working with people, managing self and personal development, facilitating change, using resources, providing direction and achieving results, all of which are examined in this book.

In this section, we trace the origins and trajectory of these developments, and propose a new framework to help you think about the nature of management. This framework draws on different ideas from some of the leading thinkers on management, and will provide the basis for much of the subsequent discussion in this course.

Reviewing the literature on the future of management some years ago, Harry Scarborough (1998) described two schools of theory on management. These are still relevant today. The first is the *empiricist* perspective, which attempts to address the question: What do managers do? This stream of writing is best exemplified by the various studies of effective managers' roles and behaviour, such as Henry Mintzberg (1973/2011), John Kotter (1990) and the recently deceased Rosemary Stewart (1979). These writers developed rich descriptions of managerial behaviours and practices, classified them according to the functions they perform for organizations and developed prescriptive theories of what managers should do. Probably the best known of these was Mintzberg's (1973) analysis of managerial work, which has formed a point of departure for subsequent discussions of management, and is still relevant today in describing what managers do (see Box 2.1 and Mintzberg, 2011).

BOX 2.1 Mintzberg (1973/2011) – Managerial work: analysis from observation

Based on a one-week observation of the chief executives of five medium-to-large organizations in the early 1970s, Mintzberg suggested an answer to the question: 'What do managers do?'

He described the characteristics of the work of these managers in the following terms and found no reason to change this list more than forty years later when he conducted a larger follow-up study:

- Managers performed a great quantity of work at an unrelenting pace.
- Managers' activity was characterized by variety, fragmentation and brevity.
- Managers preferred issues that were current, specific and ad hoc.
- Managers sat between the organization and a network of contacts.
- Managers demonstrated a strong preference for the verbal media (telephone and meetings, as opposed to mail and tours).
- Managers appeared to be able to control their own affairs (despite the fact that they have so many obligations).

Mintzberg broke down the content of the work of a manager into the following roles:

- Interpersonal roles – arise directly from his formal authority and involve basic interpersonal relationships:
    - Figurehead: a symbol, attends ceremonial events, signs legal documents.
    - Leader: motivates subordinates, develops the work milieu.
    - Liaison: horizontal communication with other managers, informal relationship.

- Informational roles:

  - Nerve centre (monitor): the focal point for the movement of non-routine (internal and external) information, including contacts with people who are nerve centres in other organizations.
  - Disseminator: transmission of information and values to subordinates.
  - Spokesman: transmission of information to outsiders.

- Decisional roles:

  - Entrepreneur: looking for opportunities and potential problems that may cause him to initiate improvement projects.
  - Disturbance handler: handling situations that are not covered by the routine rules.
  - Resource allocator: scheduling his own and his subordinates' time, and authorizing all significant decisions before they are implemented.
  - Negotiator: as part of being the organization's legal authority, its spokesman and its resource allocator.

The second of the schools identified by Scarborough was the *essentialist* perspective, the various strands of which are characterized by the attempt to uncover the 'essence' of management and its relationship to the underlying functions management performs for organizations, such as controlling employees. This essentialism is closely related to the developments by the early writers on management, such as Taylor, Ford and Fayol, to uncover a one-best-way or science of management (Clegg *et al.*, 2011). Such a perspective has a long history, and is underpinned by the universalistic principles discussed in Chapter 1.

Both perspectives have weaknesses, one of the most important of these being their neglect of the national institutional and cultural contexts in which management is practised. As we have already seen from the illustration on Germany in Chapter 1, there has been resistance to management practices developed in the USA. Similarly, private sector practices, developed in contexts for which profit maximization or shareholder value are the dominant concerns, may have less relevance in the public sector. The public sector tends to be characterized by multiple stakeholders, all of whom are deemed to have legitimate claims on organizational goals and resources (see Chapter 11). Finally, neither perspective has much to say about the kinds of personal characteristics or competencies required of effective managers in different situations, a topic that has been the subject of work on leadership (Finkelstein *et al.*, 2009) and emotional intelligence (Goleman *et al.*, 2002), and one to which we shall return in the next chapter. In the remainder of this chapter, we have put together a framework for thinking about management which draws on the ideas of the eminent management thinkers who are widely acknowledged to have made a major contribution to the literature on management and organizational behaviour.

CASE 2.1 USING MINTZBERG'S DESCRIPTORS

1 Using the description of Mintzberg's work in Box 2.1, would you expect to find significant differences between managing in the public sector and managing in the private sector? If so, which roles would you expect to be more important in the public sector?
2 Again, using the description of Mintzberg's work in Box 2.1, think about someone who has had responsibility for your work. Which of the roles did he or she tend to perform most effectively and least effectively? How did his or her performance in these roles affect your work?

A FRAMEWORK FOR UNDERSTANDING THE ROUNDED MANAGER

Introduction to the rounded manager

Any selection of thinkers on management is bound to be restrictive, because writing about the topic has become 'big business' and, as we noted in Chapter 1, there is a growing guru industry that has developed to meet the insatiable demand for new insights into management. High on anyone's list of experts would be Henry Mintzberg, a Canadian whose earlier work we have already discussed. Mintzberg has spent much of his academic career studying managers in context and developing models of management, with a view to setting out his ideas for a 'well-rounded manager' who would be able to function effectively in most business situations.

As we have already seen earlier in this chapter, Mintzberg's earliest work during the 1970s helped map out the territory by describing a number of roles that managers performed during his studies of managers. This work was notable because it was based on observation and what managers did in practice, not on what managers were supposed to do. However, in a more recent formulation of the nature of management, Mintzberg (1994/2011) attempted to 'round out the manager's job'. Prompted by criticisms of the 'atomistic' listing of managerial roles and competences, taken by many organizations, Mintzberg offered a more holistic approach to management. He argued that the listings of well-documented roles and competences 'even if joined up in a circle' did not capture the integrated nature of a manager's job. Nor did they attempt to explain how different competences related to each other, except in a very general sense. For example, such a criticism could be made of the older version of the UK Management Standards, developed by the Management Charter Initiative in the early 1990s. In these standards, competences were categorized together under roles such as managing people or managing resources. Little or no attempt, however, was made to show how the competences related to each other, except as part of managing people, etc., or to show how the roles themselves related to the overall job of managing in different contexts. The new version of the standards, however, has gone some way to meeting these shortcomings.

Mintzberg's rounding out of the manager's job is a holistic explanation going beyond a description of management. Building on his ideas, those of other key writers in this field and some of our own research (Martin *et al.*, 2015), we have set out in Figure 2.1 a revised and extended model of his rounded-out manager. This new model also draws on Keith Grint's (2010) four approaches to studying leadership (see Figure 2.1) – management as a position, management as a person, management as results and management as a process – and the work of other key writers and researchers in this field. While this framework is what we call an *entitative* framework, a logical abstraction that treats managers as a homogeneous group, we have tried to show how the context in which management is performed, and the vertical and hierarchical divisions among different levels and kinds of managers, shape managerial effectiveness.

The person in the job

The framework begins with Mintzberg's (2011) notion of 'the person in the job'. People come to take on managerial jobs with an already formed self-concept or identity of who they are, a set of values about what is right and wrong, and ideas about acceptable behaviour for managers. They also bring with them a set of prior experiences that have helped them create a set of job and personal competences, and a body of job-related knowledge, such as professional standards, for example, those required by the Chartered Institute of Personnel and Development (CIPD) in the UK for entry into the HR profession. And, as we saw in Chapter 1, such knowledge and experience also help them develop frames of reference or mindsets through which to view their world and fashion solutions to the problems they face. These mindsets are a way of seeing, and can lead to lots of creative insights, but they are also a way of not seeing (Morgan, 1997). For example, managers who lack knowledge and experience outside their own specific functions, organizations or countries can run into trouble. If you can see from only one perspective, for example as an accountant in XYZ organization in the UK, every problem will be framed in this way, summed up in the aphorism 'If you only have a hammer, every problem is likely to become a nail'. Mintzberg (2011), Finkelstein *et al.* (2009) and others suggest that specific combinations of individual differences, such as personality characteristics, values, experiences, competences, knowledge and mental models all go to make up a manager's personal style, which strongly influences how he or she tackles a job.

In terms of individual differences there are three key debates that we wish to raise because they are highly significant to practising managers. The first is the contribution of emotional intelligence, which has become a widely accepted term amongst managers and the subject of much research (Goleman *et al.*, 2002); the second is managerial judgement (Weick, 2001); while the third is the perceptions that managers bring to bear on what they see and how they see (Finkelstein *et al.*, 2009). The basic argument in support of emotional intelligence is as follows. Managers usually need fairly high levels of what we call cognitive intelligence, which comprise a number of mental abilities associated with learning and performing, for example, numerical and verbal reasoning. This kind of intelligence has been shown to be a very good predictor of management success, as measured by achievements in levels of income and job status (Judge *et al.*, 1999). However, cognitive intelligence is not regarded as sufficient to predict how well a manager will be able to perform in different organizational contexts. So, researchers then turned to examine the impact of personality factors such as the so-called 'big-five' (neuroticism, extraversion, openness to experience, agreeableness and conscientiousness) on management outcomes (Barrick and Mount, 1991). They found, for example, that factors such as conscientiousness were positively related to managers' career success while neuroticism (emotional instability and reactive to stress) was negatively related (Judge *et al.*, 1999).

More recently, writers such as Goleman *et al.* (2002) have argued that emotional intelligence, which focuses on key personal qualities that managers bring to a job, is what will help managers

TABLE 2.1 The rounded manager

Person in the job	Frame	Context	Style	Level	Roles and associated competences (note that some competences are associated with two or more roles)	
Their values	Purpose of the job creation, maintenance, adaptation	Agenda of the work	Which role they favour: science, craft or art	Managing information	Conceiving	Creating and innovating, exercising judgement
Their experience		Managing inside			Communicating	Effective oral and written communication, interpersonal effectiveness
Their knowledge		Managing within			Controlling	Creating a performance culture
Their models					Scheduling	Project management, strategic flexibility
Their degree of emotional intelligence	Purpose of the job creation maintenance, adaptation	Managing outside	How they perform the roles	Managing people	Linking	Building teams, managing conflict, networking, interpersonal effectiveness
Their self-development		The nature of the organization			Leading	Strategic flexibility, delegating, managing change, giving and receiving feedback, creating a performance culture interpersonal effectiveness and intrapersonal effectiveness, making wise judgements and decisions
		The nature of the industry	The relationships among the roles	Managing action		
Their 'attitude of wisdom'	Position the product/market strategy, structures and systems of the business	The national institution and cultural context			Doing	Building teams, coaching, dealing with ambiguity, creating and innovating

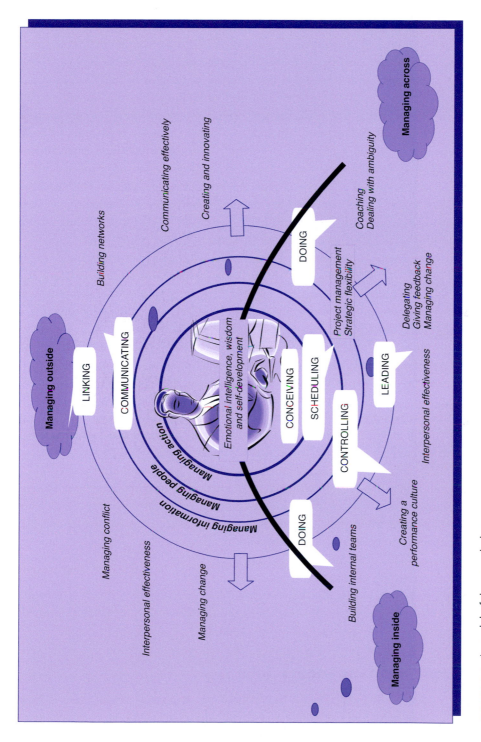

FIGURE 2.1 A model of the rounded manager

perform effectively. Emotional intelligence has been defined by Goleman as an individual's potential for mastering the skills of self-awareness, self-management, social awareness and relationship management. These skills, in turn, become the basis for learned abilities or competences. For example, self-awareness provides an accurate means for an individual to self-assess his or her strengths and weaknesses, a competence that is essential for someone seeking to manage a career. Emotional intelligence, however, is not something that one is necessarily born with, nor is it a fixed personality trait. One of its key features is that it can be developed, in some people quite substantially. Quite how emotional intelligence differs from, and adds to, what the big-five personality factors are able to predict has been a subject of recent research. These works suggest that there is no strong evidence showing that emotional intelligence is able to predict key leadership and management outcomes beyond those already predicted by the big-five personality factors and cognitive intelligence (Harms and Credé, 2010). Indeed, some researchers have argued that emotional intelligence may be counter-productive because managers who are too sensitive to others' and their own emotions may be unable to make untroubled and dispassionate decisions (Antonakis, 2009).

A second feature that forms an important input into what a person brings to a job is judgement, which has a number of dimensions to it, including wisdom (Weick, 2001), managerial hubris (exaggerated self-confidence) and overconfidence (Finkelstein *et al.*, 2009). Again, we will discuss these in more detail later on in this chapter; at this stage, however, it is worth pointing out that the abilities to reflect critically on what one has learned during the course of taking action and to be able to exercise sound judgement in making decisions are core skills that shape managerial performance in the long term. It may also be evident to you that there is a close relationship between wisdom, self-awareness and the ability of managers to reflect critically on their actions, again a point to which we shall return later in this chapter.

A third set of important person-related features that influence how managers do their jobs and the outcomes they achieve are what Finkelstein *et al.* (2009) call *key perceptual filters*. These draw on classic work by Herbert Simon (1916–2001) on managerial decision-making, and include:

- bounded rationality, which refers to cognitive limits on managers' comprehension or biases over important elements that might influence decisions, for example, recent research has shown how physically attractive people do better at job interviews than unattractive people, even when attractiveness has no bearing on job performance;
- selective perceptions, for example, what managers choose to 'notice' in memos, meetings, interpersonal relations, etc.; and
- interpretation of stimuli or signals, which refers to the meanings they attach to these stimuli or signals, for example, the extent to which they see other managers or employees as helping or hindering their work, or the regard they hold them in.

The components of managers' jobs

Mintzberg's (2011) next key contribution lies in analysing managerial jobs into three components. The first is the *frame* of the job, the second is the *agenda* of the work to be undertaken and the third is the *context* in which the work takes place.

The frame of the manager's job

The frame of the job is defined by its purpose, perspective and position. *Purpose* refers to what a manager is attempting to do with the unit he or she is managing. For example, the frame might be to run a business school to produce high-quality education, or to manage a hospital ward, or to run a whole organization. Usually, the job is circumscribed by the collective *perspective* the organization has taken on the unit or department's role and how it fits into its 'theory of the business', or what has become known in everyday business language as the 'business model'. For example, the US-based Sears organization developed a customer–service–profit chain to describe how all units might work together to create profits through high levels of customer satisfaction (Heskett *et al.*, 2008). This idea has underpinned the business models of many retailing and service companies over the last few decades. The final aspect of the frame of the job is its *position*, which broadly refers to how an organization or unit locates itself in its external product–market environment and how it proposes to do business. Michael Porter, a well-known writer on strategy, developed a positioning model of competitive strategy in the 1980s that is still used extensively today. It poses three alternatives, all of which will have different implications for managers and how they manage people. These alternatives are seeking to compete by: (1) being cost-effective throughout the value chain, (2) being different from competitors in terms of quality or services or (3) focusing on niche segments in the market either through costs or quality.

The frame of the job gives rise to the first of Mintzberg's key managerial roles in his original work, which is *conceiving*. This role is defined as 'thinking through the purpose, perspective and positioning of a particular unit to be managed over a particular period of time' (Mintzberg, 1994, p. 13). As he also suggests, managers interpret their jobs differently depending on their style and on the circumstances of the organization. For example, some managers are forced to adopt a particular style because of external requirements or tight internal controls, whereas others are able to be more creative. Managers also vary according to how vague or sharp their frame is; some frames are characterized by a highly focused aim, such as achieving x per cent in sales revenue, whereas others are characterized by a more flexible desire to become the best company in a particular industry.

What does this conceiving role mean in practice? Gareth Morgan (2003) has described two general managerial competences that help managers 'imaginize' through new mindsets. These are:

- creativity and innovation (which we explore in more detail in Chapter 9);
- strategic flexibility.

Creativity, to borrow from Marcel Proust, a nineteenth-century philosopher, is a voyage of discovery, and consists not in seeing new lands, but in seeing with new eyes. In his earlier well-known work, Morgan (1997) developed a range of different metaphors or 'eyes' for reframing problems, based on the rationale that a way of seeing is also a way of not seeing. According to him, if organizations are to survive in an increasingly changeable world, managers need to use multiple lenses to analyse problems and be able to reframe them to produce novel and compelling solutions. More recently, he has relabelled these metaphors as *mindsets*, the concept we shall use in this book to describe different ways of seeing.

Being *strategically flexible* involves an attitude of mind as well as employing a number of practical competences. These include thinking about problems as opportunities for learning, anticipating major problems before they happen, learning through strategic planning by using techniques such as scenario planning and search conferencing, using multiple perspectives to analyse and solve problems, and challenging conventional organizational wisdom before it becomes a kind of 'psychic prison' that traps managers and their organizations into outmoded ways of working. For example, it has now become commonplace in industries such as air travel to 'put customers first' by creating a business class for those who wish to pay the extra money for such a service, but this was not always the case. Passengers in the 1980s were 'cargo to be transported rather than customers to be pleased', with engineering and logistics dominating airlines' policies rather than marketing and customer considerations (Pascale *et al.*, 2000). As a consequence, airlines that failed to adopt a new 'customer-first' perspective have gone out of business. Similarly, those retailers that have been slow to adapt to the Internet have suffered badly in terms of market share because consumers' shopping habits have been changed by the online business models of firms like Amazon.

The agenda of the work

A number of management researchers, including Mintzberg (1994/2011), Kotter (1990) and Grint (2010), have pointed to the importance of agenda-setting as a key influence on managers' jobs. As Kotter cogently stated, agenda-setting refers to 'figuring out what to do, despite all the uncertainty of what is going on inside and outside the organization'. Managers have to respond to particular issues that are framed by the job, in terms of position, purpose, perspective and also their preferences, which are essentially dictated by their style. Such issues are usually 'chunked' into manageable tasks, where the key managerial role associated with setting and carrying out an agenda is *scheduling*. Scheduling is likely to involve prioritizing activities and allocating time and resources to carrying out these activities on a day-by-day and week-by-week basis. In addition to strategic flexibility, project management skills are likely to be essential. The kinds of skills involved here will include: defining the scope and mandate for the project and developing a project mission, producing a project plan, creating and deploying a project team, keeping track of the project progress and being able to close the project once the goals have been achieved.

CASE 2.2 **A CERTAIN KIND OF MANAGER**

Mario Moretti Polegato, who was 62 in 2014, is the owner of Geox footwear, an Italian company making sports shoes. His company has grown rapidly from a company that began life in 1997 as a 'hobby', employing five young people, into an established global retailer that employs 30,000 people in 1,300 outlets worldwide.

However, according to an *Economist* article (March 2004), Polegato had a number of advantages. First, he is Italian, and Italy has led the world in footwear design and manufacture, especially in the region around Venice. Second, he brought some innovation to the business by attempting to solve the problem of foot odour and clamminess around the toes. This interest in solving the problems of sweat derive from his personal experience of running in America, during which time he developed an idea of a 'membrane that fitted between the sole and the foot and stopped water from getting in through the holes, but allowed the vapour from perspiration to get out'.

He patented this idea and others, which he took to the branded designers of sports shoes, including Nike and Adidas, but without success. So he turned to design and production himself, with his staff of five who still work with him. Polegato stressed the need for innovation in a BBC interview in 2014. He claimed that Italian schools and governments don't support innovation and that, although Italian entrepreneurs do well overseas, the political system discouraged innovators like him. Thus he has had to battle against the tide and events such as the Eurozone crisis.

Like any business in the fashion industry, and sports shoes are a major part of it, tastes and circumstances can change. So Polegato now plans to close down some of his outlets in Europe and open up 400 new stores in Asia.

1 What are the kinds of values and experiences that Mario Polegato has brought to his job, and how have they shaped his business?
2 How does he display creativity and strategic flexibility?
3 Thinking about your thoughts on management, what values are likely to influence you as a manager – either now or in the future?

The context of the manager's job

So far, we have been describing the core of the manager's job, the person in the job, within a frame made operational through an agenda. We should note, however, that the core of a manager's job is located *inside*, *within* and *outside* the organization (Mintzberg, 2011). The inside context is the department or unit in which the manager works, over which he or she may have direct control, and this context is often the main focus for many middle managers. However, managers also have to work within an organization and liaise with other departments to achieve their objectives. For example, sales managers have to work with production departments, and HR managers rarely enjoy direct authority over other departments but have to liaise with these managers and their units to achieve their HR objectives. Finally, managers achieve their objectives by working with people and resources outside the organization, often relying on these to get the job done, despite having no formal authority or leverage to draw upon to achieve their objectives. So, for example, the main activities of a chief executive often involve sitting on national committees, or developing close relations with key customers or partners, rather than in managing his or her executives. This external context can provide the most difficult challenges to a manager, and requires *networking, communications and interpersonal* competences of a high order to achieve success. Nowadays, recruiters in the UK who are responsible for taking on graduate management trainees emphasize communications and personal skills, rather than the class or type of degree, precisely because so much of modern work requires three types of networking: operational networking with the people you have to work with to get the job done; personal networking with people from outside of the organization to learn from them; and strategic networking with senior managers inside and outside of your field to look for best practice and beyond the industry (Ibarra, 2003).

Managing on three levels

To be effective, managers have to translate their personal qualities (or, as they are sometimes known, personal competencies) into effective behavioural skills (or behavioural competences) inside, within and outside their organizations. According to Mintzberg (1989/2011), managers demonstrate these behavioural competences on three planes (or levels), moving outwards from the conceptual plane to the doing or action plane (see Figure 2.1). Thus, managers not only conceive and schedule, as we have just discussed, but also:

- manage *action*, by doing things directly themselves;
- manage *people* to get things done through others;
- manage *information* to influence people to take action.

As Mintzberg pointed out, managers can choose to operate at any of these planes, but need to understand any action taken at one plane has 'knock-on' consequences for action taken on other planes. Managers are also stylized by the level they prefer to work: some administrators, accountants or planners prefer to work at the informational level; 'people-oriented' managers prefer to work through others; whereas 'doers', often in front-line supervision, 'roll their sleeves up' and take direct action. In his 2004 book, Mintzberg reworked these issues of preferences in managerial styles and levels into a model of three poles of managing: management as a science, management as a vision and management as a craft (see Figure 2.2).

Managers who prefer to work at the informational level are often influenced by the idea of *management as a science*, which involves applying rational techniques and thinking about leadership and strategy, best achieved through systematic assessment and planning. Managers who prefer to work through people are more likely to be influenced by the idea of *management as an art*, which relies on creative insights and holding out a novel and compelling vision that others can buy into. Managers who prefer to work through action are influenced by the idea that *management is a craft*, learned and practised through direct experience, experimentation and action.

The critical point, according to Mintzberg, is that the rounded manager needs to function effectively at all three levels and achieve a degree of balance among the three poles in Figure 2.2. He contended that there were three balanced styles:

- A *problem-solving style*, which combines the strengths of rational analysis with practical experience (and presumably just enough people-management intuition thrown in). Such a style, common among middle-level managers in production and engineering environments, is reminiscent of the Germanic model of management.
- An *engaging style*, which is people oriented and experience based, but with just enough science to take it out of the 'gifted amateur' category. Such a style is associated with those managers who prefer to coach and facilitate, and is reminiscent of a British cultural stereotype of good managers.
- A *visionary style*, which is strong on art and vision, but is also rooted in experience, again with just enough science thrown in to give the ideas credibility. This style is one that is associated with successful entrepreneurs, and is close to a stereotype of an American model of good management.

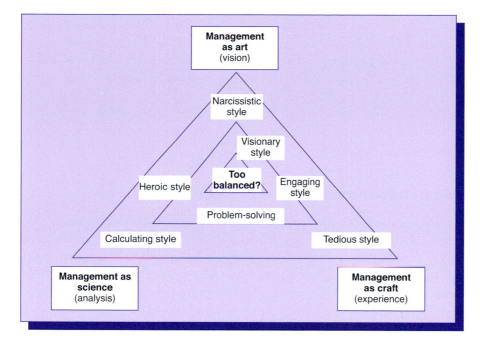

FIGURE 2.2 Managerial styles

(*Source:* adapted from Mintzberg, 2004, p. 93.)

Note that his idea of balance among styles, however, lay in reconciling two out of the three, with just enough of a third style to keep things in check. His view was that if we try to achieve a balance among all three simultaneously, we run the risk of either having no style at all or of not making a choice over how to manage.

Mintzberg also highlighted the dangers of too little a balance in styles. *Calculating* managers who manage purely at the informational level run the risk of dehumanizing the situation and lacking sufficient grounding in experience. This charge has often been made against the recruitment strategies of firms that target inexperienced MBA graduates and provide them with high degrees of responsibility early on in their careers. In Chapter 3, we shall look at the idea of talent management and some of its problems that exemplify this danger. *Tedious* managers, on the other hand, are often guilty of not being able to see the big picture because they rarely move out of their own comfort zone of experience. Often, this charge is made against engineers or other professionals who are promoted because they have been good at their professional 'craft', but who fail to provide people with a compelling vision or well-worked-out strategy. *Narcissistic* managers run the danger of being strong on vision, but with little else. Narcissism among managers has become a widely discussed topic among management researchers (Claxton *et al.*, 2015), often associated with executives who become out of control and impulsive, lose contact with reality, have excessive confidence in their own judgement and are disproportionately focused on image. Finally, *heroic* managers, according to Mintzberg (2011), are perhaps the most dangerous of all. Their style is influenced above all else by the need to promote shareholder value, which has involved a shift away from hard analysis but not from calculation. This time, however, the calculation is about how best to promote their careers (such as the account of Elton Mayo in the last chapter). The heroic style is largely about providing drama, rather than true art, and is focused on selling stories without substance to the investment community. Mintzberg's 'tongue-in-cheek' characterization of heroic leaders involves: (1) looking out rather than in; (2) ignoring existing business, because anything established takes time to fix; then (3) doing anything you can to get the stock price up and cash in before you are found out.

We are now in a position to attach behavioural competences to each of these three levels of managing and their associated poles.

Managing by information and the problem-solving style

The first broad category of competences is *communication*, which is the collection and dissemination of information. John Kotter (1990), in his seminal work on general managers, pointed out that much of communication wasn't written and formal but oral and informal, sometimes operating at the non-verbal level – joking and kidding and talking about anything and everything remotely connected with the business with people inside and outside the organization. Mintzberg (2011) reinforced this point when he suggested that nearly every serious study of managerial communications has stressed the informal and face-to-face nature of communications. However, given the availability of e-mail, other electronic means of communication such as mobile (aka cell) phones, video-conferencing and social media, and the growth in 'virtual' organizations and globally distributed working that makes face-to-face communication more difficult, the emphasis on developing skills in electronic communication is likely to become more important (see Chapter 8). Regardless of the medium, much of managerial work is concerned with building human networks to access information, sifting through this information and sharing what is relevant with outsiders and insiders. Given this key role, communicating effectively through formal and informal means and acquiring interpersonal effectiveness skills are essential to effective managerial performance.

Gareth Morgan (2003) and Mintzberg (2011) have provided some excellent insights into what managers need to be able to do to communicate effectively. There are at least three clusters of competences associated with effective communication. These are:

- developing self-awareness, self-regulation, motivation, empathy and social skills such as influencing and listening;
- monitoring all forms of useful information concerning internal and external events to become the 'Nerve Centre' of the organization;
- communicating effectively by tailoring the message, ensuring clarity of communication, engaging in two-way listening, receiving feedback well and understanding non-verbal communication;
- giving feedback to your boss, to colleagues, subordinates, etc., and being able to deliver good news, bad news and constructive criticism.

The second broad category associated with the informational role is using information in a *controlling* sense to get people to act. Such action is provoked by developing information systems, by designing structures of control and by issuing directives for people to follow. For example, managers often spend lots of time creating and using planning and performance control systems, including budgets and appraisal. By defining responsibilities and creating hierarchies, they indirectly influence information flows. Managers can also issue instructions and directives, although, as researchers have surprisingly pointed out, this directive style of management is not usually favoured in a Western context, which tends to regard authoritarian leadership as toxic (Chhokar *et al.*, 2008), nor is it the traditional Japanese way of managing, which is focused more on managing by consensus.

There is little doubt, however, that one of the key competences associated with controlling is the ability to create a performance culture in an organization. In addition to the three sets of competences above, Morgan (2003) has stressed the following sets of skills that managers need to be able to:

- Promote quality and continuous learning as core values in an organization.
- Create stretching benchmarks by measuring performance against practices from other organizations or industries and continuously raising the standards of these comparisons.
- Use problems as opportunities by using them as springboards for future success rather than treating them as barriers to change.
- Unlearn to create room for new developments, because progress often requires managers to take a couple of steps back and unlearn previously held beliefs and attitudes in order to go forward.
- Challenge conventional wisdom by looking outside an individual or organization's conventional mindset for new solutions and ways of thinking, or by appointing 'deviants', 'heretics' or 'court jesters' to think and say the 'unthinkable'.
- Improve performance through action-based learning, which uses real, workplace-based problems facing the organization as the basis for learning and aims to produce solutions to these problems, rather than to use 'schooled' learning that is remote from practice.
- Understand and deal with resistance to change, by 'knowing where people are coming from' and attempting to 'reframe' problems as opportunities for interested parties.
- Think 'win–win', by ensuring that all parties can achieve something of their aims, without any one party being seen to dominate the agenda.
- Manage projects, using the skills outlined in the previous section.

Managing through people and the engaging style

The second plane on which managers have to act is through people, which is more direct than managing through information but not as direct as managing by action. As Mintzberg (2011) suggests, the focus here is on helping other people make this happen – in other words *affect* not *effect*. Once again, most of the studies of management have stressed that much of managers' time is taken up with managing people over whom they have no direct control, such as those individuals and groups within and outside the organization. However, you would not get this impression from reading many of the management texts, which lay great stress on the relationship between superiors and subordinates, and are rooted in a model of pyramid-style organizations. Such a focus on hierarchical relationships, while not outmoded, is likely to form even less of a manager's time in the new forms of organization, such as the virtual and networked companies that are beginning to appear in many industries. We shall look at these new organizational structures in Chapter 4.

We can identify at least three broad sets of competences associated with managing people within and without organizations. These are *leading*, *linking* and *networking*, which have received lots of attention in the business literature. Of these three, leading is the one that has received most attention, and would require a book in itself to do this subject justice. For our purposes, however, we wish to treat leadership as a subset of management rather than as something distinctive in its own right. You cannot manage without leading just as you cannot lead without managing. Managers have to exercise leadership at the individual, group and unit levels in their organizations. *Individual leadership* refers to the ability of managers to inspire, motivate, coach, develop, drive, push and mentor people. Morgan's (2003) model also highlights these competences, many of which are associated with managing change and developing people. *Group leadership*, which according to some researchers is the most important level at which leadership can be exercised, became a popular focus of attention following the 'rediscovery' of teamworking in the 1980s by Japanese organizations. Thus, building and managing teams (Morgan, 2003) are key competences for group leadership. However, managers also have to provide a different kind of leadership at the unit level, which is sometimes differentiated from the personal or group level by applying the label 'strategic leadership' (Schoemaker *et al.*, 2013). Often, as we noted earlier, managers act as figureheads or in a symbolic role as strategic leaders, representing the organization to the outside world or at ceremonial events such as graduations. This level of leadership requires managers to be strategically flexible and resolute at the same time by creating a strong, performance-based culture (Morgan, 2003). In doing so, it also requires mangers to be comfortable in challenging their own and others' assumptions (an idea close to the notion of reflexivity we discussed in the first chapter) to learn from their mistakes and to deal with what Keith Grint has described as 'wicked problems' rather than 'tame' ones. As Grint (2005) has argued, wicked problems are:

- complex in that any action taken to solve a problem is likely to affect the environment which gave rise to the problem in the first place;
- often intractable, since there is no obvious relationship between cause and effect, and thus can't be solved purely through rational analysis – what kind of problem you have depends on who and what you already know.

In essence, wicked problems are inherently contested and are often only resolved temporarily through political solutions. Such problems, almost by definition, are best tackled by the team rather than individual managers, since no single person has the knowledge and abilities to address these by him or herself.

Following on from this need for managers to resolve wicked problems, Mintzberg (2011) has argued that nothing legitimizes managers' positions and image more than their ability to connect and network with the world outside of their organizations or units. The exercise of leadership by advocacy of the managers' unit and by being the focal point of external pressures and information coming inwards is a core managing people competence. Such a role is often underplayed in the texts on leadership, but is increasingly important in complex organizational networks and in newer forms of networked organization. For example, many managers spend much of their productive time promoting their units with managers of other units or with potential customers. At the same time, they act as a buffer or protector of their units from external pressures, such as the manager who spends his or her time taking criticism directly from irate customers when things go wrong as a result of actions taken by staff. Mintzberg used the metaphor of the manager as a valve to capture the essence of this role, which is probably more accurate than the use of the term 'gatekeeper'. Key competences associated with this linking and networking role are *interpersonal effectiveness*, *managing conflict* and *communicating effectively*. It also requires elements of emotional intelligence. The dimensions of emotional intelligence most associated with the linking and networking roles include a high degree of self-awareness, empathy and social competence. The networking aspect of the role also requires managers to create and develop a wide range of contacts to lobby effectively, provide information and set agendas for action, as well as mediate between the pressures coming in from the outside by disseminating information and delegating effectively. This is part of what has become know as a manager's social capital, which is defined as the ability to build 'bridges and bonds' with people inside of and outside of the organization. Social capital has been found to be one of the most important drivers of organizational knowledge creation and in creating positive external images of the organization (Martin *et al.*, 2011).

Managing action and the visionary style

To manage effectively, managers have to take a direct involvement in actions. This is a controversial topic, with some writers preferring managers to be thinkers rather than doers. However, in most Western industrialized settings, managers are required and respected for being able to take action, which includes leading by example and avoiding being seen as disconnected from colleagues (Martin *et al.*, 2015). As we have already discussed, the debate over managers as thinkers rather than doers is reflected at the national institutional level. For example, one researcher who studied how British employees in Japanese-owned factories felt about Japanese managers concluded that Japanese managers were more likely to obtain respect from their British employees because they were willing to become directly involved in sorting out problems on the shopfloor, reflecting an engaging style. Similarly, senior German managers in manufacturing industry tend to be highly qualified engineers who are able to solve technical problems themselves, reflecting a problem-solving style. This ability to take direct action was contrasted with senior British managers in UK manufacturing firms, often with no technical background (Stewart *et al.*, 1994). Mintzberg labelled this the *doing* role, which refers to getting closer to the action, sometimes managing the doing of action directly in a supervisory sense and sometimes doing the job themselves. Doing can be 'inside', carrying out projects and solving problems, substituting and doing regular work such as a surgeon leading a medical team during a complex operation or a professor leading a research team by directly undertaking the work him or herself. In addition, doing can be 'outside', in the sense of doing deals and handling negotiations, essential components of many managers' jobs. Competences associated with this action level are being able to deal with ambiguity and helping others deal with ambiguity. On many occasions, especially during significant change, people will feel uncomfortable about the lack of clarity and certainty in their jobs. These feelings are related to personality and preferred learning and thinking styles. Understanding your own personal tolerance for ambiguity, and being able to strike the right balance with others between imposing structure on the one hand and creating an atmosphere of openness and flexibility on the other, are essential skills.

CASE 2.3 EXERCISE ON THE DISTINCTION BETWEEN MANAGEMENT AND LEADERSHIP

Background

In the preceding paragraphs on the nature of management, we have alluded to a distinction that is sometimes made between management and leadership, although our position is that leadership is really a subset of management. Nevertheless, it is widely believed that management and leadership are quite distinctive in some ways. This following exercise is designed to help you examine this binary distinction. However, it also highlights the problems of binary thinking by pointing to possible overlaps between what might be labelled as management and leadership. It also helps to identify how you can implement leadership in your day-to-day jobs.

We know that organizational performance is increasingly a product of the engagement, motivation and focus of the people the organization employs. We have also argued that a major influence on people's engagement, motivation and focus is the quality of managerial performance, of which leadership is a key element in our model. Consequently, encouraging managers, supervisors, team leaders, etc., to be better leaders is an important and continual theme in management education and training.

Task 1

In Table 2.2 is a list of activities, some of which could be classified as managerial, some of which could be classified as leadership, and some of which could fall into both categories. Use Table 2.3 to position these activities.

Task 2

Reflect on why you have placed these activities in the various categories. What makes them management or leadership oriented? If you have placed some of the activities in the middle, why have you done so?

Source: adapted from Gillen, 2004.

TABLE 2.2 Lists of managerial and leadership activities

Delegate tasks	Act as interface between team and outside
Use analytical data to support recommendations	Plan and prioritize steps to task achievement
Motivate staff	Explain goals, plan and roles
Ensure predictability	Inspire people
Appeal to people's emotions	Coordinate effort
Coordinate resources	Share a vision
Provide focus	Give orders and instructions
Guide progress	Monitor feelings and morale
Create a 'culture'	Monitor progress
Check task completion	Create a positive team feeling
Follow systems and procedures	Ensure effective induction
Monitor budgets, tasks, etc.	Provide development opportunities
Unleash potential	Use analytical data to forecast trends
Monitor progress	Look 'over the horizon'
Take risks	Appeal to rationale thinking
Be a good role model	Build teams

TABLE 2.3 Worksheet for Task 1

Very high on management	Managerially oriented	Strong elements of both management and leadership	Leadership oriented	Very high on leadership

THE ROUNDED MANAGER

The process of rounding out the manager

It should now be evident that effective management requires the role holders to be 'rounded out'; managers who emphasize one set of roles, style or preferred level of managing at the expense of others are likely to become unbalanced, and may fail to perform in the medium or long term. This is not to say that context and preferred style are unimportant – indeed, as we have already argued, the opposite is the case – but that a rounding out of a manager is likely to enable him or her to be able to meet changing contexts and preferences by those for whom they are responsible and accountable. A similar point has been made by Gareth Morgan (1997) whose seminal work on metaphors in management argued that managers need to be able to read situations through multiple lenses and act on these more complex readings to organize and manage effectively. He quoted F. Scott Fitzgerald, an eminent American writer during the 1930s, who suggested that the sign of intelligent people was the ability to hold two or more contrasting ideas at the same time and work with them. This is a key competence for managers, and is obviously linked to the ability to deal with ambiguity and uncertainty (Morgan, 2003).

As Mintzberg (2011) cautions, slavish adherence to some of the well-worn nostrums produced by the management gurus and leading practitioners – such as 'don't think, do', 'steady, fire, aim' or 'it's all about communications' – is inconsistent with rounded managers. Moreover, although it is possible in conceptual terms to analyse managerial jobs into distinctive roles and knowledge-based competences, it is close to impossible to distinguish them behaviourally, because work is not practised as a set of independent or atomistic lists of competencies but as a whole. Thus, managers who think 'their way into acting' at the expense of 'acting their way into thinking' or who manage well on the outside but fail to manage on the inside will, more or less inevitably, be unable to achieve significant results in the long run. Similarly, the core roles of leading, communicating, conceiving, linking, controlling and doing cannot in practice be separated into outside and outside roles, nor can they be separated from each other, because they tend to infuse each other and blend into a mix of all.

If this is true of the key managerial roles, it is equally true of the competences associated with them. For example, interpersonal effectiveness is as important to linking and doing as it is to leading. Similarly, creating a performance culture and managing change are part of the roles most associated with managing on the outside as well as managing on the inside. Of course, how managers ultimately perform will be shaped by their preferred style as well as context. As Mintzberg argued, style will influence which roles a manager tends to stress, how he or she acts out these preferred roles, and how one role relates to another. For example, our research has shown that managers in the UK healthcare sector tend to prefer linking rather than leading, because they are often dealing with autonomous and relatively powerful professionals who have been brought up in a fragmented culture in which doctors have considerable personal and positional power (Martin *et al.*, 2015). On the other hand, the preferred management style in the US privatized healthcare sector, which has less of a history of employing autonomous, powerful and highly rewarded professionals, is more likely to emphasize leading and controlling. In terms of the acting out of roles, managers in small organizations and entrepreneurial firms will probably favour more doing than conceiving. As Weick (2001) points out, however, these roles are related. Acting your way into thinking about strategy, if done reflectively, has major benefits for managers over the think–lead–act style. The most obvious of these advantages is that it requires managers to learn through incremental actions and experience rather than implement abstract principles or theories without having knowledge beforehand of how they may influence outcomes.

Making wise decisions

Making sound judgements

We have already introduced this idea when discussing the person in the job in an earlier section. Surprisingly, making wise decisions thorough sound judgement is rarely discussed in the management literature. There were some early attempts to deal with this issue in the 1950s and 1960s, when a group of researchers at American universities set out to find a more scientific method to make judgements. They created a discipline called 'decision science', which aimed to take the human element out of risk analysis, claiming it would provide a way of making soundly based decisions for a future fraught with uncertainties. This approach involved using computer models for forecasting, estimating the probabilities of possible outcomes and determining the best course of action, thus avoiding the various biases that humans bring to decision-making. Such models, the researchers believed, would provide rational answers to questions such as whether and where to build a factory, how to deal with industrial relations negotiations and how to manage investments.

Many business schools adopted management science as part of the core curriculum, in part because it gave them some legitimacy with their science colleagues, and even some senior policymakers were persuaded by the arguments. Decision science's highpoint was probably during the Vietnam war, in the 1960s and 1970s, when Robert McNamara, then America's Defense Secretary, used such techniques to forecast the outcome of the conflict (though, as it turned out, without much success). But, for the most part, the approach did not quite catch on, especially in the less rationally oriented countries such as the UK. Decision-makers, whether in business or politics, were loath to hand over their power to computers, preferring instead to go with their gut instincts (*The Economist*, 22 January 2004). If this lack of faith in the application of rational sciences to business was evident in the last few decades of the twentieth century, it is even more so now as we operate in an increasingly unknowable and unpredictable world, disrupted ever more frequently by technology and global events. As a consequence, many managers have been grappling with the problem of how to exercise judgements that strike a balance between overconfidence and over-cautious doubt.

Reflection and judgement

Karl Weick (2001) began an engaging discussion on this issue when proposing that having an attitude of wisdom would be one of the key management competences in the 'increasingly unknowable world'. Drawing on case research from studies of disaster management, when decisions can have immediate and life-threatening consequences, Weick examined 'wise' practices. So, for example, firefighters cited in his research operated by a maxim 'don't hand over a forest fire to an incoming crew during the heat of the day' because that was when winds were strongest, the temperature at its hottest and humidity at its highest. Thus, a handover during the evening gave the incoming crew more time to learn and adjust to the conditions of uncertainty. Such maxims, he argued, revealed two initial properties of wisdom – *reflection* and *judgement*.

Reflection referred to a way of considering events in the light of their consequences in a wholly systemic fashion; in other words, it is about making considered decisions by articulating the 'big picture'. If reflection, as Weick argued, dealt with the substance of decision-making, judgement was more about the process involved in coming to reflective decisions. Judgement has often been thought of as 'gumption' or 'common sense', which to most of us means bringing to bear common knowledge to the decision-making process. However, Weick believes bringing judgement to the reflective decision-making process is more than mere common sense and must involve using the 'non-obvious, significant, shrewd and clever' characteristics of decisions that deal simultaneously with *knowing* and *doubt*.

This process of judgement exercised during reflective decision-making, according to Weick, focuses not so much on what is known but on how knowledge is held, shared and put to use. And, for him, having an attitude of wisdom is the key to exercising sound judgements, which is succinctly defined as knowing without excessive confidence or caution. Overconfidence, he argues, arises because managers and entrepreneurs find it difficult to doubt what they 'know' or admit to themselves that they can know only a small part of what is knowable about any situation. We have seen many examples of such overconfidence in events leading up to the Global Financial Crisis in 2007–8, when banks such as the Royal Bank of Scotland, which sought to become a global player, continued to make acquisitions of other banks despite being warned by investment analysts that they were playing a dangerous game (Fraser, 2014; Martin and Gollan, 2012). Once people made confident decisions, they became excessively attached to them, defending their positions even in the light of contradictory evidence. Such commitment to a course of action inevitably leads to blind spots and inattention to questions and alternatives, yet in business circles committed action is usually seen as preferable to doubt. This is because, as many writers have suggested, businesses and managers value action and anything that gets in the way of action – including reflection and wisdom – is likely to be discouraged.

If we accept the notion of excess confidence, though as we have pointed out this is less likely to be defined as a problem by practitioners, we can also be excessively cautious. On this last topic, there is a much larger literature, because it is seen by managers and businesses as a greater threat to action. This is reflected in their criticisms of business schools, which have been characterized as institutions that produce analytical thinkers rather than 'doers' (Mintzberg, 2004). Excess caution, according to Weick, is a relative concept, depending very much on the position one starts from. So if we admit we don't know (the answer), or if we notice we fail to notice (I've just discovered I was wrong and I should have accepted your alternative answer – you were right!), we begin to doubt ourselves. If those doubts begin from a position of overconfidence, then we move towards wisdom; if, on the other hand, we are too cautious to begin with, then we move further away from being wise. In short, wisdom is a fulcrum around which attitudes vary, and people make sense of their worlds differently, depending on which side of the knowing–doubting scale they place themselves.

Improvisation and wisdom

The main problem for managers, according to Weick, is to act their way into confidence when confidence is already high, because that is a position from which they will find it difficult to return. Instead, Weick, rather controversially, argues that the point of balance between knowing and doubting is best summed up as an intended oxymoron – the 'achievement of ignorance'. This he defines as the ability to act while remaining doubtful. And achieving ignorance, the sign of the wise manager, is based on his or her ability to *improvise* – the metaphor of the manager as a craftsman. Such improvisation is not the ability to make something from nothing, as is sometimes believed, but is the ability to rework existing knowledge and materials to deal with unanticipated ideas and problems during the course of work. In doing so, we produce relatively unique solutions to 'local' problems set in particular contexts, rather than use preplanned recipes in an inflexible way (think again about the saying 'give someone a hammer and every problem becomes a nail'). To give an example, the wise manager is one who when presented with a novel problem – say, the need to get academics or doctors to become more business oriented – is able to use his or her knowledge of people, whether formally or informally derived, and to fashion a solution that will work in a particular context. Thus, in the case of academics and doctors, financial gain may work with some people at certain stages of their lives, whereas the opportunity for flexible work arrangements or to travel may work with others at different points in their careers. Such a wise course of action is qualitatively different from that taken by a manager who, following attendance on a business course where he or she read up on some theory or best practice on motivation through incentive schemes, then tries to apply these without regard to the local circumstances, history or culture of the organization. Such an approach is to treat his or her knowledge as infallible. Instead, wise managers treat their knowledge as fallible, but at the same time have sufficient confidence to take what knowledge they have and combine it with other aspects of their repertoire to deal with new circumstances and problems. In short, this is a learning strategy, in which managers can act their way into thinking as much as they think their way into acting.

In a special issue of a well-known journal devoted to wisdom in management, the editors (Nonaka *et al.*, 2014) have summarized our discussion of wisdom in proposing that being a wise manager requires us to be able to cope with the unexpected and unknown by exercising two types of judgement. The first is an evaluation of what the experience actually means, not by relying on habit or previous experience but by sensitizing oneself to what is going on, often from multiple perspectives and 'listening to a situation from within' (p. 373) before acting – a kind of cool and considered reflection. The second is to act by 'making a stand' so that the situation is changed into an 'event with focus' (p. 374), which allows those whom we manage to read into the situation in a novel, credible and, hopefully, compelling story. In the case that follows, we ask you to apply some of these ideas to the case we researched of the Royal Bank of Scotland.

CASE 2.4 FRED GOODWIN AND THE ROYAL BANK OF SCOTLAND

The case of RBS has become a well-known landmark in management and organizational studies because it became the biggest failure in British corporate history in 2008 and almost led to the collapse of the UK economy. The excellent journalistic accounts of RBS, including two books by Ian Martin (2013) and Ian Fraser (2014), and our own research (Martin and Gollan, 2012; Martin et al., 2013), all point to the role of erstwhile RBS CEO, Fred Goodwin, as a major factor in causing the demise of what was at the time the largest bank in the world with assets of three trillion pounds.

Goodwin is portrayed in most accounts as a kind of pantomime villain, who enjoyed his nickname of Fred the Shred bestowed on him by employees in his former bank for his ruthless cost-cutting approach to corporate turnaround. His background was modest and not untypical of middle class children in the West of Scotland. Goodwin's academic career culminated in a law degree at the University of Glasgow, which he followed up by training as an accountant, working in the profession and then being appointed to a key role in the Clydesdale Bank based in Glasgow. He was subsequently headhunted by Sir George Mathewson in 1998 and promoted to CEO in 2001. This promotion coincided with the spectacular rise of RBS, for which he received much credit.

The Bank was deemed to be a small regional player from its inception in the early 1700s in Edinburgh right through until the late 1990s. Along with Mathewson, Goodwin set about the 'great aggrandisement' of the Royal Bank of Scotland (a name reduced to RBS for marketing purposes), through an ambitious, and some have argued nationalistic, program of acquisitions of mainly financial institutions throughout the world. This began with a hostile takeover of NatWest, a bank three times its size, which propelled it into becoming a global player, i.e. Europe's second largest bank and the fifth largest in the world by market capitalization. Goodwin and his board went on to make further acquisitions, especially in the USA, culminating the takeover of ABN Amro in 2007, just prior to the Global Financial Crisis.

Yet, only a short time earlier, he hadn't even been a banker. In his early forties, he was feted by the British establishment and world financial press. In 2003, *Forbes* magazine awarded him the accolade of global businessman of the year, which was followed up by a report by Harvard Business School, which described him and his team as the 'masters of integration'. Perhaps understandably, Goodwin's ego entered the stratosphere, which was evidenced by the new headquarters built on the outskirts of Edinburgh, close to the airport which housed his private jet. Goodwin became notorious for his obsessive attention to detail in designing the new building, including choosing the colour of carpets, the design of fountains. He also took a near intrusive interest in the commissioning and operation of the RBS Business School, which extended to making decisions on which cases his senior and middle managers should or should not study (one of our interviewees told us that Goodwin had written on a Post-it note that a case of a top British retailer was unsuitable!).

Despite these obsessions and his notorious bullying behaviour towards his managers, which occurred weekly in the 'Monday Morning Beatings', 'everyone wanted a slice of him'. This included the royal family, the Chancellor of the Exchequer, Gordon Brown and other members of the British establishment that saw financial services as a way of restoring Britain's economy. So in 2005 he was awarded a knighthood, which, according to his close colleagues, only fuelled his ego.

Goodwin's strategy appeared to be defined by a fixation on growth, despite warnings by financial analysts and his promises to his own board that he wasn't planning further acquisitions.

Yet, he continued to plan for growth, often unknown to his board members. This culminated in the purchase of ABN Amro, a large Dutch-based bank, with interests in the USA and Asia. Although analysts warned against such a purchase and a major report on banking behaviour in 2000 recommended that banks should be restrained from becoming too big to fail, encouraged by politicians and his confidence, Goodwin was attributed with persuading his board in 'a moment of collective madness' (a description by one of our interviewees who was at the meeting when the decision was taken) to sanction the acquisition without performing the usual level of 'due diligence'.

A few months later, as the 'credit crunch' that led to the Global Financial Crisis began to take hold, the takeover of ABN Amro tipped RBS over the edge. It had extended itself financially to make the purchase during a period when it could not borrow the short term money it needed to survive and discovered it had acquired a huge amount of toxic assets through its purchase and previous forays into investment banking, a field that Goodwin did not understand. The UK government, in one of the closest calls in history in which Britain came close to bankruptcy, was forced to bail out RBS.

Goodwin was eventually sacked and lost his knighthood, but retired on an annual pension of £700,000. Yet, as Ian Martin (2013) pointed out, to focus only on Goodwin and let his board, the City and government figures get away 'Scot free' was wrong. At the time of writing, none of the bankers who caused the crisis have gone to jail, huge incentives to engage in similar behaviour have not diminished despite attempts to curb bonuses, and regulation has amounted to tinkering rather than major institutional change.

1 How does our discussion of wisdom help explain what happened at RBS?

A MODEL OF EFFECTIVE MANAGEMENT

Bringing these ideas together on the rounded manager, we can map out the relationship between the person in the job (i.e. what managers bring to a job) and their effectiveness as managers. The core relationship is set out in the horizontal sequence of boxes in Figure 2.3.

So, what we propose is that effective management performance is related to the person in the job, including:

- their values, previous experience, age, career stage, their models of management (assumptions);
- their degree of emotional intelligence and their self-development;
- their perceptual filters, which include their frames of reference and how these affect their interpretation of signals from external stimuli, bounded rationality and biases, and selective perceptions.

However, it is also clear from the previous discussions that the relationship between these personal qualities and management performance is directly influenced by two key *mediating* factors, which are:

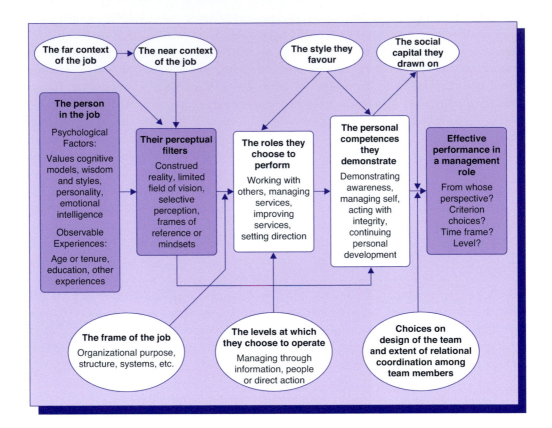

FIGURE 2.3 Modelling the relationship between the manager in the job and effective managerial performance

- the roles they are required to play as part of their work, which include conceiving, communicating, controlling, linking, leading and doing, and their identities – who do they want to be?
- the level of associated behavioural competences they demonstrate in performing their new roles, including creativity and innovation, communicating, creating a performance culture, project management, strategic flexibility, managing conflict, building teams, networking, having an attitude of wisdom and making wise decisions.

In addition to this direct 'line of sight' between what managers bring to the job and their effectiveness, the different contexts in which individual managers work will have an important *moderating* influence on this relationship. Moreover, within given constraints, managers have a choice in which roles they emphasize in their work and how they perform these roles (e.g. some managers are noted for emphasizing close control over the work of their colleagues, whereas others prefer to delegate). These *contexts* and *choices* give rise to three related sets of moderating factors that we can place above and below the core, horizontal axis or line of sight in Figure 2.3:

- *The frame of the job.* This refers to its purpose as set out by the organization, the particular theory of the business employed by the organization (its assumptions regarding success and its business model), and its product/market position, structure of controls and systems, etc.;
- *The near and far contexts of the job.* The near contexts include the agenda set by the manager's bosses, the problems of managing inside the manager's department, the problems of managing within and across the organization, and the problems of managing outside the organization, including dealings with customers, suppliers, government departments and employer's associations. The far context refers to the nature of the organization, including its structure, etc., the nature of the industry (product/services/consulting, etc.), and the national and institutional framework in which the manager is undertaking his or her work.

The choices that managers can make can be set out in terms of the two interrelated factors that Mintzberg identifies as style and level. Most managers have a degree of discretion over:

- Their preferred *style*, including the roles they prefer to perform, how they perform their roles, and how they choose to configure and relate one role to another. The choice is between how they achieve balance between the three polarities of management – management as science, craft or art.
- The *level* at which they choose to operate, which reflects their assumptions and preferred style of managing. They can choose to manage action directly, they can choose to manage other people taking action, or they can influence other people by managing the information flows surrounding their jobs so that they take necessary actions.

Finally, our research over the past five years has pointed to two further moderating factors. The first is the *social capital* they draw on to make decisions, which refers to their ability to incorporate ideas from key people inside and outside the organization, and to the good relations and trust they may have built in the units they manage and with the people inside and outside with whom they network. The second is the degree of *relational coordination* they build in their teams, which refers to the intensity and nature of communications within the team and the levels of respect they have for each other. We discuss these concepts further in the next chapter.

Of course, there is little point in studying and theorizing about management if we are unable to specify the outcomes of good management, which is an industry in itself. However, this is not so easy as it seems, because there are many issues to bottom out before we can do this. One is specifying good performance from whose perspective: often what senior managers regard as good performance is at odds with what their employees might see as good performance. Another is the choices and numbers of criteria that might be used, for example, 'hard', quantitative measures or 'soft', qualitative measures. There has been a tendency in recent times to focus on the former, but we must be mindful of the adage, 'what is measurable isn't always meaningful, and what is meaningful isn't always measurable'. Yet a further problem of specifying outcomes is the time frame. Often the results of managerial action or inaction can only be known fully after many years, yet organizations seek to performance manage and reward managers on a yearly or even more frequent basis. Finally, there is the issue of level: Do we use the same criteria for senior, middle and junior managers, or are performance outcomes attenuated by the level at which managers operate and the discretion they are allowed in their jobs? You may now be more aware or some of the problems of evaluating the performance of managers and leaders, which is one of the reasons why some consulting firms are moving away from attempting to regularly appraise their managers and reward them on the basis of short-term outcomes. Perhaps when we come to write a third edition of this book, performance appraisal of managers may look fundamentally different from where it is now.

Let's see if you can apply this model to understanding your job as a manager or a manager with whom you are familiar.

TIME OUT Self-reflection

Thinking either about yourself or a manager who is, or has been, close to you, use Figure 2.3 to analyse the relationship between what you (or they) bring to the job and your rating of yourself (or their) effectiveness as a manager. Use a sheet of paper to redraw and annotate the diagram, because it will take up quite a lot of space if you do this correctly. Doing so should be a useful exercise in understanding yourself or your managerial colleagues, and can lead you to think about your own self-development.

Questions

1 What personal qualities might you (or they) need to perform more effectively as a manager?
2 Which roles do you (or they) choose to emphasize more than others in your (or their) managerial work? Are these the right choices for managerial effectiveness, given the context of the job?
3 What are the most important contextual factors that influence how you (or they) perform their jobs? What can be done to influence these (if anything)?
4 How does the frame of the job influence the roles you (or they) perform? And can anything be done to shape the frame of the job to make you (or them) more effective as a manager?
5 What about your (or their) preferred style and the level at which you (or they) mainly operate at, i.e. through information, people or directly through action? How can that be changed to make you (or them) more effective as a manager?
6 What are your (or their) key competences? Where are your (or their) shortcomings, and what can be done to improve them?

Doing this exercise should prove to be very useful in understanding yourself or your managerial colleagues, and can lead you to think about your own self-development or the development of others.

LEARNING SUMMARY

The key learning points from this chapter are:

- The rounded manager brings values, attitudes and experiences to the job, two of the most important of which are levels of emotional intelligence (in addition to cognitive intelligence) and the abilities and attitudes to engage in critical self-reflection and make sound judgements, which balance overconfidence and doubt.

- The frame of a manager's job, which includes its purpose, the mission of the organization or department and the position of the organization in its chosen market milieu, will have an important influence on how the manager performs his or her key roles, and the roles the manager chooses to play.

- Managers spend much of their time in figuring out what to do, or in setting agendas and priorities. Particularly at senior levels, they are rarely told what to do directly.

- How managers perform their key roles and the types and levels of competences they demonstrate will be influenced by the near and far contexts of their work. Effective management is strongly embedded in context, and being good in one situation doesn't always mean that someone will be good in another situation.

- Managers can operate at three related levels, indirectly through manipulating information flows, more directly through getting other people to act, or acting oneself. Effective managers operate at all three levels, depending on the context of the job and tasks at hand.

- Management is sometimes distinguished from leadership, in the sense that management focuses on stability and control whereas leadership is necessary to produce change. The well-rounded manager has to have both of these characteristics in his or her repertoire.

- Having an attitude of wisdom, which means having enough self-confidence to take action while remaining doubtful, is a key feature in effective management. Acting one's way into thinking can sometimes be a more effective strategy for managers than thinking one's way into action. The former is a learning approach whereas the latter is a planning approach. Usually, however, managers need to be good at both.

REVIEW QUESTION

During your appraisal, your boss tells you that he wants you to develop a 'performance-oriented culture' in your department. He then asks you for ideas on how to achieve this at the next meeting. How should you respond?

REFERENCES

Antonakis, J. (2009) "Emotional intelligence": What does it measure and does it matter for leadership? In: G. B. Graen (ed.), *LMX Leadership–Game-changing designs: Research-based tools* (Vol. VII), pp. 163–192. Greenwich, CT: Information Age Publishing.

Barrick, M. R. and Mount, M. K. (1991) The big five personality dimensions and job performance. *Personnel Psychology*, 44 (1), 1–16.

Cairncross, F. (2003) *The Company of the Future: Meeting the management challenges of the communications revolution.* London: Profile Books.

Chhokar, J. S., Brodbeck, F. C. and House, R. J. (eds). (2008) *Culture and Leadership across the World: The GLOBE book of in-depth studies of 25 societies.* New York: Taylor & Francis.

Claxton, G., Owen, D. and Sadler-Smith, E. (2015) Hubris in leadership: a peril of unbridled intuition. *Leadership*, 11(1), 57–78.

Clegg, S. R., Kornhauser, M. and Pitsis, T. S. (2011) *Managing and Organizations*, 3rd edn. London: Sage.

The Economist (2004) Freud, finance and folly: human intuition is a bad guide to handling risk. 22 January. Economist Newspapers, print edition.

The Economist (2004) The Ferrari of footwear. 11 March.

Finkelstein, S., Hambrick, D. C. and Cannella Jr, A. A. (2009) *Theory and Research on Executives, Top Management Teams, and Boards.* New York: Oxford University Press.

Fraser, I. (2014) *Shredded: Inside RBS, the bank that broke Britain.* Edinburgh: Birlinn.

Gillen, T. (2004) *Leadership or Management: The differences.* Wimbledon: CIPD.

Goleman, D., Boyatzis, R. and McKee, A. (2002) *Primal Leadership: Realizing the power of emotional intelligence.* Cambridge, MA: Harvard Business School Press.

Grint, K. (2005) Problems, problems, problems: the social construction of leadership. *Human Relations,* 58 (11), 1467–1494.

Grint, K. (2010) *Leadership: A very short introduction.* Oxford: Oxford University Press.

Harms, P. D. and Credé, M. (2010) Remaining issues in emotional intelligence research: construct overlap, method artifacts, and lack of incremental validity. *Industrial and Organizational Psychology: Perspectives on Science and Practice,* 3 (2), 154–158.

Heskett, J. L., Jones, T. O., Loveman, G. W., Sasser Jr, W. E. and Schlesinger, L. A. (2008) Putting the service-profit chain to work. *Harvard Business Review*, July–August.

Ibarra, H. (2003) *Working Identity: Unconventional strategies for reinventing your career.* Cambridge, MA: Harvard Business School Press.

Judge, T., Higgins, C. A., Thoresen, C. J. and Barrick, M. R. (1999) The big five personality traits, general mental ability, and career success across the life span. *Personnel Psychology*, 52 (3), 621–652.

Kotter, J. (1990) *A Force for Change: How leadership differs from management.* New York: Free Press.

Martin, G., Gollan, P. J. and Grigg, K. (2011) Is there a bigger and better future for employer branding? Facing up to innovation, corporate reputations and wicked problems in SHRM. *The International Journal of Human Resource Management,* 22 (17), 3618–3637.

Martin, G. and Gollan, P. J. (2012) Corporate governance and strategic human resources management (SHRM) in the UK financial services sector: the case of the Royal Bank of Scotland. *International Journal of Human Resource Management,* 23 (16), 3295–3314.

Martin, G., Siebert, S., and Bozie, B. (2013) Re-conceptualising organizational trust repair: the case of repeated transgressions. Academy of Mangement Proceedings, January, Meeting abstract summary, doi: 10.5465/AMBPP. 2013.10446-abstract.

Martin, G., Beech, N., MacIntosh, R. and Bushfield, S. (2015) Potential challenges facing distributed leaders in health care: evidence from the UK National Health Service. *Sociology of Health and Illness*, 37 (1), 14–29. doi: 10.1111/1467-9566.12171.

Martin, I. (2013) *Making It Happen: Fred Goodwin, RBS and the men who blew up the British economy*. London: Simon & Schuster.

Mintzberg, H. (1973) *The Nature of Managerial Work*. London: Harper & Row.

Mintzberg, H. (1989) *Mintzberg on Management: Inside our strange world of organizations*. New York: Free Press.

Mintzberg, H. (1994) Rounding out the manager's job. *Sloan Management Review*, 36 (1, Fall), 11–25.

Mintzberg, H. (2004) *Managers not MBAs: A hard look at the soft practice of managing and management development*. Harlow, Essex: Pearson Education/Financial Times.

Mintzberg, H. (2011) *Managing*. Harlow, Essex: Financial Times/Prentice Hall.

Morgan, G. (1997) *Images of Organization*. London: Sage.

Morgan, G. (2003) *New Mindsets*. Available online at www.newmindsets.com.

Nonaka, I., Chia, R., Holt, R. and Peltokorpi, V. (2014) Wisdom, management and organization. *Management Learning*, 45 (4), 365–376.

Pascale, R. T., Milleman, M. and Goija, L. (2000) *Surfing the Edge of Chaos: The law of nature and the new laws of business*. New York: Three Rivers Press.

Scarborough, H. (1998) The unmaking of management? Change and continuity in British management in the 1990s. *Human Relations*, 51 (6), 691–716.

Schoemaker, P. J. H., Krupp, S. and Howland, S. (2013) Strategic leadership: the essential skills. *Harvard Business Review* (January–February).

Stewart, R. (1979) *The Reality of Management*. London: Macmillan.

Stewart, R., Keiser, A. and Barsoux, J.-L. (1994) *Managing in Britain and Germany*. London: St Martin's Press.

Weick, K. E. (2001) *Making Sense of the Organization*. Oxford: Blackwell.

Chapter 3

Managing in the individual–organizational context

LEARNING OBJECTIVES

At the end of this chapter you should be able to:

- understand and apply the concept of psychological contracts to work situations;
- recognize good practice in managing psychological contracts in organizations, and take steps to influence these unwritten contracts;
- understand the problems of managing talent, careers, employee engagement and work–life balance;
- use theories of employee engagement in your organizations to impact on key individual and organizational outcomes.

INTRODUCTION

In the previous chapter, we focused on managers' needs to understand themselves and to reflect on how they can be more effective by managing at different levels and in different contexts. Our model of the rounded manager also highlighted a requirement for managers to develop their emotional intelligence, leadership competencies and decision-making skills by developing an attitude of wisdom. In this chapter we shall develop some of these ideas, but this time focus on how managers can better understand the individual–organizational relationship and how they can provide more effective leadership that is sensitive to people's engagement with work, with each other and with their employers.

This topic is potentially vast, and is usually covered by conventional texts and courses on organizational behaviour, which concentrate on understanding individual differences, motivation and job satisfaction, learning, group dynamics, leadership and the like. We shall not attempt to repeat what is already well documented in such books. Instead, we examine a key question, the answers to which have enormous importance for managers:

- What is the nature of the relationships between individuals and organizations, how has it changed and how is it likely to change in the future?

In addressing this question we shall make use of two concepts that have become popular in the human resource management literature, and are supported by research for the Chartered Institute of Personnel and Development (CIPD) in the UK as key ideas in understanding the individual–organizational linkage. The first is the *psychological contract*, which we shall define and use to examine issues such as 'talent' management, careers, employee commitment and identification, and the problems of over-identification, such as workaholism and burnout. The second is the related notion of employee engagement, a consultancy generated term that has been promoted heavily to the UK government through the website Engage for Success as a way of aligning individual and organizational goals (Albrecht *et al.*, 2015; see also www.engageforsuccess.org).

Let's begin by looking at some of the issues involved by examining the case in Box 3.1, which is based on some work one of us carried out on employee relations in the UK offshore oil industry (Martin *et al.*, 2003). Although our research took place quite some time ago, we think it is still an excellent case for understanding the psychological contracts of employees in an important sector in UK industry – the extraction of oil and gas – because it had an important impact on what subsequently happened in the management of employee relations in the sector.

BOX 3.1 'Psychological contracts' among oil workers in the UK offshore drilling industry

The offshore drilling industry

In 1999 the industry comprised 14 companies employing some 6,000 men and a limited number of women in onshore and offshore operations. The work of the offshore drilling employees is usually depicted as hazardous, involving long hours in shifts and working away from home. The majority of employees on the drilling rigs are semiskilled roustabouts, supervisors, and drilling technicians and technologists, most of whom have worked in the industry for a number of years. Despite the contracting nature of employment conditions, some employers and many employees tend to treat the industry as a source of a traditional career rather than as a pure wage-for-work relationship with limited job security and no career progression. Though mobility between companies was a feature of employment in the industry because of the contract nature of the work, many of the employers had an implicit policy of retaining good employees because of their personal knowledge of particular drilling rigs. Consequently, it was common practice in the industry to attempt to offer a degree of security during slack times by standing down men for a period on limited pay until new contracts became available. Such work protection practices, however, were not a feature of all companies, and this became a source of difference among employers, from the perspective of both employees and of clients, who were the oil 'majors' operating in the North Sea, including companies such as BP, Shell and Exxon. These client companies regarded a degree of employment continuity among the contractors' workforces as sufficiently important that they would sometimes 'foot the bill' to keep good workers on the books of drilling contractors, especially if a new contract was imminent. Traditionally, these workers had also been highly compensated in relation to comparable jobs onshore, though through time the differentials had been eroded to a point where recruitment had become difficult in 2000.

The UK offshore oil and gas industry as a whole had been traditionally hostile to unions and union representatives. As a consequence, in the drilling industry, unionization was actively discouraged and no company gave any form of recognition to the unions with members in the industry. In 1998, however, the UK government's White Paper on *Fairness at Work* was introduced with provisions to reintroduce the rights of unions to pursue recognition claims if they could be justified in terms of union membership.

The UK offshore drilling contractors, which operated drilling rigs on behalf of the oil and gas majors in the North Sea oil and gas fields, immediately saw themselves at risk to predatory unions because they had been subject to attempts by a hostile union called OILC to organize members on the drilling rigs. So, when the employers became aware of the union recognition provisions of the White Paper, they perceived the threat of OILC for disruption as 'mission critical', particularly if the union was able to recruit sufficient members and gain recognition under the legislation.

As a consequence, the drilling companies combined themselves into a consortium, with the help of consultants, to decide what their stance should be. The first step the consultants recommended was that they should undertake an attitude survey of all employees in the industry to assess their general perceptions of what they wanted from work, what they saw as the key obligations of their employers, and whether these obligations were being met by their employers. The consultants also wanted the firms to understand the attitudes of workers to trade unions, so that they could advise the companies on how to proceed with union recognition. This survey involved all employees in the industry and achieved a relatively high response rate of more than 60 per cent.

TABLE 3.1 Selected data from the employee survey on key elements of the psychological contract

(Scale: 1 = strongly agree; 3 = neutral; 5 = strongly disagree)

For the purposes of interpreting these mean average responses, you should treat any result lying outside the range 2.4 to 3.6 as statistically significant. Any figure lying within this range should be treated as similar to the mean average, given the sample size.

Question	Mean average response of all employees on a five-point Likert scale
As far as could be expected the company has provided me with a reasonably secure job.	2.55
The company has provided me with fair pay for the work I do.	3.06
The company has provided me with good career opportunities.	2.94
The company has provided me with interesting work.	2.54
The company has ensured my fair treatment by managers and supervisors.	2.67
The company has helped me with the problems I have encountered outside work.	3.14
The company always provides me with a safe working environment.	2.33
The company provides me with good training for the job.	2.43

The employee survey phase as a means of intervention

The survey data provided a wealth of information on employee perceptions. Tables 3.1 and 3.2 provide a selection of these data, which were presented to the drilling contractors' HR managers.

TABLE 3.2 Selected data from the employee survey on the need for union representation

(Scale: 1 = strongly agree; 3 = neutral; 5 = strongly disagree)

Question	Mean average response of all employees on a five-point Likert scale
Employee relations in this company would be improved by having an employee representative who could speak to management on our behalf.	2.20
Management in this company usually consult employees on issues that affect them.	3.01
Management in this company usually give employees plenty of opportunity to comment on proposed changes at work.	3.16
Having an employee representative would generally be beneficial in securing fairer terms and conditions of employment.	2.31
There is definite need for better representation in this company to give voice to employee wishes and grievances.	2.18

Based on these data and other findings and forms of analysis from the survey, the headline conclusions from the study, which were reported to the HR managers and their senior managers, were as follows:

- The standard predictors of why employees in non-union companies show little interest in joining unions are: (1) high levels of job satisfaction; (2) positive beliefs about existing communications, consultation and grievance-handling procedures; and (3) negative instrumental beliefs about the ability of unions to improve pay and conditions. From Tables 3.1 and 3.2, it can be seen that job satisfaction was not significantly high and that positive beliefs about existing communications were not high. Furthermore, unions were seen positively as a means of providing a voice on key issues and, of lesser significance, in improving terms and conditions of employment.
- Employees did not perceive that they were well managed, particularly in relation to supervisors treating people poorly and to perceptions of a lack of trust in supervisors to work in employees' best interests.
- Employees were particularly interested in future employability, and the perception of a lack of career development by employees was strongly associated with positive attitudes to unions as a means of representation and participation in decision-making.
- The lack of interactional justice (perceptions of fair treatment by the company and the lack of trust in managers) and the lack of affective commitment (attitudes towards the companies) were associated with positive attitudes to unions as a means of representation and participation in decision-making.
- Expectations of job security were relatively low and, at the time of the survey, were worsening.

Source: adapted from Martin *et al.*, 2003.

THE PSYCHOLOGICAL CONTRACT

The case discusses the levels of employees' attachment to their work and to the companies employing them. We want to use the case to introduce the notion of psychological contracts and show how useful it can be in explaining the relationships between employees and their organizations. First, however, we need to define what we mean by psychological contracts, look at how they are formed and then transformed.

Defining and forming psychological contracts

Psychological contracts have been used to describe the expectations and beliefs that employees hold about the mutual obligations between themselves and their organizations, such as expectations about fair pay or career opportunities provided by their companies, or the amount of effort they might reasonably be expected to exercise in performing their work (Conway, 2015; Conway and Briner, 2005). So, the psychological contract mirrors the explicit legal contract by focusing on largely implicit and unwritten reciprocal obligations, though certain writers have included written 'promises' by employers, such as those evident in mission statements, e.g. to treat people with dignity and fairness. Here is a basic but useful definition of psychological contracts:

> '. . . the employee's beliefs regarding the promises of the reciprocal exchange agreement between the employee and organization' (Suazo *et al.*, 2009, p.154).

This definition needs some elaboration to tease out the key features of such contracts. To help us, we can draw on the insights into psychological contracts and the employment relationship provided by Neil Conway (2015) and, earlier, by Sparrow and Cary Cooper (2003). These researchers have highlighted four key aspects of psychological contracts and how they come to be formed and changed:

- They are *subjective, unique and idiosyncratic*, in the senses that: (1) they reside in the subjective expectations and perceptions of employees (and employers); (2) every individual has his or her own interpretation of these expectations and perceptions; and (3) they vary from one person and organization to another. Therefore, you can gain an insight into psychological contracts by questioning only one party to the relationship, because the contract 'is in the eyes of the beholder'.
- They are *reciprocal*, in the sense that they emerge in the context of a *specific* mutual employment relationship. As there are two parties to this relationship, they each have their own expectations about the specific employment relationship (but not employment relationships in general).
- They are not objective 'facts', but based on *beliefs and perceptions* held by individuals. However, because people act on their subjective perceptions, they are no less real in their consequences than if they *were* fact.
- They arise from beliefs and perceptions of *obligations* that, in the case of employees, are what they believe they are entitled to as a consequence of perceived *promises*, either explicit or

implicit, made by the employer. In that sense, a psychological contract is more than just a set of expectations that can arise in the absence of a promise. Only expectations relating to perceived promises are entitled to be considered as part of the psychological contract. Just what these promises look like in practice and how they arise are illustrated in Box 3.2.

BOX 3.2 'Promises' in the employment relationship that create obligations

Promises arising from spoken and written communications:

- strategic documents, employer commitments to certain courses of action, mission and values statements, agreements, pledges, speeches;
- financial statements or employer reporting statements;
- statements made on application forms, etc., by employees.

Promises arising out of behaviour and actions:

- observations of management or employee actions, e.g. how managers and employees act in relation to one another in treating each other with respect;
- interactions with manager or employee representatives, such as how recruiters behave during the interview process.

Breach and violation of psychological contracts

Like legal contracts, psychological contracts can be breached or violated if employees feel that the significant terms have been broken, or that perceived obligations are unmet (Conway *et al.*, 2011). The distinction between breach and violation is largely one of degree; breaches are treated as minor, more short term and less significant, whereas violations are seen as more serious, more long term and significant in terms of outcomes. It is to the violation of psychological contracts that many researchers attribute major breakdowns in employee relations, or failures in organizational change programmes. For example, violation of psychological contracts has been used to explain strike action and rises in absenteeism and employee turnover; at the same time, violation has been used to explain rising levels of cynicism about never-ending 'programmes' of organizational change and lack of trust in managers to 'walk the talk' (see Chapter 10) (Martin *et al.*, 1998).

One way of thinking about employee responses to contract violation is to distinguish between active and passive 'actions' on the one hand and positive and negative 'actions' on the other (see Figure 3.1). Note how apparent loyalty or silence by employees may occur as a response to management actions that breach, or even violate, expectations regarding promises. This can be treated as

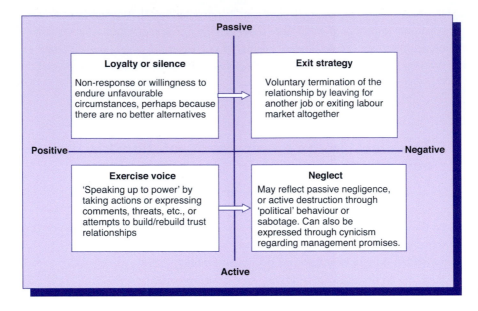

FIGURE 3.1 Range of employee responses to psychological contract violation

(*Source*: based on Turnley and Feldman, 1998.)

a positive response to changes managers may make in the psychological contract, because they have built up a store of trust and a reputation for integrity in the past. However, it may also be seen as negative, because employees endure what they perceive as unfair treatment as they are unable to foresee alternatives to their current employment. When the employment situation changes, however, they are very likely to adopt an exit strategy if the breaches continue. A further implication of this framework is that managers should do all they can to encourage employees to 'speak up to power', rather than suppress discontent. By encouraging such actions, managers are able to rebuild trust, an essential component of employment relations (Siebert *et al.*, 2015). Otherwise, they run the risk of employees adopting a negative, 'neglect' strategy.

Conway and Briner (2002) attempted to understand why and what happens when management actions, through design, accident or miscalculation, result in breaches being treated as violations. They pointed to four characteristics of perceived promises that can have a major impact on employee responses to breach or violation:

- the degree of explicitness of a perceived promise – the more explicit the promise, the greater the sense of injustice and the more active (positively or negatively) the employee response;
- attributions of personal responsibility for contract breach or violation – the more personally responsible a manager or party is held to be for the perceived breach, the more intense the other party's reaction;
- the unexpectedness or infrequency of the breach – the more unexpected or infrequent the breach/violation (a break with past behaviour), the more intense or active the response will be from employees;

- the degree of importance the party attaches to the goal or relationship breached – the more important the interest/relationship breached, the more likely it will be treated as a significant violation and, hence, provoke a negative response.

EXERCISE 3.1

Drawing on the previous discussion on psychological contract breach and violation, do you think that the drilling companies should have recognized a union for bargaining purposes?

Types of psychological contract

Though psychological contracts are individual in nature, resulting in as many contracts in an organization as there are people, psychologists have tried to classify some of their more general features. Three such classifications have emerged in the extensive research in this area. These are set out in Table 3.3 and reflect changes taking place in organizations and the wider economy.

During the 1990s in the USA, it was argued that the traditional, relational contracts that many, mostly white-collar, employees held with their employers – based on commitment in return for job security and career prospects – could no longer be sustained because of increased global competition (Cappelli, 1999). Consequently, it was suggested this traditional, relational contract became replaced by a more transactional contract, but one with a slight twist on the model highlighted in Table 3.3. Organizations recognized that they could no longer offer stable employment to all, nor could they guarantee careers to all, even though they wished to retain the benefits of relational contracting from employees working 'beyond contract' and showing high levels of (temporary) commitment. Consequently, the notion of *employability* came into common usage: employers sought temporary commitment from employees as long as they remained in the job, but offered in return the opportunity for employees for self-development and to hone their skills on interesting and demanding projects. This employment proposition, which was a form of 'come and work for us and learn', was attractive to many mobile employees in fields such as computing and software development because it made them more employable for their next job. In effect, their career paths became boundaryless, because they moved in and out of organizations and even occupations. This notion of employability, however, was much less widespread than much of the literature would have had us believe, especially outside what became known as the 'new economy' organizations based in the hi-tech regions of the USA (see Chapter 4). We shall examine this idea of changed psychological contracts later in this chapter, and in other parts of this book, when we look at new forms of organization, technological change and the knowledge and innovation contexts.

Many organizations, however, seek through their mission and value statements to go beyond even relational contracts and create ideological relationships with individuals. Mission-driven organizations aim to captivate employees by having them believe that they are working for a greater or higher-level purpose, even in relatively low skilled industries such as retailing. For example, Wal-Mart, the

TABLE 3.3 Different types of psychological contract

Dimension	Transactional	Relational	Ideological
Organizational obligations	Degree of job security, safe work and a 'fair day's pay'	To provide a career with training and education, promotion opportunities, interesting work and long-term employment prospects	Demonstrate credible commitment to a valued cause
Individual obligations	'A fair day's work'	Go beyond contract by doing excellent work and demonstrating high commitment and identification with organization	Participate fully in the organizational mission/ cause by being a good organizational and societal citizen
Beneficiary	Self	Mutual interest between self and organization	The organization and employee share same passion/cause
Beliefs about human nature	Self-interested, instrumental worker who works for money	Socialized employee, who is collectively oriented and finds satisfaction in work itself	Principled involvement
Characteristics of violation	Black and white	Grey areas, which are negotiable	Grey (negotiable) but also non-negotiable, moral 'hot-buttons'
Typical response to violation	Leave organization	Withdraw commitment and revert to a transactional exchange	Principled organizational dissent
Basis of attachment to work and organizations	Compliance and focus on the job	Identification with organ- ization and career	Work as a calling

Sources: based on Thompson and Bunderson, 2003, p. 575; Conway and Briner, 2005; Rousseau, 1995.

world's largest retailer, tries to engage employees by convincing them that they have the opportunity to 'give ordinary folks the chance to buy the same things as rich people'. In Chapter 6, we shall examine just how effective such employer branding propositions are in the development of ideological psychological contracts. However, it should be obvious to most readers that ideological contracts are more likely to be found amongst higher-level professionals in occupations with a sense of vocation, such as medicine, teaching, religion and even politics, or in voluntary organizations such as Save the Children or Cancer Research.

EXERCISE 3.2

Drawing on the material in this last section, how would you describe the psychological contracts of most employees in the North Sea oil drilling industry, based on Table 3.3?

Measuring psychological contracts

From a manager's point of view it is clearly useful to be able to gain insights into employee perceptions of perceived promises, because they have extremely important consequences for understanding the effectiveness of people management strategies and management actions. Figure 3.2 shows the relationship between what some researchers have found to be the important factors which shape psychological contracts, the key components or content of psychological contracts themselves, and positive and negative outcomes associated with the way in which psychological contracts are managed.

What most employees appear to expect from employers and what they regard as the most important employer obligations have been identified by a number of researchers. These items are often used in surveys to determine the health of psychological contracts in organizations:

- to provide an adequate procedure for induction into the job and training to make people more effective and safe;

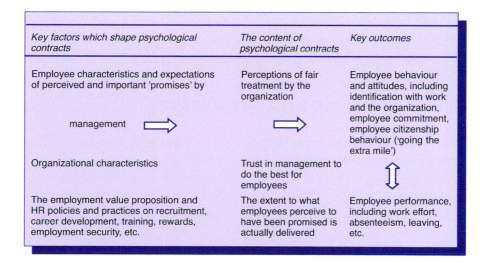

FIGURE 3.2 Inputs, content and outputs of the psychological contract

(*Sources*: based on CIPD, 2003; Conway and Briner, 2005; Martin *et al.*, 1998.)

- to ensure that the procedures for selection, appraisal, promotion and lay-offs are fair;
- to provide justice, fairness and consistency in the application of important rules and on discipline and dismissal;
- to provide equitable treatment on pay and rewards in relation to market circumstances and to be fair in the allocation of non-pay benefits to individuals and groups;
- to provide interesting work where possible;
- to provide fair pay for taking on responsibility in the job;
- to provide career development and support for employees to learn new skills;
- to allow people reasonable time off and flexibility to meet family and personal needs;
- to consult and communicate effectively on matters affecting employees;
- to allow employees reasonable autonomy in how they *do* their jobs;
- to act in a personally supportive way to employees;
- to recognize loyalty and reward special contributions;
- to provide a safe and friendly work environment;
- to do what they can to provide employment security;
- to ensure that managers keep their promises and commitments and do their best for employees.

Employers, on the other hand, expect that employees will work extra hours when needed, take on work outside their responsibilities when circumstances dictate, look for better ways of undertaking the job and suggest improvements, be flexible, save costs and adapt to changes in the work environment.

EXERCISE 3.3

Thinking back to the North Sea oil industry case in Box 3.1, design three written survey questions that might identify key elements of employees' psychological contracts.

MANAGING PSYCHOLOGICAL CONTRACTS

Managing the individual–organizational relationship by shaping the psychological contracts of employees in a positive manner comprises many elements. In this section, we want to discuss five important ones, especially in the light of recent and forecasted changes in employment and in the nature of organizations:

- managing talent;
- managing careers;
- managing organizational identification;
- managing work–life balance;
- managing employee engagement.

These five management issues of the individual–organizational relationship have been the subject of intense research and speculation, and are at the core of modern human resource management. As Brown and Edwards (2009) have argued, the *individualization of the employment relationship* has been one of the most important developments of recent times among organizations in most developed countries, evidenced by the decreasing influence of trade unions and the increased use of nonstandard forms of employment contracts. Such developments towards individualization can be seen in two ways. On the one hand, some writers and critics have highlighted the negative side by pointing to how modern national states and large organizations have rejected their responsibilities for providing employment security and passed the onus on to individuals to make themselves employable through calls for self-development and displays of flexibility. On the other hand, some proponents of these changes have argued that many employees are increasingly motivated by the need for autonomy, and actively seek more career flexibility and the opportunities to follow rather different, boundaryless career and work patterns from those of their predecessors, a point discussed in the previous section. McKinsey, a large consulting organization, labelled this relationship as an important feature of the 'Gig Economy' (*Financial Times*, 05/07/15). Many such individuals tend to work in knowledge-intensive occupations and organizations, business and financial consultants, professional engineers, entertainment, education and healthcare. Because these people have such different orientations to work and because they tend to be in short supply, organizations increasingly find themselves competing for talent and having to devise new ways of managing them.

Managing talent

What is talent management?

The term 'talent management' has come into popular usage as a direct result of a major study by McKinsey consultants Ed Michaels, Helen Handfield-Jones and Beth Axelrod, who undertook their original work in 1997 on the impact of how companies managed their leadership talent on corporate performance, and have subsequently followed this study up with further research (Michaels *et al.*, 2001). Prior to the bursting of the dot-com bubble in the USA in early 2000, the recruitment of talented people was seen to be the biggest single issue facing US business. Based on some in-depth research among business leaders these writers concluded that the 'war for talent' was, and would continue to be, one of the most important problems facing industry and commerce in developed countries. The changed labour market circumstances following the downturn in economic prosperity in the USA associated with the dot-com collapse did nothing to diminish their beliefs, and subsequent research by them provided strong support for their thesis in certain industrial sectors and certain countries. Their work showed that only a small proportion of senior managers believed their organizations: (a) recruited talented people (their A-class high performers); (b) did all they could to identify and retain these talented performers, and to develop performers with potential (the B class); or (c) undertook to remove or replace low performers (whom they called C-class performers).

TABLE 3.4 The new talent mindset

Old HR mindset	New talent mindset
The vague leadership and HR rhetoric of 'people being our most important asset'	A deeply held conviction that talented people produce better organizational performance
The responsibility for people management lies with HR	The responsibility for managers to do all they can to strengthen the talent pool
Small-scale and infrequent programmes for succession planning and training managers in acquiring and nurturing people	Talent management as a central component of the business and part of the ongoing role of senior leaders
Managers have to work with the people they inherit	Managers constantly taking active and bold steps to attract and develop their talent pool and actively manage low performers

Source: adapted from Handfield-Jones *et al.*, 2001, p. 4.

Talent management, they argued, required a new talent mindset among business leaders, because it was so 'mission critical', and therefore could not be left to HR departments. Instead, it required the direct support of the organization's board and needed to be made a core element of the work of business leaders (see Table 3.4).

These authors proposed that organizations that sought to become top performers should implement three elements of a talent management strategy. There should be:

- disciplined talent management, through rigorous and continuous assessment, development of managers and matching them with jobs;
- creative recruitment and retention through refined and meaningful *employee value propositions* (EVPs), which we shall discuss more fully in Chapter 6 on corporate reputation, branding and HR;
- thoughtful executive development, using coaching, mentoring and on-the-job experiences at key points in managers' development.

New approaches to talent management

A theory of talent management

Gradually, this 'Hollywood' metaphor term has entered the lexicon of many global companies to refer to the appointment and management of key people (Collings *et al.*, 2015). While a somewhat cynical interpretation of the talent management bandwagon focused on the HR function's attempts to rebrand itself, we believe there is more to talent management than HRs' needs for legitimacy. David Collings and Kamel Mellahi (2009) have made a good case for strategic talent management, which is based on organizations' needs to compete in labour markets for valuable and scarce staff. They define it as:

'activities and processes which differentially contribute to the organization's sustainable competitive advantage, the development of a talent pool of high potential and high performing incumbents to fill these roles, and the development of a differentiated human resource architecture to facilitate filling these positions with incumbents and to ensure their continued commitment to the organization' (p. 305).

The first core element in their argument is the notion of an HR architecture, which differentiates the contribution and management of people according to the value they add to organizational performance and their scarcity in the labour market (Lepak and Snell, 2002). This approach segments the internal labour market of an organization into four quadrants (see Figure 3.3), all four of which require a focused approach to the recruitment, retention, development and motivation of staff.

So, because knowledge-based workers in the top right-hand box are capable of adding value to the strategic objectives of an organization and are scarce or unique in some cases, they require significant investment in their development and retention. Good examples would be senior professionals such as engineers or scientists in high-tech or science-based industries, geologists and geo-physicists in oil and gas companies, senior doctors or academics in hospitals and universities, top footballers and, in some cases, high level managers. Workers in the bottom-right box are capable of adding strategic value but are not so scarce; thus they are recruited, developed and managed to perform pre-determined jobs, such as craftsmen, technicians or middle/junior level managers and administrators. Workers in the bottom left-hand box are neither high-value adding nor scarce, so

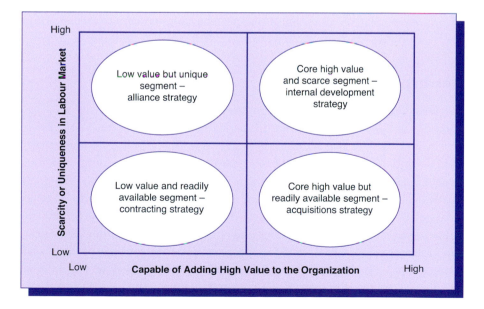

FIGURE 3.3 Segmented human resource architecture

they are likely to be employed on contracts or be outsourced, with little or no investment in their training and development. Good examples include most workers in call centres, security staff or semi-skilled labourers on building sites. Finally, workers in the top left-hand box may be scarce and talented but are not core to the strategic mission and operation of an organization. Examples of such workers can include professionals such as accountants, HR staff and computer programmers in certain types of organizations, and most of the management consultants brought into an organization from time to time to help out with special projects. These employees rarely enjoy significant career development although they may be rewarded highly for their contribution.

The second core element is the notion of a talent pool, which is the internal reservoir of high potential and high performing employees that organizations usually rely on to undertake so called 'pivotal' roles (Boudreau and Ramstad, 2007) in the top right-hand box of the diagram in Figure 3.3. Creating a talent pool by recruiting and developing talented individuals 'ahead of the curve' allows an organization to implement succession plans and develop new lines of business or ways of working. Sometimes, this means that organizations recruit high quality staff for which no current job or vacancy exists; instead they buy them in to develop their own role in the organization. This is a strategy frequently used by universities, the science and computing sectors, all of which rely on constant innovation to compete in their respective marketplaces for ideas.

Bringing these ideas together, Collings and Mellahi (2009) have proposed a new theory of strategic talent management, which can be depicted in Figure 3.4. They argue that the first step in talent management should be to identify the pivotal roles and pivotal performers in an organization – the so called 'A' stars and 'A' positions, which correspond closely to the top right-hand box of the differentiated HR architecture in Figure 3.3. These positions are filled by a strategy of recruitment of high performing individuals to the talent pool from an organization's internal and external labour market. In turn, they predict that this exclusive strategy should lead to high performance through improved work engagement, retention and extra-role behaviour, sometimes labelled as organizational citizenship.

Employer branding

One of the most important developments in talent management in recent years has been the incorporation of the language and theories of marketing into HR (Martin *et al.*, 2011; Edwards, 2013) (see Chapter 6). This is most obvious in the recruitment process, which is seen by many companies as too important to be left to HR practitioners, especially those untutored in the language and methods of developing strong corporate reputations and brands. Marketing theories are increasingly evident in the proposals to segment internal labour markets, such as the architectural model described above, with firms attempting to differentiate employer value propositions (EVPs) for each major segment or unit of labour. This idea of differentiating workforces internally to reflect the multiple, differentiated external strategies of companies has become one of the key HR messages in recent times. Mark Huselid and Brian Becker (2011) have argued that a differentiated HR architecture is necessary to support the implementation of firms' strategies. They focus on the need to identify strategic capabilities and strategic jobs as the most essential tasks on designing a 'workforce management system' design rather than use traditional hierarchies as the basis of segmenting the

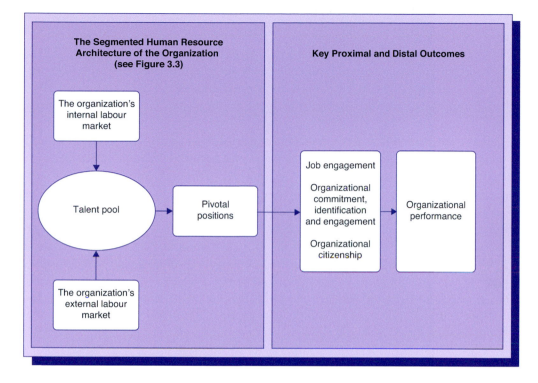

FIGURE 3.4 A model of talent management

workforce. This has two implications. The first is that managers are not necessarily seen as core employees and may not be part of the talent pool; the second is that there is a need to develop employer brands and EVPs that appeal to an exclusive segment of core employees who have the necessary job-related, social and networking skills to create high value. In effect, we are increasingly witnessing an increasingly exclusive approach to talent management and employer branding which is at odds with the more traditional inclusive approaches that firms have usually followed (Thunnissen et al., 2013). Huselid and Becker's thesis is that 'best employer' schemes, which operate in many countries, are counterproductive because they attempt to appeal to, and include, all employees as 'talent' rather than a select group. As a result, they contend that organizations following undifferentiated talent management and employer branding approaches place 'golden handcuffs' on mediocre employees, while at the same time failing to attract and retain high value creating talent through a differentiated strategy. This language of differentiation mirrors the ideas of psychological contracting in recognizing the individual nature of psychological contracts and the different types of contracts. We return to this issue in the next section on managing careers.

Criticisms of talent management

Exclusive approaches to talent management and employer branding typically imply price segmentation in the form of highly differentiated rewards strategies in organizations. Given that talent is, by definition, in short supply or, in the language of economists, inelastic, in the short to medium term, the price of talent has risen quite markedly over the last few decades in many countries. Thus, organizations are increasingly 'paying for the person' rather than having fixed rates and bands for staff, and the differentials between high performers and average performers are gradually increasing to reflect market values and the kinds of economic rent that accrue to factors in short supply. There is certainly evidence of this having occurred since the 1980s, with ratios of salaries between the top-paid managers and the average salaries of employees having increased significantly in most countries. So, for example, the independent High Pay Centre (2015) in the UK reported that CEO salaries among the top FTSE 100 firms in Britain were 130 times their average employees', with some firms paying their CEO several hundred times the average worker salary. These trends in rewarding talent in an increasingly global world, in which executives are highly mobile, are associated with rapidly increasing inequality in many countries in the developed world. In Britain, for example, the share of income earned by the top 1 per cent has more than doubled from 6 per cent to 14 per cent, although the general public seems to be unaware of this trend in believing that social inequalities are diminishing (High Pay Centre, 2015).

These trends and the discourse of talent management have affected how all of us think about the increasingly individualized nature of the employment relationship, careers and rewards in organizations, which may explain why societies seem to be more tolerant or even ignorant about growing inequalities. Such a discourse and set of associated HR practices, however, have not captured the imagination of all commentators and practitioners, especially critical theorists (Thunnissen *et al.*, 2013). The case below points to problems that can arise when individual talent management is overemphasized, especially at the expense of other members of the organization (Collings *et al.*, 2015).

CASE 3.1 THE DARK SIDE OF TALENT MANAGEMENT

The 'talent mindset' is the new orthodoxy of American management. It is the intellectual justification for why such a high premium is placed on degrees from first-tier business schools, and why the compensation packages for top executives have become so lavish. In the modern corporation, the system is considered only as strong as its stars, and in the past few years this message has been preached by consultants and management gurus all over the world. None, however, spread the word quite so ardently as McKinsey and, of all its clients, one firm took the talent mindset closest to heart. It was a company where McKinsey conducted 20 separate projects, where McKinsey's billings topped $10 million a year, where a McKinsey director regularly attended board meetings and where the CEO himself was a former McKinsey partner. The company, of course, was Enron.

The Enron scandal is now a famous watershed in corporate governance history. The reputations of Jeffrey Skilling and Kenneth Lay, the company's two top executives, were destroyed. Arthur

Andersen, Enron's auditor, was effectively driven out of business, and attention turned to Enron's investment bankers. The one Enron partner that escaped largely unscathed, however, was McKinsey, which is odd, given that it essentially created the blueprint for the Enron culture. Enron was the ultimate 'talent' company. When Skilling started the corporate division known as Enron Capital and Trade in 1990, he 'decided to bring in a steady stream of the very best college and MBA graduates [he] could find to stock the company with talent'. During the 1990s Enron was bringing in 250 newly minted MBAs a year. 'We had these things called Super Saturday', one former Enron manager recalls. 'I'd interview some of these guys who were fresh out of Harvard, and these kids could blow me out of the water. They knew things I'd never heard of'. Once at Enron, the top performers were rewarded inordinately and promoted without regard for seniority or experience. Enron was a start system. 'The only thing that differentiates Enron from our competitors is our people, our talent', Lay, Enron's former chairman and CEO, told the McKinsey consultants when they came to the company's headquarters in Houston. Or, as another senior Enron executive put it to Richard Foster, a McKinsey partner who celebrated Enron in his 2001 book (co-authored with Sarah Kaplan) *Creative Destruction*, 'We hire very smart people and we pay them more than they think they are worth'.

The management of Enron, in other words, did exactly what the consultants at McKinsey said that companies ought to do in order to succeed in the modern economy. It hired and rewarded the very best and the very brightest – and it is now in bankruptcy. The reasons for its collapse are complex, needless to say. But what if Enron failed not in spite of its talent mindset but because of it?

1   Can organizations overrate talented people? What does the case highlight about the dark side of talent management?

Source: based on Gladwell 2002.

Well-known American academics such as Boris Groysberg (2010) in the USA have pointed out the dangers of talent management and the trends toward individualization of the employment relationship. The main thrust of their criticisms is that the competition created by talent management practices harms everyone, and not just the 'losers' or 'C' performers. This is because it undermines organizational loyalty, team-working, knowledge sharing and the organization's overall ability to turn knowledge into action. To many people in the USA and UK, management practices that produce internal competition are so common nowadays that they seem unexceptional. Examples of such talent management practices include recognition awards given to individuals, such as 'employee of the month or year programmes'; forced distributions of individual merit raise budgets, so what one person receives another cannot; contests between departments or individuals for prizes; and published rankings of unit or individual performance. These practices often create a zero-sum contest in which the success or rewards of one person or department must come at the expense of another, and thus there is a built-in disincentive to share knowledge. Other problems identified by Groysberg (2010) and others include the following:

- The focus on hiring outsiders plays down the abilities of insiders, who can rapidly become demotivated and often leave. Organizations that 'enjoy' such a reputation for favouring external 'new talent' can attract poor reputations among potential recruits as a 'hire-and-fire' company, as well as among dissatisfied insiders (a point to which we shall return in Chapter 6).

- The focus on hiring outsiders leads senior managers to expend considerable effort in finding the 'right people'. Such a commitment leads them to rationalize their efforts by placing high value on talented outsiders and to assume they are better than insiders. Sometimes we refer to this as the 'neglect of prophets in their own land' syndrome. This syndrome is exemplified by the current fashion among some football clubs for recruiting football managers and football stars from other countries, which is often played out in the popular press by a 'will they come, won't they come' storyline and frequently leads to a bidding war in which outsiders are paid much more than insiders. Such strategies often lead not only to internal dissatisfaction but to a mercenary culture, because talented individuals who are attracted by money are equally likely to leave for money.

- Focusing on individual talent often results in playing down the need to repair problems with the organization as a whole, such as the 'fit' among individuals, business processes, organizational cultures and structures. Again, the football team example highlights the problems of relying on recruiting star players, a strategy that doesn't always lead to success.

- Arrogance and elitism often follow the recruitment of talented individuals – part of the problem at Enron. Such attitudes and behaviour run counter to the attitudes of wisdom, a delicate balance between knowing and doubting and one of the hallmarks of good managers and leaders (see Chapter 2).

- The stars' 'shine' typically begins to decline because they are uprooted from their supportive, previous organization and workgroups and replanted, often in infertile soil. Stardom is over-attributed to personal qualities and under-attributed to the organizational context. Moreover, the performance of the group that has to work with the new star usually suffers because of declining morale, communication problems and interpersonal conflicts. These two consequences have related to declining valuations of companies following publicized appointments of stars in the financial services industry (Groysberg, 2010).

Managing careers

We have already raised some of the issues concerned with managing newer patterns of careers in the previous sections. However, there are issues requiring more elaboration so that managers are better able to understand and deal with the problems they are likely to face, both now and in the future. These issues can be subsumed under the general trend in career patterns towards fragmentation, segmentation and/or idiosyncrasy.

The notion of boundaryless careers, employability and the individualization of employment have already been introduced in previous sections. Though there is still some argument over the objective evidence on the extent to which individual career expectations have changed, and whether there have been markedly different career behaviours exhibited by the majority of employees, there is little doubt that the *rhetoric of careers* has changed since the 1990s (Arthurs, 2008). What seemed to be a widespread trend, among developed economies at least, was for employees to begin their disengagement from careers at an increasingly early age (Sparrow and Cooper, 2003). However, given demographic trends, changing attitudes towards older employees by employers and projected labour shortages in certain countries over the next few decades, many people are remaining at work well beyond traditional retirement age, with legislative changes making later retirement mandatory in countries with ageing populations, e.g. Greece in 2015. Moreover, Bal *et al.* (2012) found that new, flexible and development-oriented deals and supportive organizational climates motivated older workers to continue their careers beyond retirement age.

In the 1980s, Ed Schein (1990) developed the idea of people having different *career anchors*, relatively stable orientations to one's organization and one's career(s). He identified eight such anchors (see Box 3.3), which have been widely used to analyse career development and to provide advice to managers, including, for example, assigning individuals to employment in other countries (Cerdin and Le Pangneux, 2012).

However, other researchers have shown the permanence implied by the notion of career anchors may be a little misplaced (Arthurs, 2008). For example, Arthurs *et al.* (1999) found that 75 participants in their in-depth, longitudinal study over a period of ten years were less likely to involve upwards progression and were much less linear and idiosyncratic than most career theory had suggested, often involving movements outside the labour market and downwards and sideways moves. Thus, careers, they argued, sometimes lacked the objective rationality that was implied by these anchors, or else revolved around individuals' desire for personal fulfillment or maximization of their earnings or education, depending on their ambitions at a particular point in time.

BOX 3.3 Schein's career anchors

Edgar Schein identified eight career anchors, and has shown that people will have prioritized preferences for these. For example, a person with a primary theme of security/stability will seek secure and stable employment over, say, employment that is challenging and riskier. Career anchors, he argues, are relatively stable, and people tend to stay anchored in one area, which will be reflected in their career and job choices.

- *Technical/functional competence.* This kind of person likes becoming expert at something, and will work to this end. They like to be challenged and then use their skill to meet the challenge, doing the job properly and better than almost anyone else.
- *General managerial competence.* Unlike technical/functional people, these folks want to be managers (and not just to get more money, although this may be used as a metric of success). They like problem-solving and dealing with other people. They thrive on responsibility. To be successful, they also need emotional intelligence competences.
- *Autonomy/independence.* These people have a primary need to work under their own direction, rather than be controlled. They avoid standards and prefer to work alone.
- *Security/stability.* Security-focused people seek stability and continuity as a primary factor of their lives. They avoid risks and are generally 'lifers' in their job.

- *Entrepreneurial creativity*. These people like to invent or innovate, be creative and, most of all, run their own businesses. They differ from those who seek autonomy in that they will share the workload to accomplish things. They find ownership very important. They easily get bored. Wealth, for them, is a sign of success.
- *Service/dedication to a cause*. Service-oriented people are driven by how they can help other people, often more than using their natural talents (which may fall in other areas). They tend to work well in public services such as education and healthcare, or in management occupations such as HR.
- *Pure challenge*. People driven by challenge seek constant stimulation and difficult problems that they can tackle. Such people will change jobs when the current one gets boring, and their careers can be very varied.
- *Lifestyle*. Those who are focused first on lifestyle look at their whole pattern of living. They not so much balance work and life as integrate it. They may even take long periods off work in which to indulge in passions such as sailing or travelling.

In relation to psychological contracting, research has found highly varied attitudes and expectations of such contracts, even within the same industry (retail banking) and in the same country (the UK) (Sparrow and Cooper, 2003). Once we move outside similar contexts, we are likely to find increased variations among typical psychological contracts (Herriot, 2001). For example, US researchers have found significant differences among career orientations and career-oriented behaviours of knowledge workers and managers in leading technology companies in America, Europe, Asia and Israel (Finegold and Mohrman, 2001) (see Table 3.5).

This last piece of work not only focused on what employees say in interviews about expectations and desires, but has also examined the relationship between key behaviours and levels of employee retention and commitment. The key point for managers from this research reinforces the idea introduced in the previous sections that organizations need to use their data on employees to refine their understanding of changing and varied employee expectations, psychological contracts and career-driving behaviours, and to segment their workforces and develop appropriate EVPs and employer brands.

Arthurs (2008) has identified a broad category of contemporary careers, which are responsive to: (1) changing boundaries in occupational, organizational, national and global ways of working, (2) greater uncertainty arising from increased knowledge and (3) increased choice among individuals consequent on changing occupational, organizational, national and global boundaries and the greater range of job experiences available to people.

Thus, one general trend is for people to seek more flexibility in the type of employment relationship and psychological contract they have with their employers. Such flexibility is more likely to be sought and negotiated by people whose skills are highly valued and who are in a relatively powerful position to negotiate flexible deals. They are usually high-status employees who are also highly mobile and marketable, including doctors, some academics and other professionals or high added value contractors in short supply (Barley and Kunda, 2006). Denise Rousseau (2001), one of the most influential researchers of psychological contracting, has called this process *idiosyncratic dealing*. These deals are different from psychological contracts because they are based on more than employee expectations and arise only when individuals actually negotiate different treatment from their employers than is normally the case with comparable others. Examples of such deals often involve working less than full-time contracts so they have time to work on their own behalf with other clients, or can enjoy 'portfolio' careers, working significant time at home and negotiating special monetary and non-monetary arrangements, including special performance or commission arrangements, pension deals, vacation time, etc. (Collins *et al.*, 2013). Idiosyncratic dealing, however, creates a number of problems for employers because it gives rise to a 'star' system that breaks normal conventions and can lead to some of the problems associated with talent management discussed earlier.

Finally Feldman (2007) argued that older workers over the age of 50 are more likely to change career paths if they are motivated to change and have the ability to change. Such motivation and ability is negatively related to their career embeddedness, which is shaped by their lack of external networks, their fit with their current career, the sacrifices they would have to make if they decided to change careers and the barriers to entry to alternative careers.

TABLE 3.5 Potential variety in psychological contracts and career expectations

Sparrow's contractual deal (UK retail banking)	Herriot and Pemberton's career contracts (UK retail banking)	Finegold and Mohrman 'What employees really want' (Technology industry/ cross country)
Still ambitious – accept constraints of new deal but believe they can still advance	Career development core deal – organization sought flexibility, commitment, involvement and performance, while employees accepted this and sought trust, security, employability and career development	Early career employees (30 and under) seek career advancement, satisfaction with professional work environment, influence within organization and to work for innovative company. Security less important
Frustrated mobile – disengaged mentally because managers did not understand need, and were on constant job search	Autonomy – organization looked for specific, short-term, project-type skills and capability to work unsupervised, while employees sought autonomy, freedom to do work and challenging projects	Mid career employees (31–50) seek degree of autonomy to manage own careers and professional satisfaction
Passively flexible – understood requirements for being flexible, but no enthusiasm for it	Lifestyle or part-time deal – organization wanted flexibility to match workload and part-time, and usually high-customer service skills while employees wanted flexible work patterns and workloads to match their lifestyle loads	Late career employees (over 50) These employees seek security above all else. Professional satisfaction and autonomy less important

continued . . .

TABLE 3.5 Continued

Sparrow's contractual deal (UK retail banking)	Herriot and Pemberton's career contracts (UK retail banking)	Finegold and Mohrman 'What employees really want' (Technology industry/ cross country)
Lifers – respected old relational contracts, and not impressed with high pay and employability. Believed technical competence was sufficient reason for advancement		
Buy me out – sought a deal to leave, but waiting for right offer from employers		
Guidance seekers – sought and needed help to understand their career possibilities		
Don't push me too fast – understood need for change but thought it was going too fast, too far		
Just pay me more – transactional outlook, and would accept most changes but at a price		

Source: adapted from Finegold and Mohrman, 2001; Sparrow and Cooper, 2003, p. 131.

EXERCISE 3.4

Think about your career. Which description, if any, fits your own career pattern or expectations? Would you say that your career expectations have changed over time?

Managing organizational commitment and identification

We have repeatedly come across or used terms such as commitment, identification, citizenship or engagement; these are different ways of describing the nature of the linkage between an employee and his or her organization and the factors that influence this relationship. For managers, it is important they understand the differences in these linkages, especially what they refer to and their implications for practice (see Table 3.6). For example, commitment, identification and citizenship each have their own specific meaning, antecedents and consequences, yet each is used to describe the nature of psychological contracts and the strength of employee brands or EVPs. Furthermore, many employee surveys conducted by 'blue-chip' organizations fail to distinguish between them or, even worse, confuse them. As a consequence, HR managers often have to rely on measures for A (e.g. identification) while hoping for B (e.g. commitment). In this section, we shall look briefly at organizational commitment, organizational identification and the notion of psychological ownership, the three most important of the individual–organizational linkages (Sparrow and Cooper, 2003) before moving on to discuss the newer concept of employee engagement.

Organizational commitment

In the case on the North Sea oil industry, our measures of employees' relationships with their organization focused mainly on commitment, a term that is used to refer to a number of different types of attachment to work, including commitment to work itself, to specific jobs, to the union or workgroup, to a career or professional calling, or to the employing organization(s). It is the last of these that has received most attention because it has promised much in terms of desired organizational outcomes, such as loyalty, 'going the extra mile' (organizational citizenship behaviour), low absenteeism and good performance.

Organizational commitment is usually defined in terms of the reasons underlying people's wish to join and remain with an organization and their feelings towards it (Sparrow and Cooper, 2003). It is sometimes thought to have three components, which are set out in Box 3.4. An individual's commitment can be made up of one or more of these types of commitment, and usually a composite measure of all three is provided in general surveys.

BOX 3.4 **Three types of organizational commitment**

1 *Affective (or attitudinal) commitment*, which is based on a willing acceptance of the organization's goals and an identification or emotional attachment with the organization and its values. Measures include items like 'I really feel as if this organization's problems are my problems'.

2 *Continuance commitment*, which refers to the extent to which employees are bound to the organization in terms of their intention to remain or leave. This may result from a weighing-up of the costs and benefits of staying or leaving, such as perceptions of alternative jobs, or the financial hardship associated with leaving. Measures include items like 'I would continue to work for this organization even though I received a better offer from another employer'.

3 *Normative commitment*, which refers to an individual's perceptions of obligation or loyalty to the organization. Measures include items like 'This organization deserves my loyalty'.

Source: based on Meyer and Allen, 1991.

There are several problems, however, with the notion of organizational commitment that render it a less useful concept in describing the strength of the relationship between individuals and their organization, especially in contemporary contexts (Swailes, 2002). First, it is used as both an explanation and an outcome of individual–organizational linkages, which can cause confusion in trying to establish the causes of commitment. Second, the notion that individuals may be committed to only one organization, especially in the light of recent changes towards networking in organizations (see Chapter 4), and in the light of boundaryless careers discussed earlier, may be becoming outmoded (Arthurs, 2008). Third, the goals and values of a large organization are likely to vary from one part to another, such as in those organizations that have strong lines of business brands, and rejection of one specific value (or line of business brand) may coexist with the acceptance of other values (or other lines of business). This could be the case, for example, with organizations that have ethically dubious products such as cigarettes as part of their portfolio.

Perhaps more than anything, however, the reason to be a little wary of the concept of commitment is its promised and expected relationship with desired organizational outcomes. Although high levels of continuance commitment are related to lower labour turnover and absence, and affective commitment is associated with job performance, the links between organizational commitment as a whole and job and organizational performance are really quite weak (Sparrow and Cooper, 2003). And given the changes in the nature of employment and careers, even this weak relationship may diminish over time.

Organizational identification

This concept has become more widely used over the last decade or so because of its more direct links with values-based management, EVPs and employer branding (see Chapter 6). It differs from commitment, which is a more general term, and refers to only one component or type of commitment. However, psychologists who are experts in identity theory have claimed that organizational identification is a deeper and richer concept than the one measured by commitment scales. It also has a specific meaning. So, for example, He and Brown (2013) have defined identification in organizations as *'the extent to which an organizational member defines himself/herself with reference to his/her organizational membership'* (p. 12).

Social identity theory, the basis of this idea, suggests that we define our self-concept through the links we have with important reference groups by forming a relationship in our minds between the identity of those groups and ourselves. We tend to highlight the similarities between our own self-identity and those of the group we aspire to relate or belong to, and emphasize the distinctiveness between ourselves and those groups that do not fit in with our self-identity – in other words, who we are not (Hatch and Cunliffe, 2013). For example, in recent studies we have conducted into the work of senior doctors in the National Health Service in Scotland, we have found a significant division in attitudes to their jobs and organizations between hospital consultants who had worked in a medical management role and those without such experience (Martin *et al.*, 2015). Many consultants in the latter group regarded consultants who had become medical managers as having undergone a significant identity change, one that was inconsistent with patient care as the primary goal of healthcare organizations. Medical managers were often described as having 'crossed a line in the sand' or having gone over to 'the dark side'. So, the less individuals believe the norms and values of an organization represent their own norms and values, the less will be their level of organizational identification, which was certainly the case in our research.

From the perspective of managers, organizational identification theory holds some promise, because strong levels of identification have a potential capacity to be positively related to employee self-esteem, greater satisfaction and motivation, perceived superior job performance by managers, high levels of loyalty, a more attractive place to work, organizational citizenship and working beyond contract. However, the links between it and financial performance are weaker and limited (He and Brown, 2013). Research also shows that measures of organizational support, especially employees' perceptions of the extent to which the employer values their contribution and care for their well-being, have a positive effect on organizational identification (Edwards and Peccei, 2010), a finding we take up later in this chapter.

Psychological ownership

Jon Pierce and his colleagues (2001) have argued that, although commitment and identification are important constructs for understanding the relationships and attachments between individuals and their organizations, neither is a complete or even necessary explanation of psychological ownership, which they define as follows:

> 'As a state of the mind, psychological ownership . . . is that state in which individuals feel as though the target of ownership (material or immaterial in nature) or a piece of it is "theirs" (i.e. "It is MINE!"). The core of psychological ownership is the feeling of possessiveness and of being psychologically tied to an object.'
>
> (Pierce *et al.*, 2001, p. 299)

These authors contend that 'mine' is a small word, but with enormous consequences for organizations. Psychological ownership arises because people have an innate need to possess, or because it satisfies certain human motives, which are either socially derived or genetic (Avey *et al.*, 2009; Van Dyne and Pierce, 2004). These include:

- *self-efficacy*, which refers to individual's beliefs that they can achieve success in a specific task;
- the need to *control and be accountable*, in which ownership confers on us certain rights and abilities to shape our environment so that we can become more effective – for example, the degree to which we can determine our working times;
- *self-identity*, which is formed partly through our interactions with what we possess and our reflections on what they mean – for example, company cars;
- the need to have a *place*, 'home' or 'territory' that we can call our own, which is not only a physical but also a psychological space – for example, employees not only seek office or work spaces they can call their own, but also look for 'soul mates' they can metaphorically set up a home with at work.

Ownership is achieved by three 'routes', involving:

1   Having a strong degree of control of the object of our ownership, such as the job or the organization and its performance.
2   Coming to know the object of our ownership intimately by having a 'living' relationship with it – for example, the academic who comes to feel the university department belongs to him or her, having achieved tenure and worked in it for a long time.
3   Investing the self into the object of our ownership. Through time as we expend effort into shaping, creating or making something we feel that we come to own what we have shaped, created or made, such as machines, ideas and even people.

TABLE 3.6 The differences between commitment, identification and psychological ownership

Criteria for distinctiveness	Organizational commitment	Organizational identification	Psychological ownership
Core proposition of concept	Desire to remain with organization	Use of organization's identity to define oneself	Possession of the 'organization', job or area of work
Questions answered for individuals	Should I remain?	Who am I?	What is mine?
Motivational bases	• Security • Belongingness • Beliefs and values	• Attraction • Affiliation • Self-enhancement	• Control • Self-identity • Need for place
How it develops	• Decision to remain with organization	• Incorporating organizational values into self • Affiliation • Emulating organizational characteristics	• Active imposition/ investment of self on organization
Main consequences for practitioners from research findings	• Organizational citizenship behaviour ('going the extra mile') • Intention to leave or remain • Attendance and absenteeism	• Support for organizational values and participation in its activities • Intention to remain • Frustration/stress • Alienation • Lack of integration into organizational values/culture	• Development of employee rights and responsibilities • Promotion of/ resistance to change • Frustration, alienation and sabotage • Integration of employees with work • Organizational citizenship behaviour

Sources: adapted from Pierce *et al.*, 2001, p. 306; Avey *et al.*, 2009.

The consequences of psychological ownership are to create among individuals a set of perceived rights and responsibilities that help explain why individuals promote and resist change. Thus, change that is self-initiated by employees who have high levels of psychological ownership is more likely to be promoted and accepted because it enhances feelings of self-efficacy and control. Likewise, imposed change is likely to be resisted because it diminishes feelings of self-efficacy and self-control. This concept is extremely important in understanding the success or otherwise of stock or share ownership in organizations, often given as a form of reward to individuals and as a way of creating organizational identification. As a number of researchers have concluded, share ownership without psychological ownership will not produce the hoped-for benefits of greater organizational identification and motivated behaviour (Sparrow and Cooper, 2003).

Finally, however, it is also worth noting that high levels of psychological ownership can also create pathological responses among those people who become separated from the objects of their ownership. For example, many years ago one of us worked as a personnel manager in a construction company. Some senior managers in that company proposed laying off a large number of young electricians who had spent many months installing electrical wiring in a new and high-profile building, on which many of these apprentice electricians were naturally proud to have worked. On hearing of the proposed lay-off, in a deliberate act of sabotage these young electricians systematically removed all the cabling and equipment they had installed.

Pierce and his colleagues have compared and contrasted the three concepts of commitment, identification and ownership, the outcomes of which are highly relevant to managers who hope to manage psychological contracts and individuals' attachment to their organizations. We have adapted their table and work by Avey *et al.* (2009) in Table 3.6 to highlight the most important practical implications.

Over-identification and workaholism

In the previous section we touched on negative consequences of high levels of psychological ownership in terms of stress and sabotage. One of the most popular discussions among the organization and families of many employees, however, is the subject of workaholism, which tends to be treated as a pathological response to the pressures of organizations on individuals and as a form of addictive behaviour, like drug taking. A definition by Schaufeli *et al.* (2008) seems to capture the idea succinctly, when they describe it as 'a compulsion or uncontrollable need to work incessantly' (p. 175). The prevalence of workaholism, especially among professional workers and certain cultures, has been estimated in some studies to be around 20 per cent of employees in the groups studied. So, for example, one early study in the USA estimated that whereas 5 per cent of the population might be classified as workaholics, 23 per cent of a sample of doctors, lawyers and psychiatrists were high on workaholism measures. Similarly, a study in 1996 of Japanese managers found that 21 per cent of the sample were workaholics (Burke, 2000). These figures have been confirmed by other surveys reported by Griffiths (2015), who sees workaholism as a form of addictive behaviour, similar to gambling and playing video games.

For managers, it is important to be able to identify workaholic behaviour (especially among themselves), to understand its positive and negative consequences and how it can be managed for the good of both the organization and individual. However, when we discuss workaholic attitudes and behaviour, though, we usually refer to the negative aspects, including long work hours at work and at home, waking times, refusal to delegate, not taking holidays, low levels of trust in others, perfectionist behaviour and a range of attitudes associated with such behaviours.

Drawing on earlier work, Shimazu and Schaufeli (2009) suggested that a typical work addict is driven by strong internal factors that individuals are unable to resist, such as a desire for career advancement, rather than external factors, such as financial problems or organizational culture. They also distinguished workaholism from other types of engaged work behaviour in three ways. The first is the excessive amount of time workaholics spend on discretionary work – the behavioural dimension. The second is that workaholics are reluctant to disengage from work involvement, even thinking about work when not at work – the cognitive dimension. The third is that workaholics work beyond what could reasonably be expected of normal people to meet deadlines – the compulsive dimension. The outcomes of workaholism are often high levels of psychological distress and, often, health problems. These factors are often associated with low levels of job satisfaction and life satisfaction (Shimazu and Schaufeli, 2009). However, we know less about the impact of workaholism and job performance, leading some researchers to speculate that workaholics may well be poor performers, or at least not necessarily good (Schaufeli *et al.*, 2008).

The lessons for practice from this research suggest that workaholism is associated with what Shimazu and Schaufeli (2009) call 'unwell-being' as distinct from well-being. These authors echo the epithet that the avoidance of workaholism and achieving work–life balance calls for 'working smart' rather than 'working hard', which leads us neatly into the next section.

Work–life balance

Work–life balance has become a major issue in many developed countries, with legislation being passed in the EU to limit the length of time spent at work by people in all kinds of employment (Walsh and Bartikowski, 2013). The basis for much of the debate is over the 'long hours culture' of some countries and of certain organizations within these countries, which is attributed to the adoption of new information and communications technologies, global competition and job restructuring, and has resulted in greater pressure on employees to work harder and more flexibly. Tables 3.7 and 3.8 show the variations in average hours worked and annual leave entitlements among selected countries, and also show how working hours have varied over time. Recent evidence has shown that American workers don't use up the holidays to which they are entitled, largely because they aren't entitled to be paid for these holidays (Ray and Schmitt, 2007).

The debate, however, has a number of angles to it. The proponents suggest that work–life balance as a concept implies a balanced relationship between paid work and life outside work, with a presumption that the two are distinct and that people have and should seek a degree of control over their working lives. Often, the term is used in the context of an agenda that seeks to preserve the institutions of family life, caring for children and older people, and one that seeks to promote genuine equality of opportunity for women. Set against this balance are the forces of technology and more intensive competition discussed in the previous section on workaholism, which have led some organizations to exercise pressures for long working hours, even though these extra hours may not be productive. For example, managers often talk about cultures of 'presenteeism', referring to situations where employees present themselves for work but don't actively engage in productive work ('there in body but not in mind'). As a consequence of this tension, governments and some organizations have introduced policies to help mitigate the 'colonization' by long working hours and the increasing length of working lives over non-working hours and non-working lives. Central to this balancing act is the idea that the individual–organizational employment relationship should be a negotiated psychological and legal contract that meets the expectations and obligations of both parties (Walsh and Bartikowski, 2013). The increasing degree of autonomy and control provided by this revised psychological contract is brought about by:

- increasing the variety of ways individuals are able to integrate work and non-work activities by giving them choices over working hours or job sharing;
- changing how employees balance work and non-work by constructing their own boundaries between work and non-work activities, such as working at home, tele-commuting, sabbaticals, extended leave, unpaid leave, parental leave and extended breaks for family responsibilities.

Policies that organizations develop to provide employees with these two forms of control have become more common. Box 3.5 illustrates how one UK company has attempted to put some of these ideas into practice.

Despite the volume of research conducted on the relationship between working hours and key outcomes, including health and general well-being, few strong conclusions can be drawn (Sparrow and Cooper, 2003; Walsh and Bartikowski, 2013). A meta-analysis conducted in 1997 found only a small, statistical correlation between working hours and health (Sparks *et al.*, 1997), which was supported by a later meta-analysis by Faragher *et al.* (2005). This latter work, however, found that job satisfaction was an important influence of the health of workers. Other studies have concluded that perhaps the main justification for companies to introduce such programmes may be more to do with attracting and retaining non-traditional employees to organizations and contributing to meeting the expectations of individuals with respect to modern employment conditions.

As we have already mentioned, however, there are some strong criticisms of the work–life balance agenda that suggest why the idea may have limited appeal to some organizations and to some employees. The first of these is the impact on productivity and output. Critics of work–life balance point to the example of the USA, which has the longest working hours in the developed world, but also has among the highest levels of productivity growth. Indeed, this comparison has influenced the French government to change its legislation on working hours by increasing them only shortly after having reduced them. Another example of the importance of flexibility over working hours to productivity was an agreement negotiated by Volkswagen, the German motor vehicle company, with its German employees to trade flexible working (longer hours when required) for guarantees on job security.

The second criticism is the rather arbitrary distinction between work and life outside work, which the notion of work–life balance implies (Walsh and Bartikowski, 2013). Many employees see work and life as overlapping, since what they do for work often is the main source of meaning in their lives, whether or not they are being paid handsomely for it. This is often the case with professionals in the fields of medicine, academia and in some of the creative professions, such as architecture and art, who are often seeking a form of community engagement (Adler *et al.*, 2008). In essence, work–life balance is a subjective concept and will vary from one person to another. However, most commentators and governments would agree that organizations and their senior managers are obliged to ensure that they are not placing undue pressure on people to see the balance in such a way that it leads to ill-health and the detriment of family relationships.

TABLE 3.7 Annual total hours actually worked

Country	2000	2004	2007	2010	2013
Japan	1821	1787	1785	1733	1735
Australia	1780	1741	1719	1695	1676
France	1535	1513	1500	1494	1489
Germany	1471	1436	1422	1405	1388
Korea	2512	2392	2306	2187	2163 est.
Poland	1988	1983	1976	1940	1918

Source: OECD. Sat Extracts.

TABLE 3.8 Annual leave and paid public holidays in the EU and USA

Country	Average annual leave entitlement	Paid public holidays per year
Austria	30 calendar days (22 work days); 36 after 6 years	13
Belgium	20 working days	10
Denmark	30 working days	9
Finland	4 weeks (five after a year)	9
France	30 working days	1
Germany (west)	4 weeks (up to 5 for younger workers)	10
Greece	4 weeks (plus 1 day after 2nd and 3rd years)	6
Ireland	4 weeks	9
Italy	4 weeks	13
Netherlands	4 weeks	0
Portugal	22 working days	13
Spain	22 working days	12
Sweden	25 working days	0
UK	4 weeks	0
USA	0	0

Source: Ray, R. and Schmitt, J. (2007) A comparison of leave and holidays in OECD countries, *European Economic and Employment Policy Brief*, No 3, ISSN 1782–2165.

BOX 3.5 Work–life balance programmes in the UK

Constructing a better balance in Balfour Beatty. When Balfour Beatty Civil Engineering Major Projects surveyed their employees in 2012, it found that an overwhelming majority liked working for the company but that for 62 per cent, work–life balance was a problem. 'I love my job and feel proud when I drive past a bridge and know that I helped to build it,' says engineer Chris Till, 'but I live in Preston and working on the M1/M25 means I live on site during the week and it can take me four hours to get home on a Friday.'

Balfour Beatty took these concerns seriously. 'We are always striving to improve both our service to our customers and the well-being of our employees,' said Commercial Director Nigel Roberts. 'A contented workforce leads to better productivity and fewer accidents on site.'

The Company employed flexible working specialists, Swiftwork, to help improve work–life balance. Working initially with the project team on the M1 construction site, the concept was tested. 'We had to be clear that the business case for this significant culture change was sound,' says Nigel Roberts. 'We wanted to ensure that performance was maintained and that our customers and suppliers needs were met. But we were also hoping that this would have a positive impact on recruitment and retention in an increasingly competitive market for highly skilled employees.'

Following a senior manager workshop, schemes were developed by local teams, to target specific work and individual requirements. Each team devised new ways of working that suited its business needs. Most were variations on flexitime and, for some, compressed hours over the working week were introduced. One team developed cross-skilling to offer a broader depth of service to internal clients across the whole day. Cost savings were also made to night services supplied using a flexitime scheme that had previously been provided by an external consultant.

For Balfour Beatty, the business case is proven. 'We have realised operational improvements in efficiency,' says Nigel Roberts, 'for example, there is better interdependence and communication between teams, time recording is better, health and safety cover has increased – not decreased – with more flexibility. Now we're hoping to build on this and develop even smarter ways of working.'

Lynette Swift, of consultants Swiftwork, is confident that new ways of working have huge potential for achieving productivity gains and reducing costs. 'If it's not improving performance, you're not managing it right,' she says. 'To succeed, new initiatives should be people driven but also business focused, not just about acceding to individual requests for flexible work patterns.'

Source: adapted from 'Constructing a better Balfour Beatty,' available online at www.flexibility.co.uk/cases/balfour-beatty.htm.

BOX 3.6 **The importance of flexible working hours – VW in Germany**

A report in *The Economist* in late 2004 suggested that Volkswagen, Europe's largest vehicle manufacturer, was in trouble, especially with the Volkswagen brand. Losses had amounted to a €47 million operating loss for the period January–September in 2004. The article pointed out that its production was less efficient than other German car-makers, including BMW and Chrysler Benz, with labour costs 11 per cent more than their competitors and wages 20 per cent higher than the union average. Nevertheless, this fact didn't stop unions putting in for an above average 4 per cent pay increase. But, like all German industrial workers, the article went on to say 'what they really crave is job security', which has persuaded the workers to modify their demands and accept more flexible hours, sometimes translating into longer hours and a wage freeze until 2007, in return for job security until 2011.

VW's response was to pay its 100,000 plus workers €1,000 each in cash as a flat-rate bonus, which it hoped would cut its labour costs by 10 per cent. However, this was only a small dent on its longer-term target, which was to reduce its wage bill by 30 per cent by 2011. The reaction of the investment markets to this news was to punish VW by devaluing its share price by 3 per cent for the 'compromise' deal that wouldn't go anywhere near to solving its long-standing productivity problem.

As *The Economist* noted in 2004, 'It sees that long hours are not enough to satisfy investors in Germany who also want to see traditional job security deals removed.'

As a consequence and after many years of negotiation with its unions and Works Council, Volkswagen has developed a new working time model with its union representatives. According to the company website in 2015, this model:

> 'offers its employees a high level of flexibility. Daily working hours are as variable as the number of shifts. Company weekly working hours – adjusted to market requirements and depending on the working time model – can be defined within a working time corridor of 25 to 34 hours per week. In addition, working time accounts ensure flexibility for the individual employees and the entire team over long periods . . .
>
> Volkswagen can therefore react flexibly to fluctuations in demand and offer its employees a number of working time models without having to constantly recruit staff or make existing employees redundant. In this way, jobs and the knowledge capital of employees are secured for the long term. Customers, the company and employees benefit as flexibility is an important aspect when it comes to reconciling work and family life' (Volkswagen Personnel Policy, 2015).

Sources: adapted from *The Economist*, 'Darwin meets job creationism', 6 November 2004, and Volkswagen Personnel Policy, 2015 [available online at www.volkswagen-karriere. de/en/what_we_stand_for/personnel_policy/flexibility.html.]

MANAGING EMPLOYEE ENGAGEMENT

Since writing the first edition of this book, the topic of employee engagement has generated enormous interest among practitioners and, more recently, academics as a way of integrating many of the ideas discussed in the chapter (Albrecht *et al.*, 2015; Peccei, 2013). While retaining a degree of scepticism over 'the desire to pour old wine into new bottles' by the management consultancy industry, we believe that the notion of employee engagement has much to offer as a way forward for understanding and managing individual–organizational relationships. This is especially relevant in economies, industries and organizations that have relatively poor records of productivity growth and ensuring work–life balance, which has been recognized by the UK government in its funding of the 'Engage for Success' programme (see www.engageforsuccess.org).

In our research into hospital consultants (Martin *et al.*, 2015), we drew on a set of ideas from contemporary research into employee engagement (Albrecht *et al.*, 2015; Farndale *et al.*, 2014; Sparrow, 2014; Truss *et al.*, 2013) to develop a framework that might help us think about employee engagement more generally (see Figure 3.5). Basically we proposed that employee engagement should be thought of in terms of four distinctive but related levels. The first is the well-researched and empirically verified concept of *work engagement* (Schaufeli, 2015). The second level is *engagement with each other*, especially in interdependent workgroups, which draws on the notion of relational coordination, a construct that was been found to have a significant impact on performance outcomes in a range of industries (Gittell *et al.*, 2010). The third level is *organizational engagement*, initially developed by consultants but which is now being treated in academic literature as an important driver of organizational performance (Farndale *et al.*, 2014; Sparrow, 2014). The fourth level is *industry engagement*, which can be important in explaining employees' attachment to their work in certain sectors of economic life.

Work engagement

Work engagement studies are increasingly based on a *demand-resources model of work engagement* (Schaufeli, 2015). This model has identified three forms of connections that people have with their work: the *vigour* employees invest in doing the job, their levels of *absorption* or immersion and attachment to their work, and their *dedication* to their work. Work engagement has been shown to predict valuable outcomes such as positive evaluations of organizations, lower job turnover and higher levels of individual and unit performance (Albrecht *et al.*, 2015). It is also positively associated with key job resources and challenging work. However, vigour, absorption and dedication in work, if taken too far, can lead to over-engagement (or over-identification as we have discussed in this chapter) or employee burnout. High levels of work engagement also tend to be associated with 'cosmopolitan' career orientations, which typically refer to the external career orientation of professionals such as the doctors in our own research (Martin *et al.*, 2015) as distinct from the 'local' or internal career orientations of occupational groups such as health service managers.

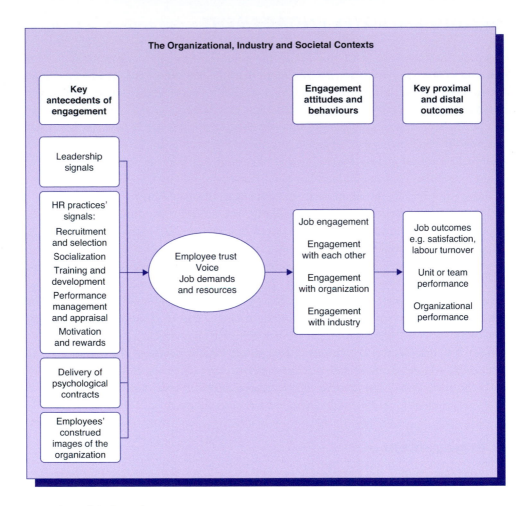

FIGURE 3.5 A model of employee engagement

Engagement with each other

Relationships among employees at a group or team level have also been found to lead to effective organizational performance. This has traditionally been theorized in terms of social capital and networking among employees to facilitate group and organizational learning. More recently, Gittell *et al.* (2010) have developed a theory of relational coordination to explain the impact of effective coordination among task interdependent groups on achieving soft and hard desirable organizational outcomes. They define relational coordination as 'a mutually reinforcing process of interaction between communication and relationships carried out for the purpose of task integration' (Gittell, 2002, p. 301), which involves groups engaging in frequent and high-quality communications, sharing goals and knowledge, and showing mutual respect for each other. While these authors restrict their analysis to the coordination of 'highly interdependent, uncertain, and time-constrained work', we argue that the concept of relational coordination is relevant to most forms of work in modern organizations. It also provides an explanation of the link between the individualistic focus of employees' engagement with their work and employees' engagement with their organization and its senior management.

Organizational engagement

Recent academic work has sought to define organizational engagement in terms of emotions and attitudes (state engagement) and behaviour engagement (the traditional interest of management consultants) (Farndale *et al.*, 2014). Key components of these different types of engagement with the organization include organizational satisfaction and commitment, vigour and absorption displayed towards an organization and positive organizational citizenship behaviours (Albrecht *et al.*, 2015). To these we would add employee identification with an organization, drawing on the well-established concept of organizational identification we discussed earlier in this chapter. As we noted, Martin Edwards and Ricardo Peccei (2010) proposed a three-factor explanation of employee identification with their organizations. The first factor refers to how employees self-categorize their personal identities. As noted earlier, employees differ in their career orientations and the extent to which their employing organization helps define their identities. The second refers to their sense of attachment and belonging to their organizations, often related to how long they have worked in it. The third refers to the extent to which employees share the goals and values of the organization and incorporate them into their own goals, values and beliefs. In these studies, high levels of organizational identification were shown to predict all categories of workers' helping behaviours, turnover intentions and feelings of being involved in the organization.

Industry engagement

Employees in particular industries often tend to identify with the sector in which they work rather than the firm, which reflects the notion of cosmopolitan versus local orientations to work discussed in the section on work engagement. Thus we found in our study of the changing work experience of hospital consultants in the National Health Service in Scotland that many of these senior doctors were more attracted by working in the sector than any particular employer within it. Engagement with the sector was high but engagement with their employers was only low to moderate (Martin *et al.*, 2015). Moreover, we also found that consultant doctors identified more the democratic values of the healthcare sector in Scotland than the more market-oriented healthcare system in England, even though the two sectors are part of a UK-wide National Health Service. Industry engagement can also be explained by the notion of a *construed image*. What employees think about the industry and the organization in which they work is influenced by how significant others, including close friends and family, the media and the general public, rate an industry's or organization's reputation. So, for example, financial services rated only marginally better in reputation rankings than government and tobacco (Harris Poll, 2015), while the general public in the UK have high levels of trust in doctors in the National Health Service.

State and behavioural engagement

Another element of engagement is the distinction made between state engagement, which refers to employees' attitudes and emotions (e.g. sharing the values of the organization), and behavioural engagement, which refers the kinds of behaviours employees report when feeling engaged or disengaged (e.g. I often recommend my employer as a place to work). These distinctive *foci of engagement* (Farndale *et al.*, 2014) are very important in making engagement a worthwhile and useful subject of study and practice, since most of the previous research into individual–organizational relationships have focused on attitudes and emotions rather than the arguably more important behaviours that employees display in their work.

The drivers of engagement and their impact on employee trust, voice, and job demands and resources

Our framework also identifies some of the most important antecedents of these different types of engagement discussed in this chapter. From our reading of recent research, the ones that have the most impact are: (1) signals sent out by the rhetoric and actions of senior leaders in the organization, (2) the signals sent out by the kinds of HR practices employed in the organization, (3) the extent to which the psychological contract is delivered and (4) employees' construed image of the organization or industry. The rhetoric–reality gap between what leaders pronounce (usually a 'soft' version of people management as 'resourceful humans') and how they behave both personally and in directing their organizations (a 'hard' version of people as 'human resources' or 'capital') has been a constant source of tension in organizations (Legge, 2005).

We have covered the nature of signals sent out by senior managers and/or leaders in Chapter 2, and the delivery of the psychological contract and the notion of a construed image in this present chapter, so little more needs to be said about these 'drivers' of engagement. However, the nature of human resources practices requires further elaboration. Albrecht *et al.* (2015) have usefully categorized these as recruitment and selection, socialization, training and development and performance management, including motivation and rewards, and appraisal. To these we would add talent management and employer branding, job design and employee relations' practices, including the means and media used to secure employees' involvement and cooperation. However, it is not just the fact or existence of such practices, individually and collectively, regardless of their sophistication, that is important, but the honesty of the signals they send out to employees and how these signals are sensed or interpreted by them (Martin and Cerdin, 2014). This highly subjective process of interpretation by employees of the honesty or authenticity of signals sent out by the organization shaped three key intermediate variables. These are: (a) employees' trust in the organization and its leaders, (b) the extent to which they feel free to exercise voice and participate in decision-making and (c) their perceptions of demands placed on them and the quality of the resources available to them to do their jobs.

Employee trust has become one of the most widely researched and sought after phenomena in HR and organizational studies (Siebert *et al.*, 2015). Trust is manifested when employees place themselves in a vulnerable position and have to rely on their managers' competence, integrity (honesty) and benevolence (good intentions) towards them. Since the Global Financial Crisis of 2007–8, employee trust has been at a premium, especially in sectors badly affected such as financial services and the energy industries. Instead of trust, we may be witnessing high and stable levels of distrust as the norm in many sectors of the economy rather than lowering levels of trust. Our study of de-professionalization among hospital consultants could be read that way, which showed a remarkable level of distrust of non-clinical managers as a consequence of the 'dishonest' signals deliberately sent by recent government and managerial strategies to reduce the, once sacrosanct, professional autonomy of the doctors in healthcare (Adler *et al.*, 2008).

Employee voice is also a major influence on employee engagement at different levels. This has been defined as 'the right to express opinions and have meaningful input into work-related decision-making, which includes individual and collective voice, union and non-union voice, and voice mechanisms that cover not only employment terms, but also work autonomy and business issues' (Budd, 2014, p. 477). Voice researchers concern themselves with whether employees feel free and able to speak up or remain silent, whether voice is exercised in a socially constructive manner to improve decision-making, or as retributive justice exercised by employees over managers and the organization, and the extent to which employees enjoy democratic rights in their organizations and are able to exercise a degree of control or task autonomy in their work situations (Wilkinson and Fay, 2011). This literature has distinguished between direct, indirect and hybrid voice channels, with the last of these represented by managers' attempts to secure employee voice through union or representative channels. In our study of doctors' de-professionalization, we found the lack of voice, individually and collectively, to be the most important factor in leading consultants to express low-to-moderate levels of engagement with their employers.

Of the theories that attempt to explain work engagement and its antithesis – burnout resulting from over-engagement – perhaps the most widely cited is the job-demands-resources model (Schaufeli, 2015). This model is based on the idea that resources can be of two types – functional job resources consistent with achieving work goals, personal growth and/or reducing job demands and personal resources, associated with personal resilience and self belief in being able to control their immediate work environment. You might be able to think of the kind of resources your employer or university could provide you with to help you meet the demands of your job and career, such as appropriate technology, time to do the work and low levels of bureaucracy; or, in the case of academics and students, a self-belief in their ability to produce good quality research papers in spite of what reviewers and tutors might write about you. However, if you perceive the demands are too great and your resources are insufficient, then this is likely to lead to health impairment, disengagement and eventually to burnout. In our study of hospital consultants, greater demands for more intensive working and increased bureaucratic control over resources were also an important influence on their low levels of engagement with their employers. Nevertheless, this imbalance between demands and resources did not impact on work engagement or their engagement with colleagues in clinical teams.

The outcomes of engagement, improving engagement and the influence of context

The research into engagement has predicted and shown positive effects on job, unit/team and organizational performance (Albrecht *et al.*, 2015). At the level of the job itself, improved satisfaction, commitment and lower levels of labour turnover have resulted from actions designed to raise engagement levels, such as providing the optimal mix of job demands and resources, enabling employees to improve their personal resources through training and encouraging employees to engage in what are called 'job crafting' behaviours. Reminiscent of the job redesign movement of the 1960s and 1970s, job crafting focuses on the ability of employees to shape their jobs by choosing particular tasks or specialisms that match their interests and abilities, negotiating different job content to enhance their skills, and by assigning greater meaning to their jobs (for example, being seen as a mentor to less-experienced people).

At the level of the team or work unit, improving relational coordination has been shown to have a highly significant impact on key outcomes. So, for example, improving the frequency, timing, accuracy and quality of communications between doctors, nurses, social workers, physio-therapists and managers, supported by shared goals, shared knowledge and mutual respect in these clinical teams, has a remarkable effect on surgical performance, as measured by patient satisfaction, post-operative freedom from pain and functioning, and the days spent in hospital (Gittell *et al.*, 2008).

Finally, Albrecht *et al.* (2015) report some research findings that suggest higher levels of engagement can lead to greater organizational innovation, operational performance, financial returns and competitive advantage. While these so called 'distal' measures of performance are certainly desirable, for the most part they remain part of the rhetoric of the 'engagement industry' rather than the reality on the ground, because organizational-level outcomes cannot easily be attributed to individual attitudes and behaviour such as leadership or employee engagement. Two examples might suffice to illustrate this point. First, from our research into organizational trust, we concluded that inaction can sometimes be a better strategy for repairing trust than direct action. Time can often be a great healer and taking direct action usually has unforeseen and, indeed, unknowable consequences (Siebert and Martin, 2014). This conclusion is supported by the so-called 'too-much-of-a-good-thing effect' in HR, which refers to the diminishing and indeed negative returns that often accompany programs such as appraisal, rewarding people for performance and communications (Pierce and Aguinis, 2013). Secondly, organizational success is often down to external factors such as the vicissitudes of markets or, in the case of our doctors, factors outside of their control such as political priorities in spending. In other words, and to return to a central message of this book, context (and time) matters! Which is why we circumscribed the variables in Figure 3.5 by a box representing different levels of context – the societal, industry and organizational levels.

In the next chapter, we will discuss organizational contexts and show how organizational structures and processes shape people's attitudes, identities and engagement. In Chapter 5, we examine the impact of societal level institutions and national cultures on these same factors. And in Chapters 7 and 9, we look at the industry level when discussing knowledge workers and creative workers, whose attitudes, identities and what they are engaged with are often very different from other types of employees.

LEARNING SUMMARY

In this chapter we began by examining the idea of psychological contracts as a way of understanding the relationships between organizations and individuals at work. The concept of psychological contracts has become a popular one with practitioners and academics alike, and should help you understand your own relationships with your employer or potential employer. You should have learned how to apply the idea of psychological contracts in analysing and designing work situations, including the importance of recognizing the different types of contract – transactional, relational and ideological – the potential outcomes of breaching and violating contracts, and the questions used to measure psychological contracts.

We then examined the problems of managing psychological contracts at work, which include managing talent, managing careers, managing different kinds of individual–organizational linkages and managing work–life balance.

Talent management has become one of the major issues for many employers in developed countries; it is generally defined as the ability to attract, inspire and retain high-performing employees, and develop others so that they can perform more effectively. We examined the elements of a talent management strategy and new thinking in talent management, which focuses on segmentation of internal labour markets and using different approaches to recruiting, developing and retaining these groups. However, talent management has a dark side, especially if it focuses on external recruitment to the detriment of growing people inside the organization, and you should be aware of the shortcomings of many talent management programmes.

Managing careers has been characterized by general trends towards fragmentation and individualization. The notions of employability and boundaryless careers have been used to illustrate these changes in psychological career contracts between employers and employees. There is little doubt that the evidence supports these changed expectations among employees who are seeking different things from careers at different stages of their working lives, and possibly greater variety, flexibility and autonomy at work. Employers need to be aware of these changes, and design contracts to reflect the different groups within their workforces.

Psychological contracts can also be applied to the measurement of different kinds of individual–organizational relationships, including commitment, identification and psychological ownership. The importance of these three concepts to managing relationships between people and their organizations cannot be overestimated; too many organizations engage in surveys of employees in which they are unclear as to what they are measuring and attempting to manage. Often, they measure and manage one aspect of individual–organizational relationships while hoping for positive outcomes from some other, quite different, feature. Commitment is essentially focused on whether people will remain with the organization; identification focuses on a person's sense of who they are and the extent they can use the organization's values to define their identity; psychological ownership indicates the extent to which an individual sees that organization as part of him or herself. These different constructs are associated with different outcomes, with identification arguably the most important when examining the extent to which individuals will provide behavioural support for the organization's values and branding strategies.

An area we also examined was the problems of over-identification and workaholism. Workaholism has been seen as a major problem by many employers and governments, which are attempting to reduce the negative consequences of people being too attached to their work. Workaholism has been attributed to three causes: family background and how young people learn addictive behaviour; personal beliefs and fears; and organizational values that encourage high levels of attachment. Many organizations have put programmes into place to deal with various dysfunctional consequences of workaholism, including flexible working, home-working and culture changes focusing on working 'smarter' rather than 'harder'.

Finally, we examined the role of employee engagement, which has become a way of thinking about how employees connect with their work, each other, their organizations and their chosen employment sector. We presented a model of engagement at these different levels, explained some of the antecedents of engagement, such as leadership, HR practices, delivery of the psychological contract and construed image, and how they might work through employee trust and voice to impact on desired organizational outcomes. In summary, we have explored a wide range of ideas, research and concepts that should be useful to you in practising management and in any writing you need to do for your courses.

REVIEW QUESTIONS

1 An exclusive approach to talent management is the way forward for organizations looking to gain competitive advantage. Discuss.
2 Workaholism is not necessarily a bad thing. Discuss.
3 Can employees ever be over-engaged?

REFERENCES

Adler, P. S., Kwon, S.-W. and Hecksher, C. (2008) Professional work: the emergence of collaborative community. *Organization Science*, 19 (2), 359–376.

Albrecht, S. L., Bakker, A. B., Gruman, J. A., Macey, W. H. and Saks, A. M. (2015) Employee engagement, human resource management practices and competitive advantage. *Journal of Organizational Effectiveness: People and Performance*, 2 (1), 7–35.

Arthurs, M. B. (2008) Examining contemporary careers: a call for interdisciplinary enquiry. *Human Relations*, 61 (2), 163–186.

Arthurs, M. B., Inkson, K. and Pringle, J. (1999) *The new careers*. London: Sage.

Avey, J. B., Avolio, B. J., Crossley, C. D. and Luthans, F. (2009) Psychological ownership: theoretical extensions, measurement and relation to work outcomes. *Journal of Organizational Behavior*, 30 (2), 173–191.

Bal, M. P., De Jong, S. B., Jansen, P. G. W. and Bakker, A. B. (2012) Motivating employees to work beyond retirement: a multi-level study of the role of I-deals and unit climate. *Journal of Management Studies*, 49 (2), 306–331.

Barley, S. R. and Kunda, G. (2006) *Gurus, Hired Hands, and Warm Bodies: Itinerant experts in a knowledge economy*. Princeton, NJ: Princeton University Press.

Boudreau, J. W. and Ramstad, P. M. (2007) *Beyond HR: The new science of human capital*. Cambridge, MA: Harvard Business School Press.

Brown, W. and Edwards, P. (2009) Researching the changing workplace. In: W. Brown, A. Bryson, J. Forth and K. Whitfield (eds), *The Evolution of the Modern Workplace*. Cambridge: Cambridge University Press.

Budd, J. (2014) The future of employee voice. In: A. Willkinson, J. Donaghey, T. Dudon and R. B. Freeman (eds), *Handbook of Research on Employee Voice*. Cheltenham: Edward Elgar, pp. 477–488.

Burke, R. J. (2000) Workaholism in organizations: concepts, results and future research directions. *International Journal of Management Reviews*, 2 (1), 1–16.

Cappelli, P. (1999) *The new deal at work: managing the market-driven workforce*. Cambridge, MA: Harvard Business School Press.

Cerdin, J.-L. and Le Pangneux, M. (2012) Career anchors: a comparison between organization-assigned and self-initiated expatriates. *Thunderbird International Business Review*, 52 (4), 287–299.

CIPD (2003) *Managing the Psychological Contract*, Factsheet. Wimbledon: CIPD.

Collings, D. G. and Mellahi, K. (2009) Strategic talent management: a review and research agenda. *Human Resource Management Review*, 19, 304–313.

Collings, D. G., Scullion, H. and Vaiman, H. (2015) Talent management: progress and prospects. *Human Resource Management Review*, 25 (3), 233–235.

Collins, A. M., Cartwright, S. and Hislop, D. (2013) Homeworking: negotiating the psychological contract. *Human Resource Management Journal*, 23 (2), 211–225.

Conway, N. (2015) The psychological contract. In: C. Cooper (ed.), *Wiley Encyclopedia of Management*, 3rd edn. Chichester: John Wiley.

Conway, N. and Briner, R. B. (2002) A diary study of affective response to psychological contract breach and exceeded promises. *Journal of Organizational Behaviour*, 23, 287–302.

Conway, N. and Briner, R. B. (2005) *Understanding Psychological Contracts at Work: A critical evaluation of theory and research*. Oxford: Oxford University Press.

Conway, N., Guest, D. and Trenberth, L. (2011) Testing the differential effects of changes in psychological contract breach and fulfillment. *Journal of Vocational Behavior*, 79 (1), 267–276.

The Economist (2004) Darwin meets job creationism. 6 November.

Edwards, M. R. (2013) Employer branding: developments and challenges. In: S. Bach and M. R. Edwards (eds), *Managing Human Resources*, 5th edn. Chichester, Sussex: Wiley, pp. 389–410.

Edwards, M. R. and Peccei, R. (2010) Perceived organizational support, organizational identification, and employee outcomes. *Journal of Personnel Psychology*, 9, 17–26.

Faragher, E. B., Cass, M. and Cooper, C. L. (2005) The relationship between job satisfaction and health: a meta-analysis. *Occupational and Environmental Medicine*, 62, 105–112.

Farndale, E., Beijer, S., Van Veldhoven, M., Kelliher, C. and Hope-Hailey, V. (2014) Work and organization engagement: aligning research and practice. *Journal of Organizational Effectiveness: People and performance*, 1 (2), 157–176.

Feldman, D. C. (2007) Career mobility and career stability among older workers. In: K. S. Schultz and G. A. Adams (eds), *Aging and Work in the 21st Century*. New Jersey: Lawrence Erlbaum Associates, 179–197.

Financial Times (2015) The GIG economy. 5 July. London: Financial Times Newspapers.

Finegold, D. and Mohrman, S. (2001) *What Do Employees Really Want? The perception vs. the reality*. Report presented at the World Economic Forum 2001 Annual Meeting. Los Angeles: Korn/Ferry International.

Gittell, J. H. (2002) Relationships between service providers and their impact on customers, *Journal of Service Research*, 4 (4), 299–311.

Gittell, J. H., Weinberg, D., Bennett, A. and Miller, J. A. (2008) Is the doctor in? A relational approach to job design and the coordination of work. *Human Resource Management*, 47 (4), 729–755.

Gittell, J. H., Seidner, R. and Wimbush, J. (2010) A relational model of how high-performance work systems work. *Organization Science*, 21 (2), 490–506.

Gladwell, M. (2002) The talent myth. 22 July. *The New Yorker*.

Griffiths, M. (2015) Workaholism – a 21st century addiction. *The Psychologist*. Available online at https://the psychologist.bps.org.uk/volume-24/edition-10/workaholism—21st-century-addiction.

Groysberg, B. (2010) *Chasing Stars: The myth of talent and the portability of performance*.Cambridge, MA: Harvard Business School Press.

Handfield-Jones, H., Michaels, E. and Axelrod, B. (2001) Talent management: a critical part of every leader's job. *Ivey Business Journal*, November/December. Available online at www.iveybusinessjournal.ca/view_article. asp?intArticle_ID=316.

Harris Poll (2015) Americans report declining trust in banks. Available online at www.theharrispoll.com/business/ Americans_Report_Declining_Trust_in_Banks.html.

Hatch, M. J. and Cunliffe, A. (2013) *Organization Theory: Modern, symbolic and postmodern perspectives*. Oxford: Oxford University Press.

He, H. and Brown, A. D. (2013) Organizational identity and organizational identification:a review of the literature and suggestions for future research. *Group and Organization Management*, 38 (1), 3–35.

Herriot, P. (2001) *The Employment Relationship: A psychological perspective*. Hove: Routledge.

High Pay Centre (2015) WPP CEO paid an astonishing £43 million in 2014. Available online at http://highpaycentre. org/blog/wpp-ceo-paid-an-astonishing-43-million-in-2014.

Huselid, M. A. and Becker, B. E. (2011) Bridging micro and macro domains: workforce differentiation and strategic human resource management. *Journal of Management*, 37 (2), 421–428.

Legge, K. (2005) *Human Resource Management: Rhetorics and realities*, anniversary edition. Palgrave Macmillan: New York.

Lepak, D. P. and Snell, S. A. (2002) Examining the human resource architecture: the relationships among human capital, employment and human resource configurations. *Journal of Management*, 28 (4), 517–543.

Martin, G., Staines, H. and Pate, J. (1998) The new psychological contract: exploring the relationship between job security and career development. *Human Resource Management Journal*, 6 (3), 20–40.

Martin, G., Pate, J. M., Beaumont, P. B. and Murdoch, A. (2003) The uncertain road to partnership: an action research perspective on new industrial relations in the UK offshore oil industry. *Employee Relations*, 25 (6), 594–612.

Martin, G., Gollan, P. J. and Grigg, K. (2011) Is there a bigger and better future for employer branding? Facing up to innovation, corporate reputations and wicked problems in SHRM. *International Journal of Human Resource Management*, 22, 3618–3637.

Martin, G. and Cerdin, J.-L. (2014) Employer branding and career theory: new directions for research. In: P. Sparrow, H. Scullion and I. Tarique (eds), *Strategic Talent Management: Contemporary issues in international context*. Cambridge: Cambridge University Press, pp. 151–176.

Martin, G., Siebert, S., Howieson, W. B. and Bushfield, S. (2015) The changing work experience of consultants in NHS Scotland. Report for the British Medical Association. Available online at http://www.gla.ac.uk/schools/ business/research/publications/management/.

Meyer, J. P. and Allen, N. J. (1991) *Commitment in the Workplace*. London: Sage.

Michaels, E., Handfield-Jones, H. and Axelrod, B. (2001) *The War for Talent*. Cambridge, MA: Harvard Business School Press.

Peccei, R. (2013) Employee engagement: an evidence-based review. In: S. Bach and M. R. Edwards (eds), *Managing Human Resources*, 5th edn. Chichester, Sussex: Wiley, pp. 336–364.

Pierce, J. L., Kostova, T. and Dirks, K. T. (2001) Towards a theory of psychological ownership in organizations. *Academy of Management Review*, 26 (2), 298–310.

Pierce, J. R. and Aguinis, H. (2013) The "too-much-of-a-good-thing" effect in management. *Journal of Management*, 39, 313–338.

Ray, R. and Schmitt, J. (2007) No-vacation nation USA – a comparison of leave and holidays in OECD countries. *European Economic and Employment Policy Brief,* No 3. Available online at www.law.harvard.edu/programs/lwp/papers/No_Holidays.pdf.

Rousseau, D. M. (1995) *Psychological Contracts in Organizations: Understanding written and unwritten agreements*. Newbury Park, CA: Sage.

Rousseau, D. M. (2001) The idiosyncratic deal: flexibility versus fairness. *Organizational Dynamics*, 29 (4), 260–273.

Schaufeli, W. B. (2015) Engaging leadership in the job demands-resources model. *Career Development International,* 20, 446–463.

Schaufeli, W. B., Taris, T. W. and Van Rhenen, W. (2008) Workaholism, burnout and engagement: three of a kind or three different kinds of employee well-being. *Applied Psychology International Review*, 57, 173–203.

Schein, E. (1990) *Career Anchors*. San Diego, CA: University Associates.

Shimazu, A. and Schaufeli, W. B. (2009) Is workaholism good or bad for employee well-being? The distinctiveness of workaholism and work engagement among Japanese employees. *Industrial Health*, 47, 495–502.

Siebert, S. and Martin, G. (2014) People management rationales and organizational effectiveness: the case of organizational trust repair. *Journal of Organizational Effectiveness: People and Performance*, 1 (2), 177–190.

Siebert, S., Martin, G., Bozic, B. and Docherty, I. (2015) Looking 'beyond the factory gates': towards more pluralist and radical approaches to intra-organizational trust research. *Organization Studies,* 36 (8), 1033–1062.

Sparks, K., Cooper, C. L., Fried, Y. and Shirom, A. (1997) The effects of hours of work on health: a meta-analytical review. *Journal of Occupational Psychology*, 70, 391–408.

Sparrow, P. (2014) Strategic HRM and employee engagement. In: C. Truss, R. Delbridge, K. Alfes, A. Shantz and E. Soane (eds), *Employee Engagement in Theory and Practice*. Oxford: Routledge, pp. 99–115.

Sparrow, P. and Cooper, C. (2003) *The Employment Relationship: Key challenges for HR*. Oxford: Butterworth-Heinemann.

Suazo, M. M., Martinez, P. G. and Sandoval, R. (2009) Creating psychological and legal contracts through human resource practices. *Human Resource Management Review*, 19, 154–166.

Swailes, S. (2002) Organizational commitment: a critique of the construct and its measures. *International Journal of Management Research*, 4 (2), 155–178.

Thompson, J. A. and Bunderson, J. S. (2003) Violations of principle: ideological currency in the psychological contract. *Academy of Management Review*, 28 (4), 571–586.

Thunnissen, M., Boselie, P. and Fruytier, B. (2013) A review of talent management: 'infancy or adolescence?'. *The International Journal of Human Resource Management*, 24 (9), 1744–1761.

Truss, C., Shantz, A., Soane, E., Alfres, K. and Delbridge, R. (2013) Employee engagement, organizational performance and individual well-being: exploring the evidence, developing the theory. *International Journal of Human Resource Management*, 24 (14), 2657–2669.

Turnley, W. H. and Feldman, D. C. (1998) Psychological contract violations during corporate restructuring. *Human Resource Management*, 37 (1), 71–83.

Van Dyne, L. and Pierce, J. L. (2004) Psychological ownership and feelings of possession: three field studies predicting employee attitudes and organizational citizenship behavior. *Journal of Organizational Behavior*, 25, 439–459.

Volkswagen Personnel Policy (2015) Available online at www.volkswagen-karriere.de/en/what_we_stand_for/personnel_policy/flexibility.html.

Walsh, G. and Bartikowski, B. (2013) Employee emotional labour and quitting intentions: moderating effects of gender and age. *European Journal of Marketing*, 47 (8), 1213–1237.

Wilkinson, A. and Fay, C. (2011) New times for employer voice? *Human Resource Management*, 50(1), 65–74.

Chapter 4

Managing in the organizational context

LEARNING OBJECTIVES

At the end of this chapter you should be able to:

- understand the problems created by organizational structure, systems and processes in achieving strategic aims;
- identify different types of organizations and know when they are appropriate to changing strategic environments;
- apply three well-known frameworks to the analysis of organizational problems;
- suggest creative solutions to these problems, based on rigorous research;
- understand why organizations change from simple to more complex structures, and the problems accompanying these changes;
- understand the strengths and weaknesses of new organizational forms, including virtual and networked structures;
- apply a rigorously researched test of effective organizational design to your own organization or one with which you are familiar.

INTRODUCTION

According to John Child (2015), one of the best-known organizational theorists, the most fundamental task of senior managers is to set the strategy of the organization and design the organizational structures, systems, culture and processes to deliver the strategy. While even the best organization in the world cannot make up for an unsound strategy, 'superior organization offers one of the best sustainable sources of competitive advantage' (Child, 2015, p. 4). Designing organizations and managing in the organizational context refers to the tasks of understanding, analysing and designing structures, systems and processes to coordinate and motivate large numbers of people undertaking interconnected activities, often in different locations (Roberts, 2004). At this level, managers have to take more macro-level decisions than those affecting only individuals and teams. These decisions can have significant consequences for the strategic aims of the organization, because it is through organizational structure that strategy becomes realized. Consequently, it is extremely important that you understand some of the basic design principles of organization and the potential advantages and drawbacks of adopting different organizational forms, including some of the newly emerging ones that have captured the imagination of the business press. So, in this chapter we shall attempt to address the practical problems of organizational design, first by examining a case study and, second, by introducing you to some concepts and models that will help you understand the problems faced by senior managers in designing organizations and the solutions available to them.

You should read the case study of Innovative Petroleum Engineering, a pseudonym for an oil services company we shall use throughout this chapter to help you understand and apply key concepts. Your ability to understand some of the choices that managers face in designing organizations, analyse the problems faced by the case company and your choice of design solutions should improve as you work your way through the chapter. We shall also look at cases of newer forms of organization that are becoming more popular in certain contexts and industries, especially those connected with knowledge-intensive, technologically based and creative organizations, which are discussed in Chapters 7, 8 and 9 of this book.

CASE 4.1 INNOVATIVE PETROLEUM ENGINEERING – AN INTEGRATIVE CASE STUDY

Innovative Petroleum Engineering is the pseudonym of a major subsidiary of a US multinational operating in Europe. It produces sophisticated drilling equipment, which is used by other major firms in the Oil and Gas industry. Its parent company is a well-known *Fortune* 500 company, with interests in many countries, and which is highly regarded in published lists of the 'Best Places to Work' in many of these countries. It has diversified into a number of related fields in recent years.

Innovative is an important part of the parent company's core business but over the last five years its performance has been patchy, owing largely to the downturn in the market for certain of its core products. The company built its reputation on technological breakthroughs in bits, tools and other drilling products, based on extensive research and development. Each decade since the 1950s had seen success, with employees benefiting from financial success. The company adopted an 'employer of choice' policy, in which highly talented people were recruited at all levels in the company and were paid well. These employees were treated well by Innovative, enjoying major benefits and privileges, internal career advancement and time off to undertake education and training. It became known as one of the best places to work in the region, with a strong internally focused promotion and benefits system, which was associated with high levels of employee commitment and identification with the organization.

With the downturn in the segment of the oil and gas market they served since 2005, Innovative was forced to rationalize its activities and introduce a small number of compulsory lay-offs for the first time in its 55-year history. Headcount management from the US parent company, which was also experiencing problems, made the situation worse a year or so later, when more lay-offs were implemented. However, the senior management at Innovative was confident matters would improve once the business cycle began to move into an investment phase for their principal customers, and employees were encouraged to 'weather the storm'. The company still continued to pursue its 'employer of choice' policy, keeping benefits and career development at relatively high levels in anticipation of better times.

As the decade wore on, however, things didn't really improve. The technical developments by Innovative didn't really seem to be attractive to existing and new customers, and the company became ever more open to threats from new competitors. The mixture of less innovative developments and new competition resulted in losses being posted for the years 2005–2010 of more than 15 million euros per year, against a gross yearly revenue of between 450 million and 500 million euros. The real state of affairs, however, is unknown because of internal transfers between companies in the group of which Innovative was a part. Innovative was forced to use many of the services of sister companies, and paid a premium price for some of these services, including some of the research and development on which technical breakthroughs were achieved. Innovative's management believed that real losses were probably much less than the 15 million euros per year, with the figure being 2 million euros according to the senior managers.

The US parent company urged Innovative to maintain greater control of variable costs, mainly labour costs, and set it targets for increased sales revenues. However, the US parent also insisted it use the centralized research and development services and keep local research to a minimum. This was troublesome for a number of reasons to Innovative's managers, most importantly because US products were not always suited to the mainly European markets served by Innovative. Consequently, they had always followed a local policy of encouraging new business ventures that showed promise to work around the parent company strictures. However, cash constraints now prevented them from following this local product development strategy, and Innovative found itself having to make do with the core products that seemed to be unsuited to the local markets or required modification.

Innovative Petroleum's management team were mainly highly technically competent engineers. They regarded themselves as working for a leading-edge engineering company operating in the expanding upstream Oil and Gas Industry, with first-class products, and despite current problems always saw light at the end of the tunnel. The corporation was organized as a traditional bureaucracy, set within a global matrix structure. This meant that subsidiary companies such as Innovative were given responsibility for a specific geographical area, but were expected to replicate the functional structure of the US parent company. Thus people at the top levels of the organization and the functional heads dominated, and power had been concentrated in the hands of a powerful CEO at Innovative, who integrated the fragmented functions.

The CEO's power and control were exceptionally great, and he exercised his leadership through a careful reporting system of performance, costs and other policies. He was also the single most important interface between the company and the US parent company, and was also HQ's ambassador to Innovative. He had been in post for 15 years, and more or less followed the US parent company's policies to the letter without making local amendments. Though delivering excellent returns for the first ten years of his reign, like Innovative, his performance had suffered recently. His successor was John Fox, a 52-year-old British engineer, who had substantial experience in the US parent company in marketing. He had seen the problems of the ageing product range at Innovative and was committed to a turnaround, but didn't really want to do anything that rocked the boat. He was also of the opinion that the company had to be research and technology driven, like his senior management in the parent organization. Fox suffered the problems faced by all senior managers in subsidiary companies caused by the tensions between demands for corporate control and local autonomy. However, in the final analysis his decisions reflected the need to satisfy his career and senior management team in the US.

Soon after his arrival, Fox had begun to make changes to the bureaucratic structure of Innovative by trying to foster closer collaboration between marketing, research and development and the traditionally powerful production, sales and engineering functions. He set up management teams incorporating these functional heads and new appointees to HR and Finance and gave them the mandate to work towards a more collaborative organization by 2016. Only the HR manager was female. This development was enabled by management 'away-days', based on a new vision and values framework, plans and objective-setting. The head of HR experienced some problems with the male-dominated, 'football-club' atmosphere, but gradually became used to the culture and worked her way into a powerful position, along with the new, 45-year-old Head of Finance and Accounting.

There were still lots of problems, however, partly associated with Fox's inability to 'walk the talk' (as the Americans say) through his actions. Although espousing teamwork values, he wasn't seen to be a good team player himself. When times were difficult, which was more and more frequent, he resorted to authoritarian behaviours and a 'bottom-line' performance mentality – 'it's the shareholders and parent company that pay your salary.' In addition, given the resource constraints of the US parent, there were problems associated with allocation of resources among departments. Competition among departments led some members of the management team to pursue their own departmental interests and those of staff in their departments at the expense of overall company cohesion and team spirit. Thus certain departments began to be run as personal 'fiefdoms', rather than contributing to the overall mission and goals of Innovative.

After some time functioning like this, the management team made a decision to embark on a continuous improvement (CI) programme, which they labelled 'Project 2016', signifying the desire to have this change programme last beyond the normal one or two years of many other initiatives introduced by the company. Continuous improvement through Project 2016 gave rise to a number of project teams that looked at issues such as quality improvement, Six Sigma, production improvement schemes, suggestion schemes, organizational development and HR initiatives. The middle-level managers who staffed these teams were all sent on courses to develop their under-standing of team-working and to help them develop new team-working skills. Being selected for one of these project teams was seen as having 'arrived', because the management team selected only the fast-track, high-quality managers who were seen to be going places. Almost without exception, these people were highly committed to the company, technically very well qualified, and ready to go 'beyond contract' for the sake of the company and their careers.

The first year of this CI programme produced some excellent outcomes, with project team members being seen as highly engaged and highly productive in their tasks. However, not many of the team recommendations were taken up, except in a watered-down fashion. The management team was always full of praise, but usually found reasons not to implement recommendations, usually because of budgetary reasons, the time not being right, or that they didn't quite fit the strategic plans. This lack of implementation began to generate a great deal of cynicism and mistrust, not only among the middle managers on the project groups but also among the members of the management team, who felt that the project teams weren't pursuing the interests of the company, nor were they coming up with the kinds of improvement that the management team would have suggested. Instead, they felt that nearly all improvements were 'bids for resources', rather than genuine, cost-effective improvements.

Project team members began to complain to each other that they didn't have the necessary information or policy guidelines to do their jobs effectively. The management team was rarely seen to issue 'straitjackets' (dictums that had to be followed) but let it be known through innuendo and hints what was and wasn't acceptable. Consequently, project teams often had to go through a number of iterations of improvement plans to learn what might really be acceptable. Most of the time, what they found out was rarely radical but only marginal improvements on the status quo. Complaints made along these lines to the management team caused the senior members of management to take a much more controlling approach to the workings of the project teams, often by dropping in on team meetings and overriding their discussions.

Gradually the project teams began to become more sceptical of the management team's objectives, which they determined weren't really about improvements but about socializing them into the ways of Innovative Petroleum – what was acceptable and what wasn't. Naturally enough, those groups of middle managers who wished to get on began to play the game, which was concerned more with style than with substance, and 'second-guessing' what might be acceptable to their sponsoring managers in the management team. Over the period of the next year or so, however, the project team members put in less effort and less commitment to the CI programme. As this project work wasn't rewarded in any specific way, and was over and above their departmental responsibilities, most project team members put their efforts into attaining good appraisals for their regular jobs.

After a further year of operation and wavering commitments by the management team and the project team members, it became clear that the CI programme wasn't going to deliver much in the way of transformational change, and even when the management team espoused the rhetoric of creativity and innovation, teams rarely believed that was what was required. Often they ended up repackaging and producing 'old wine in new bottles', because, although innovation was called for, it was rarely implemented and never really rewarded tangibly or intangibly. This rather depressing vicious circle of cynicism was made worse by the management team's informal feedback sessions to the CI project teams, which, though designed as 'full and frank' discussions, often turned out to be blame sessions and calls for the teams to develop more teamworking skills and controls – this despite the company having a 'no-blame' culture as one of its aspirational values.

Following a further year of operation, the CI programme was still officially in existence but was essentially moribund. Few ideas that had been produced had been implemented, and although there were a few examples of success in quality controls, the senior management team had spent a lot of money on training and culture change for very little reward. If anything, they had produced a cynical and somewhat demoralized middle management group who played the game but weren't really committed. The management team settled down into a comfortable way of working with each other, in which formal relations were good but there was little in the way of team camaraderie. Fox's beneath-the-surface authoritarian streak and the latent rivalries within the management team continued to plague developments in Innovative, and gradually their expectations of Project 2016 became much more modest.

At the time of writing, the company has shown little in the way of significant improvements, and most work is carried on through the formal, hierarchical structure of reporting relationships. The company management team continues to talk about innovation, entrepreneurship and 'break-throughs' from HQ, which will guarantee its future but know that the rhetoric bears little relationship to the reality of how they are doing.

Based on your current understanding of organizational design principles, and before you read the following text, answer the following questions:

1 How would you describe the organization of Innovative Petroleum Engineering?
2 What are the causes of the problems?
3 What changes would you make to the organizational structure to improve things?

ORGANIZATIONAL STRUCTURES

To help you provide an in-depth and more informed analysis of the problems faced by organizations such as Innovative Petroleum Engineering, we should begin by looking at some basic ideas from the organizational design literature. A constant theme of the book is that there is no one best way of managing and organizing; ultimately, firm performance and problems that arise in organizations such as Innovative depend on the degree of *fit* between the organizational design solutions, the strategies being pursued and the context or environment in which they arise. This is a contingency theory of organizations that implies that there are no right answers, only those that fit the context (Child, 2015). Contingency theories arose as a challenge to the 'one best way or organizing' school associated with classical organizational theories such as bureaucracy and scientific management that we met in Chapter 1. So to help us understand the case more fully, we should begin by defining different types of organizational structure, the problems to which they give rise and the contexts that seem to influence their effectiveness.

Determinants of organizational structures

One very useful starting point is to consider the 'star model' of Amy Kates and the late Jay Galbraith (2007) to the design of organizations. They outlined the following six influences or 'shapers' of organizational forms relevant to the contemporary business environment:

- *Buyer power.* The new rules of competition, aided by access to information and communications technologies (ICT) and global sourcing, have shifted power to consumers and buyers, who are learning how to use that power effectively. As a consequence, we are seeing a shift in organizations to reflect the desires of key customers and market segments.
- *Variety and solutions.* In response to customer demand and the segmentation of markets, organizations have developed an increased numbers of products and services, and have shown

a willingness to customize their offerings. To do this, however, managers must be able to deal with ever more information, make more decisions and set priorities – this means that more people have to be involved in the decision-making process. Increasingly, business customers are seeking integrated solutions to their problems, not merely bundles of products and services. To provide such solutions organizations have to develop cross-product and cross-functional teams.

- *Information and communications technologies.* As we shall see in Chapter 8, the Internet has been an incredibly powerful influence on organizations, especially in creating web-based portals and new business models such as those used by Amazon, Dell, eBay and new technology intermediators such as the 'e-lancing' firm Uber (Aguinis and Lawal, 2013). The new economics of information have altered the old-style trade-off between 'reach and richness' of information, allowing firms to do more of both simultaneously, which has had the result of deconstructing traditional industries (Christensen and Horn, 2008). Also, increasingly customers and staff require a single point of contact for their problems, so the functions of the organization, such as sales, delivery, call centre operations and HR, have to be coordinated.
- *Complexity.* Like many other writers in this field, Kates and Galbraith (2007) identified environmental complexity, or what they label as 'multiple dimensions', as a key factor in shaping organizations. Originally, companies were structured along functional lines, but as the environment became more complex, so organizations began to develop divisional (multi-product or multi-region) structures to reflect customer segments. Throughout the last century and the early part of the present one, the environments of organizations have become more complex in terms of the products, markets and geographical regions they are serving; organizational structures have had to reflect this complexity.
- *Change.* One of the nostrums in business of the last few decades has been 'the only constant is change', also a recurring theme of this book. As Hatch and Cunliffe (2013) have argued, organizations are better thought about from a process perspective, in which organizations are always in a state of 'becoming' rather than as static 'beings'. This process philosophy has important implications for how we study organizations and organizing, which do not sit comfortably with some of the design principles we have outlined in this chapter but is very important in understanding organizational change and development. So, for example, it is very important to consider how the pace and direction of change in organizational environments have had a marked influence on how organizational structures and cultures have changed over time, particularly with regard to information flows and decision-making structures. Changing environments have been at the heart of developments towards decentralized structures and cross-functional/departmental teamworking designs.
- *Speed.* The pace of change in customer demands and tastes has caused organizations to design along more flexible lines to meet these challenges. Demands for reduced operations and production cycle times and shorter lead times to market – for example, in the motor vehicle industry – have led to organizations changing their structures to cope with less inventory and increased response times. Thus, speed is associated with developments in outsourcing and decentralized structures, as well as increased take-up of ICT.

Kates and Galbraith (2007) have argued that organizational designs able to meet the demands of these organizational 'shapers' are a source of real competitive advantage that cannot be easily copied, because they are a delicate and complex mix of different design features. They see the choice of organization as a design issue in much the same way that buildings and machinery are designed to meet competing and often contradictory claims, in which trade-offs have to be made. For example, balances have to be struck between time to market, with the focus on reduced design and production cycle time, and production organizations that achieve cost advantages through scale economies. Consequently, the effective organizational design is a constantly evolving balancing act between these environmental pressures and the policies that senior managers can use to influence appropriate design solutions. These policies are summarized in their 'star model', set out in Figure 4.1.

Corporate *strategy* refers to the mission, goals and objectives of the organization, and sets out its basic direction. Business-level strategies refer to the products, services and markets the organization seeks to serve. Different organizational designs are appropriate to different centralized decision-making, whereas innovative strategies are likely to be better served by decentralized decision-making. Following a debate between outside-in and inside-out approaches to strategy in the 1990s (Child, 2015) and the growing importance attached by scholars to dynamic capabilities (Teece, 2009), Kates and Galbraith added the idea of strategic capabilities to the original model to refer to the internal capabilities that firms use to differentiate themselves from their competitors. Dynamic capabilities refer to an organization's capacity to seek and create new opportunities by learning quickly, and to reconfigure internal assets such as knowledge, technologies, people and processes to ensure sustainable strategic advantage in rapidly changing environments.

Structure is concerned with the distribution of power and authority in organizations (Child, 2015). The following are its main dimensions:

- *Hierarchy* – the hierarchical ordering of positions that give rise to the chain of command.
- *Specialization* – the number of jobs and job specialists found in an organization.
- *Span of control* – the number of people reporting to any specialist manager.

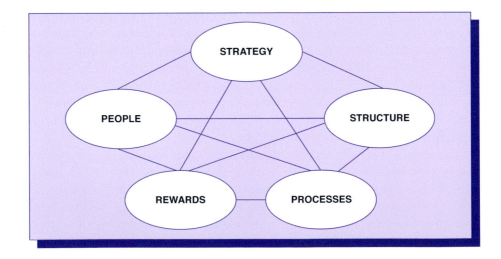

FIGURE 4.1 The star model

(*Source*: adapted from earlier work by Galbraith, 2002, p. 10.)

- *Distribution of power* – this can be both *vertical*, referring to the levels of hierarchy in an organization, and *horizontal*, which refers to how close a particular department or manager is to the core, mission-critical decisions.
- *Departmentalization* – the basis on which departments are developed, which can be functional, product based, workflow based, market or geographically based.

DEFINITION Processes

Processes refer to the information and decision-making processes that are the lifeblood of any organization. Again, these can be vertical, reflecting hierarchical power, or lateral, with teamworking being a good example. *People* policies are one of the main subjects of this book, one that we have and will elaborate on in great detail in later chapters. It is perhaps sufficient to point out at this stage that different structures require people with often contradictory abilities to make them work, with team-based organizations being a good example. Such organizations rest on the ability of people to *cooperate* rather than compete with one another, but at the same time people in teams have to show individual *initiative* (Fjeldstad et al., 2012). Selection and development policies for team selection have to reflect these potentially opposing characteristics. Finally, the purpose of a *rewards* system is to align the needs and motives of employees with the goals and structure of the organization. To reuse the teamworking example, reward systems, which can be both monetary and non-monetary, have to be designed to facilitate interpersonal cooperation as well as be motivating to individuals.

Apart from warning us that the process of organizational design is a constant balancing act between the nature of the environment and the five policy areas of the framework in Figure 4.1, one of the main implications of the star model is that too much time is spent on designing structures on paper and not enough time is given to thinking about how they might align with processes, people and rewards. Given the pace of change facing many organizations, Kates and Galbraith (2007) have suggested that process, people and rewards are more important in organizational design than the formal reporting structures because they have the most direct impact on organizational performance and culture. However, they also recognize that the five points of the star have to be dynamically aligned (see Figure 4.2).

EXERCISE 4.1

1 What are the key shapers of the organizational structure of Innovative Petroleum Engineering?
2 How does the star model in Figure 4.1 help us understand the problems of Innovative Petroleum Engineering?

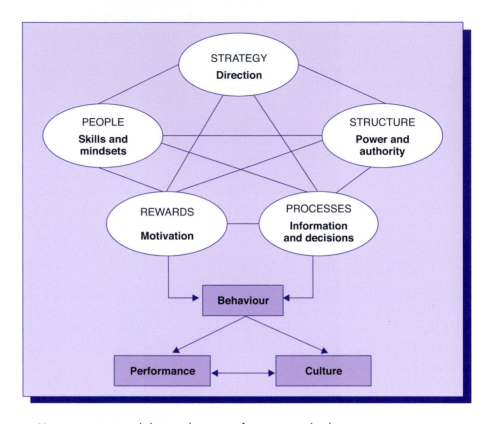

FIGURE 4.2 How organizational design shapes performance and culture
(*Source*: adapted from Galbraith, 2002, p. 15.)

Mintzberg's different types of organizational structure

There have been a number of very useful attempts to classify structures according to how they relate to the nature of the environment in which they operate. Two such attempts have attained 'classic' status precisely because they are so useful in helping us understand the kinds of problems set out in our introductory case. The first is by Henry Mintzberg (1993), whose work on different forms of organization is one of the most often cited and is reflected in his thinking about management which we discussed in Chapter 2. The second is by Raymond Miles and Charles Snow (1984) whose work has stood the test of time and, through constant revisions, once again, have much to say about the problems faced by modern organizations (Child, 2015).

Like Galbraith, Henry Mintzberg sees an organization's structure as shaped largely by the degree of environmental variety it faces. For Mintzberg, environmental variety was determined by *environmental complexity* and the *pace of change*. He identified five organizational forms, four of which were associated with different degrees of complexity and change (see Figure 4.3).

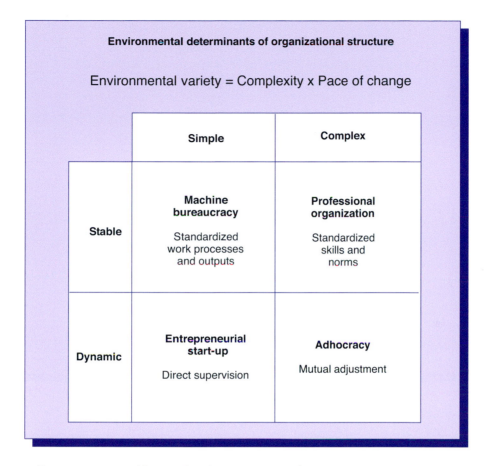

FIGURE 4.3 Four organizational forms related to environmental variety

To explain the shape of these four organizational forms, Mintzberg set out five basic organizational component subunits: the strategic apex, the technostructure (the technically qualified planners and analysts), the support staff (as distinct from line managers), the middle line (the line managers) and the operating core (the 'doers') (see Table 4.1). The relative importance of these five component subunits in any organization helps define its overall shape (see Figure 4.4).

The real insight of Mintzberg's work was in linking the importance of different mechanisms of coordination to the four organizational forms depicted by his typology in Figure 4.3 and Table 4.2. His argument was that these four forms were dependent on fundamentally different mechanisms for coordination, which could vary from direct supervision through to the standardization of operating norms or culture (see Figures 4.5 and 4.6). Furthermore, in each particular form, different subunits tend to have greater influence.

TABLE 4.1 Basic component units of an organization

Component subunit	Possible positions from a firm such as Innovative Petroleum
Strategic apex	Board of Directors, Chief Executive Officer
The technostructure	Planning, HR, Research and Development, engineering managers
Support staff	Legal Department, Public Relations, Marketing
Middle line	Vice Presidents of Production, Marketing and Sales
Operating core	Purchasing administrators, machine operators, assemblers, sales staff, dispatch staff

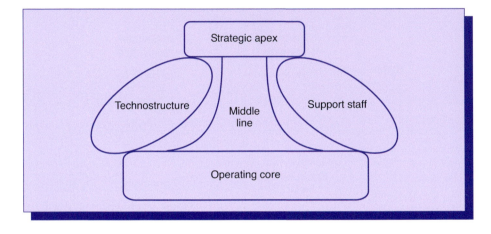

FIGURE 4.4 The shape of a typical organization

TABLE 4.2 Linking organizational form to coordinating mechanisms

Organizational form	Coordination mechanism
Machine bureaucracy	Standardized administrative procedures, work processes and outputs, e.g. through quality assurance manuals, procedures manuals and strict templates for production or services (the nature of a telephone call in a call centre or the final product from an assembly line)
Professional bureaucracy	Standardized professional skills through education and training and operating norms through culture management techniques (e.g. a hospital or university that relies on the professional training and norms of medical or teaching staff)
Entrepreneurial organization	Direct and personal leadership, supervision and control from the CEO (e.g. a newly formed business or a new department in an established organization)
Adhocracy	Mutual adjustment of ad hoc work teams (e.g. teams brought together to work on a one-off construction or engineering project, which have to develop their own ways of adjusting to each other, or a crew brought together to make a film, create a major conference or sporting event)

The basic shapes of the four organizational forms, reflecting the relative importance of the component subunits and dominant mechanisms of coordination, are shown in Figure 4.6. Note how Mintzberg implied the importance of the operating core (e.g. the people who actually produce the services) in professional bureaucracies (e.g. hospitals and universities), and how unimportant they were in some versions of an adhocracy where many of the operations could be routinized or mechanized. Also note how he considered the strategic apex of an organization was less important in coordinating professional organizations and adhocracies, both of which form the basis of many knowledge-intensive and creative organizations discussed later in this book. However, it is fair to say that traditional professional bureaucracies are under increasing challenge from managers' attempts to control them, make them more accountable and to introduce into them an entrepreneurial spirit, especially in sectors such as healthcare and universities.

EXERCISE 4.2

How would you describe the organization of Innovative Petroleum using Mintzberg's design framework? What are the principal methods of coordination used and are they appropriate to the teamworking structure?

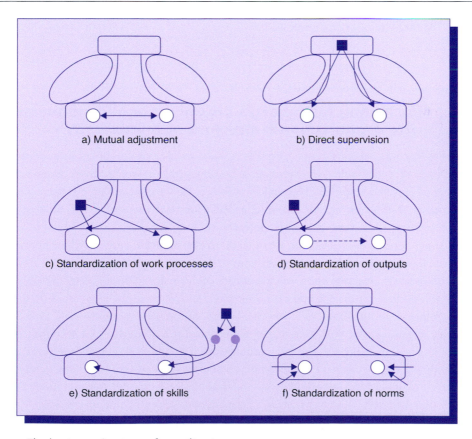

a) Mutual adjustment

b) Direct supervision

c) Standardization of work processes

d) Standardization of outputs

e) Standardization of skills

f) Standardization of norms

FIGURE 4.5 The basic mechanisms of coordination

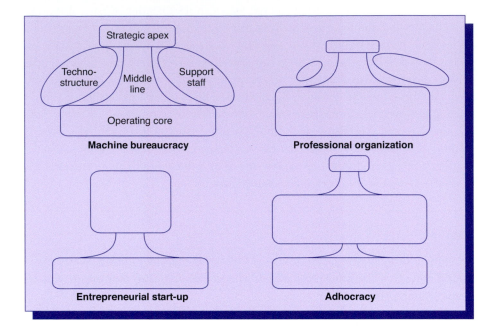

FIGURE 4.6 The basic forms of organizations

BOX 4.1 Illustrating Mintzberg's organizational configurations – the organizational structure of a university

Universities, such as the ones in which both of us work, used to be thought of as good examples of a professional organization or professional bureaucracy, dominated by academics and the core work of creating and disseminating knowledge. However, academic support units may be composed of other forms. For example, support units such as student accommodation or the maintenance department, which perform routine functions, may have a machine bureaucratic management structure, while technocratic subunits, such as HR or finance, may be administered as professional organizations themselves or as adhocracies.

As a university struggles to cope with the introduction of new information technologies in the areas of HR, student admissions and online learning, and to the constant pressures to transform itself to improve reputational rankings, its overall organizational form may tend towards adhocracy in the form of new project teams. But the stress of working in an adhocracy puts pressure on the organization to organize subunits according to one of the other forms. In other words, specialist departments are set up to take on board these new functions. One good example is international recruitment departments, recently established by many Western universities in the USA, UK and Australia to capture a share of the lucrative overseas student market.

Finally, the logic of professionalism, which shapes the orientation of academics toward autonomy and in the types of decisions they make, has come under increasing challenge from governments and managers, whose decision-making is governed by market and bureaucratic logics. This political and managerial agenda has constituted students as customers, engendered competition through research and student experience rankings between universities, and seeks to create a disciplined compliance with quality and operating procedures. As a consequence, universities are better characterized as hybrid organizations, attempting to align conflicting institutional logics, which they sometimes do successfully but more often than not end up failing to reconcile them for any length of time, so leading to further change intervention – 'the more things change, the more they remain the same'.

Miles and Snow's strategy, structure and process model

Alongside Mintzberg, Miles and Snow's 'strategy, structure and process' model of organizations is the best known and one of the most useful to managers who wish to improve their organization's competitive position through new organizational structures and processes. First developed in 1978 and refined in 1984, this model has stood the test of time and has been revised to show its application to contemporary circumstances (Miles *et al.*, 2010).

Their original contribution began by setting out the idea of an adaptive cycle, which referred to how organizations adjust to changes in their environment (note, once again, the importance of matching organizations to their environments). The key proposition was that successful organizations needed to develop consistency among their strategy, their business model, which included the dominant form of technology, and their organizational capabilities, including human resource management practices. They viewed the adaptive process as addressing three problems – the entrepreneurial, engineering and administrative problems – that an organization had to solve in a coherent way (see Table 4.3):

- The *entrepreneurial problem* focused on the choices of products/services and markets the organization would serve. In established organizations these choices are constrained by history, and discussions typically focus on creating new ventures.
- The *engineering problem* focused on putting into operation the solutions to the entrepreneurial problem. Choices here revolved around which business model and types of technology to adopt and implement. The engineering problem is one that has been identified in many studies as one of the most critical in determining the success of organizations (Nohria *et al.*, 2003).
- The *administrative problem* related to the structure and processes of the organization, including its design and people management policies, the topic of this chapter.

Miles and Snow's next contribution lay in developing a set of categories for organizations based on how they responded to the adaptive challenges. These categories were not intended to be static

TABLE 4.3 The four organizational types

	Defender	Prospector	Analyser	Reactor
Entrepreneurial problem	Narrow market focus	Broad market focus	Multiple markets, both stable and dynamic	Poorly articulated or ambiguous strategy with no clear direction
	Limited external analysis	Broad range of external analysis	Steady growth through penetration of existing markets, with some product development	Often following strategic paths that are out of date
	Penetration of existing markets	Growth through development of new markets and new products	Fast-follower strategy, rather than innovator	
	Limited development of existing products	Search for new technologies		
Engineering problem	Single core technology	Multiple technologies	Dual technologies, stable core and innovative periphery	No clear business model
	Relatively low on knowledge creation and work	Low degree of routine operations	Moderate degree of knowledge creation and work	
		High on knowledge creation and work		
Administrative problem	Functional organization	Product/geographical divisional structure	Matrix structure	Organizational features not consistent with strategy
	Production and finance are predominant functions	Marketing and R&D heavily influential	Marketing and applied research are main influences	Organizational features not consistent with each other

Relational psychological contracts and traditional careers	Transitory management structures and job tenure	Moderately centralized control	Persistent strategy–structure imbalance of degree of fit
Centralized control	Many task forces and project teams	Complex coordination and planning	
Coordination through standards and schedules	Non-traditional careers and range of psychological contracts		
Intensive planning	Decentralized control		
	Extensive rather than intensive planning		
Risks and benefits Good for defending existing markets and in conditions of little change	Effective in dynamic environments but vulnerable because of low profitability and focus	Robust portfolio but needing constant review	Inability to respond to market changes
Unable to exploit new markets		Complex internal environment	Poor performance

Source: adapted from Miles and Snow, 2003.

representations of reality, but integrated organizational strategy/structure/process configurations that changed in a dynamic interaction with their environment. They identified four such archetypical configurations – the defender, the prospector, the analyser and the reactor – the first three of which were coherent and sustainable in the long run. The reactor, by contrast, was incoherent and fragile (see Table 4.3).

EXERCISE 4.3

1 Based on Miles and Snow's typology, how would you classify Innovative Petroleum?
2 What would their typology suggest about the changes that need to be made in Innovative to make it more effective?

Developments from simple to more complex structures

These two approaches to understanding and designing organizational structures are relatively simple in the sense that they focus on single businesses or narrow product–market segments. Mintzberg's machine bureaucracy and even Miles and Snow's innovator organizational configurations are good examples of such designs. As early as the 1930s, however, organizations such as General Motors began to adopt an organizational design based on divisionalization, which served a more complex, multi-product–market environment. This form of multidivisional structure (the M-form organization) became known as a *strategic business unit* (SBU) structure, and was, and still is, the dominant form of organizational design (Child, 2015). These SBUs had the following characteristics (Goold and Campbell, 2002):

- They were market or customer focused, serving specialist customer segments, e.g. small, family motor cars in Europe.
- They were largely autonomous, usually having a CEO, general manager or president (or management team) who had the responsibility and authority to make key strategic and operating decisions that affected the results of the SBU.
- They generated revenues, incurred specific costs and were accountable for profits from serving their customer segments, and their managers were held to account for these revenues, costs and profits (or losses).

Having such characteristics, SBUs developed a specific focus and were delegated sufficient control and authority to make key decisions without interference from the parent company. In effect, the role of the parent company (corporate headquarters) was to act as a central banker, allocating funds to the various SBUs on a strict 'return on investment' basis. Such SBU-based organizations were managed as portfolios of assets by the parent company, which treated the individual SBUs as independent businesses. As such they provided an ideal training ground for general managers, who could step up to the problems of leadership at corporate level.

However, SBUs also gave rise to the following important management challenges (Miles *et al.*, 2010):

- Choosing the appropriate market focus for the SBUs and weighing up the trade-offs in such decisions. For example, some organizations have chosen to focus on geographically based customers, allowing them to develop local expertise in customs, cultures and tastes. However, such a focus makes it more difficult to develop global products, develop global sourcing of materials or reap the benefits of global branding.
- Silo management and achieving cooperation between SBUs. Organizing along SBU lines provides the advantages of local autonomy and the motivation for local managers to display initiative, but inevitably creates 'silo' mentalities among SBU managers as they compete for resources from the parent company. This is another example of the cooperation–initiative dilemma referred to earlier. SBU managers are often accused of managing their own personal 'fiefdoms', like medieval barons, often striving to achieve their own units' objectives at the expense of others and the company as a whole. Achieving coordination between these units, especially when they act as internal suppliers or customers to one another, or are required to share common services such as research and development or HR, is a frequent problem in many organizations.
- Parenting SBUs by adding value to them through, for example, setting stretching business objectives, providing shared critical services, such as research or marketing, or creating a powerful global brand reputation. Tensions often arise between the value-creating actions of the parent company and what SBUs may regard as local interference or value-destroying activity. For example, global brands can be perceived both as a strength and as a weakness, especially if they do not take into account local tastes.
- Adapting to changing circumstances. Although SBUs are not inherently inflexible, they can become over-adaptive to local circumstances, or tied by design to particular customer segments that may decline in the long run. Such situations lead to 'skilled incompetence', in which SBUs become locked into their own 'psychic prison' and deny the existence of a changing world outside their purview. In effect, they become very skilled at what they have always done and incompetent at changing course.

To cope with the problems presented by SBU-based organizations, while retaining the benefits, large companies began in the 1970s to develop more complex structures, most of which revolved around the idea of a matrix structure (Miles *et al.*, 2010) (see Figure 4.7). In Figure 4.7 we have simplified the original structure of a UK bank for the purposes of illustration into three autonomous customer segments – retail banking, corporate banking and a small number of overseas clients who warranted special attention. Gradually this bank has expanded into the US and continental Europe, creating multiple dimensions of focus, but wished to retain the benefits of common marketing and product design, a shared IT platform and shared HR services, including the e-enablement of HR, training and development, and reward management. Figure 4.7 shows a simplified version of its structure in 2008.

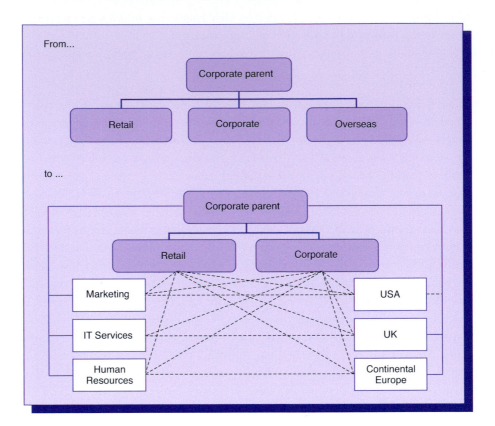

FIGURE 4.7 Evolving from a simple SBU structure to a more complex, interdependent structure

These more complex structures have the following characteristics:

- Multiple dimensions of focus, usually linked to serving differently defined market segments such as products, specific geographical areas or industry groupings.
- Overlapping responsibilities, in which units will be much less self-contained and autonomous and more likely to work in collaboration with other units, or work in integrated project teams.
- Shared accountabilities, in which units are accountable for their own results and for how well they contribute to the work of other units and the company as a whole. This is a concept far removed from the profit and cost accountability of SBUs.

Like SBUs, however, these more complex structures pose significant management challenges (Child, 2015; Miles *et al.*, 2010). First, decision-making can be slow and complicated, because the consensus is often required between the various units. Originally, the theory of matrix structures suggested a *balance* of authority between the different units so that, for example, country managers and customer managers would have an equal say in the marketing of a new product. Such balanced authority relationships have come to be seen as unworkable and time-consuming in resolving disputes, with the main focus now on deciding which units will have the authority. These newer structures, however, are faced with the problems of either (a) deciding on the main sources of sustainable competitive advantage, or (b) being able to change structures to reflect a competitive context in which there is no sustainable source of advantage, e.g. where new technologies or sources of knowledge become readily available to all would-be competitors. Often, this means that organizations need to be designed on a *reconfigurable* basis, such as that described by the notion of dynamic capabilities discussed earlier (Teece, 2014), to reflect changes in the competitive environment, and enormous resources are now being put into organizational change or 'reinvention'.

Second, complex organizations have to deal with the challenge of coordination and collaboration across unit boundaries (Fjeldstad *et al.*, 2012). Such coordination and collaboration is rarely achieved through mutual self-interest, and has to be designed into organizational structures. Sometimes this is achieved through developing informal networks, but more often team-based or project-based methods of coordination are used to ensure that units collaborate to share knowledge. For example, customer teams can be set up if the main source of competitive advantage lies in serving a few, large, global customers well. An alternative solution might be to create a new role of global account manager to ensure that country managers focus on globally important customers.

Third, more complex structures lead to less obvious accountabilities and are less exposed to market disciplines and self-correction when things go wrong. Complex structures mean that simple performance measures, such as unit profitability, are less relevant, and that there is a need for more rounded measures that take into account the ability of a unit to collaborate and share its knowledge. As we shall see in Chapter 7 on managing knowledge, there are measures that can assist in this process, based on ideas such as a balanced scorecard. These types of measure may reward unit managers and their teams for balancing the interests of key customers, geographical units and product groupings, as well as implementing corporate HR and IT policies.

EXERCISE 4.4

Can some of the problems of Innovative Petroleum be attributed to the problems of the 'global matrix structure' of which the company is a part?

NEW APPROACHES TO ORGANIZATIONAL DESIGN

New organizational forms and networks

The approaches to analysing and designing organizations we have discussed have stood the test of time, and provide excellent insights into most conventional forms of organizational structure. The principles underlying these structures, however, are based on hierarchy as a governance and control mechanism. During the 1980s and 1990s the notion of flexibility became a much more important design principle, and organizations began to adopt more flexible structures, as presaged by both Mintzberg and Miles and Snow's earlier work on adhocracies and innovative organizations. Writing in 1984 in the UK, John Atkinson proposed the model of the flexible firm, based on the distinction between core and peripheral tasks. He noted that organizations were progressively segmenting their workforces between those employees who were 'mission critical' to the core tasks of producing and selling the key products and services of the company, and those employees who were peripheral. These peripheral employees were to be found at all levels in the organization. For example, they could be people such as accountants and HR staff, whose work could be outsourced, or whole departments, such as estates management or even manufacturing, if the organization saw its main capability as the marketing, design or development of products and services, such as the sportswear firm Nike. The periphery could also include work that could easily be undertaken by temporary employees who could be hired and fired when needed. The principle underlying this form of flexible firm, which is similar in many ways to the architectural model of strategic human resource management we discussed in Chapter 3, was to translate as much of the fixed labour costs as possible in an organization into variable costs that could be adjusted to the fortunes and circumstances of the organization.

Around the same time, writers in the US, such as Rosabeth Moss Kanter (1989) and Miles and Snow (1984), were proposing a model of the networked organization, based on the theory of loosely coupled systems of organization that operated throughout the value chain. Networked organizations began to develop in a number of forms (Child, 2015). These included organizations that outsourced and offshored many of the functions, such as manufacturing in the case of consumer electronics and motor vehicles to Eastern Europe and China, and customer services, such as call centres to India. They also included so-called virtual organizations, which exist in space but are not bound by physical and legal structures – so-called imaginary structures. Child uses Dell Computers as an example of a virtual organization because it sold direct to the final customer, so cutting out distributors and

KEY CONCEPT Tight and loose coupling

According to Aldrich (2008), a tightly coupled system is one where any changes in the organization's environment or design, or the fit between them, will result in compromised performance. In effect, organizations are designed to be aligned with one set of competitive circumstances, such as large-scale and hierarchical production plants, which used inflexible assembly line forms of manufacture to produce single models of motor vehicles for the mass-consumption markets in America during the 1970s and 1980s. Such tight coupling works well until the competitive conditions change, when the organizational design becomes a liability by preventing a change in strategy.

Loosely coupled systems are more flexible in design. They are less attuned to a particular set of competitive circumstances, and offer the possibility of more rapid change when the environment changes. This is the thinking underlying the design of many modern motor vehicle plants, including the Toyota production system that we shall discuss in Chapter 8. We also raise it in Chapter 9 on creativity and innovation.

retailers. We shall discuss these later in the chapter. Finally, networked organizations also include strategic alliances, which covers situations where organizations engage in medium or long-term collaborations to realize the strategic objectives of all partners. Good examples of such alliances are to be found in oil and gas exploration, and in the staging of major international events such as the World Cup or Olympics.

The ideas underlying many of these networked organizations emerged from places such as Silicon Valley in California, where rather unusual organization structures were being developed to take advantage of the rapid change associated with the high-technology environment. Agility and versatility became the bywords for organization design, rather than hierarchy and control. Many of these new organizations were more akin to loose federations or constellations of business units that relied on each other for expertise and know-how (Fjeldstad *et al.*, 2012). One good example, though not based in Silicon Valley, was Microsoft with its Certified Partners programme. The illustration in Box 4.2, taken from Microsoft's website, gives you some insight into how organizations such as Microsoft have grown through networking with smaller organizations that can provide expertise in helping them develop their products and services and by providing channels to market for Microsoft products.

Goold and Campbell (2002), well-known authorities on organizational design, have suggested that the kind of example set out in Box 4.2 is one of the most compelling images of organizations in the twenty-first century – the idea of such self-managed networks, free from bureaucracy, built on expertise and highly motivated, creative units interacting with each other in a mutually adjusting fashion (see also Case 4.2 on TCG). The image is particularly attractive because it contrasts markedly with the conventional, bureaucratic form many of us are used to working in, which is often characterized by a lack of innovation and by internal political behaviour. Table 4.4 sets out

---

BOX 4.2 **An example of growth through networking**

This is an extract taken from Microsoft's website for its partnership programme.

Microsoft Partner Program builds relevance and value into all the tools and resources we provide to help you thrive in the market. You'll find benefits and resources to support all stages of your business cycle, helping you to:

- *Plan your business.* The tools and resources to help you grow and develop your business.
- *Build and maintain expertise.* Assistance in building and maintaining expertise in your particular areas of specialization through training resources and access to Microsoft software for development, support, sales or internal-use purposes.
- *Market and sell.* Marketing activities and resources to help you create demand and build sales around Microsoft software launches and new marketing initiatives.
- *Provide service and support.* The tools and services you need to aid in delivering and supporting Microsoft software and solutions.
- *Retain your customers.* Tools to help you connect with and strengthen your customer relationships.

TABLE 4.4 Contrasting old and new organizations

Organizational activity	Conventional organization characteristics	Emerging organization characteristics
Strategic management, goal-setting and implementation	Top-down, centralized decision-making, tightly coupled	Decentralized goal-setting, loosely coupled
	Concentrated power and authority	Distributed power and authority, and freedom from hierarchy
	Preference for large units and wide-scope SBUs, with single-dimension focus to reflect relatively stable and simple environments	Preference for smaller units and multidimensional focus to reflect more complex and changing environments, need for constant renewal and 'reconfigurability'
	Leader control, monitoring and specific objective-setting through use of formal authority	Leaders provide guidance and support, but also manage conflict and act as brokers
	Vision dictated by senior managers	Vision emergent often from middle
	Knowledge routine and knowledge secrecy	Knowledge intensive and knowledge sharing
	Focus on costs and 'playing within the rules of the game'	Focus on innovation and 'changing the rules of the game' by setting stretching targets
Maintaining necessary integration within organizational boundaries and defining organizational boundaries	Firms or SBU as unit of analysis	The value chain or network as the unit of analysis
	Boundaries of organization clearly specified and durable, with most support services undertaken in-house	Boundaries of organization permeable, fuzzy and flexible, with more outsourcing and markets for spin-offs and buy-outs
	Standards, reliability and replicability as key bywords for managers	Flexibility as key management principle
	Vertical communications	Horizontal communications
	Rules and procedures dominant	Relationship based and personal networking
	Assets, budgets and investment decision linked to organizational units	Assets, budgets and investments independent of organizational units and often focused on projects and initiatives

continued . . .

TABLE 4.4 Continued

Organizational activity	Conventional organization characteristics	Emerging organization characteristics
Maintaining necessary differentiation with the organization, including functions and roles, duties and rights, and governance	Specialized roles and detailed division of labour, with people hired for jobs	General roles and little heed paid to division of labour, with people hired to fit organization
	Clear job and function definitions	Fuzzy job and function definitions
	Uncertainty absorption	Adaptation
	Relative permanence of jobs and careers, based on relational psychological contracts	Relative impermanence of jobs and boundaryless careers, based on transactional psychological contracts and employability
	Efficiency orientation	Innovation oriented
Modes of integration		
Networking	Only with major stakeholders	Integral to the value chain
Outsourcing	Vertical integration into large units, little or no outsourcing	Horizontal integration between smaller units, non-core activities outsourced
Alliances	Avoided due to fears of loss of control	Extensively used
Organizing across borders	Either a loose financially coordinated conglomerate or coordinated via an international division	Complex multidimensional organization that attempts to gain the benefits or global integration and local responsiveness

Sources: based on Aldrich, 2008; Child, 2015; Miles *et al.*, 2010; Goold and Campbell, 2002; Malone, 2004; Roberts, 2004.

the contrast between conventional and emerging network-based organizations in more formal terms. The table contrasts the two forms on the basis of three dimensions: the process of strategic decision-making; how integration is achieved between units; and how the necessary differentiation is achieved within the organization. On this last point, note the implications for careers and attachments to organizations, and the changed basis of the psychological contracts discussed in previous chapters.

The virtual organization and networking

As noted earlier particular constellations of networked organizations can come together to create a *'virtual firm'*. Such organizations are usually defined by what they are not (Aldrich, 2008). That is, they are not the conventional, vertically integrated and directed organizations described earlier in this chapter. Instead, they are 'virtual' in the sense that all or most of the activities in the value chain, from acquiring raw materials to customer relationships, are contracted out and loosely coupled. The result is a series of networked companies, focusing on doing what they can do most effectively and acting *as if* they were a single organization. In this sense, the network *simulates* a single company, which is why we use the term 'virtual'. Such organizational structures aren't new, as many industries have operated on the basis of contracting out for many years. The construction industry is one such example, often with the architect acting as the network *'integrator'* on behalf of the client and managing the supply chain from design, through construction to handing over the building to the customer. The main advantages of this kind of organization lie in specializing in what they are good at and in being comparatively small when it is advantageous to be small, while being able to scale up when size and scope are important.

Besides Dell and Nike, good examples of well-known virtual organizations are Benetton, the Italian fashion house. All of these organizations contract out most, if not all, manufacturing, and act as network integrators in bringing together all aspects of their respective value chains to provide distinctive value propositions to their customers. It is not only organizations that are becoming virtual, but also major functions such as HR. For example, BT, the global communications technology company, reduced its HR department from employing nearly 14,500 HR staff in 1991 using 26 separate HR systems to 550 executives to concentrate on strategic HR issues by July 2005 (Hunter and Saunders, 2007). Like all virtual organizations, the operations of Benetton, Dell and BT's HR departments have been made possible by new information and communications technologies in linking the various companies and outsourcing contractors together to provide a seamless service to their respective customers. One good example is the so-called e-Lancing firm Uber (see Box 4.3 below).

BOX 4.3 *Uber – a technology mediator*

Danial Pink wrote a book entitled *Free Agent Nation* in 2001 but could hardly have foreseen how technology would change the nature of freelancing to e-lancing. One company that has featured heavily in this new 'sharing' economy is Uber, a web-based taxi company that customers access through an app on their mobile phones. It originated in San Francisco in 2009 and became one of the fastest-growing technology start-ups by 2015, operating in 229 cities in 46 countries with a business model that has become a marker for many other firms.

Using an app on smartphones, Uber allows passengers to call drivers directly 'from the comfort of a sofa or bar stool', which has caused a major shake-up in the taxi market. The interesting aspect organizationally is that Uber does not own taxis but connects passengers with e-lancers, individuals who use their own vehicles in their own time to supply the rides.

For this service, Uber charges a fixed 20 per cent of the fare. The strong networking effects of this type of business allow Uber to recruit more self-employed drivers, many of whom are part-time, which reduces pick-up times and thus attracts more passengers.

However, Uber is not without its critics, especially from the existing taxi companies and from some of its e-lancers. It is known for being a ruthless competitor in its market with its surge pricing model – raising rates during peak times to encourage more drivers on the roads – and also ruthless in its dealings with e-lancers. So in June 2015, the Labor Commissioner in California ruled that a former driver was an employee and not a subcontractor, and thus entitled to be paid expenses for her mileage. This ruling has set off a class action by drivers who are seeking to be regarded as employees rather than e-lancers, receiving, for example, all tips. Such a decision, if repeated in other US states or other countries, could represent a major threat to Uber's business model, and to those companies that have adopted it.

Moreover, while e-lancing can be liberating for some, for others it can be a source of anxiety for two reasons. Schonfeld and Mazzola (2015) have shown how anxiety follows from the self-employed not knowing 'whether one is doing enough, or good enough work' because they lack a reference point with employee norms. In addition to performance anxiety (being good enough), Gianpiero Petriglieri from Insead described an existential anxiety (Who am I and why am I doing this – is it valuable?). One consequence is burnout, because as Standing (2009) has suggested the 'profician' (e.g. lawyers, sports stars, IT professionals who are self-selling entrepreneurs) 'has to live a very frenzied and opportunistic life'.

As the above case highlights and as several writers have pointed out, virtual corporations have a number of disadvantages and face many challenges (Child, 2015; Pettigrew *et al.*, 2000):

- The loss of proprietary knowledge, when providing information and learning to other members of the network. For example, when IBM contracted out its software and processor manufacture to Microsoft and Intel, they effectively gave away core competences. BT also suffered from losing control of proprietary knowledge in outsourcing much of its HR function to Accenture during the 1990s, a problem that took many years to overcome (Martin *et al.*, 2008).
- The more an organization contracts out, the more potential profit through value-added services it loses. For example, in the IBM case in the previous bullet point, both Microsoft and Intel became larger than IBM. Perhaps as important, contracting out means that an organization has less control over the business process. If even one of these processes is 'mission critical', any conflict that arises from disagreements can damage the reputation of the whole virtual network.
- The feasibility of networks, which depend on the attitudes of partners and the information available to them. In a virtual organization, success often depends on the personalities, emotional intelligence, motivations and career trajectories of individual managers. It may be difficult for managers brought up in large SBU organizations, many of whom have been used to relatively rich resources, stable career paths and competition, to work in smaller, often resource-poor, organizations with very different career structures, and expect them to collaborate and share their knowledge.

- A final problem with networks arises from the time and effort often required to create them. Because of the initial investment in management time, they are likely to become closed systems, resistant to new partners and to future change.

Thus, designing effective virtual organizations is very much based on effective partnering, which writers such as Child (2015), Galbraith (2002) and Miles *et al.* (2010) see as addressing the following issues:

1   Creating a partnership strategy, in which companies play appropriate roles. These roles can range from being a specialist contributor, who performs only a few activities such as payroll services, to a network integrator such as Uber, Nike, Benetton, Dell or even Boeing, the aircraft company. As discussed above, the network integrator has to balance contracting out mission-critical and potentially profitable activities against the value of having expert outside suppliers contribute to the network.

2   Designing appropriate external relationships and coordination mechanisms, which can vary according to (a) the degree of control the integrator has or desires over other companies in the network, (b) the levels of day-to-day coordination necessary and (c) the value the network integrator wishes to capture from the partnership: this refers to the proportion of total value added by the network supply chain that the network integrator seeks to appropriate for itself.

3   The design choices available range from developing pure *market or contracting relationships*; through *sourcing and alliance partnerships*, often found in motor vehicle manufacture; *equity relationships*, in which an integrator may take out a financial stake in the other companies; to outright *ownership* of the other companies. As all of these choices have their strengths and weaknesses, solutions are specific to the context of the partnership. For example, BT set up an equity relationship with Accenture in the 1990s to deliver HR services to other companies, which it relinquished later on in part because of problems of lack of trust between the partners.

4   Partner selection is another and often critical design issue. In many respects, the issues here are similar to those involved in selecting individuals to fit organizations, and revolve around having common aims and compatible cultures or characters. As Child (2015) suggests, firms skilled at creating alliances, whether they be networks, sourcing alliances, joint ventures or equity partnerships, spend a lot of time and effort evaluating potential partners for 'fit' during the selection process, to ensure that all issues that may cause the partnership to go wrong are uncovered during the 'courtship' process.

5   Finally, supporting policies for people and reward policies, key components of the star model in Figure 4.1, are critical design choices. As noted above, the success of partnerships depends on the qualities and motivation of the managers who have to make them work; these qualities are often different from those that are successful in competitive contexts. Key skills include the ability to influence without authority, negotiating and working with people from different corporate and international cultures. They also include the ability to be able to cooperate and reveal information, as well as retain information that is confidential. Reward systems, like cooperating skills, have to be based on the idea of a win–win scenario in which the deals and arrangements struck bring benefits to all parties.

CASE 4.2 **TCG – AN EXAMPLE OF A VIRTUAL ORGANIZATION BASED ON CELLULAR PRINCIPLES**

Technical and Computer Graphics (TCG), an Australian privately held information technology company based in Sydney and founded in 1971, is a classic example of a virtual organization, based on cellular principles. As Miles *et al.* (2010) concluded since revisiting their original research in the firm in 1997, TCG has certainly evolved. In the 1990s it focused on developing a wide variety of products and services, including portable and hand-held data terminals and loggers, computer graphics systems, bar-coding systems, electronic data interchange systems, and other IT products and services. More recently, it has moved into the development of business accelerators and technology parks, and business services. The network originally comprised 13 individual small firms as partners, the basis of the cellular approach. Drawing on the biological metaphor of a living organism, each firm or 'cell' had its own aims and can live independently from the others, but all share a common bond with other network members. For example, some TCG firms specialized in one or more product categories, whereas others specialize in hardware or software.

At TCG, the various partners had existing high levels of technical and business competence. However, the ambitions of the network were to ensure system-wide competence for the group as a whole. The process used to develop this overall partnership competence was called triangulation; it was the means by which TCG developed new products and services.

Triangulation was based on a partnership model with three components: (a) a partnership with one or more TCG firms; (b) an external joint-venture partner, such as Hitachi, which may provide equity to the venture; and (c) a principal customer or client that can provide large orders and additional cash and resources to the partnership in return for contractual and intellectual property rights for the innovations or developments.

The process of venturing was critical to the partnership, with all TCG networked firms expected to search continually for new product and service opportunities. Once there was some interest shown by a potential client, the initiating TCG firm acted as project leader for the remainder of the venture. The first step in the triangulation process was to identify and collaborate with a joint-venture partner that has specialist competence in the underlying technology or process involved. TCG sought some funding for the project from the joint-venture partner and also gained access to the key technology, etc. The second step was to locate and work with a potential customer for the new product, for whom they agreed to custom-design a product. By working with the joint-venture partners and end-user, TCG could produce high-technology solutions and products that met the particular demands of a client who is not taxed with having to set up a specialist in-house organization to innovate.

The credo of TCG ensures that the project leader firm in the network partnered with other firms in the group, not only for their specialist contribution, but so that the collective competence and knowledge base of the network was enhanced. Triangulation thus served a dual purpose of building on collective expertise and also enhancing it by diffusing the learning gained from business development, partnering and project management. The principles of networking were interconnected at TCG and serve to reinforce each other to bind the network together. First, acceptance of entrepreneurial responsibility is required for admission to the group and is increasingly enhanced by the triangulation process. Second, the principle of self-organization gave the individual firm both the ability and the freedom to adapt to changing partner and customer needs. Third, each firm's profit responsibility, as well as the guaranteed ability to take out equity in other TCG firms, provided the motivation and rewards for overall collective growth and use of each other's specific competences.

In revisiting this well researched case, Miles *et al.* (2010) concluded that the process of multi-firm collaboration at TCG was mutually reinforcing, with knowledge sharing a key feature of this continuing collaboration (as stated in its website in 2015). Fjeldstad *et al.* (2012) proposed that such collaborations were built around organizational architectures that embodied three key features:

- organizational actors in the firms who had the capabilities and mindsets to self-organize,
- a common approach to accumulating and sharing resources,
- enabling structures and processes that facilitated multi-actor collaborations.

Sources: adapted from Fjeldstad *et al.*, 2012; Miles *et al.*, 1997; Miles *et al.*, 2010.

1   To what extent does the TCG network embody effective partnering? Can you foresee any problems?

TESTS OF EFFECTIVE ORGANIZATIONAL DESIGN

So what have we learned about the kinds of problems faced by organizations such as Innovative Petroleum Engineering, and what can we do to help them restructure more effectively? During this chapter, you have been introduced to a number of ideas that might suggest useful ways forward from the perspective of Innovative and its parent company. You have also learned about the virtues of new organizational forms that companies like Innovative may consider. However, we want to reiterate there is no single solution for organizations such as Innovative. Instead, there are only sensible general questions we can ask, the answers to which may help us design an organization appropriate for a particular context and time frame. To help us ask and answer such questions, we have integrated Goold and Campbell's (2002) nine design tests with those of Child (2015) and others (e.g. Fjeldstad *et al.*, 2012), on the basis of two basic concepts in organizational design:

- *fit*, which is based on the idea that organizations should be fit for purpose;
- *design principles*, which have been distilled from previous 'promising' practices in organizational design. Note we do not use the term 'best practice', because we do not believe there can be practices that are 'best' for all contexts, other than at a very general level.

The four drivers of fit and the five design principles are best defined by the nine tests that Goold and Campbell associated with them (see Figure 4.8 and Table 4.5). Again, we believe these design tests have stood the test of time since writing the first edition of the book and remain extremely useful because they can be used to assess the strengths and weaknesses of existing organizations, those of major changes to an existing organization, or proposals for new organization forms such as the ones we have discussed in this chapter.

This practical set of principles would be a good place to begin to evaluate your own organization, focusing on its existing structure or on any proposed changes. Returning to the case of Innovative

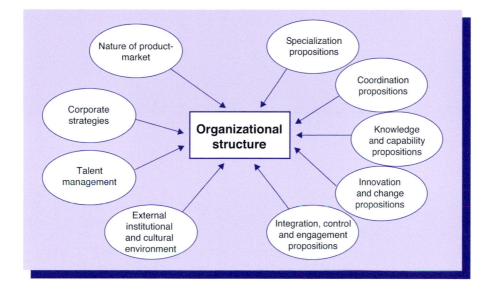

FIGURE 4.8 The relationship between fit shapers, design propositions and organizational structure (*Sources*: based on Child, 2015; Goold and Campbell, 2002; Fjeldstad *et al.*, 2012 and our own researcher.)

TABLE 4.5 Fit shapers and design propositions

The shapers of organizational design	Design propositions
Product–market propositions	1. Management should focus on the operating priorities and sources of advantage in each product market segment? 2. Structures should focus on customers' requirements in each product–market segment served by the organization, which may cause divisional structures to look different and have different connections to corporate headquarters
Corporate strategies	1. The organizational design should reflect corporate headquarters support for operating units and reflect key strategic initiatives or actions planned by the company, e.g. implement a corporate-wide brand, outsource all call handling
Talent management	1. The design should be able to secure the core talent needed to deliver the strategic aims currently and in the future 2. The design should align with the values, motivations and expectations of existing and potential core talent, but not to the exclusion of other value creating segments of the workforce

continued . . .

TABLE 4.5 Continued

The shapers of organizational design	Design propositions
External institutional and cultural constraints	1. The design should be feasible in taking into account external institutional and cultural constraints that might make it unfit for purpose 2. The design should ensure that the external environment has been interpreted and sensed to identify all possible legal, institutional and national cultural constraints in which the company operates

Design propositions	
Specialization propositions	1. Specialist sub-unit culture units should have flexibility and authority to protect themselves from domination by the corporate culture
Coordination propositions	1. The design should ensure through protocols coordination benefits that will be difficult to achieve on a voluntary networking basis, especially in areas such as critical quality standards and ethical standards that would be difficult to achieve on an informal basis?
Knowledge and capability propositions	1. All levels of the managerial hierarchy and all managerial roles in the hierarchy should add value through specific knowledge and capabilities 2. Organizational design should ensure appropriate physical and virtual spaces where actors can accumulate and share knowledge and resources? 3. The design should ensure that all employees are given sufficient opportunity and encouraged to engage with decision-makers and express their legitimate voice without fear of retribution or blame
Integration, control and engagement propositions	1 The design should facilitate integration and control processes for each unit, which are appropriate to their roles and responsibilities, and economical to implement 2. The design should reflect the need for distributed leadership to ensure that everyone with expertise is able to contribute? 3. The design should be compatible with the need to create high intra-organizational engagement and trust dynamics by ensuring all integration and control processes are seen as high trust initiatives by senior management
Innovation and change propositions	1. The design should facilitate help the development of new strategies and be flexible enough to adapt to future changes 2. Locations and the architecture of buildings should be designed to encourage innovation, formal and informal knowledge sharing among employees 3. Innovative units should have appropriate access to talent to meet demands for new products or services, and rewarded for learning, passing on their learning and for putting learning into practice in the form of innovations 4. In a multinational context, attention should be paid to reconciling needs for global integration, local responsiveness and identity, and transferring knowledge across borders

(*Source*: based on Child, 2015; Goold and Campbell, 2002 and Fjeldstad et al, 2012 and our own research.)

Petroleum, managers in the company would be well advised to look at these design principles before continuing with their changes to the organizational structure. At the time of putting this book together, however, there is little sign of them doing so.

LEARNING SUMMARY

In this chapter we looked at the kinds of problems faced by many large organizations that can cause them to underperform and, possibly, go out of existence. We looked at three well-known frameworks that help us understand organizational analysis and design, and applied these to the problems faced by Innovative Petroleum Engineering, a pseudonym for a real firm undergoing problems of change.

We have also examined developments in organizational forms, beginning with changes from simple to more complex structures, including the M-form and matrix structures. We also focused on the more recent introduction of virtual organizations and networking. These latter types are not yet widespread, but evidence suggests that they will become more common in all countries, creating new opportunities for businesses but also presenting new problems for managers, especially in managing in situations with traditional levels of authority and power.

Finally, we looked at a highly practical test of good organizational design that we hope you will use in your future career to analyse the problems faced by the organization you work for or any changes proposed for its future.

REVIEW QUESTIONS

1 What are the key environmental factors that influence organizational design?
2 What are the strengths and weaknesses of new organizational forms?

REFERENCES

Aguinis, H. and Lawal, S. O. (2013) eLancing: A review and research agenda for bridging the science-practice gap. *Human Resource Management Review*, 23 (1), 6–17.

Aldrich, H. A. (2008) *Organizations and Environments*. Stanford, CA: Stanford University Press.

Atkinson, L. (1984) Manpower strategies for flexible organizations. *Personnel Management*, August, 28–31.

Child, J. (2015) *Organization: Contemporary principles and practices*, 2nd edn. Chichester, Sussex: John Wiley.

Christensen, C. M. and Horn, M. (2008) *Disrupting Class: How disruptive innovation will change the way the world learns*. New York: McGraw-Hill.

Fjeldstad, D. O., Snow, C. C., Miles, R. and Lettl, C. (2012) The architecture of collaboration. *Strategic Management Journal*, 33 (6), 734–750.

Galbraith, J. (2002) *Designing Organizations: An executive guide to strategy, structure and process*, new and revised edition. San Francisco, CA: Jossey-Bass.

Goold, M. and Campbell, A. (2002) *Designing Effective Organizations: How to create structured networks.* London: John Wiley.

Hatch, M. J. and Cunliffe, A. (2013) *Organization Theory: Modern, symbolic and postmodern perspectives.* Oxford: Oxford University Press.

Hunter, I. and Saunders, J. (2007) *Human Resource Outsourcing: Solutions, suppliers, key processes and the current market.* Aldershot, Hants: Gower.

Kanter, R. M. (1989) *When Giants Learn to Dance: Mastering the challenges of strategy, management, and careers in the 1990s.* New York: Simon & Schuster.

Kates, A. and Galbraith, J. R. (2007) *Designing Your Organization: Using the star model to solve 5 critical design challenges.* San Francisco, CA: Jossey-Bass.

Malone, T. W. (2004) *The Future of Work: How the new order of business will shape your organization, your management style, and your life.* Cambridge, MA: Harvard Business School Press.

Martin, G., Reddington, M. and Alexander, H. (eds) (2008) *Technology, Outsourcing and Transforming HR.* Oxford: Butterworth Heinemann.

Miles, R. E. and Snow, C. C. (1984) Fit, failure and the hall of fame. *California Management Review,* 26 (3), 10–28.

Miles, R. E. and Snow, C. C. (2003) *Organizational Strategy, Structure and Process: A Stanford Business Classic.* Stanford, CA: Stanford University Press.

Miles, R. E., Snow, C. C., Mathews, J. A. and Miles, G. (1997) Organizing in the knowledge age: anticipating the cellular form. *Academy of Management Executive,* 11 (4), 7–24.

Miles, R. E., Snow, C. C., Fjeldstad, O. D., Miles, G. and Lettl, C. (2010) Designing organizational to meet 21st century opportunities and challenges. *Organizational Dynamics,* 39 (2), 93–103.

Mintzberg, H. (1993) *Structure in Fives: Designing effective organizations.* Englewood Cliffs, NJ: Prentice-Hall.

Nohria, N., Joyce, W. and Robertson, B. (2003) Driving success in your business. *Harvard Business Review,* 81 (July), 52–53.

Petriglieri, G. (2015), cited in *Financial Times,* The silent anxiety of the sharing economy, 25 June, available online at www.ft.com/cms/s/0/e61ca2e2-18f0-11e5-a130-2c7db721f996.html#axzz3vtR4411d.

Pettigrew, A. M., Massini, S. and Numagami, T. (2000) Innovative forms of organising in Europe. *European Management Journal,* 18 (3), 259–273.

Roberts, J. (2004) *The Modern Firm: Organizational design for performance and growth.* New York: Oxford University Press.

Schonfeld, I. S. and Mazzola, J. J. (2015) A qualitative study of stress in individuals self-employed in solo businesses. *Journal of Occupational Health Psychology.* Online first publication, 23 February, http://doi.org/10.1037/a0038804.

Standing, G. (2009) *Work after Globalization: Building occupational citizenship.* Cheltenham, Gloucester: Edward Elgar.

Teece, D. J. (2009) *Dynamic Capabilities and Strategic Management: Organizing for innovation and growth.* Oxford: Oxford University Press.

Teece, D. J. (2014) A dynamic capabilities-based entrepreneurial theory of the multinational enterprise. *Journal of International Business Studies,* 45, 8–37.

Chapter 5

Managing in an international context

LEARNING OBJECTIVES

At the end of this chapter you should be able to:

- understand the problems of 'going international' and the implications for managers;

- understand the forces for convergence and divergence in international management;

- apply the ideas of national cultural differences to the analysis and solutions of international management problems;

- apply the ideas of national business systems to the analysis and solutions of international management problems;

- identify key international management competences, and use these to reflect on your ability to become a more effective international manager;

- understand the problems of developing managers for international assignments, and construct appropriate management development programmes and activities to help them become more effective overseas;

- construct a learning agenda to build your own international management competencies.

INTRODUCTION

During the first four chapters of this book, we have discussed how important it is to understand business and management from an international perspective. As noted earlier, one of the dominant trends in the development of modern economies is the increased 'globalization' of business, though as some writers have pointed out, this trend is the subject of a number of myths and misunderstandings (Mendenhall *et al.*, 2007). Leaving aside its economic and cultural impact, globalization has a significant influence on how we manage, not only in multinational enterprises (MNEs) but also in our home-based companies as, increasingly, we borrow ideas on promising practices from companies in the advanced industrialized countries. Much of this borrowing has come from

US-based companies that are headlined in the international business press and much of the US-based academic literature as models of excellence, for example, Apple, Google and Amazon as leaders in their fields. Nevertheless, some researchers have argued that US companies, partly because of the US government's generally isolationist approach to world affairs throughout much of its history (at least until the Second World War), were among the least well-equipped organizations to conduct effective global management in a multinational context. In essence, the argument is that US companies are 'reluctant globalizers'. For example, only two US-based companies featured in the 'Global Top 100 Non-Financial Trans-National Corporations ranked by Foreign Assets in 2013' list – General Electric and Exxon Mobil. At a more prosaic, though no less important, level, it was pointed out that only 50 per cent of US senators held passports in the 1990s, supposedly indicating their lack of interest in foreign affairs. However, that figure is reported to have increased markedly to near 100 per cent over the last two decades, which may also indicate changes in American business interests and foreign policy.

Yet at the same time a number of major US organizations have been at the forefront of the internationalizing (if not globalizing) process, initially in Britain and the rest of Europe after the Second World War, and more recently in their operations in the Asia-Pacific region. Such efforts at internationalization, although generally successful in bringing economic success to the USA and to the host countries of US subsidiaries, have been plagued by problems. These problems are often the consequence of US 'exceptionalism' (a belief in the superiority of their own values), ethnocentrism and the attempt to export US-style 'best practice' in management to other countries, especially in the field of human resource management (Lawler and Boudreau, 2015). As a consequence, major mistakes have been made by US companies in working overseas. By no stretch of the imagination, however, is such exceptionalism and ethnocentrism unique to America and American organizations. The political and economic history of the last 400 years is characterized by problems experienced by companies based in Europe, Japan and the so-called 'newly emerging economies' such as China, Korea and Thailand in internationalizing (Jones, 2003; World Trade Organization, 2014). Perhaps the most notable example of internationalization was the British Empire, in which the UK attempted to create a world in its own image and which reached its apogee in the early 1900s, comprising 25 per cent of the world's land mass and 25 per cent of its population. This was internationalization on a scale never seen before or since, and virtually every lesson in how to conduct global management – good and bad – can be drawn from Britain's imperialist era (Ferguson, 2003, 2004). Like the British East India Company, which once controlled most of India, European organizations have sometimes found that their internationalization strategies have failed because of their excessive commitment to parent company values and practices, and a failure to understand the institutional and cultural characteristics of host countries and their subsidiaries. Amusing examples of such problems include the early attempts by Marks and Spencer, one of the world's largest retailing organizations, to set up operations in France during the 1980s. So entrenched were their British values that they tried to operate a 'buy British' campaign in a country that has competed with England for hundreds of years (including a 100 years war), and to sell Christmas puddings, a uniquely British dish, without any cooking instructions. French customers bought them and ate them cold, which only confirmed their already low opinion of British food products.

Thus, we face the possibility of companies throughout the world destined to repeat many of the mistakes of history when operating in each other's territories. As a consequence, it is critically important for globalizing firms to make sensible and contextually sensitive decisions in key areas of marketing, knowledge management and human resource management: decisions that take into account institutional, cultural and psychological differences between parent company institutions, values and practices, those of host countries and those of third country nationals employed to work in global organizations. And because there are so many lessons that can be drawn from the past, we shall spend a little time taking a historical perspective.

In this chapter, then, we shall explore the international context of business and management and address three key questions often asked of practising managers and of academics who research in this interesting area:

1   To what extent do countries differ in their business environments, and how does this affect the practice of management in these countries?
2   What has been the impact of the internationalization of business and the growth of so-called global firms on the practice of management?
3   What lessons can we learn from research and practice about managing people in an international environment?

The problems of internationalization and its implications for management

In our academic and knowledge exchange roles with experience of living and working in a number of different countries, we have been asked to provide advice to a small number of US 'start-up' companies in the technology field thinking about setting up operations in the UK and continental Europe. These companies and their managers are not naive and appreciate the problems of 'going international', especially in countries of which they have little knowledge. Academics traditionally referred to this practical problem as the 'liability of foreignness', which is the cost of doing business abroad arising from the unfamiliarity of the environment, from cultural, political and economic differences, and from the need for coordination across geographic distances. However, as Johanson and Vahine (2009) have pointed out, this liability of foreignness may have given way to the liability of 'outsidership', i.e. being locked outside of networks of firms related to each other in complex and often invisible ways.

KEY CONCEPT The liability of foreignness

This was originally defined by Zaheer (1995) as 'the costs of doing business abroad that result in a competitive disadvantage for a multinational enterprise (MNE)'. These costs broadly refer to all of the additional costs that a firm operating in a market overseas incurs that a local firm would not incur. Four such categories of costs are likely to arise:

1   Costs directly associated with distance, such as the costs of travel, transportation and coordination over distance and across time zones.

2 Firm-specific costs based on a particular company's unfamiliarity with and lack of roots in a local culture and business system.
3 Costs resulting from the host country environment, such as the lack of legitimacy of foreign firms and economic nationalism among governments and people.
4 Costs imposed by home country governments on doing business overseas, such as the restrictions on high-technology or weapons sales to certain countries.

The relative importance of these costs, and the choices that firms can make to deal with them, will vary by industry, firm, host country and home country. Regardless of its source, the liability of foreignness suggests that, other things being equal, foreign firms will have lower profitability than local firms and, perhaps, a lesser chance of survival.

As a consequence, many companies seek to exploit their assets by trading across international boundaries. In doing so, however, they are challenged by four basic questions. The first two relate to the now classical integration-responsiveness problem, which largely focus on economic or profit advantages for MNEs (Rosenzweig, 2006), the second two focus on a need to develop intellectual and social capital in MNEs (e.g. Johanson and Vahine, 2009; Legnick-Hall and Legnick-Hall, 2012):

1 To what extent can or should they *standardize* their operations across national boundaries to exploit existing products and services, brands, intangible assets and human resource management practices?
2 To what extent can or should they exploit the benefits of *localization* by adapting these products and/or services, and policies to fit in with their overseas markets?
3 How can they best leverage their knowledge and learning in one part of the company to other units?
4 To what extent can they build trust and commitment to develop the necessary bonds and bridges between the firms in their network of relationships?

The balance between standardization and localization a firm eventually settles on (and it usually is some form of balance) is based on the extent to which organizations assess their liability of foreignness or liability of outsidership in different market circumstances. Among other considerations, this calculation turns on whether these organizations assume that the countries they seek to enter are similar (convergent) to their own national cultures or are dissimilar (divergent) from their own national culture. The internationalization strategies that organizations might choose can take a range of forms (see Table 5.1), dependent on the extent to which they seek to have equity (ownership) in their overseas ventures. However, all such strategies rest on the liability of foreignness perceived by a firm and their convergence–divergence assumptions. Should, for example, an internationalizing firm invest in recruiting, developing and rewarding managers in their own country so that they can be sent overseas to transfer their knowledge and practices to the local situation? Or should they rely on the 'insider' judgement of local managers and their knowledge and practices? If, as organizations are increasingly seeking to (or are required to) partner with local firms, should they enter into a joint venture or a full-blown merger, and should they attempt to impose a homogeneous organizational culture by transferring home-based practices into the local firm?

Increasingly, however, MNEs are being challenged by host countries to address a fifth question, which focuses on a need to act responsibly and ethically by adopting a stakeholder approach to their overseas operations (see Chapter 11). Often this requires them to contribute to the development of local businesses and economies of the countries in which they locate through so-called 'local content' agreements. Moreover, they have to comply with legislation on local labour, local cultural issues and health and safety. Increasingly, MNEs also seek to compete on the extent to which they implement socially responsible and socially sustainable policies and practices, which address the needs of local stakeholders by engaging in corporate citizenship activities and contributing to environmental improvements (Kujala and Sajasalo, 2009).

NATIONAL DIFFERENCES IN THE BUSINESS ENVIRONMENT

Converging or diverging cultures?

To answer the questions posed in the previous sections, we need to understand not only how societies differ but also whether these differences are significant and if, as a result of globalization, these differences are likely to diminish. For instance, some people believe that societies are becoming alike, so understanding international differences and developing strategies to take these into account will be much less relevant in the near future. On this issue, informed opinion is divided over the extent and rate of convergence of national economies as a consequence of these changes. It splits between those who emphasize the forces for *convergence*, most notably the globalization of business, and those who emphasize the forces for *divergence*, principally the existence of strong national institutions (e.g. legislation, religion, consumer culture, patterns of business ownership, education, etc.), that constrain change (Wilkinson *et al.*, 2013). We shall examine this very important institutionalist perspective on why change is difficult later in this chapter.

Convergence and globalization

The *convergence* 'thesis' has become an established paradigm in the management literature: it is based on evidence that organizations and their managers around the world embrace many of the same values, attitudes and behaviours, and are increasingly likely to do so given the internationalization of technology and markets. Convergence exists, it is argued, despite the influence of obvious historical differences in national culture and key institutions in these countries, such as the legal, political and educational systems. A modified and more recent form of the convergence thesis is the *globalization* 'thesis', which has been used to herald the creation of worldwide markets and the growth of huge corporations with few roots in, or ties to, a specific country, some of them with revenues greater than many countries (Joynt and Warner, 2002). According to some writers, globalization is an overworked concept, because economic activity has always taken place across borders, and truly

TABLE 5.1 Entry strategies into overseas markets

Non-equity modes

Forms	*Characteristics*
Exporting	Selling overseas, which is usually low risk and requires little investment
Licensing	Giving a local firm legal rights to produce or sell a product or service, which is usually low risk but may lead to problems of local quality control
Franchising	Providing local firms with a complete package of trademarks, products and services, and operating principles
Contract manufacturing and service provision	Contracting out non-core business activities to overseas operations, which requires no local ownership or investment. Problems associated with quality control and contracting out 'moral responsibilities' to local entrepreneurs who may have different standards and attitudes to labour management

Equity modes

International joint ventures	An agreement by two or more companies to produce a product or service together, usually involving an equity-sharing arrangement between a local partner and an MNE. Provides rapid entry into new markets and local knowledge, but often associated with political problems between partners over the sharing of core technology and knowledge
Fully owned subsidiaries	Can take the form of an overseas acquisition or merger, or a new business start-up. Acquisitions provide ready markets and local knowledge, but present major difficulties in merging cultures and creating new identities. New start-ups are most costly in terms of management time and highest risk, given levels of investment. However, they are often preferred as they minimize the cost of transferring knowledge to partners and of sharing technologies.

global companies, which are not tied to their home country in important ways, are limited in number (Sparrow *et al.*, 2004). These writers also point out the more negative connotations of globalization as a form of neocolonialism and as a set of transformative social forces that lead to exploitation of labour in the developing world (see Wilkinson *et al.*, 2013) and major environmental problems such as global warming and depletion of natural resources. However, despite these arguments over the meaning of globalization, most writers broadly acknowledge the increased permeability of traditional boundaries of almost every kind, including those more tangible ones (time and space, nation-states and economies, industries and organizations) and less tangible ones (cultural norms and assumptions of 'how we do things around here'). Thus, the proponents of this globalization thesis propose that convergence among nations is occurring as a result of the globalization of economies, techniques and communications, and that national mindsets and institutions are less important in understanding the nature and effects of international business and management. Perhaps more importantly, it is sometimes argued by enthusiastic 'globalizers' – for example, the International Monetary Fund (IMF)

– that in a global economy national institutions and mindsets are an impediment to the modernization and interests of business in a specific country (see Box 5.1). One good example was the insistence on the part of Greek creditors, especially the IMF, to reform the Greek economy during 2014–15 by demanding pension reforms and the privatization of businesses rather than increased taxes on the rich.

One of the main engines for convergence and/or globalization has been the role played by large, transnational corporations such as the Ford Motor Company, Toyota and DaimlerChrysler in the cross-border transfer of products, ideas and processes to their subsidiaries, and indirectly to other

---

BOX 5.1 Kultur clash

An *Economist* article in 2004 pointed out that Mannesmann, a leading German company, was taken to court in 2004 accused of breaches of German securities law, but not so serious to warrant any individual being convicted of a criminal breach of trust. This followed the Vodafone takeover in 2000 and the accusations against six senior managers of committing or abetting a breach of trust in awarding bonuses worth €57 million to themselves.

The issue was portrayed in the German media as 'corporate greed' on trial and as a clash between two business cultures: the importation of Anglo-Saxon capitalism into the more socially oriented Rhineland variety. As an *Economist* article pointed out, 'Big German firms have traditionally been run by consensus: a German executive board has no real CEO, in the American sense. Each executive is directly answerable to the supervisory board, which contrasts with the autonomy enjoyed by the boards of American and British companies.'

In German companies, however, it was unusual for a senior executive to be sacked, US style, by the supervisory board, though there have been some examples of this occurring. The article cited Ulrich Schumacher as one example, the American-influenced leader of Infineon, a semiconductor firm, when he was abruptly ousted by his supervisory board for his reputation for, among other things, lecturing his own executives 'like children'.

The norm in Germany was that some managers who may have been sacked under an Anglo-American regime would survive because they were adept at playing consensus politics with the supervisory boards, including Jurgen Schrempp, head of loss-making DaimlerChrysler. But, according to the article, if the Mannesmann trial led to a more widespread adoption of Anglo-American management governance practices in Germany, it should also highlight the need to govern well, since 'the supervisory board of Mannesmann has been revealed as "Germanically" sloppy . . . Adding American methods to traditional German business strengths may be a better strategy.'

There is evidence that just such a trend has begun to take root in German companies (Hilger, 2008). To fend off the US challenge, German companies began to adopt US style management practices and, to an extent, corporate governance practices, as a way of catching up. So is this a case of convergence around the American Business Model?

Sources: adapted from *The Economist*, 3 April 2004, and Hilger, 2008.

organizations in those countries that copy them or are subject to their influence. For example, many multinational corporations seek to promote a corporate brand image and culture across all of their subsidiaries; this practice sometimes extends to suppliers of those subsidiary companies and to local companies that imitate their 'winning formula' (see Chapter 6). Few such MNEs exemplify the globalization thesis as well as McDonald's, the food retailing organization, which has had an enormous impact on eating habits and on business practices around the world. Until a change in strategy during the early 2000s, McDonald's, one of the world's most recognizable brands, was associated with promoting an American way of life around the globe and a one-best-way formula for fast-food retailing and for managing a franchise operation (see Case 5.2 for an example of recent changes at McDonald's).

In addition to MNEs, another important engine, as we have pointed out, has been the growth in global management education and the growth of global consulting firms in the transfer of ideas and best practices (Khurana, 2007). Sparrow *et al.* (2004) referred to this argument as the development of a 'like-minded international cadre', a class of managers whose thinking has become 'de-nationalized' as a result of attendance at international business schools that broadly followed a similar syllabus and ethos of business in their MBA programmes or internal consultancy training. Since these authors reported on the effects of global management education producing more standardized managers, the situation is likely to have become even more pronounced with the growing influence of 'triple' accreditation bodies for business schools, including the American Association of Collegiate Schools of Business (AACSB), the European Foundation for Management Development's EQUIS programme and the Association of MBAs (Wilson and McKeirnan, 2011).

Divergence, culture and institutions

Although the convergence and globalization theses have had many adherents, some writers believe that differences between national cultures and institutions have remained relatively marked and consistent over time. These writers adhere to the *divergence thesis*, which is premised on two sets of observed and relatively enduring differences among societies. The first of these differences comprises the strength of locally held *cultural values* and their impact on management practices, despite obvious and growing economic and social similarities among nations (Hofstede *et al.*, 2011). Such business-related cultural values typically include the extent to which national cultures endorse individualism and individual freedoms, the extent to which risk-taking behaviour by individuals is encouraged and rewarded, attitudes towards inequality and to competitive behaviour, conceptions of time and attitudes towards the open display of emotions (Trompenaars, 2012; Trompenaars and Hampden-Turner, 2004; Hofstede *et al.*, 2011). We look at this cultural values approach in more detail in this chapter.

The second relates to the historically embedded *institutional differences* among countries (Morgan and Whitley, 2012; Whitley, 2008). These institutions refer to the social, political, economic, business and labour market features of a country or region that have historically interacted to create a distinctive national business system. So, for example, we often talk about a distinctive American business system, Asian business systems or the Chinese diaspora (Witt and Redding, 2014).

This *national business systems approach*, which has become more influential in the management literature since the 1990s, is a broader concept than culture and has emphasized the difficulties in borrowing and diffusing best practices from overseas countries created by enduring institutional differences (Morgan *et al.*, 2010). Though competition among national business systems at the international level has led to borrowing and copying of practices, this process of diffusion does not necessarily result in convergence, because the embedding of such practices has to occur in pre-existing and nationally distinctive configurations of business practices. The consequences of this line of thinking for organizations seeking to export their values and practices are threefold: (1) they need to be aware of the historical and institutional configuration of the business system in which they seek to operate; (2) they are likely to meet with institutional resistance to such 'foreign' practices; and (3) even if companies are initially successful in implanting their home-grown practices, they can never be sure how these transferred practices will interact with the existing systems to produce anything like the originally intended outcomes. Again, we shall examine these ideas in more detail later in this chapter.

To help you understand the role of institutional constraints, read the case of Wal-Mart's entry into Germany (see Case 5.1).

CASE 5.1 **WAL-MART AND OVERSEAS EXPANSION**

Traditionally, retailers are not very good at going abroad. Wal-Mart is no exception. It has done well in America's border countries. It has been successful in Canada, for instance, and in Mexico, where Wal-Mart is the biggest private employer.

But, in Germany, Wal-Mart ended up with egg on its face. Wal-Mart entered Germany, the third biggest retail market after America and Japan, in 1997–98 by buying two local retail chains, Wertkauf and Interspar, for $1.6 billion. Whereas Wertkauf was well known and profitable, Interspar was weak and operated mostly run-down stores. Wal-Mart has lost money in Germany ever since. Problems have included price controls preventing below-cost selling, rigid labour laws and tough zoning regulations that make it extremely difficult to build big stores.

Wal-Mart also faced well-established rivals in Germany, such as Metro, and hard discounters such as Aldi and Lidl, already comfortable with razor-thin profit margins. Many retailers in Germany are owned by wealthy families, whose business priorities are not always consistent with maximizing shareholder value.

But there was more to it than that. Wal-Mart's entry was 'nothing short of a fiasco', according to the authors of a 2003 study at the University of Bremen. At first, Wal-Mart's expatriate managers suffered from a massive clash of cultures, which was not helped by their refusal to learn to speak German. The company has come to be seen as an unattractive one to work for, adds the study. In part, this is because of relatively low pay and an ultra-frugal policy on managers' business expenses.

Wal-Mart eventually pulled out of Germany in 2006, with losses estimated by analysts at $200–300 billion per annum. The company also had problems in Japan, because of a failure to understand different consumer preferences and the preferred retail environment, and problems in gaining access to existing powerful supply chain networks. It has been claimed that Japanese consumers preferred to buy more frequently in smaller quantities and tend to equate high quality with high prices. Moreover, it persuaded Seiyu, its partner in Japan, to dismiss 25 per cent of headquarters staff and managers, which was a cataclysmic decision in a country known for lifetime employment practices. Similarly, Wal-Mart had problems in South Korea because of a claimed failure to understand local consumer preferences for fresh food and for stores to be based in cities rather than the outskirts where Wal-Mart sited most of its stores. Along with the French supermarket Carrefours, it pulled out of South Korea in 2006.

This contrasts with Wal-Mart's much smoother expansion into Britain, where it bought ASDA for $10.7 billion in 1999. ASDA already had a strong business competing on price, and it has since overtaken struggling J. Sainsbury to become the second biggest supermarket chain after Tesco. But that may say more about Sainsbury's difficulties in overcoming its problems than ASDA's successes. Unlike Tesco, under its boss Sir Terry Leahy, Sainsbury was slow in responding to Wal-Mart's expected arrival in the British market. In particular, it was late in expanding into non-food goods, the source of much of Tesco's growth.

1 What institutional features of the German system have prevented Wal-Mart from making a successful entry into that country?
2 What could they have done to overcome these problems in Germany, Japan and South Korea?
3 Why do 'smart managers', such as those at Wal-Mart, seem to do 'dumb things'?

More pragmatically minded writers have argued that the convergence–divergence debate isn't particularly helpful because it casts everything in terms of 'either/or' scenarios. Instead, they make a case for 'both/and' thinking in which nation-states, industries and organizations deal with the tensions promoted by convergence and divergence in new, more appropriate ways. So, for example, nearly all MNEs seek to secure global economies of scale, to promote consistent brand images, and have employees align with a single corporate identity and set of values. At the same time, they also seek to secure the benefits of differentiating their products and services in local markets and in respecting local product and labour market circumstances by developing locally relevant practices. For these reasons, we have witnessed the development of 'think global and act local' policies by some MNEs, sometimes referred to as 'glocalization' (Martin and Hetrick, 2010) (see Case 5.2 on McDonald's in Europe).

It is argued by some writers that such a glocalization orientation is possible if organizations make a distinction between business *principles* and *practices*. Principles and values that many large MNEs espouse, such as respect for individuals and trustworthiness, tend to be more general and universal in application, but local context, contingencies and firm-specific aspirations are likely to shape the practices that arise from such principles and value frameworks. In the remainder of this chapter we shall expand on the problems of cultural differences, institutions and business systems, and how managers should address these differences.

CASE 5.2 **CHANGES AT MCDONALD'S: BACK TO THE FUTURE**

McDonald's set out a new strategy in 2015 to reverse years of underwhelming results and customer loss. In an *Economist* article published in 2004, McDonald's appeared to be performing well in the USA but its European operations were not so good, except in the most unlikely country – France. The article attributed the French performance to its French CEO, Denis Hennequin, who ran McDonald's in France, and had been made head of McDonald's European operations.

Given the French love of *haute cuisine*, 'le fast food' was not expected to take off. Yet, the article claimed that 'France is the only place in Europe that has consistently loved McDonald's since the first outlet opened there in 1979.' Contrary to the popular image of the French distaste of everything American, particularly its pop culture, French families and children seemed to love McDonald's: so much so that it outperformed all its indigenous fast-food rivals and is the most profitable European subsidiary.

The answer, according to the article, lay in Hennequin's strategy for France as 'upgrading and transparency'. Put simply, restaurant décor were improved, the menu was widened and enhanced with better quality products, and relations with the difficult French unions over low pay – an often-made criticism of McDonald's – became relatively cordial.

The article also claimed that McDonald's was clever in adapting food and décor to local tastes and concentrating on children. The ham-and-cheese 'Croque McDo' was invented as McDonald's version of a *croque monsieur*, a French favourite. McDonald's teamed up with French companies to offer local fare – for instance, fruit yoghurts produced by Danone, coffee from Carte Noire and the French soft drink Orangina. McDonald's in France also sourced most of its raw material from local farmers and has used this fact to enhance its reputation as a socially responsible company – at least in French eyes.

Hennequin aimed to use the McDonald's France formula in the rest of Europe, where sales had dwindled. His innovations included a 'food studio' and a 'design studio' near Paris to research and innovate new products and interior designs for Europe's restaurants, under the supervision of a top French Michelin-star chef. One of the newest innovations was 'Salads Plus' to provide a number of healthier options to the often-criticized traditional McDonald's fare of burgers and fries. These were previously tried out in America, to stave off litigation over its contribution to American levels of obesity. McDonald's calls the new salad menu 'a strategic change in the positioning of its menu in Europe'.

In 2015, a *Time Magazine* article reported that McDonald's has experienced five years of underwhelming results and an exodus of customers due to increased competition and a 'menu that had grown bloated'. Is this a case of the more things change, the more they remain the same?

Sources: adapted from 'Burger and fries a la Francaise', *The Economist*, 17 April 2004, and 'How McDonalds plans to make a turnaround', *Time Magazine*, 4 May 2015.

NATIONAL CULTURAL VALUES

Understanding national cultural values

We have already introduced the importance of national cultural values as a key factor in explaining the relatively enduring differences among countries and their approach to business and management. This 'cultural' school, which began with the work of Hofstede in the 1960s (Hofstede *et al.*, 2011), continued with Trompenaars (Trompenaars, 2012) and has been extended by the so-called 'Globe' studies of leadership and organizational effectiveness (House *et al.*, 2004), has resulted in many cross-cultural studies, usually comparing values and practices in a range of countries to shed light on the difficulties that organizations may face in doing business outside their own territory, or to provide advice for managers on how to behave with 'foreigners'. The cultural values approach has been extremely influential in the management literature, but it is not without its critics, some of who believe the 'national cultural card' has been overplayed (Baskerville-Morley, 2005). In this section of the chapter we shall review the work of two of its most influential theorists, and point out its limitations. First, however, we should describe what culture means in an international context.

Generally, in the management literature at least, culture refers to 'systems of meanings' – values, beliefs, expectations and goals – shared by a particular group of people distinguishing them from members of other groups (Gooderham and Nordhaug, 2003, p. 131). Ed Schein, one of the founding fathers of cultural studies in management, has defined culture as:

> 'a set of basic assumptions – shared solutions to the universal problems of external adaptation (how to survive) and internal integration (how to stay together) – which have evolved over time and are handed down from one culture to another.'
>
> (Schein, 1985)

This definition is appealing for two reasons. First, it links (a) the external but universal problem that all organizations face in searching for effective strategies and ways of addressing markets and customers with (b) the internal and often unique solutions of designing effective organizations and appropriate people management practices. Second, it points to the internalized ways in which people behave and in what they believe and value. Schein usefully distinguished between different levels of culture in an organizational setting (see Figure 5.1). These distinctions can also be applied to the international context, and indicate how we might discover these behaviours, values and beliefs and the basic assumptions that underlie them.

Thus, translating Figure 5.1 into a national setting, the most visible levels of cultural artefacts might be exemplified by traditional modes of greeting each other, forms of address and title, dress codes, national symbols such as flags and buildings, etc. For example, many emerging countries seek to create buildings of national significance to reflect their aspirations to be a modern economy – the building of the Petronas Towers in Malaysia in 1998, the Clock Building in Saudi Arabia in 2011 and Burj Khalifa in Dubai in 2012 are good illustrations. Older countries also use architecture to signify something distinctive about their national identity, such as the new Scottish Parliament Building in Edinburgh, Scotland, the Guggenheim Museum in Bilbao, Spain, and the Pompidou

Centre in Paris, France. In greeting each other, Japanese business people bow to show respect; the lower one bows the more respect one is showing, usually to seniors. Titles are used quite differently in different cultures, with Germans usually insisting on the use of titles such as professor and doctor in social as well as work situations, whereas in the USA the title 'doctor' may be dropped because it has elitist connotations. In the UK such a title, used in a non-medical context, may even have negative connotations that reflect the historically low value placed on higher education beyond first degree level (though this is changing). Office architecture is another good example of artefacts that reflect values, so in Germany one is likely to find enclosed offices with official titles on the doors, whereas in the USA open-plan is quite normal (though people do attempt to personalize these spaces) (Hatch and Cunliffe, 2013).

Espoused values and beliefs in a national setting refer to the goals, norms of behaviour and everyday philosophies that guide actions in a particular country – for example, in relation to making money, displaying wealth and promoting entrepreneurship in a society. As an illustration, it is widely accepted that national cultures vary in their beliefs and values about the criteria for success, with America well known for its business culture that promotes the 'divine rights' of shareholders, risk-taking behaviour, materialism and open displays of wealth. In other countries such beliefs and values would be anathema, with the Japanese valuing customer service, market share and obligations to colleagues, Swedes valuing the rights to be consulted, job security and social benefits, and the Germans (and Swedes) valuing product quality. German managers in manufacturing industry will often place the high-quality design and reliability of their products over shareholder interests or

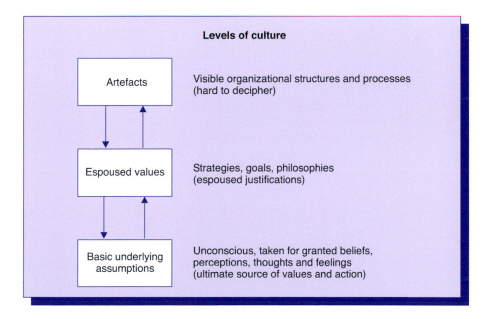

FIGURE 5.1 Different levels of culture
(*Source:* adapted from Schein, 1985.)

customer satisfaction; engineering, producing and selling are functions valued much more highly than marketing or finance. In France, the beliefs and values in technological leadership are paramount, with a high premium placed on engineering and science degrees, in sharp contrast to the UK, where engineering has enjoyed low status for many years.

At the deepest level, basic underlying assumptions refer to the unconscious, taken-for-granted beliefs, perceptions, thoughts and feelings that shape values and guide actions. Schneider *et al.* (2014) have organized this idea of basic assumptions into three overlapping domains (see Figure 5.2). Two of these we have already discussed – how different cultures manage relationships with the environment (external adaptation) and how different cultures manage relationships with people (internal integration). The third domain is a set of linking assumptions on how different societies regard time, space and language.

It is worth setting these assumptions out in a little more detail.

Environmental assumptions

Societies differ according to beliefs in their ability to *control nature*. So, for example, the notion of management implies control over nature, even though some economists argue that managers and

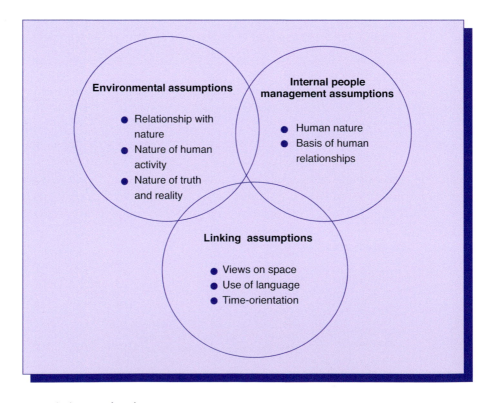

FIGURE 5.2 Underlying cultural assumptions
(*Source*: based on Schneider *et al.*, 2014.)

management can exercise little such control in reality (since, according to one school of thought at least, it is markets and competition that shape economic activity, not managers). However, most Americans believe in the ability of managers to shape their destiny, so leadership has become a major preoccupation in US business teaching and practice. In contrast, fate or destiny is seen by Islamic cultures to be predetermined, so that assumptions regarding the power of leadership to shape the future, especially leadership of a secular kind, are limited. The burial in 2005 of the King of Saudi Arabia in a modest grave illustrates this point. Linked to this belief in fate are beliefs in the power of *human activity*. So, for example, beliefs in control over the environment go hand in hand with taking action and making decisions – to act one's way into thinking as Karl Weick (2001) insightfully put it.

It is also linked to the idea that achievement is a result of what a manager accomplishes. Contrast this 'American Dream' with societies that believe more in predetermined destiny. Such is the case of French managers, who value reflection, analytical thinking and planning – 'thinking their way into action' – and in 'being', which reflects the quality of their education and who they are rather than what they do. Finally, societies differ according to their assumptions about *truth and reality*. Anglo-Saxon cultures place emphasis on facts and science, whereas Asian, Latin European and Latin American cultures are more likely to assume that truth(s) can be uncovered by intuition, feelings and spiritual means – for example, by astrology, graphology or fortune-telling in Brazil, France and China respectively (Schneider *et al.*, 2014).

Internal people management assumptions

Societies differ according to their views of *human nature*, with some believing in the virtuous side of people (mainly those of a Protestant persuasion) and their ability to do 'God's work' on earth by achieving material wealth through hard work. This argument has been used to explain why the UK, USA and Germany were the first countries to industrialize compared with the mainly Catholic countries like France and Spain. In these latter countries, there was (and is) a greater expectation of people sinning, repenting and being forgiven by spiritual means, rather than earning forgiveness through secular hard work (Anthony, 1977; Weber, 1930). Societies also differ in their assumptions regarding the relationships of people to tasks or to people. In the USA, a task orientation is pre-eminent, and 'getting things done' and 'strictly business' are guiding principles. Contrast this with the more relationship-oriented Latin cultures in which business cannot be done effectively unless strong personal relations are established between people. Associated with these ideas about task and relationship orientations are the assumptions about taking care of people in business. In 'feminine' societies (see Hofstede below), there is an assumption that the role of business is, in part, to improve the quality of life and nurture relationships, whereas 'masculine' cultures assume that competition, assertiveness and winning are important. Finally, societies differ in their assumptions regarding the importance of hierarchy in structuring relationships between people. In France, hierarchy and the power of the senior individual manager are enshrined in law, business practice and the higher education system, whereas in northern European countries, such as Sweden and Denmark, hierarchy is played down to a much greater degree.

Linking assumptions on space, language and time

Societies differ in their assumptions about *space*, which are expressed in the areas of architecture, personal space and public–private space. For example, North Americans, probably because land is plentiful and available, place a great deal of emphasis on privacy and on geographic and professional mobility. In Japan and countries such as Hong Kong, where space is limited, assumptions regarding privacy and mobility are somewhat different.

DEFINITION Language

Language is another, and critically important, linking assumption, because it helps us shape our thoughts as well as express them. So, for example, it is often claimed that Inuits who live in snowy climates have many different words to express snow, which help them 'see' different kinds of snow and convey their meanings to others. In 'high-context' cultures, communications between people are highly dependent on the person and the situation, so a great deal can be communicated by what is not said and how it is said, such as in Japan. In 'low-context' cultures, the assumptions are that language and communications are means of expressing precisely what is meant, regardless of who is doing the saying and the nature of the situation. Such is the case in the USA, where short, to-the-point, written and oral communications are the norm. It is in such a society that PowerPoint slides have become the basis of classroom presentations, the bullet-point nature of which tend to exasperate and bore managers in the UK and continental Europe ('death by PowerPoint').

Finally, different cultures have quite different conceptions of time. The usual distinction is made between *monochronic and polychronic conceptions of time.* In Anglo-Saxon and northern European cultures time is seen as a limited commodity and the clock as a crucial device in educating people about the value of time. Arguably, Anglo-Saxon capitalism could never have developed without the invention of the clock and synchronous time. Time tends to be thought of in a linear sequence, with strict scheduling, clocking-in and time management features of such societies. Being 'on time' is an extremely important signifier of efficiency and in your respect of other people's limited time – the more important the person you are to meet, the more likely you are to be 'on time'. This contrasts with cultures in which time is seen as expandable to accommodate different activities concurrently. For example, in Latin and Middle Eastern cultures, engaging in several activities at the same time, without bothering too much about punctuality, would be the normal way of working, as we have discovered to our frustration, when working in Cyprus, Greece and Saudi Arabia. Assumptions also vary in relation to the importance of past, present and future time, with older cultures such as the UK revering their past and tradition, whereas the Americans look to the future (Schneider *et al.*, 2014).

Classifying national cultures according to fundamental dimensions such as values and beliefs has been of great importance to practitioners, if only to explain the notion of cultural distance. This

---

BOX 5.2 Cultural assumptions and education

One good example of a basic national assumption over which societies differ is the belief in education as a way of advancement. In Chinese societies, learning and education are held in high regard, both as an end in themselves and as ways of advancement. Consequently, Chinese families are willing to sacrifice a lot for the education of their children, and educationalists, especially top-level university scholars, are held in great esteem (Zhang and Martin, 2003). By contrast, education in England (as distinct from Scotland), at least historically, was not believed to be of such great value in defining who a person was and, consequently, as a way of advancing themselves in society (Weiner, 2004). This rather negative view of education as a way of getting on applied most notably to vocational education, such as engineering and, more recently, business studies (which began in earnest only in the 1960s in the UK compared with the late 1880s in the USA). Thus, vocationally based higher education in the English universities and the academics who work in vocational subjects have not been held in high regard by the academic community or by the general public at large in rankings of social esteem. It is these underlying assumptions that are the most pervasive aspects of national culture but which are the most difficult to surface and most resistant to change. Such is the legacy of the 'English disease' and its assumptions and attitudes to vocational education that nearly all governments since the 1960s have been forced to bring in one programme or another to generate interest in vocational subjects and vocational careers in areas such as engineering or, more recently, entrepreneurial activity (Wolf, 2002).

---

concept is self-explanatory, and refers to the distance between one national culture and another in terms of values, beliefs and deep-rooted assumptions. Thus, for example, the UK and USA share a common history, certain religious beliefs, language and legal system, and it should come as no surprise that the dimensions on which these countries are deemed to differ reveal very little cultural distance. The writers most associated with explaining national cultures according to key dimensions are the Dutchman Geert Hofstede and the Anglo-Dutch cooperation between Fons Trompenaars and Charles Hampden-Turner.

Hofstede and cultural values

Geert Hofstede began his work in 1967 on a large research project into national culture differences across subsidiaries of IBM, the computing MNE, in 64 countries. According to Hofstede, this original work and the follow-up studies by him and his colleagues have identified and validated five independent dimensions of national culture differences (see Box 5.3).

His extensive research and further replication studies by other people showed countries differ significantly along these dimensions, the ranking of which can be seen in Table 5.2.

Hofstede found that power distance scores tend to be high for Latin, Asian and African countries and smaller for Germanic countries. Individualism prevails in developed and Western countries,

BOX 5.3 **Hofstede's cultural values**

Power distance

High- and low-power distance refers to the extent to which the less powerful members of organizations and institutions such as the family accept and expect that power is distributed unequally. This bottom-up view suggests that a society's level of inequality is endorsed by the followers as much as by the leaders. Power and inequality, according to Hofstede, are fundamental facts of any society, and experience of living in different societies will lead anyone to the conclusion that all societies are unequal, but some are more unequal than others.

Individualism

This dimension is defined in contrast to *collectivism* and refers to the degree to which individuals are integrated into groups. In individualist societies the ties between individuals are loose: individuals are expected to look after themselves and their immediate family. In collectivist societies people from birth onwards are integrated into strong, cohesive groups, more often than not in extended families, which provide protection and a level of identity in exchange for unquestioning loyalty. Notions of the American and Sicilian Mafia come to mind here. It should be noted that Hofstede did not intend the notion of collectivism to have a political meaning, such as occurred in the old USSR. It refers to the group, not to an official state ideology.

Masculinity and femininity

Hofstede attracted much criticism for his use of terms here, especially from writers concerned with gender studies. However, he claims that he has been misunderstood or misinterpreted. His argument was that different societies distribute roles between the genders in different ways. His IBM studies revealed that: (a) women's values differ less among societies than men's values; (b) men's values from one country to another contain a dimension from very assertive and competitive (and very different from women's values in a country) to modest and caring (and similar to women's values in that country). The assertive pole he called 'masculine' and the modest, caring pole 'feminine'. The women in feminine countries he described as having the same modest, caring values as the men; in the masculine countries they are somewhat assertive and competitive, but not as much as the men, so that these countries show a gap between men's values and women's values.

Uncertainty avoidance

This refers to a society's tolerance for uncertainty and ambiguity and how it deals with these issues. According to Hofstede, it refers ultimately to a society's search for and belief in a universal truth, and indicates the extent to which a country's culture mentally programmes its members to feel comfortable in unstructured situations. Unstructured situations refer to new and perhaps surprising ones, different from those usually experienced. Uncertainty-avoiding cultures try to minimize the possibility of such situations by imposing laws and rules, safety and security measures, and at the philosophical and religious level by a belief in absolute truth. People in uncertainty-avoiding countries also tend to show more emotions in everyday interactions. By contrast, uncertainty-accepting cultures tend to be more tolerant of different opinions and new ideas, have fewer rules and value rule-makers less, and on the philosophical and religious level they are more relativist in their views (see Chapter 1). People within these cultures are more matter-of-fact and tend not to express emotions openly.

Long-term versus short-term orientation

This fifth dimension was brought to public notice by one of Hofstede's colleagues, Michael Bond, in a study among students in 23 countries around the world, using a questionnaire designed by Chinese scholars. Values associated with long-term orientation are thrift and perseverance; values associated with short-term orientation are respect for tradition, fulfilling social obligations and protecting one's 'face'. Both the positively and the negatively rated values of this dimension are found in the teachings of Confucius, the influential Chinese philosopher who lived around 2500 years ago. However, the dimension also applies to countries without a Confucian heritage.

TABLE 5.2 Country rankings according to Hofstede's values

Country	Power distance	Individualism	Uncertainty avoidance	Masculinity	Long-term orientation
Arab countries	80	38	68	53	
Argentina	49	46	86	56	
Australia	36	90	51	61	31
Austria	11	55	70	79	
Belgium	65	75	94	54	
Brazil	69	38	76	49	65
Canada	39	80	48	52	23
Chile	63	23	86	28	
China, mainland	No data available	118			
Colombia	67	13	80	64	
Costa Rica	35	15	86	21	
Denmark	18	74	23	16	
East Africa	64	27	52	41	

continued . . .

TABLE 5.2 Continued

Country	Power distance	Individualism	Uncertainty avoidance	Masculinity	Long-term orientation
Ecuador	78	8	67	63	
Finland	33	63	59	26	
France	68	71	86	43	
Germany FR	35	67	65	66	31
Great Britain	35	89	35	66	25
Greece	60	35	112	57	
Guatemala	95	6	101	37	
Hong Kong	68	25	29	57	96
India	77	48	40	56	61
Indonesia	78	14	48	46	
Iran	58	41	59	43	
Ireland	28	70	35	68	
Israel	13	54	81	47	
Italy	50	76	75	70	
Jamaica	45	39	13	68	
Japan	54	46	92	95	80
Malaysia	104	26	36	50	
Mexico	81	30	82	69	
Netherlands	38	80	53	14	44
New Zealand	22	79	49	58	30
Norway	31	69	50	8	
Pakistan	55	14	70	50	
Panama	95	11	86	44	
Peru	64	16	87	42	
Philippines	94	32	44	64	19
Poland	No data available	32			
Portugal	63	27	104	31	
Salvador	66	19	94	40	

continued . . .

TABLE 5.2 Continued

Country	Power distance	Individualism	Uncertainty avoidance	Masculinity	Long-term orientation
Singapore	74	20	8	48	48
South Africa	49	65	49	63	
South Korea	60	18	85	39	75
Spain	57	51	86	42	
Sweden	31	71	29	5	33
Switzerland	34	68	58	70	
Taiwan	58	17	69	45	87
Thailand	64	20	64	34	56
Turkey	66	37	85	45	
Uruguay	61	36	100	38	
USA	40	91	46	62	29
Venezuela	81	12	76	73	
West Africa	77	20	54	46	16
Yugoslavia (former)	76	27	88	21	

whereas collectivism prevails in less developed and Eastern countries. Japan takes a middle position on this dimension. Masculinity is high in Japan, in some European countries such as Germany, Austria and Switzerland, and moderately high in Anglo countries. It is low in Nordic countries and in the Netherlands and moderately low in some Latin and Asian countries such as France, Spain and Thailand. Uncertainty avoidance scores are higher in Latin countries, in Japan and in German-speaking countries, but lower in Anglo, Nordic and in countries with a dominant Chinese culture. A long-term orientation is found mostly in East Asian countries, in particular in China, Hong Kong, Taiwan, Japan and South Korea.

These rankings allowed Hofstede to map countries on two dimensions at a time to create typologies of cultural systems or maps. Perhaps the best known is his mapping of uncertainty avoidance and power distance, which was particularly relevant in explaining the relationship between national culture and organizational structures (see Figure 5.3). Countries that were high on both power distance and uncertainty avoidance, such as France and most South American countries, tended to favour bureaucratic or mechanistic organizational structures. This grouping was labelled the *pyramid of people*. Countries that were the opposite – low on both of these dimensions, such as Denmark and Sweden and, to a lesser extent, the UK and USA – tended to favour more flexible, decentralized, organic organizations that were less bound by rules and procedures. This grouping

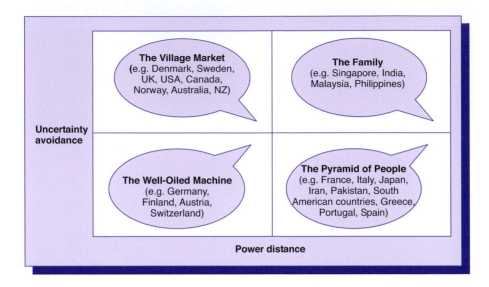

FIGURE 5.3 Hofstede's mapping of uncertainty avoidance and power distance

was called the *village market*. Countries high on uncertainty avoidance but low on power distance were called the *well-oiled machine*. These were located mainly in the Germanic region and were high on routines but low on the needs for centralized leadership. Finally, those countries high on power distance and low on uncertainty avoidance tended to be located in South East Asia and exhibited the *family like* tendencies of Chinese cultures. Organizations in these countries operate on the basis of centralized personal leadership rather than on routines and rules.

More recent research has confirmed many of Hofstede's findings (Schneider *et al.*, 2014). This research described variations in 'implicit' organizational models found in different cultures that closely resembled the pyramid of people in France, and the well-oiled machine in Germany. The UK organizations researched in the study were found to reflect the more flexible village market, with British managers more willing to fit organizations to people, rather than the other way around. Similarly, studies in Asia have confirmed the family model in the Indian, Singaporean and Hong Kong banking systems.

Trompenaars and Hampden-Turner and cultural values

Trompenaars and Hampden-Turner's (2004) work can be compared with Hofstede's approach in so far as they both used bipolar dimensions to classify cultures. However, Trompenaars and Hampden-Turner began from a different position in drawing on ideas from sociology rather than empirical studies. Subsequently, they have tested their ideas on cultural dimensions with 30,000 managers in companies across 28 countries. They have identified seven value orientations. Some of these value orientations described below are nearly identical to Hofstede's dimensions, whereas others offer different insights into culture.

- *Universalism versus particularism*. In universalist cultures there is an emphasis on formal rules and contracts regardless of circumstances. Universalist countries take contracts very seriously and employ lawyers to make sure that the contract is kept. A good example is the USA, with probably the highest rates of lawyers per capita. Particularist countries think that the relationship is more important than the contract and that a good agreement does not require a written contract; the relationship and trust between particular people and the particular situation are more important than universal rules. Particularist countries include Russia, China and India.

- *Communitarianism versus individualism*. Very similar to Hofstede's individualist/collectivist dimension, in communitarian cultures people stress allegiances to groups first and foremost, whereas in individualist cultures people stress individual freedoms, rights and effort. Alongside Israel and Denmark, the USA is regarded as an individualist culture, with China and Germany seen as communitarian cultures.

- *Neutral versus emotional*. This value dimension refers to the extent to which emotional behaviour is used freely and openly in a business situation. In a neutral culture, emotions would not be seen as acceptable in interpersonal relations. Most South American and Latin European countries would be regarded as emotional, whereas China, Japan and India would be regarded as neutral.

- *Diffuse versus specific*. A specific culture can be regarded as one in which a strong separation is made between work and private life, so that the authority relationship that exists in a work situation is not carried over into wider social life. A manager is only a manager at work and not in the social community in which he or she lives. In diffuse cultures, authority relationships carry over into the wider social situation, where formal relationships are maintained. The USA would be regarded as a specific culture, whereas China, Russia and Japan might be regarded as diffuse cultures.

- *Achievement versus ascription*. This value refers to the basis on which societies accord status to individuals. An achievement orientation is based on performance at work and through education, with the USA, UK and Denmark scoring highly on achievement. An ascription orientation allocates status on the basis of factors such as age (China), kinship (India) and gender (Japan). Other status factors also come into play, including the kind of school attended by children – private v. state (the UK).

Trompenaars and Hampden-Turner also refer to the two key dimensions of time and human nature, which we discussed in the earlier section on understanding cultures.

Of these seven value dimensions, two closely mirror the Hofstede dimensions of collectivism/individualism and, to a lesser extent, power distance. Trompenaars and Hampden-Turner's communitarianism/individualism value orientation seems to be virtually identical to Hofstede's collectivism/individualism. Their achievement/ascription value orientation, which describes how status is allocated in society, reflects Hofstede's power distance index, at least if one accepts that status is accorded by nature rather than achievement, and that this reflects a greater willingness to accept power distances. It is, however, not a complete match, as Hofstede's power index relates not only to how status is accorded, but also to the acceptable power distance within a society. Trompenaars and Hampden-Turner's other dimensions seem to focus more on some resulting effects of underlying value dimensions. For example, their neutral/emotional dimension describes the extent to which feelings are openly expressed, i.e. a behavioural aspect rather than a value in itself. Their universalism/particularism value orientation, describing a preference for rules rather than trusting relationships, could be interpreted as part of Hofstede's uncertainty avoidance dimension on the one side, and to some extent the collectivist/individualist dimension. However, their diffuse/specific value orientation, describing the range of involvement, seems to have no direct link to any of Hofstede's dimensions.

The GLOBE studies

The GLOBE studies, begun by Robert House *et al.* (2004), were an extension of Hofstede's work in showing how national cultures were both different and similar to each other. Built on an enormous body of research, this project identified nine dimensions of cultural similarity and difference in relation to norms, values and beliefs. These were:

1   Power distance – The degree to which members of a collective expect power to be distributed equally.
2   Uncertainty avoidance – The extent to which a society, organization or group relies on social norms, rules and procedures to alleviate unpredictability of future events.
3   Humane orientation – The degree to which a collective encourages and rewards individuals for being fair, altruistic, generous, caring and kind to others.
4   Institutional collectivism – The degree to which organizational and societal institutional practices encourage and reward collective distribution of resources and collective action.
5   In-group collectivism – The degree to which individuals express pride, loyalty and cohesiveness in their organizations or families.
6   Assertiveness – The degree to which individuals are assertive, confrontational and aggressive in their relationships with others.
7   Gender egalitarianism – The degree to which a collective minimizes gender inequality.
8   Future orientation – The extent to which individuals engage in future-oriented behaviours such as delaying gratification, planning and investing in the future.
9   Performance-orientation – The degree to which a collective encourages and rewards group members for performance improvement and excellence.

Based on these dimensions, the many researchers associated with this project have been able to cluster cultures, most importantly to provide the basis for showing similarities and differences in outstanding leaders. These clusters were: Germanic Europe, Anglo American, Nordic Europe, Latin America, Confucian Asian, Middle East, Eastern Europe, Latin Europe and Sub-Saharan Africa, which closely resemble a geographic description. The GLOBE researchers further identified how individuals in these clusters held implicit theories of leadership, showing how leadership is contextually embedded, eventually reducing the myriad of styles to six. A charismatic/value based style and a team-oriented style appeared to be common to nearly all cultures, while participative, humane, self-protective (procedural, status conscious) and autonomous (individualistic) styles varied in importance in the various cultural clusters identified above. So for example, English speaking Canadians viewed a participative style as very important in contributing to outstanding leadership with a self-protective style inhibiting outstanding leadership, whereas Albanians and Egyptians tended to view self-protection as important in effective leaders. These studies have been claimed to be the most rigourously researched and still attract a lot of attention in cross-cultural studies, but like all such studies they have their critics.

Problems with the cultural values approach

Hofstede's work, in particular, has been subject to a number of criticisms, which he has acknowledged in his recent writings. Five of the most important are discussed below (Baskerville-Morley, 2005), some of which also apply to Trompenaars and the GLOBE studies, though with less force.

- Hofstede generalized about the culture of national populations on the basis of a small number of questionnaire responses of one organization, IBM, in particular countries. Small-sample research is prone to error. In addition, attempting to describe national variables while undertaking research at the level of the firm is a dangerous strategy. The corporate culture of the firm is always likely to influence respondents' answers.
- Nation states are a relatively recent and often changing phenomenon, and sometimes don't have a national culture as such. Cultural differences within nation states are often as great as differences between them!
- Hofstede didn't acknowledge the variation in cultures within countries that, as noted earlier, can often be greater than the variation between countries.
- Questionnaires are not a good means of identifying deep-rooted concepts such as culture. Many academics claim that survey methods only tap the surface of culture, which can only be fully understood by more in-depth qualitative research, or by living in a culture in the way anthropologists do.
- Hofstede claimed that cultures were largely immutable.

These criticisms have sparked off a greater interest in qualitative and historical approaches to understanding national differences, including interest by Hofstede himself. We can now turn to this focus on institutions and business systems.

INSTITUTIONS AND BUSINESS SYSTEMS

A definition of business systems

Sociologists often refer to institutions in their analysis of societies, by which they typically mean the key 'pillars' of society such as the family, religion, education, the mass media, business and financial institutions, labour movements, the state and its agencies, and so on. These key institutions both shape and are shaped by national cultural beliefs, assumptions and values (Morgan *et al.*, 2010). We have already seen this process at work when describing how the cultural values concerning education in different countries have been related to business success. In addition to the national institutional framework, we also have to consider the role of supranational institutions, which include bodies such as the European Union (EU), the World Trade Organization (WTO) and the North American Free Trade Association (NAFTA). Thus, it is possible to make an analytical distinction, at least, between the more abstract notion of national culture, with its emphasis on values, assumptions and beliefs, and the more concrete notion of institutions that refer to the particular organizational forms and structures of behaviour that define a society.

In the business literature, institutional analysis has been used to describe the variety of national or regional models that provide alternative and often competing modes of operating in the global economy (Bjorkman and Gooderham, 2012). We touched on this concept in Chapter 1 when examining the sources of ideas on management. As we have suggested, competition between national systems has led to much borrowing and diffusion of practices, but these cross-border developments have not resulted in the wholesale convergence predicted by the globalization thesis. Institutionalists accept that national systems are increasingly inter-linked and interdependent, and that we are witnessing greater mutual influence among such national systems, but they also point out that the picture is of a more complex pattern of simultaneous *convergence* and *divergence* in any system (Whitley, 2008). A little like the GLOBE researchers, these institutionalist writers have introduced the concept of national (or regional) *business systems* to describe these complex patterns, now an accepted way of comparing and contrasting business and management issues in countries and regions of the world. We can get a better idea of what a business system might comprise by examining the following definition.

DEFINITION A national business system

National business systems comprise the formal interlocking institutions, structures, patterns of behaviour and norms and values that shape the markets, nature of competition and general business activity of a country (or region) in capitalist economies. These institutions include: the industrial relations system; the systems of training and education of employees and managers; the typical structure of organizations; the typical relationships among firms in the same industry; typical firms' relationships with their suppliers and customers; the nature of financial markets of a society; the conceptions of fairness and justice held by employers and labour; the structure of the state and its policies for business; and a society's idiosyncratic customs and traditions, as well as norms, moral principles, rules, laws and recipes for action.

Four elements are used to distinguish between national business systems: (1) the nature of property ownership (e.g. private, collective or state), (2) access to capital (e.g. state, capital markets, banks, etc.), (3) the degree of integration of production and product markets into local, national or international systems and (4) relations between the state and the economy.

Sources: based on Hollingsworth and Boyer, 1997, p. 2; Martin et al., 2011; Whitley, 2008.

As you can see, this definition refers to the cultural features of society, such as assumptions about fairness and justice, norms, moral principles and recipes for action, but it also highlights the specific organizational forms, relationships and systems that both reflect and give rise to these cultural features of a nation's or region's business system. Like a number of authors, we believe this wider conception of business systems and how they develop provides additional insights for practitioners, making the approach indispensable to gaining a deep understanding of how to manage in specific countries. There are at least five characteristics of a business system approach that are worth highlighting:

1   The importance of a historical perspective.
2   The systemic and enduring nature of business systems.
3   The role of critical turning points in changing systems.
4   The basis for comparing business systems.
5   The interaction of national systems with regions and industry systems.

The importance of a historical perspective

The first of these insights is the emphasis on the *historical development of business systems*, an area that psychologists interested in international comparisons and cultures have either neglected or played down. To those of us who have lived and worked in different countries, this neglect of history may seem strange, as people in everyday situations are often proud of their history when describing their countries' distinguishing achievements. For example, ask the Scots, Israelis or Greeks, all inhabitants of small countries with a tradition of educational excellence and a belief in the values of education as a way of getting on in life, what they have done for the modern world and they will point out a long list of mainly historical inventions, ideas and people that they have 'gifted' to the 'New World'. Thus, 31 US presidents have claimed Scottish descent, as well as inventors of the telephone (Alexander Graham Bell), the steam engine (James Watt), the television (John Logie Baird), and the sciences of economics (Adam Smith) and sociology (Adam Ferguson) (Herman, 2001). So, to stick with these countries for the moment, it seems inconceivable that we could understand how international firms with origins in Scotland, Israel or Greece operate abroad without some form of historical understanding of the relationships between education, innovation and export of people for which these countries were, and still are, noted.

To widen the discussion, we might ask the question: Why is it that two countries as geographically (and, in some respects, as culturally) close as the UK and Germany have developed distinctively different forms of economic organization, industrial relations and attitudes to management, particularly managing people? The answer requires an insight into the timing of industrialization in these two countries, their relationship to the development (or absence) of political parties that supported the working classes, the development of trades unions, approaches to the development of managers and the legacy of major events such as the two world wars during the twentieth century. As some researchers have pointed out, trade unionism in the UK developed prior to mass industrialization in the eighteenth and nineteenth centuries to provide support for craft-based workers, and predated, by many decades, the political party (the Labour Party) that was created to support mass working-class interests. As a consequence, the structure of trade unionism in the UK has been complex, with large numbers of unions pursuing different aims and often competing with each other for members and for pay. Historically, many of these unions have had a strong political agenda because they were formed before the Labour Party, the consequences of which, according to some commentators, served only to increase the conflict between management and labour for most of the twentieth century in Britain. Strike activity, particularly unofficial strike action by small groups of workers, became a marked feature of industrial conflict after 1945, at least in the minds of the popular press, and gave birth to the phenomenon known as the 'British disease'.

Overlaid on these political and labour factors was a traditional approach to recruiting and developing business leaders and managers in the UK (predominantly England) who were not experts in the task they were managing (witness the previously described attitudes to vocational education), but were noted more for social skills and graces, for which their education and social class backgrounds partially equipped them. It is not surprising that these 'gifted amateurs' defined their roles predominantly in terms of people management and external networking, rather than as managing through taking direct action or by managing sophisticated information flows, except in the field of accounting information (see Chapter 2). What might be more surprising, given the people-management bias of the traditional British manager, is that so much industrial conflict resulted. This can be partly explained by the historically marked differences in social class values that permeated UK management and labour. These differences exacerbated the 'arm's length' relationship created by the relative inability of managers to relate to their workers in terms of expertise or the task (Stewart *et al.*, 1994).

By contrast, much of German industry and its labour movement had to be reconstructed from scratch, following the demise of Hitler and the Nazi Party and the devastation caused by the Second World War. The German trade unions were purposely reorganized, with British help, along industrial lines, so that the competition between unions for members and pay never developed to the same extent that it did in the UK. These factors, coupled with the return to a supportive system of labour legislation that had been developed by the social democratic political party prior to the 1940s and the new capital formation associated with much of German industry, resulted in a relatively peaceful industrial relations system for many decades. This state of relatively harmonious industrial relations has provided the stability necessary for rapid German economic development since 1945, and consensus between management and labour continued to be a feature of German industry even when economic development slowed down during the late 1990s.

Overlaid on these industrial relations factors and the effects of the Second World War is the traditional German attitude to education, particularly engineering education, and the beliefs of German managers in expertise and the importance of the task. German managers are noted for not distinguishing technical work from managerial work. Management is necessary to get things done, is not 'over and above' technical work, and is best done by taking action themselves (see Chapter 2 and the well-rounded manager model), rather than necessarily working, once removed, through other people (Lawrence, 2000). Such an attitude, coupled with the much higher technical education of many German managers, meant that they were able to define their jobs less as people managers and more as experts. So, given a more harmonious context, higher level of technical capability and the greater respect from workers for this ability, it is not difficult to explain why the German business system might be very different and why British managers may have difficulty in such a system.

The systemic and enduring nature of business systems

A second feature of business systems is the *interlocking and enduring nature of business-related institutions* in any country or region over time. Often, we find that new industries, developing in a particular country or region, call for new kinds of skills and work patterns. Good examples of such developments during the latter part of the twentieth century include call centres and software

BOX 5.4 **A business history approach**

In an interview, Harvard Business School Professor Geoffrey Jones was asked what his research had told him about the success and impact of businesses around the world. He replied as follows:

'[It] shows how entrepreneurs and firms have occupied centre stage in driving the wealth of nations. It also demonstrates that there has never been a single model for successful or unsuccessful capitalism.

To give only one example, business and economic historians have often taken a sceptical view of the merits of family owned and managed firms. Harvard Business School's Alfred Chandler, the doyen of business historians, famously ascribed Britain's relative economic decline to the United States from the late nineteenth century to that country's proclivity towards family or "personal capitalism".

This was contrasted with the separation of ownership and control and the growth of professional management seen in the United States. That debate continues. But this book does report compelling research that shows that, historically, family ownership and management in many countries has been a dynamic force. Leading firms such as Michelin in France, Heineken in the Netherlands, or Cargill or Mars in the United States are the tip of a huge iceberg of successful and long-lived family firms worldwide. Even today around a third of *Fortune* 500 companies are family controlled.

It may sound a simplistic conclusion that there has never been "one best way" of achieving business success. However, this historical experience stands as a powerful corrective to over-simplistic management fads and fashions, and to slavish transfers of management systems and practices that might work well in one country but can be disastrous in another.

. . . I intended our chapter comparing British and Dutch business history to be provocative. The business historians of these two countries have frequently made comparisons with the United States, and sometimes Germany. Generations of British business historians explained their country's economic "failure" by establishing what it did "wrong" compared with US or German business. They then explained this by identifying idiosyncratic factors in Britain's development, such as the class system, or an alleged industrial "anti-industrial" bias of its social elite, or the post-1945 flirtation with socialism and extensive state intervention. We maintain that comparisons which use the United States as a benchmark can be misleading. The United States is an idiosyncratic country by virtue of its size and growth, high levels of entrepreneurial energy, legalistic culture, and a number of other unusual features.

In our work, we show that the business systems of Britain and the Netherlands shared many similarities. Both countries had an imperial and mercantile heritage. Family business stayed important. The service sector was strong. Multinational activity was extensive and persistent. The two countries even shared the ownership of two of the world's largest multinationals, Shell and Unilever. Many allegedly distinctive features of British and Dutch capitalism turn out to be part of a wider pattern for countries with shared geographical positions, cultural orientations, and historical patterns of development.'

Source: adapted from an interview with Geoffrey Jones, available online at
http://hbswk.hbs.edu/item.jhtml?id=4106andt=bizhistoryandnl=y.

development in India, electronics manufacture in Malaysia, computer and mobile phone manufacture in China, and motor vehicle manufacturing in the southern states of the USA. These new industries and the typical kinds of employment policies and practices associated with them were necessarily overlaid on the existing, dominant system of older industries and human resource management patterns. Although changes occurred in the business systems of the affected areas of India, China, Malaysia and the southern USA, these changes were constrained by previous institutional frameworks, such as the dominant patterns of worker organizations, including trade unions, legislation and patterns of business ownership (e.g. the importance of family owned firms in Malaysia and the state ownership of traditional Chinese firms). For example, foreign companies wishing to set up in China were required to form a relationship with a local partner to form a joint venture, though this requirement was relaxed as a result of legislation in 2004. Such joint ventures were governed by a system of regulations on employment practices regarding contracts, union recognition and safety that continue to reinforce the role of national and regional governments and the control of the Communist Party on economic development (Zhang and Martin, 2003). Thus, it has often been the case that the rise of new industries and associated employment practices may herald some significant changes in certain aspects of the business system, but because these changes do not fit closely with the previously dominant business institutions, the interlocking and conservative nature of these previously dominant institutional arrangements means that the existing system remains largely intact, albeit in a modified form.

Some companies have understood this problem of institutional inertia only too well when setting up new facilities overseas. For example, most Japanese car manufacturers that entered the US market during the 1980s set up their production facilities in southern locations to avoid many of the institutional constraints associated with typical US vehicle manufacturing in the northern states of the USA. Indeed, some researchers have pointed out that these Japanese firms tended to locate not in the major centres of population in these southern states but in formerly rural small towns to source employees without previously formed expectations of a manufacturing environment and without a previous history of trade union membership. Such was the case with Toyota, which set up one of its major US plants in Georgetown, Kentucky, a small town quite far removed in distance and 'mentality' from the major centres of vehicle manufacture in Michigan and neighbouring Ohio.

The role of critical turning points and changes in systems

A third feature of a business systems approach is the importance of aptly named *critical turning points* in bringing about radical change. These turning points include wars, economic crises and political upheavals. For example, Christian Caryl (2013) cited the election of Margaret Thatcher as Prime Minister in Britain, Deng Xiaoping's liberalization of the Chinese economy, Khomeini's establishment of an Islamic republic in Iran and the rise of the Mujahideen in Afghanistan, all in 1979, as the return of the market and religion with a vengeance. Such events have often revealed severe problems in previously dominant systems and resulted in transformational institutional change. The new institutional frameworks imposed, for example, following the election of Margaret Thatcher redefined the pre-existing relationship between employers and employees. As a consequence, the changes in management–employee relationships became embedded in institutional arrangements (e.g. laws, bureaucratic systems, lobbying bodies) that persisted long after the upheavals giving rise to them. Another excellent example from the USA is the New Deal era, following the critical turning point of the Great Depression in the 1930s that led to a new industrial relations framework, based on a highly codified system of collective contracts and trade union recognition, which exists to this day in the northern US states. As the inwardly investing Japanese car manufacturers attempted to point out in their location decisions, the New Deal institutional arrangement might have been appropriate during an era of mass production with an emphasis on a standard and limited product range and cost containment, but was not suited to their novel 'lean production' strategy of providing high levels of quality, a wider product range and even lower costs.

A more complex basis for comparing and contrasting international business systems

A fourth feature of the business systems approach is to allow comparisons of different national systems on a more complex range of key dimensions and, at the same time, to reveal their unique nature. These key dimensions for comparison cover major institutional arrangement such as the nature of product, labour and capital markets, the organization of firms, the role of the state, systems of vocational education and training, and industrial relations. However, the unique character of any one system is guaranteed by the particular configuration of what dimensions are important and their interaction over time. In the example of the development of the US business system below, the timing or 'path dependence' of each of the key features of the system means that the US business system is unique (Jones, 2003), even though we can use most of these dimensions to compare it with other capitalist systems (see Box 5.5).

BOX 5.5 **Business systems analysis and the USA**

Work by Davis (2009), Ferner (2001), Mayer (2013) and Khurana (2007) show how different aspects on the American business system can be analysed using an institutionalist approach and how the features of this system affect managers of US multinationals managing overseas and recent developments in the global economy such as the Global Financial Crisis of 2007–8. For example, Ferner identified eight key components of the US business system that help to compare and contrast it with other national systems, and provide an explanation of current events:

- the development and nature of firms and product markets;
- the development and role of the state and interest associations;
- the development and nature of financial markets;
- the development and nature of labour markets;
- the developing relationship between capital and labour;
- the nature of work organization, the education and training system, and skills;

- the nature of management;
- the development and organization of the HR function.

Firms and product markets

There were a number of key features of the ways in which US firms have developed, especially in their relationships with product markets:

1 The early emphasis on market competition and managerial capitalism as the main ethos in organizing economic competition and organizations, compared with the more cooperative form of market competition of Germany and the 'personal' form of capitalism that characterized the UK.
2 The early development of mass markets in the rapidly growing US, mass marketing techniques, such as the development of catalogue retailing and large stores, and the rise of multidivisional organizational structures associated with companies such as General Motors.
3 The mass production, standardization and large-scale organizations associated with the development of the application of scientific management and the moving assembly line in motor vehicle manufacture – for example, Ford in the 1920s.
4 The early development and rise of a managerial class, functional management, including the growth of accountants and sales specialists, and the beginning of the separation of control by professional managers from the ownership of these large-scale organizations by financial institutions.
5 Early diversification overseas, including some of the earliest MNEs.

The role of the state and employers' associations

Historically set out as an argument between 'big' and 'small' government in the USA, the state has been characterized by relatively weak central government as an economic actor, with a fragmented federal/state structure. Its role has been limited to creating a favourable climate for private sector investment and providing a limited safety net for its inhabitants. There was no explicit industrial policy, in contrast to countries such as Germany, Japan, France and Singapore. The USA has embarked on brief periods of direct global intervention, (e.g. Marshal Aid and GATT in the 1940s and 1970s, and more recently through the World Bank, IMF, etc.), but has traditionally been reluctant to provide economic aid to overseas countries or to become involved in major initiatives on limiting the effects of global warming. Its relatively weak business associations and industry groups reflect the historical weakness of organized labour. The USA, more than any other country apart from the UK (Mayer, 2013), has promoted the idea of economic coordination and performance through market forces and contractual relationships rather than trust-based long-term relationships.

Financial markets

There has been a historical absence of close relationships between financial organizations and industry, with Wall Street having an arm's length relationship with corporate organizations.

In comparison to other countries, the central bank and the banking system have been historically weak and have not intervened in industry. Apart from the UK, there has been a strong market for corporate control, involving many takeovers and mergers. Corporate control has been a key method of disciplining underperforming companies. This market for corporate control, coupled with the early development of equity markets, has led to a rapid turnover of shares and charges of short-termism. The impact on long-term investment in areas such as strategy, R&D and training has been noticeable. Since the late 1970s, this system was associated with a focus on creating shareholder value as a mode of corporate governance, cost control and downsizing (Davis, 2009), which has become even more pronounced with the introduction of new players into the financing of businesses, such as hedge funds and private equity. However, the promise of extremely high rewards through 'playing' the financial markets has led to the large-scale development of new businesses and innovation.

Labour markets

Historically the US labour markets have been highly flexible, with few restraints and with labour bearing the brunt of market difficulties. It was no surprise that the idea of human resource management was born in the USA as costs to be cut rather than as people to be invested in. As a consequence, amongst developed economies, the skills are standardized and there is a relatively high proportion of low-skilled workers in comparison with countries such as Germany, France and Sweden. Traditionally, there have been highly rigid internal labour markets and career structures in organizations, with strong demarcation between groups, often based on education and qualifications. More recently, there has been a decline of organizational careers, with old-style psychological contracts offering job security becoming less important. Instead, there has been a growing importance in the idea of employability (a chance for individuals to learn new skills and make themselves more employable on the open labour market) in blue-collar and managerial labour markets. This is evident in the growth of self-employment and e-lancing discussed in the previous chapter. Historically, there have been few institutional constraints to flexible labour markets and insecurity apart from equal opportunities legislation. The consequence, according to some writers, has been a lack of incentives to invest in employees because of the short-termist orientation of firms and the system of standardized mass production (see section on work organization and skills).

The relationship between employers and labour

Traditionally, US employers have been anti-unionist, stemming from their beliefs in economic liberalism, which has also been the official ideology of the state. Both Democratic and Republican governments have provided state support for employers at the expense of labour, except during the New Deal era. Historically, labour relations have been marked by often violent and sustained anti-labour tactics, such as those employed by Ford during the 1930s. Apart from early flirtations with left-wing politics, the USA has lacked a radical labour movement that already had political rights. This was in contrast to the labour movements of many European countries. Such a system resulted in company-based bargaining and 'business' unionism. This lack of a working-class movement was also brought about because the USA has historically been a middle-class, wealthy society (even during the eighteenth century), with the Frontier and the West a useful safety valve for minorities, and with high rates of social mobility that allowed such minorities to pursue the 'American Dream'. There has been a relatively recent and increasing division between classes in terms of income since the 1950s, which has been a feature of the end of the New Deal. America is now one of the most unequal advanced capitalist societies in the world, which shows no signs in declining.

The non-union model or sophisticated paternalism

The last few decades have seen ever-declining levels of unionism coupled with resurgence of a sophisticated paternalism (human resources management) by naturally inclined, anti-union employers. This is a unitarist strategy, in marked contrast to the pluralist, New Deal strategy that governed much of labour relations before the 1970s. Such strategy has also been associated with the growth of US welfare capitalism, in contrast to European state capitalism (Davis, 2009). Employers have sought to employ 'high commitment strategies' designed to provide an alternative to unions, based on a heavy reliance on behavioural science techniques to secure compliance and commitment. Market-based pay became a guiding principle in the design of rewards systems, with a heavy emphasis on performance and shareholder value as criteria in determining pay differentials, which have widened markedly. This was accompanied by a decline of internal career progression and an increased reliance on recruitment from external labour markets and employability (employers offered high pay and the opportunity to learn, but no guarantee of employment security in return for high commitment from employees).

The system of work organization and skills

The US work organization and skills profile is a legacy of mass production and the application of Taylorism to many aspects of US industry. Historically, it has been marked by the assertion of managerial control and the relocation of manual skills into technology and management. Managers have played a major role in innovation and in leading teams, with the effect of broadening rather than deepening skills. The accompanying mass higher education system and the concern for vocational skills have been other marked features of the USA, with anti-intellectualism as a current in US society and the veneration of the 'practical' wo/man. This system has helped produce the focus on the external labour market and relatively low investment in training. Some economists have argued it has also produced a relatively inefficient use of cheap labour and lack of investment in technological innovation.

Organization of the HR function

The HR function historically has been proactive and quite well developed in its pursuit of high commitment and welfare strategies, with a growing professionalism, assisted by bodies such as the Society for Human Resource Management (SHRM). Some researchers, however, have argued that HR has remained a minor administrative function compared with finance and marketing, and with HRM in countries such as the UK. Because of the absence of legal constraints, HR has had wider latitude in developing procedures for labour relations, especially when compared with the bureaucratization and formalization of other countries, e.g. planning, testing, performance management, job evaluation, monitoring compliance, affirmative action. There are, however, systematic differences between union and non-union firms and the priority assigned to labour relations.

Different types of business system

Similar to Hofstede, business systems writers have attempted to classify different types of system according to key dimensions. Whitley's 2008 work is the most widely cited typology of business systems, in which he identified eight systems, four types of states and six types of innovation systems. The eight systems were:

1 *Fragmented systems*, which are dominated by small, highly competitive family businesses, with little overall coordination of economic activity, e.g. Hong Kong. Short-term contracts are the basis for cooperation and employment.
2 *Project networks*, which were set up to be short term, narrow in scope but were highly integrated into ownership.
3 *Coordinated industrial districts*, such as those existing in the northern Italian clothing industry. Here small firms are closely integrated across the value chain of an industrial sector and between sectors. High levels of employee commitment are the basis for innovation.
4 *Financial conglomerate*, in which holding companies operate businesses as financial investment vehicles. The UK has a high preponderance of such companies.
5 *Integrated conglomerates*, which are characterized by high levels of ownership integration and high levels of scope (e.g. the Korean Chaebol).
6 *Compartmentalized systems*, associated with the traditional joint stock countries of the USA and UK. Large firms dominate, and activity between and across sectors is highly integrated. However, cooperation and commitment between firms, partners and employees are based on contract rather than on trust.
7 *Collaborative systems*, such as those found in Germanic countries. Large alliances of inter-country collaborators, resting on interdependent relations between firms, managers and employees. Comparatively high level of trust.
8 *Highly coordinated systems*, such as those found in Japan after the Second World War. Highly coordinated system of alliances and networks between and within sectors of industry, with government sponsorship.

Another such approach is to compare the relative weight of different 'governance' mechanisms by which economic and business activity is coordinated in a country or region, and how these factors affect the management of people (Pendleton and Gospel, 2013). Traditional economic and organizational analysis has identified three such governance mechanisms:

1   *Market mechanisms*, which have emphasized the role of free markets, contracting and the price mechanism as the principal means of coordinating and controlling activities in organizations and economies during the nineteenth century and during the Thatcher–Reagan era of national economic policy, which was accompanied by large-scale deregulation of markets in the late twentieth century.

2   *Hierarchies*, which emphasized the increasing role of bureaucratic organizational structures, rules, rewards and traditional career systems during the twentieth century to govern organizations and regulate economies.

3   *Corporatist structures*, which emphasized the interlocking roles of the state, informal networks and associations. These corporatist arrangements have been especially important historically in the governance of European business systems and in Japan. The state refers to government and institutions, including government agencies. Informal networks refer to the loosely connected groups of key individuals and organizations in a business system that are influential in government–business relationships. These networks conduct their relations on the basis of mutual trust and confidence rather than on a legally enforceable basis, and are bound together by common values and/or dependence on resources (Ferner, 2001). Associations, of which employers' associations and unions are the most important examples in business systems, usually have a legal identity, and are interest groups that enforce cooperative behaviour on their members and engage in collective contracts with other associations on behalf of their members.

In an interesting application of governance mechanisms to human resource management, Gooderham *et al.* (2006) have identified four different contexts or business systems in Europe. They distinguish such systems according to two dimensions that reflect the ideas of Whitley and others. The first of these is the extent to which the state exercises a highly pervasive or limited role in labour relations. In turn this influences the extent to which organizations can exercise choice in how they manage people. Thus, organizations in the UK, USA, Denmark and Norway can exercise considerable freedom in human resource management, whereas firms in Germany, France and Spain are highly regulated, albeit in slightly different ways. The second, which maps onto the distinction between market and corporatist governance structures set out above, is the extent to which market individualist or communitarian infrastructures dominate in shaping business relations. Market individualism refers to the belief in self-interest, market forces and price as a coordinating mechanism, whereas communitarian infrastructures refer to a belief in high-trust informal networks and mutually obligated associations as the most effective form of shaping business relations. These writers contrast the UK and USA particularly as having a pervasive and strong market mentality that inherently leads to low-trust relations and limited cooperation between managers and their employees with countries such as Germany, Norway and Denmark, in which firms are embedded in communitarian obligations and relatively high trust relations. Figure 5.4 compares and contrasts European countries along these two dimensions.

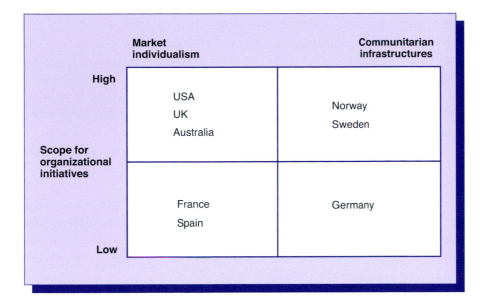

FIGURE 5.4 Comparing key countries' governance structures

(*Source*: adapted from Gooderham and Nordhaug, 2003.)

MANAGING PEOPLE IN AN INTERNATIONAL CONTEXT

In the earlier chapters, we spent some time examining the nature of management and produced frameworks for thinking about the rounded manager. In constructing these frameworks, our desire was to make you aware that effective management had to be related to the contexts in which it was practised. We referred to inner and outer contexts and to near and far contexts in these frameworks, but only touched on the international context. This chapter has been written to provide you with a much greater insight into this increasingly important international backdrop to how cultures and institutions will affect the work of managers and their dealings with others. In this section, we need to spell out in more detail what internationalization or globalization might mean for managers in their everyday working lives. We can do this by looking at the changing views of the 'international manager' and the kinds of characteristics, biographies and competences that seem to be necessary to work well in diverse cultural and institutional contexts. We can also examine how organizations best approach the development of international managers for such changing contexts.

Lessons from the field

Most companies have first learned about the international context through the stories told by expatriate managers who may have been sent out on 'expeditionary' missions to particular countries and who have returned to tell the 'horror' or 'wonderment' tales. These tales are nearly always comparatively based, and for managers from developed countries the comparison is against their own national 'benchmark' cultures and standards of behaviour. Such benchmarking is most apparent when managers are confronted with situations that touch directly on their ethical or moral positions, such as having to deal with requests for 'bribes', or where women are treated as 'second-class' citizens. These tales reflect the problems of expatriate adjustment on international assignments (Schneider *et al.*, 2014). It has been estimated that around 30 per cent of expatriates in US multinationals fail to complete their full term overseas, with a large proportion of this rate put down to the failure of *cultural adjustment*.

This process of cultural adjustment to foreign countries is often thought to follow three phases:

1   The *honeymoon*, characterized by positive feelings and optimism.
2   The *morning after*, which is a period when the charm wears off and when interpersonal and/or work experiences become unsettling or annoying. This is the phase that creates most difficulty for expatriates and can result in serious problems. Although these problems are more likely to occur as a result of a number of minor events or situations, the term 'culture shock' is used to describe feelings associated with this phase.
3   *Happily ever after*, when expatriates have become gradually adjusted to the new culture.

These phases are not universal, because expatriates have different family circumstances, prior experiences and motivations, and are placed in different work situations. Moreover, the culture shock of moving between countries is usually related to the cultural and institutional distance between them. It should come as no great surprise that US MNEs invested more heavily in the UK than in any other European country following 1945, in part because of this lack of cultural and institutional distance.

Research has shown that adjustment evolves when expatriates acquire greater knowledge of the local culture and language, and through positive work and social relations with local employees and people outside work. Stereotyping tends to diminish, and there is a greater likelihood of shared understandings and similarities. However, if work or social experiences are negative, then these tend to reinforce previously held views and make adjustment more difficult. Moreover, expatriate managers often have to resolve the dilemma of usually having formal responsibility over locals, but not having the local 'knowledge' or resources to get things done. As a consequence, they run the risk of managing at a distance, through information or through different layers of hierarchy. As we have already seen, this is inconsistent with the model of the well-rounded manager, which requires people to manage directly through action, at least on certain occasions.

International management competences

So, what is required to become a highly effective international manager, and how does this affect our model of the well-rounded manager? Again, we have to consider the contexts of such work as set out in our model of the well-rounded manager in Chapter 2. These contexts include the agenda of the work, managing on the inside and managing on the outside. In this connection, international managers have to interact with major sets of stakeholders, including:

1   *Owners*, who are mainly interested in short- and long-term returns for their investment, and are often focused on financial and cost control.

2   *Executive managers*, who are often interested in company growth and sometimes idiosyncratic issues that enhance their personal reputation and career prospects.

3   *Customers and suppliers*, whose interests lie in product/service quality, design, costs, availability and so on.

4   *Regulators and governments*, whose interests lie in compliance with legal, socio-cultural and environmental norms.

5   *Employees*, whose interests lie in being treated with respect and in having interesting and rewarding jobs and long-term careers.

6   *The general public*, who are interested in the long-term sustainability of the company and its impact on the environment.

Such a focus on these stakeholders reminds us that managing in an international context often involves managing multiple and conflicting agendas, which are set by a wide variety of stakeholders, and that successful management is as much about managing on the outside as managing inside. It concerns managing one's own career, which is increasingly becoming defined as 'boundaryless', involving less hierarchical progression within a single organization, and more national and lateral movement within and across organizational and national boundaries (and even outside organizations themselves, as people increasingly work for themselves or take career breaks) (see Chapter 3). Such career patterns are associated with changes in the willingness of organizations to guarantee secure employment, and with employees' changing career orientations, away from security to concerns with lifestyle, excitement and psychological growth (Sullivan and Arthur, 2006). According to Schein (1990), this concern for managing one's own career involves managing an 'external' career, which is concerned with objective notions of advancement upwards and between organizations, and managing the 'internal' career, which involves dealing with subjective issues such as 'Where am I going in life?' and 'What kind of person do I want to be?'

The evidence suggests that having an international career doesn't always lead to objective notions of advancement, because it will often take an individual away from the centres of key political decision-making. It comes as no surprise, then, that most lists of competences for such a career highlight the need for even greater emotional intelligence than may be conventionally inferred from our well-rounded manager model, and will include the *motivation to live overseas*, *cultural empathy* and *linguistic abilities* (see Table 5.3).

In addition to expatriate managerial competences, which refer to what is required to work in another culture, international managers are increasingly required to work across many cultures and institutional contexts simultaneously. These situations also require managers to work across levels simultaneously. Often, this means managing a project in one situation, but being a team member in another situation. This situation requires a further set of competences (see Table 5.4).

Schneider *et al.* (2014) summarize these lists of competences for being able to manage internationally at home as having a *global mindset*. This meta-competence, or umbrella concept, refers to the ability of managers to think simultaneously about integration (global or corporate issues) and differentiation (local cultural or subsidiary issues), and to understand how such answers to specific

TABLE 5.3 Competences for managing abroad

Interpersonal effectiveness	Usually seen as the key competence, this refers to the ability of managers to form relationships by building trust and getting along with others. The values of consensus and cooperation are important in developing such competences
Linguistic ability	Often, this means developing a feel for what language is important to others in a symbolic sense, and in being able to use this effectively in conversations, rather than complete mastery of a language in a technical sense
Cultural curiosity and the motivation to live abroad	Cultural curiosity of managers and families is based on genuine interest in other cultures and experiences
Tolerance and dealing with ambiguity	Recognizing that uncertainty and ambiguity is a normal state of affairs and that flexibility and multiple mindsets are necessary
Patience and respect	Again, these map onto the emotional intelligences of self-regulation (self-control) and empathy, but are even more important in an international context
Cultural empathy	Linked to the above, cultural empathy implies understanding the needs and cultural values of others without being judgemental
Strong sense of self-awareness	Another form of emotional intelligence that refers to being in tune with your emotions and recognition that negative emotions, such as insecurity and a lack of self-identity, can hinder work performance
Sense of humour	A key social skill, which acts as a coping mechanism to help gain a sense of perspective and as a relationship-building skill

Source: adapted from Schneider et al., 2014.

problems of internationalization may change over time. Returning to our discussion of multiple perspectives in earlier chapters, having a global mindset implies being able to work with competing ideas at the same time – in being open-minded rather than believing in a one-best-way. Above all, it implies a learning culture: which leads us nicely into a discussion of how we should develop managers for international roles.

DEVELOPING INTERNATIONAL MANAGERS

The problems of developing international managers

Let's begin with a short case in Box 5.6 that gets to the heart of some of the problems of developing managers for an international role, either at home or abroad.

BOX 5.6 **The problems of educating managers for international business**

An old study by Reiss and Ones (1995) is still highly relevant in showing the unforeseen consequences of educating managers for international assignments. The study reported on attempts to internationalize US undergraduate and graduate courses by including substantial information about the global environment and cross-cultural differences in a business context may have backfired! The headline findings were that:

- Ethnocentric attitudes, as measured by standard questionnaire studies, increased during the period of the course.
- Most significant increase in ethnocentrism occurred when taught by US faculty members.
- 'International' faculty members, who had been recruited specifically to provide an international perspective, were associated with neither an increase nor a decrease of the subsequent ethnocentrism of these students.

This study showed that the conventional solution of education and training may not produce the intended outcomes: developing a global mindset or 'thinking global and acting local' is not an easy skill to develop, because of the paradoxical and ambiguous nature of the problem. It requires us to link abstract issues such as global competition and outlook with concrete issues of 'place' and local identity. Moreover, as we noted in the criticisms of Hofstede earlier in this chapter, acting local usually assumes some kind of semi-fixed national cultural unity, itself a problematic concept. For example, can India, China or Malaysia really be characterized as one culture, given the various historical ethnic, religious and class divisions, despite political attempts to forge national identities. And can we reasonably talk of a British national culture, without offending the Scots, Irish and Welsh? Clearly not in the case of Scotland, which, at the time of writing, is as far apart from the rest of the UK in terms of the identity of its people and its politics than at any time in the history of the Union between Scotland and England.

Instead, in addressing this question, it is usually more useful to think in terms of the two options available to companies wishing to internationalize their managers that mirror the cooperation–initiative discussion raised in Chapter 4. The first is the *integration solution*, which focuses on creating cooperation through standardized structures, systems, processes and, especially, development and training opportunities, so that a strong corporate culture becomes the main point of reference for managers. Good examples of this integration approach include systems of managerial control, including ABB, the well-known Swiss–Swedish MNE, 'seven-ups' benchmarking system and the role played by their international management development conferences in diffusing benchmarking, and the role played by corporate universities such as Motorola in standardizing the education of managers across their various subsidiaries in different countries. The second is the *differentiation solution*, which focuses on preserving variations in international cultures and institutions that are deemed necessary for local identity and initiatives and encouraging diversity among managers.

TABLE 5.4 Competences for managing internationally at home

Understanding interdependencies	Usually seen as the ability to manage complex and interlocking systems that cut across hierarchy in organizational situations. This often means taking the lead in one situation and being a member in another
Responding to multiple cultures simultaneously	The ability to learn about multiple cultures and work with them simultaneously, which means dealing with people who are often different from each other as well as from yourself
Recognizing cultural differences 'at home'	Cultural curiosity of managers and families is based on the genuine interest in other cultures and experiences
Being willing to share power and learn from others	Recognizing that boss–subordinate relations are inappropriate in modern management situations, especially given increased educational levels and importance of subsidiaries in MNE performance. This is associated with the acceptance of the reverse diffusion of ideas and practice
Thinking and acting with 'local worldwide' mindset	The ability to understand and work with the needs of companies to differentiate by thinking local while integrating by thinking global simultaneously
Adopt a 'culture-general' approach	This means understanding the dimensions along which cultures are likely to differ, rather than having a specific understanding of one culture
Rapidly learning and unlearning	The constant challenging of old assumptions and ways of doing things, and trying out of new ideas and approaches – sometimes referred to as double-loop continuous learning

Source: adapted from Schneider et al., 2014.

One way of thinking about this problem is to use the classic distinction made by Perlmutter (1969), whose work we adapted to discuss approaches to international staffing and deployment (Martin and Hetrick, 2010). Figure 5.5 draws on these integration–differentiation dimensions:

- *Ethnocentric* approaches are characterized by organizations with little interest either in developing a strong corporate culture across subsidiaries/markets or in establishing a strong local identity. Often, they have a strong belief in the virtues of their own culture and institutions, and seek to export them overseas. The approach to staffing, deployment and development is focused on head office interests and its predominant needs to maintain financial control. 'Exporting' home managers to run local subsidiaries with little or no thought given to the role and training of local managers is the usual approach to management 'development'. They may even see educating local managers as a dangerous strategy (too much knowledge!). This approach resonates with political or economic colonial/imperialist styles of management.
- *Polycentric* approaches are characterized by firms that have little knowledge of local product and/or labour markets, or which believe in the importance of differentiation above all else. Such

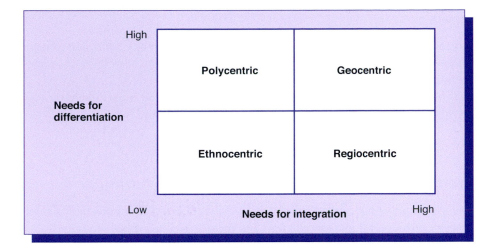

an approach is evident in the hiring of local managers, developing them locally and in 'letting them get on with the job' with minimal interference.

• *Geocentric* approaches are characterized by a belief that nationality has no place in modern business and that home office 'imperialism' is bad for business because it promotes monocultures and inhibits change. High needs for integration and differentiation are thought to be reconcilable, but such organizations are relatively rare. They believe in recruiting managers from inside or outside the company, regardless of nationality, and in developing them to have a global mindset through education in international (academic and/or corporate) business schools and through frequent assignments in different countries.

• *Regiocentric* approaches are characterized by a strong emphasis on regional integration, such as having a strong regional brand, or regional corporate culture that reflects product and/or labour market features. Japanese firms setting up in Europe are good examples. Managers tend to be recruited from the home office, deployed in a particular region and educated into a regional mindset.

It is important to note that no one solution is advocated as the best in all circumstances, although there is the implication in this kind of theorizing that the geocentric approach is the most progressive. Even the ethnocentric approach has advantages and still dominates the HR strategies of many internationalizing organizations. It also has some historical justification, as it was the basis of the British Empire's strategy for most of its 200-year dominance of world affairs (although there were periods and places when Britain pursued a more polycentric strategy). It has also been a strategy employed by many US MNEs as part of the USA's 'economic imperialism' at various points in recent history and in certain regional contexts.

EXERCISE 5.1

1 Think about the outcomes of the international management education programmes discussed earlier. Why should students have become more and not less ethnocentric during their international management courses?
2 What are the difficulties that organizations face in developing a geocentric strategy?

Management development for international managers

Developing international managers involves devising a set of policies and practices aligned with the needs of the organization for managerial talent and the needs of individual managers for continuous professional development (Harzing and Pinnington, 2014). Such a process has to be set in the external and internal contexts of an international organization. The critical factors which make management development in an international context different from developing managers for the domestic environment are: (i) the competences needed to reduce the liability of foreignness, as discussed above; (ii) the need for an international organization to create and transfer learning among its subunits for competitive reasons, often through the transfer or expatriation of managers to subsidiaries; and (iii) the embeddedness of managers in the institutions and educational systems of their own countries.

With regard to the last of these three factors, it is quite clear that management development in international companies is strongly influenced by the institutions of their home countries. It is instructive to see how countries differ in their typical approaches, and these differences raise questions about the roles of managers and about management education. For example, comparing systems of management development in the USA, France, Germany, Japan and the UK, we get quite different views on the roles of managers and management education, as we have already seen in some of our illustrations. Although there is a growing convergence in that all of these countries seem to require some form of self-development beyond their initial education, graduate education, based on the MBA model, is becoming more important in the UK, Germany, Japan and France. On-the-job development in Germany, Japan and, probably to a lesser degree, in the UK and France is more planned than in the USA (Thomson *et al.*, 2001). The UK is relatively unique in managers having low status compared with other occupational groups, traditionally a reflection of the low levels of qualifications of many managers. However, management education in Britain has improved markedly over the last two decades, in part because of systematic attempts to develop standards for management and leadership through the Management Standards Centre, established in 2000. Attempts to draw comparisons in a few paragraphs are difficult, but Table 5.5 highlights some of the important characteristics of national systems of management development, based on key features of national business systems.

The main point of this comparison of approaches to developing managers is, once again, to reinforce the idea that there is no one best way, though certain trends are observable. As we noted in Chapter 2, Henry Mintzberg (2004) is highly critical of management development that is not related to practice and context, and many of the more effective approaches to developing

TABLE 5.5 Differences among national systems of management development

	US	France	Germany	Japan	UK
Status/role of managers in society	High recognition and increasing	High recognition, the 'cadre' mentality	Medium but increasing	High status and elitist	Medium status. Gifted amateur model
Nature of labour market	Externally focused, decline of internal labour markets	Limited managerial mobility, except at top	Limited mobility, strong internal labour markets	Limited mobility but increasing. Strong internal labour markets	Changing from internal to external focus
Focus on 'off-the-job'/role of education	MBA as a screening device. Often criticized for lack of application	'Grandes Ecoles' (major universities) act as screening device. Seen as too intellectual	Middle status vocational schools providing Diplom Kaufmann. PhD for senior managers	Almost no graduate degrees in business. Undergraduate degrees as screening device	Part-time MBA increasing. Professional qualifications also important
Focus 'on-the-job' development	Little emphasis. Rise of 'corporate universities' with strong emphasis on education	Considerable proportion of wage bill spent on management development, for middle/lower managers	Strong apprentice-ship system with job rotation	Integrated career structure, planned learning and mentoring, multifunctional approach	Relatively unplanned but improving. Development of corporate universities with focus on experiential
Nature of education system/relationship to industry	Mass higher education. Rationalist focus of education. Unplanned 'system' of MD	Elitist and rationalist system of ESCs, linked to chambers of commerce. Planned system	Elitist universities supported by new polytechnic universities. Weak links with industry. Strong links with chambers of commerce and industry	Elitist universities, with strong focus on technology and business. No strong links with industry	Moving to mass higher education, with some universities having strong links with industry

Sources: based on Burgoyne et al., 2004; Lawrence, 2000, 2002; Thomson et al., 2001.

international managers require considerable periods of time spent in reflective practice while working in overseas countries. However, such reflection is aided by a critical understanding of where you stand, and one of the best exercises that can be undertaken off-the-job is to have managers understand how their views of others are influenced by the idiosyncratic nature of their institutional and cultural upbringing. To help you do this, we would like to end this chapter by asking you to engage in some personal reflection by attempting Exercise 5.2 for your own personal development.

EXERCISE 5.2 Personal reflection

1 Re-read Box 5.5 and then construct a brief analysis of your country's national business system, reflecting on:

- the development and nature of firms and product markets;
- the development and role of the state and interest associations;
- the development and nature of financial markets;
- the development and nature of labour markets;
- the developing relationship between capital and labour;
- the nature of work organization, the education and training system and skills;
- the nature of management;
- the cultural values, norms and standards of behaviour.

2 How does it differ from the example of the USA? And how do these differences influence how you see things at work?

(If you are from the USA, you can still benefit by choosing another country: reflect on how different its institutions and culture are from the USA and how that might affect how its people view American business practice.)

LEARNING SUMMARY

In this chapter we have examined the problems of organizations 'going international' and the implications for managers. We began by examining the notion of the liability of foreignness and the practical problems to which that concept gives rise, such as whether firms should expatriate their own home country managers or use mainly local managers in overseas operations. Decisions such as these depend on the different entry strategies used by internationalizing firms and on the experience and values of senior managers in the parent company.

They also depend on whether the parent company managers see the countries into which they are entering as convergent with or divergent from their own in terms of culture and institutional frameworks. So, in the middle section of the chapter we examined the nature of national cultural differences and applied them to the analysis of different countries and their organizational and management practices. We also examined the idea of national business systems and applied these to the analysis of Wal-Mart's entry into Germany to show how a lack of understanding of institutions, as well as culture, can seriously hamper ambitions to develop overseas markets. Indeed, one of the most practical exercises you can do as a manager charged with developing overseas markets or working overseas is to undertake an institutional and cultural analysis of the target country. It is also extremely beneficial for you to undertake a similar exercise on your own country, to understand more fully your own idiosyncratic views and to compare these with other countries. Such comparisons, however, are not without dangers, which are highlighted in Box 5.6 on 'The problems of educating managers for international business'.

The problems of educating international managers lead us into the final section on identifying key international management competences and developing managers for overseas assignments. The capability to think global and act local was a starting point for a more complex picture of competences required for managing abroad and for managing internationally at home. These competences are quite distinct, requiring managers not only to have an understanding of one country, but also to be able to work across many cultures and institutional contexts at the same time. As a consequence, there is no one best way to develop international managers, with different countries taking different routes to preparing managers for their jobs. However, there is little substitute for reflective practice while working overseas in making you a more effective international manager. These kinds of reflections are assisted by having a deep understanding of how to analyse the institutions and cultures of your own country as well as those overseas.

REVIEW QUESTIONS

1 How easy is it to think global and act local? What are the best ways of developing a global mindset?
2 Compare and contrast a national cultures approach to international management such as Hofstede's with a national business systems approach.

REFERENCES

Anthony, P. (1977) *The Ideology of Work*. London: Tavistock.

Baskerville-Morley, R. F. (2005) A research note – the unfinished business of culture. *Accounting, Organizations and Society*, 30 (4), 389–391.

Bjorkman, I. and Gooderham, P. (2012) International human resource management research and institutional theory. In: G. K. Stahl, I. Bjorkman and S. Morris (eds), *Handbook of Research in International Human Resource Management*, 2nd edn. Cheltenham, Glos: Edward Elgar, pp. 472–489.

Burgoyne, J., Hirsh, W. and Williams, W. (2004) *The Development of Management and Leadership Capability and Its Contribution to Performance: The evidence, the prospects and the research need*. Research Report RR560. Department for Education and Skills. London: HMSO.

Caryl, C. (2013) *Strange Rebels: 1979 and the birth of the 21st century*. Philadelphia, PA: Basic Books.

Davis, G. F. (2009) *Managed by Markets: How finance re-shaped America*. Oxford: Oxford University Press.

The Economist (2004) Kultur clash. 3 April.

The Economist (2004) Burgers and fries a la Francaise. 17 April.

Ferguson, N. (2003) *Empire: How Britain made the modern world*. London: Allen Lane.

Ferguson, N. (2004) *Colossus: The rise and fall of the American Empire*. London: Allen Lane.

Ferner, A. (2001) The embeddedness of US multinational companies in the US business system: implications for HR/IR. Paper available at the School of Business, De Montfort University, Leicester, UK.

Gooderham, P. and Nordhaug, O. (eds) (2003) *International Management: Cross-boundary challenges*. Oxford: Blackwell.

Gooderham, P., Nordhaug, O. and Ringdal, K. (2006) National embeddedness and calculative human resource management in US subsidiaries in Europe and Australia. *Human Relations*, 59 (11), 1491–1513.

Harzing, A.-W. and Pinnington, A. H. (2014) (eds) *International Human Resource Management*, 3rd edn. London: Sage.

Hatch, M. J. and Cunliffe, A. L. (2013) *Organization Theory: Modern, symbolic and postmodern perspectives*, 3rd edn. Oxford: Oxford University Press.

Herman, A. (2001) *How the Scots Invented the Modern World*. New York: Three Rivers Press.

Hilger, S. (2008) 'Globalisation by Americanisation': American companies and the internationalization of German industry after the second world war. *European Review of History*, 15 (4), 375–401.

Hofstede, G., Hofstede, G. J. and Minkov, M. (2011) *Cultures and Organizations – Software of the Mind: Intercultural cooperation and its importance for survival*. New York: McGraw-Hill.

Hollingsworth, J. R. and Boyer, R. (eds) (1997) *Contemporary Capitalism*. Cambridge, MA: Harvard University Press.

House, R. J., Hanges, P. J., Javidan, M., Dorfman, P. W., and Gupta, V. (eds) (2004) *Culture, Leadership and Organizations: The GLOBE study of 62 societies*. Thousand Oaks, CA: Sage.

Johanson, J. and Vahine, J.-E. (2009) The Uppsala internationalization process model revisited: from liability of foreignness to liability of outsidership. *Journal of International Business*, 40, 1411–1431.

Jones, G. (2003) Multinationals. In: F. Amatori and G. Jones (eds), *Business History Around the World*, pp. 353–371. Cambridge: Cambridge University Press.

Joynt, P. and Warner, M. (eds) (2002) *Managing Across Cultures: Issues and perspectives*, 2nd edn. London: Thomson Learning.

Khurana, R. (2007) *From Higher Aims to Hired Hands: The social transformation of American business schools and the unfulfilled promise of management as a profession*. Princeton, NJ: Princeton University Press.

Kujala, J. and Sajasalo, P. (2009) Reforming the integration-responsiveness framework: a business ethics perspective. *Journal of International Business Ethics*, 2 (1), 59–72.

Lawler, III, E.E. and Boudreau, J. W. (2015) *Global Trends in Human Resource Management: A twenty-five year analysis*. Stanford, CA: Stanford University Press.

Lawrence, P. (2000) Management development in Europe: a study in cultural contrast. In: M. Meddenhall and G. Oddou (eds), *Readings and Cases in International Human Resource Management*, 3rd edn, pp. 169–183. Cincinnati: South West College Publishing.

Lawrence, P. A. (2002) *The Change Game: How today's global trends are shaping tomorrow's companies*. London: Kogan Page.

Legnick-Hall, M. L. and Legnick-Hall, C. A. (2012) IHRM and social network/social capital theory. In: G. K. Stahl, I. Bjorkman and S. Morris (eds), *Handbook of Research in International Human Resource Management*, 2nd edn. Cheltenham: Edward Elgar, pp. 490–508.

Martin, G. and Hetrick, S. (2010) Employer branding and corporate reputations in an international context. In: P. S. Sparrow (ed.), *Handbook on International Human Resource Management*. Sussex: John Wiley, pp. 293–321.

Martin, G., Gollan, P. S. and Grigg, K. (2011) Is there a bigger and better future for employer branding: facing up to innovation, corporate reputations and wicked problems in SHRM. *International Journal of Human Resource Management*, 22 (17), 3618–3637.

Mayer, C. (2013) *Firm Commitment: Why the corporation is failing us and how to restore trust in it*. Oxford: Oxford University Press.

Mendenhall, M., Oddou, G. and Stahl, G. (eds) (2007) *Readings and Cases in International Human Resource Management*, 5th edn. Cincinnati: South West College Publishing.

Mintzberg, H. (2004) *Managers not MBAs: A hard look at the soft practice of managing and management development*. Harlow, UK: Pearson Education/Financial Times.

Morgan, G., Campbell, J., Crouch, C., Pedersen, O. and Whitley, R. (eds) (2010) *The Oxford Handbook of Comparative Institutional Analysis*. Oxford: Oxford University Press.

Morgan, G. and Whitley, R. (eds) (2012) *Capitalisms and Capital in the Twenty-First Century*. Oxford: Oxford University Press.

Pendleton, A. and Gospel, H. (2013) Corporate governance and labour. In: M. Wright, D. Siegel, K. Keasey and I. Filatochev. *The Oxford Handbook of Corporate Governance*. Oxford: Oxford University Press, pp. 634–657.

Perlmutter, M. V. (1969) The tortuous evolution of the multinational corporation. *Columbia Journal of World Business*, 4 (1), 9–18.

Reiss, A. D. and Ones, D. S. (1995) Does international management education work? Reduction in ethnocentrism and negative stereotyping. Paper presented to Academy of Management Conference, Vancouver, Canada.

Rosenzweig, P. M. (2006) The dual logics behind international human resource management: pressures for global integration and local responsiveness. In: G. K. Stahl and I. Bjorkman (eds), *Handbook of Research in International Human Resource Management*. Cheltenham, Glos: Edward Elgar, pp. 16–34.

Schein, E. (1985) *Organizational Culture and Leadership*. San Francisco, CA: Jossey-Bass.

Schein, E. (1990) *Career Anchors*. San Diego, CA: University Associates.

Schneider, S. C., Barsoux, J.-L. and Stahl, G. K. (2014) *Managing Across Cultures*, 3rd edn. London: Financial Times/Prentice Hall.

Sparrow, P. R., Brewster, C. and Harris, H. (2004) *Globalizing Human Resource Management*. London: Routledge.

Stewart, R., Keiser, A. and Barsoux, J.-L. (1994) *Managing in Britain and Germany*. London: St Martin's Press.

Sullivan, S. E. and Arthur, M. B. (2006) The evolution of the boundaryless career concept. Examining physical and psychological mobility. *Journal of Vocational Behaviour*, 69 (1), 19–29.

Thomson, A., Mabey, C., Storey, J., Gray, C. and Iles, P. (2001) *Changing Patterns of Management Development*. Oxford: Blackwell.

Time Magazine (2015) How McDonalds plans to make a turnaround. 4 May.

Trompenaars, F. (2012) Cultural dimensions relating to people. In: J. Dumetz, *et al.* (eds), *Cross-cultural Management Textbook: Lessons from the world-leading experts in cross cultural management*. Create Space Independent Publishing, pp. 117–146.

Trompenaars, F. and Hampden-Turner, C. (2004) *Managing People Across Cultures*. Chichester, Sussex: Capstone.

Weber, M. (1930) *The Protestant Ethic and the Spirit of Capitalism*. London: Unwin University Books.

Weick, K. E. (2001) *Making Sense of the Organization*. Oxford: Blackwell.

Weiner, M. J. (2004) *English Culture and the Decline of the Industrial Spirit, 1850–1980*, 2nd edn. Cambridge: Cambridge University Press.

Whitley, R. (2008) *Business Systems and Organizational Capabilities: The institutional structuring of competitive competences*. Oxford: Oxford University Press.

Wilkinson, A., Wood,. G. T. and Deeg, R. (eds) (2013) *The Oxford Handbook of Employment Relations: Comparative employment systems*. Oxford: Oxford University Press.

Wilson, D. and McKiernan, P. (2011) Global mimicry: putting strategic choice back on the business school agenda. *British Journal of Management*, 22 (3), 457–469.

Witt, M. A. and Redding, G. (2014) *The Oxford Handbook of Asian Business Systems*. Oxford: Oxford University Press.

Wolf, A. (2002) *Does Education Matter? Myths about education and economic growth*. London: Penguin.

World Trade Organization (2014) World trade report: trade and development, recent trends and the role of the WTO. Available online at http://www.wto.org.

Zaheer, S. (1995) Overcoming the liability of foreignness (Special Research Forum: International and Intercultural Management Research). *Academy of Management Journal*, 38 (2), 341–364.

Zhang, H. and Martin, G. (2003) *Human Resource Management Practices in Sino Foreign Joint Ventures*. Nanching, China: Jiangxi Science and Technology Press.

Chapter 6

The corporate context, organizations and managing people

LEARNING OBJECTIVES

At the end of this chapter you should be able to:

- understand the importance of the corporate context and the role of managing people in creating corporateness;
- identify the different concepts that contribute to the corporate image of an organization;
- apply the AC²ID frameworks to the analysis of organizational identity;
- understand the importance of employer-branding in organizations;
- understand the complex relationships between people management, organizational identity, corporate branding and corporate reputation;
- apply the model of the relationship between people management, organizational identity, corporate branding and corporate reputation to an organization seeking to develop a stronger corporate brand and reputation.

INTRODUCTION TO CORPORATE REPUTATION, IDENTITY, BRANDS AND PEOPLE MANAGEMENT

There can be few better justifications for a chapter in a book on management than the importance of its intended topic to the fate of a nation and its major corporations – in this case the USA. Take a few minutes to read this case, updated with new data on America's image abroad since it was originally written just after the end of the war with Iraq in 2004.

CASE 6.1 AMERICA'S IMAGE ABROAD – REPUTATION MANAGEMENT AND BRANDING

In the first edition of this book, we used a case study based on an *Economist* article written in 2004, which referred to Keith Reinhard, the chairman of DDB Worldwide, whose challenge was to sell American business and American brands to the world following the Iraq war. He exclaimed, 'I love American brands, but they are losing friends around the world and it is vital to the interests of America to change this,' in a talk to an audience at Yale University Business School during February 2004. He argued that the reputation of America abroad was at an all-time low and that this perception, however misguided, was damaging the economy.

To tackle the problem Reinhard, with senior executives in America's advertising industry and some academics, set up Business for Diplomatic Action (BDA) to improve the reputation of the USA overseas. The idea wasn't new, since President George W. Bush had speculated on the reasons as to why 'everyone hates America' after 11 September 2001. But Reinhard felt the need to use consumer research to tell American business what most people outside the USA seemed to know about America's declining image.

His worries have subsequently been reinforced by a DDB study covering 17 countries, which provided the feedback that 'America, and American business, was viewed as arrogant and indifferent toward others' cultures; exploitative, in that it extracted more than it provided; corrupting, in how it valued materialism above all else; and willing to sacrifice almost anything in an effort to generate profits'. Further evidence came in the shape of a survey of global brands by Roper ASW, which showed a marked decline in support for and trust in American brands.

Since writing this case illustration a decade ago, there have been a number of investigations into America's image abroad, including a House of Representatives hearing and conference on the topic in 2007. So, for example, Secretary of State Condoleezza Rice announced the creation of a new annual award for a company, university or other non-governmental institution that excelled in promoting America's image abroad. A public relations coalition, which was an offshoot of this initiative, argued that despite US companies and individuals donating much more money overseas than in the overall US aid budget, the image was still in decline. This decline was to be further exacerbated by the role played by American financial services companies during the Global Financial Services Crisis in 2007–8.

Since then, however, matters seem to have improved a little, at least according to Pew Research Center (2014), a think tank. Although there were major critics of America and American companies, especially in the Middle East (Egypt, Jordan, Palestine, Lebanon), Turkey, Greece and Germany, all of which had predominantly unfavourable images, there were blocks of the world where America's image and those of its companies, were generally positive, including most of Europe, Asia, sub-Saharan Africa and the traditional 'suspects' such as Israel and Italy. There were also some very surprising results on favourability, with France entering the top ten nations of 'Fans' of America for the first time. The image held by UK citizens declined markedly from 2002 until 2008, but has recovered a little since then with approximately two-thirds of those surveyed holding a favourable image of America and its companies in 2015.

Source: adapted from 'Selling the flag', *The Economist*, 26 February 2004 and 'Which Countries Don't Like America and Which Do?,' Pew Research Center, 2014.

1 In your view, what are the causes of America's poor reputation abroad in this case?
2 What should the American government and businesses do about it?
3 What role can more effective people management play in improving the brand image and reputation of American companies and America generally?

The above illustration sums up the growing realization that organizations and even nation-states need to create and maintain strong ideas of 'corporateness' for competitive advantage. The case also raises issues of America's image abroad and that of its major corporations, invoking notions such as identity, branding and reputation. These corporate-level concepts have become key areas of strategic interest among the boardrooms of companies in sectors as diverse as financial services, information and communication technology (ICT), retailing, food and beverages, hospitality and tourism, healthcare, local and national government and charities. They also provide one of the key future contexts for shaping the nature of people management (Harvey and Morris, 2012).

As we have already discussed, there are strong negative reasons driving organizations throughout the world to focus on their corporate identities, brands and reputations, including:

- *The decline in general levels of trust and consumer confidence* following the highly publicized cases of *questionable corporate governance* and *questionable ethics*. Good examples of these are the Enron, Andersen Consulting and WorldCom financial scandals during the early 2000s, British financial services companies such as RBS, the Bank of Scotland and Barclays in the lead up to and following the Global Financial Crisis, and global companies such as Starbucks and Amazon, which incurred public wrath over their attempts to minimize the taxes paid in particular countries (e.g. the UK) by legitimate but questionable tax avoidance methods.
- *Problems associated with inferior and dangerous lines of business products and services*. Examples here include BP and the Deepwater Horizon oil spill disaster in 2010, Toyota and its frequent recalls of cars from 2010 onwards, Ryanair, the low cost airline, which was named the worst company for customer service in 2015, and Tesco, whose reputation suffered markedly as a result of the UK horsemeat scandal in 2013.

More positively, however, organizations also see strong corporate brands, identities and reputations as significant intangible assets, sometimes worth up to twice the book value of their tangible assets. For instance, the world's best-known brand, Apple, has been estimated to be worth $118,863 million in 2014, and the brand images of companies such as UK-based Virgin, the budget airline EasyJet and Apple itself have allowed them to extend their product–service offerings into completely new areas of business, e.g. Apply Pay. So a firm's corporate brand and reputation can lead to significant strategic advantage through the power to differentiate itself in the marketplace (Barnett and Pollock, 2012). Moreover, this differentiation is often difficult to copy, precisely because the sources of differences are intangible and take many years to create (see Table 6.1 on the most reputable companies in 2015).

The illustration in Case 6.1 of the reputation of American organizations abroad also serves to highlight another important feature of corporate brands, identity and reputation, which is the role of *people* in creating and maintaining these valuable assets (Martin and Hetrick, 2006). Corporate image usually refers to how diverse groups of receivers react to communications of the corporate identity projected by an organization (Melewar *et al.*, 2012). It is largely created through the *unscripted and discretionary* actions, attitudes, talk and behaviours of employees, which lead customers, investors and the public at large to infer favourable or unfavourable impressions of the company (Sjovall and Talk, 2004). The key point is that it is not only the formal communication of corporate identity an organization wishes to portray that is important, it is also the informal impressions created by employees in the normal day-to-day conduct of their work that, in turn, lead key stakeholders to attribute to the company fundamental attributes, such as its culture, character or reputation. This is one of the central messages of the example of 'America abroad', particularly its conduct of recent wars, support for Israel against the Palestinians, and the actions of its managers at some multinational companies such as the Wal-Mart example in Chapter 5. So, many organizations have come to recognize that one of their few unique and inimitable assets is their *human resources* in creating *reputational capital*, because their products and services, and many of their internal management processes, including financial engineering, supply chain management and purchasing strategies, are all tangible sources of capital, so are open to copying and therefore provide little sustainable differentiation (Joyce *et al.*, 2003).

The business literature is replete with anecdotal evidence of how customer service, linked to good human resource management, makes a significant difference to consumer purchasing decisions, including a number of those firms listed in Table 6.1. However, a note of caution – since writing the first edition of this book in 2006, companies cited as excellent in regard are no longer excellent, including firms such as Nokia, British Airways, Tesco and RBS, all of which have suffered marked reputational decline. We should not be surprised at this finding, however, since it mirrors the pattern of studies of so-called excellent companies in the 1980s (Rosenzweig, 2007). Thus, we

TABLE 6.1 The world's most reputable companies

Position	Company
1	BMW
2	Google
3	Daimler
4	Rolex
5	Lego
6	Walt Disney
7	Canon
8	Apple
9	Sony
10	Intel

Source: Reputation Institute (2015) Global RepTrak® Study.

have to look for more solid justifications for this proposition in widely cited sources we examine later in this chapter. These are:

- Mary Jo Hatch and Majden Schultz's (2008/13) work on more than 100 leading companies in the USA and Europe, which found that organizations wishing to create a strong corporate brand had to align three essential, interdependent and largely intangible elements – the organization's vision, its culture and its image. These included the top management's aspirations for the company, the organization's values, the way employees felt about their organization and the image (or reputation) held of the organization by its major stakeholders – customers, shareholders, the business media and potential employees.
- Charles Fombrun and colleagues' work on corporate reputation management since the early 1990s has demonstrated a close link between the financial fortunes of companies worldwide and their reputations (Fombrun and Van Riel, 2004; Fombrun, 2012; Fombrun *et al.*, 2015). They found that bottom-line returns, operating performance cash flows and growth in market values were closely tied to their reputation quotient (RQ) measure and to their new reputation toolkit – RepTrak® – both of which include important people and culture management variables.

In this chapter we shall look at the relationship between corporate-level concepts such as brands, identity and reputations, and their relationships with human resource management, as this is one of the most important areas in which the effective management of people has been proved to impact directly on performance. First, we shall address the rather vague notion of 'corporateness' to clear up some of the confusion of ideas in this area. Second, we shall look at some of the human resource-based literature to see what it can add to our understanding. Then we shall examine a framework we have created that brings these two sections together to show the links between people management, branding, identity and corporate reputation. Finally, we shall use this model to analyse one of the cases we have researched, so that you can learn to use it in real-life situations.

DEFINING AND EXPLAINING 'CORPORATENESS'

There is little doubt that the concept of corporateness, a term coined by Balmer and Greyser (2003) to refer to a raft of corporate-level concepts, has featured more prominently in the management literature in recent years (see Chapter 11). This is because the promise of benefits derived from strong corporate brands, images and reputations for social responsibility and sustainability is now being taken seriously by businesses on a global scale. At one and the same time, the notion of corporateness provides a new and powerful lens through which to reveal how corporations can improve performance, *and* creates a good deal of confusion because of the myriad of concepts competing for prominence (Fombrun, 2012). This confusion has arisen because of the different disciplines and interests contributing to the growing body of ideas, evidence and practice that has served only to mystify practitioners and academics.

To help clear up this state of affairs, Balmer and Greyser set out six questions that remain important to anyone working in this area (see Table 6.2). These questions related to six corporate-level concepts that are often used synonymously, thus producing much of the confusion of terminology

TABLE 6.2 What 'corporateness' means: six questions and related concepts

Key question	Key concept
What are the corporation's distinctive attributes?	Corporate identity
To whom and what do/should we communicate?	Corporate communications
What is our corporate promise or pledge?	Corporate branding
What are organizational members' affinities, or 'who are we'? (see Chapter 3)	Organizational identity
How are we perceived as time goes on?	Corporate reputation
How are we perceived right now?	Corporate image

Source: adapted from Balmer and Greyser, 2003, p. 4.

in this field. When brought together, however, and defined in more exacting terms, they seem to capture the notion of corporateness.

Balmer and Greyser pointed out that each of these concepts has been popular during different time frames since the 1970s, reflecting the problems that organizations faced at the time and the various disciplinary interests and ambitions of those contributing to the debate. For example, corporate branding was the concept favoured in the last decade, perhaps because marketing specialists made an all-out attempt to colonize this field of study and practice for their own ends. Interestingly, Balmer and Greyser, both of whom are marketeers, identified a potential for bringing together these concepts and interests under the umbrella of 'identity studies', which comprise the various definitions of identity, branding and reputation discussed in this chapter. We shall return to this proposition later in this chapter. However, from our perspective, and to repeat the core message, what is common to all of these concepts is the critical importance of people in helping 'make or break' them.

Let's look at some of these definitions and distinctions in a little more detail before building our model.

Corporate branding

Branding of products and services has played a significant part in the marketing strategy of firms for many years, with a number of products and services having worldwide recognition and helping create market values well in excess of book values. A good example from the service sector is the MBA – the single most recognizable global brand in educational services. The classic case of branding lines of products, however, is associated with Procter & Gamble, the American multinational, which is attributed with 'inventing' the branded strategy for its household cleaning, personal hygiene, baby and pet care goods. Although some of its brands are global, such as Crest toothpaste, Sure deodorant and Old Spice aftershave, others are specific to particular countries.

Nevertheless, it is the *branding of companies* that has become increasingly valuable, especially in particular industries such as financial services and consumer goods and services (Schultz *et al.*, 2012;

Miller and Merrilees, 2013). Marketing jargon for company or corporate branding is *monolithic branding*, because it reduces the needs of firms to promote individual lines of business or products/services. Such developments are not new: some strong corporate brands have retained their place in the top 100 global brands for 50 years or more, including Coca-Cola, Hewlett-Packard, Gillette, Heinz, Volkswagen and Kellogg's. In the case of the MBA, it is Harvard that is mostly associated with this brand. So, to some extent at least, the fact of the continued existence of these organizations reflects the power of corporate brands to bestow the following advantages on their companies by:

- building long-term trust by increasing customer loyalty and convincing consumers of the benefits of their products and services;
- reducing customers' search costs for perceived quality products and services and also conferring on them certain psychological rewards;
- ensuring repeat purchases, assisting in the development of new product launches, facilitating market segmentation by communicating directly to the intended customers of the product or service and facilitating premium pricing.

As we noted, branding specialists began to stake out a claim for the whole area of corporate-level studies and practice, because it was a concept used more and more by organizations to express their distinctiveness. A website for a major branding consulting company put the inclusive case for corporate branding as the key unifying concept, which was, the author suggested, 'no less and no more than the face of business strategy, portraying what the corporation wants to be known for in the marketplace. The corporate brand is the overall umbrella for the corporation's activities and encapsulates its vision, values, personality, positioning and image among many other dimensions' (Hatch and Schultz, 2008).

Given its popularity and inclusiveness, Balmer and Greyser (2003) believed that the concept of the corporate branding philosophy offered the 'superior organizational lens'. It was the *explicit covenant* between an *organization and its key stakeholder groups*. The corporate brand had to articulate its agreement with these stakeholder groups – consistently and over time – to indicate that it kept its word or pledge. In this sense it was similar to the concept of corporate identity, discussed in the introduction, but was also quite distinctive in a number of important ways:

- Corporate branding usually applied only to organizations, whereas identity could apply to individuals, groups, organizations, regions and countries.
- Corporate brands usually took longer to develop than identities.
- Corporate brands focused mainly on the external world.
- Corporate brands usually attempted to achieve high visibility.
- Corporate brands typically required support through organizational communications and designers, e.g. through logos and symbols.
- Corporate brands could be portable – extended to cover new products and services – in a way that identities cannot.
- Corporate brands could be valued financially in terms of goodwill.

Corporate branding, however, is also recognized for a further, significant reason, and that is its ability to *engage* the 'hearts and minds' of employees. The reverse is also true: corporate branding *depends* on the hearts and minds of employees, because, as we have already seen, much of the value of corporate brands is delivered through people, having employees identify with the brand and align their efforts behind the brand (Martin *et al.*, 2011). Marketing professionals have become more willing to recognize the role of employees in delivering the brand: as a result, corporations have begun to use the language and tactics of branding internally, to create employers' brands, which, as we suggested in Chapter 3, is quite widespread in the USA, Europe and Asia (Martin *et al.*, 2011). One good example is the HSBC, which is a bank that grew rapidly through acquisitions on a global scale during the early part of this decade to be number one in the world as measured by Tier 1 capital (and, at the time of writing, has retained its place in the top ten banks). Part of the secret of its success was its ability to transfer the brand equity of these acquired firms into the corporate brand equity, so that customers and employees identify with the corporation rather than the local banks they used to be served or employed by. We shall return to this idea of employer branding later in this chapter.

However, not every organization wishes to, or needs to, have a corporate brand. Indeed, many large organizations have chosen to continue with a devolved branded strategy, or have gone for a halfway-house *endorsed brand strategy*, in which business units enjoy brand status in their own right but derive benefits from carrying the overall corporate brand. For example, before its rapid decline from 2008, RBS allowed its acquired brands such as NatWest, Ulster Bank and Citizens in America to retain their identities, albeit referring to the RBS Group in the strap line.

Corporate reputation and image

Organizations have always had a concern for their image and in the 1950s academics began to examine the idea of image in terms of personality theory in the retailing sector (see, for example, Martineau, 1958). This concern led a number of commercial research organizations to conduct image studies, such as Marketing and Opinion Research International (MORI) in the UK and the Opinion Research Center (ORC) in the USA. The concept of image and image research, however, has been bedevilled by a number of problems, because it has been used to refer to quite different aspects of an organization. These include the transmitted image (the visual image or desired image, transmitted by the corporate designers), the received image (how stakeholders perceive the brand, corporate reputation or the organizational symbols) and the construed image (how, for example, employees believe that customers see the organization). As a consequence, image is a concept that is difficult to pin down and, consequently, has ceded ground to the idea of corporate reputation as a more useful concept. So, from the 1990s onwards, the study of corporate reputation has grown rapidly, bringing together scholars and practitioners from marketing and branding, organizational studies, communications and strategic management (Barnett and Pollock, 2012; Fombrun, 2012) and from HRM (including our own work, e.g. Martin and Hetrick, 2006; Martin and Hetrick, 2010; Martin *et al.*, 2011).

Though branding and corporate reputation have a common origin in being concerned with the external image of an organization, corporate reputation claims to be a distinctive and, arguably, higher-order concept than either branding or image because it includes past as well as present and future impressions of a company's image, a wider range of measures of corporateness and a wider range of stakeholders. In this sense, corporate reputation currently competes with branding and identity to be the superior organizational lens. Corporate reputations have become the subject of a number of influential press ratings, including *Fortune* magazine, *Asia Business* and the *Financial Times*, which have lent it credibility with the general public and other stakeholders. As we indicated earlier, such a positive reputation can lead to significant financial advantages. However, it has also become notable because of its ability to help defend an organization when it encounters adverse publicity (Elsbach, 2012). For example, Apple was able to draw on its reputation for control, innovation and excellence following the problems experienced with the iPhone 4 in dropping calls in 2010 to convince consumers of the strengths of the Apple brand and the iPhone itself. Johnson & Johnson was also able to survive the catastrophic, malicious tampering with Tylenol, one of its core products, by recovering well from a small decline in its market value because of the company's past reputation for good business principles – its reputational capital. Other companies, when facing similar disasters, have suffered more severe and sustained declines in market value because they did not have the depth of reputational capital to sustain them through their crises. Corporate reputations have also become more important in the wake of recent corporate governance and financial irregularities following the Global Financial Crisis, because they act as a form of ethical control by creating a culture of ethical values and standards of behaviour that help guide employees in their dealings with customers, clients and governments (Barnett and Pollock, 2012). In effect, they answer the question: Would my actions be in line with the organization's reputation? An interesting example of this notion is a proposal developed by senior bankers to have their pay determined by how they advance to the 'standards' (read reputation) of their companies.

So, what do we understand by corporate reputation? Two of the most insightful scholars in the field, Mary Jo Hatch and Majken Schultz (2008/2013), saw it as a result of the interaction between the objective and subjective evaluations of existing and potential stakeholders, comprising three interrelated dimensions:

- *Informal* interactions among stakeholders – for example, through sales meetings, employee storytelling or accounts from satisfied or dissatisfied customers. These incidents strongly influence an organization's reputation or external image but are largely uncontrollable.
- *The business press*, such as the rankings of the best places to work and industry press ratings of organizations, as outlined above.
- *Potential stakeholders*, such as possible recruits, shareholders and other funders, government organizations and the community at large.

However, perhaps the best-known practitioner-oriented work on corporate reputations is by Charles Fombrun and his colleagues at the New York-based Corporate Reputation Institute (Fombrun, 1996, 2012; Fombrun *et al.*, 2015). The definition of corporate reputation used by Fombrun and his collaborators has seven characteristics:

- They are socially constructed through interactions between companies, stakeholders and environments.

- They are rooted in past actions and achievements as well as the present, and stakeholder assessments of them.
- Corporate can attract and repulse people, so they have a powerful effect on how people perceive and enact reputations.
- Because they are diversely perceived by different stakeholders, they are only partly shaped by company communications and corporate identity management.
- They are affected by the degree of alignment that develops between parts of the system and the system as a whole.
- They signal the relative attractiveness of a company to potential stakeholders and result from long-term investments in creating distinctiveness.
- They are an important intangible source of economic value for organizations and can be used to position the organization against competitors and benchmark against the best ones.

Fombrun and Van Riel (2004) originally developed a widely used measure of corporate reputation – the *reputation quotient* – which was developed into a more sophisticated consulting tool in 2010 – RepTrak® measure of global companies used in Table 6.1 (Fombrun *et al.*, 2015). This aggregate measure is based on seven dimensions of reputation (see Table 6.3) that influence the extent to which stakeholders hold the organization in high esteem, have positive feelings/emotions about it, admire it, and trust in its competence, integrity and benevolence. The RepTrak® model has been validated across five stakeholder groups in six countries, which confirmed the existence and stability of the seven dimensions of the model and so makes it a good academic and practitioner tool for measuring and managing stakeholder images of different companies.

TABLE 6.3 The RepTrak® reputation dimensions

Products and services	The organization stands behind products and services. It offers high quality products and services at good value. Meets customer needs
Innovation	Innovative products and services, and processes of producing them; first to market and quick to adapt to change
Leadership	Well organized, appealing leaders, excellent management team and a clear vision for the future
Workplace environment	Offers equal opportunities, rewards people fairly and is known for looking after employee well-being
Governance	Fair in business, behaves ethically and is open and transparent in its decision-making
Citizenship	Environmentally responsible, positive influence on society and supports good causes
Financial performance	Record of profitability, strong prospect for future growth and typically produces results that are better than expected

Source: Reputation Institute (available at www.reputationinstitute.com/about/RepTrak).

We can now define corporate reputation as 'a collective representation of a firm's past actions and results which describe its ability to deliver valued outcomes to multiple stakeholders. It gauges a firm's relative standing with employees and externally with stakeholders, in both its competitive and institutional environments' (Fombrun *et al.*, 2015).

Corporate and organizational identity

The interest in corporate reputation management had its origins in earlier work on organizational identity, discussed in Chapter 3 of this book. In a classical interpretation of the concept, there were three central principles that could be used in any assessment of organizational identity (Albert and Whetten, 1985):

- it should capture the essence or 'claimed central character' of the organization;
- it should set out its claimed distinctiveness;
- it should show continuity over time.

This last principle has been subject to challenge, especially in the modern environment of continuous change, with other writers claiming that fluidity and flexibility are requirements for organization identities to cope with environmental turbulence (Gioia *et al.*, 2013). Note, for example, how a firm such as IBM has managed to make the transition from computer hardware manufacture to business services as pressures on manufacturing costs increased as a result of global competition from countries such as China.

A second feature of identity noted by a number of authors is the notion of multiple identities: this concept runs counter to the notion of a monolithic corporateness, but is probably a more realistic image of most organizations. For example, hospitals can be seen as a business, a caring organization and a professional organization at one and the same time (Reay and Hinings, 2009). So, how you see an organization at any point in time thus depends on where you are viewing it from – from the perspective of a politician or financier looking for value and money, as a patient looking for high levels of care or as a doctor looking for a place to practise his or her craft and develop a reputation (Martin *et al.*, 2015). This feature leads us to a third characteristic, that the issue of an organization's identity surfaces and resurfaces at different points in its career or life cycle. For example, during the start-up phase the concern will be to establish an identity, whereas during a period of retrenchment the concern will be with embracing the need for change but retaining previously held identities for acting in good faith so that they are able to retain valued employees. Again, IBM is a good example of this characteristic.

However, as we have already pointed out, in addition to the notion of organizational identity, we can also talk about corporate identity. Stretching (some might say, straining) the concept even further, Balmer and Greyser (2003) contend that identity has five meanings, which incorporate the afore-mentioned notions of corporate and organizational identities but also include others that broadly coincide with our ideas of corporate image, strategic vision and corporate strategy (see Figure 6.1). They also contend that the field of corporate-level studies can cohere around the management of these *multiple identities* of a corporation, and they propose a useful multidisciplinary approach – the AC^{2}ID *framework* – to the management of image and identity.

- The *actual identity* is defined as the current attributes of the corporation, including the values shared by management and employees. It is close to, but not synonymous with, the notion of organizational identity discussed in Chapter 3, and broadly addresses the question: Who are we? The actual identity is shaped by leadership styles, organizational structure, ownership characteristics and the businesses and markets in which the organization operates, as well as the psychological contracts and motivations held by organizational members.
- The *conceived identity* refers to the perceptions of image, branding and reputation held by stakeholders. Managers have to make judgements about which of these to focus on.
- The *ideal identity*, the optimum positioning of the corporation in its given markets at a point in time, is based on an analysis of external environmental–internal resources fit. This identity is associated with the work of strategic planners, and is close to the notion of corporate strategy and strategic positioning.
- The *desired identity* is synonymous with the vision of the organization held by its leadership. It is not the same thing as ideal identity, which is mostly the result of serious analysis. The desired identity is very often a personal and egotistical statement made by senior leaders.
- The *communicated identity* is the 'official' identity put into the public domain through the corporate communications function – the official rhetoric of the organization that communicates what the organization wishes to be. It is also, however, communicated by less controllable media, such as 'word of mouth' and the financial press, which require a great deal of management time spent on internal communications and public relations.

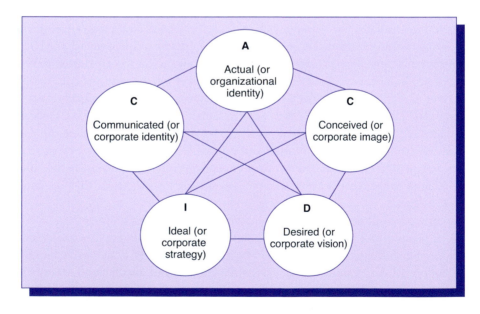

FIGURE 6.1 The AC²ID framework

(*Source:* adapted from Balmer and Greyser, 2003, p. 17.)

The main practical value of this framework is the proposition that all five identities need to be broadly aligned over time. If any two of these are out of alignment at a particular time, this is manifested as a 'moment of truth' from which a corporation's reputation is in danger of suffering serious damage. So, for example, the dangers of communicated identity (or corporate identity) running ahead of the actual identity (or organizational identity) can, as we pointed out in Chapter 3, lead to persistent cynicism among employees and also lead to a breach of trust among customers if this cynicism is communicated by disaffected employees. Another situation could be where redundancies lead to mass disaffection among employees (organizational identity) who are simultaneously being exhorted to 'live the brand' image that 'puts people first' (the conceived identity).

CONNECTING CORPORATE BRANDING, REPUTATION AND IDENTITY TO PEOPLE MANAGEMENT

Let's turn to the human resource management literature and practice to see what else we can learn about the concept of corporateness. Our key message – that good employee relations is a necessary (but not sufficient) condition for creating and maintaining corporate brands, reputations and identities – is lent considerable support by five streams of writing and practice in the HR-related fields. These are: the culture–excellence movement, the strategic HRM literature, the employer of choice thesis, employer branding and the corporate reputation management literature itself.

The culture–excellence movement

One reading of the corporate branding and marketing literature is that it demonstrates close parallels with the 'culture–excellence' movement, which dominated much of management thinking and practice during the 1980s and 1990s, and remains a cornerstone of HRM literature today (Godard, 2014). This work, which began with Peters and Waterman's (1982) well-known book *In Search of Excellence*, fuelled the idea that the search for business success began with a serious examination of the internal culture of the organization. They promoted the message that, as the environment of most organizations was increasingly unknowable and uncontrollable, the 1970s focus on 'outside-in', rational management techniques was misplaced. Instead, it was to feelings and people – the organizational culture – that they turned for an explanation of excellence. Excellence was achieved through a strong emphasis on customer focus, which, they argued, 'all began from people'. This focus on culture as a source and driver of success has re-emerged over the past two decades from its earlier human relations incarnation, which we discussed in Chapter 1 and will examine further in Chapter 10. It has influenced many of the 'business guru' writers, and has also influenced the development of the new resource-based view of strategic management, which focuses on internal resources as the key driver of competitive success.

Peters and Waterman took some of their ideas from Ed Schein (1992), who defined the major problem of organizations as one of simultaneously managing external adaptation to the changing environment of organizations with internal integration. This process of alignment, which we encountered earlier in this chapter, involved managing cultures and people to fit with the external image of the organization. However, the process is not a simple one, and requires managing dualities, paradoxes and tensions; these have become key features of the organizational change literature to be examined in Chapter 10.

The culture–excellence literature, however, has been roundly criticized by economists and strategic management scholars for its overemphasis on the internal workings of organizations at the expense of market analysis, for the belief that managers can control or shape organizational cultures and, from an ethical standpoint, by critical management writers who see culture management as little more than indoctrination (Hatch and Cunliffe, 2013) (see Chapter 10). We return to these criticisms in the Chapter 10, but there is little doubt that the managerially oriented, 'optimistic' literature on culture management has had an unquestionable influence on the practice of many organizations; culture management and its associated 'toolkit' approach has provided a strong rationale for both strategic human resource management and the corporate reputation and branding literatures with their emphasis on vision and values (Giorgi *et al.*, 2015).

The strategic management literature

A second important stream of literature is the new strategic management or *resource-based view* (RBV) of the firm (Barney, 2002; Boselie, 2013) and its derivative, *strategic human resource management* (Boxall and Purcell, 2011). This approach has developed as a counter to the traditional 'outside-in' approaches, in which the starting point for thinking about strategic management and competitive advantage is the external environment. The work of Michael Porter is most associated with this outside-in perspective. The resource-based view on strategy and, by extension, on HRM sees the fundamental, and indeed only, sustainable route to competitive advantage as arising from how you put together unique and enviable combinations of internal resources – the most important of these being people and their relationship to other key systems in the organization, such as knowledge and information. Such a perspective has led some writers to argue that the way organizational cultures are managed and employees are selected, developed, rewarded and organized is what differentiates firms, especially in knowledge-based industries or the growing service sectors in Europe and the USA (Pfeffer, 2010). Thus, the resource-based view has strong links with humanist ideas on learning organizations and organizational learning (Easterby-Smith and Lyles, 2011) (see Chapter 7).

Like the earlier outside-in approaches, however, these 'inside-out' theories have in common a tendency to offer a one-best-way solution, regardless of context, and to proselytize employees at the expense of other aspects of the business. As Porter (1996/2008) argued, resources in and of themselves are of no competitive value; it is how and in what context such internal resources are used that leads to value creation. Both camps are beginning to recognize, however, that the answer to this fundamental question of competitive strategy probably lies somewhere in the middle, with both perspectives having something to offer (Boxall and Purcell, 2011). Nevertheless, the RBV has managed to rebalance the debate, based on the rationale that you don't move a seesaw by sitting in the middle (Boselie, 2014). This view has also provided a major intellectual and empirical justification for HR and its links to key strategic decisions on issues such as branding.

Consistent with the RBV, another stream of influential strategic management literature has begun to explain effective and sustainable strategic advantage, which is based on the notion of *core internal competences* (Hamel, 2007) and the complementary idea of the *balanced scorecard* (Kaplan and Norton, 2001; Kaplan, 2008). The balanced scorecard is particularly relevant to the links between HR and branding, because it makes explicit and very practical links to balancing the needs and measurement of satisfying customers and financial objectives with the effective management and measurement of internal business processes, including people, and individual and organizational learning and growth. Kaplan and Norton have also developed a strategy map or *theory of the business* that is, in summary, a cause-and-effect model to help managers understand the relationships between critical performance drivers and their associated outcomes. Especially in the context of service industries, such as retailing and financial services, there have been a number of important contributions linking the marketing of services and customer satisfaction to internal market and human resource management. The best known of these is the old but still relevant employee–customer service–profit chain identified by the Sears corporation in the USA (Kirn *et al.*, 1999) (see Figure 6.2).

Employers of choice

As we discussed in Chapter 3, during the 1990s an important stream of literature emerged on *new psychological contracts* based on the need to become an employer of choice (Leary-Joyce, 2004). This argument served as an antidote to the business process re-engineering, delayering and downsizing exercises undertaken by many organizations during the early part of the 1990s, and has led employers to think more closely about the connections between employee satisfaction and retention, hiring, customer satisfaction, branding performance, financial performance and corporate reputation.

According to some consultants, becoming an employer of choice is a deliberate business strategy that has driven some large US and UK employers to benchmark themselves against others in rankings of the 'best place to work', published by *Fortune* magazine in the USA and *The Times* in the UK. Although such ideas and strategies have their roots in a decade of unprecedented economic growth in the USA during the 1990s, when recruitment and retention became among the most important business issues for American employers, they appear not to have diminished in importance, despite recurrent economic crises as we saw in Chapter 3.

For some organizations, following an employer of choice strategy means little more than more sophisticated and sensitive recruitment practices, such as improving recruitment design, online recruitment, sensitive induction, retention analysis, cafeteria compensation and benefits, and 'growing your own' talent (Michaels *et al.*, 2001). For others, it means a new, more contextually sensitive, version of the old-style, relational psychological contract (Cappelli, 1998) in which long-term commitment from employers, demonstrated through the organization's goals, values and trust initiatives, is matched by high-commitment and low-turnover responses from employees. Such a psychological contract is characterized by highly competitive remuneration and benefits, often including elements of contingent pay, interesting, challenging and varied projects, a commitment to training and development tailored to individual needs, flexible working arrangements, family friendly policies and a motivating work environment.

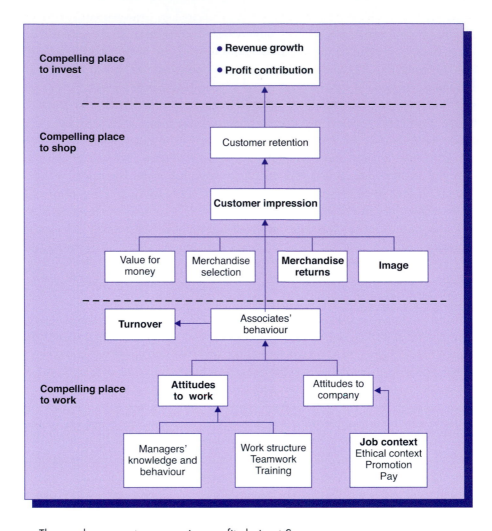

FIGURE 6.2 The employee–customer service–profit chain at Sears
(*Source*: adapted from Kaplan and Norton, 2001.)

This consulting recipe for an employer of choice strategy is reminiscent of the classical and still influential work by Pfeffer (1998), in which he identified seven practices of highly successful companies from his review of the US and European literature. The list encompassed prescriptions on: employment security, selective hiring, self-managed teams and decentralization, high compensation contingent on organizational performance, extensive training and development, reduced status distinctions and extensive information-sharing on performance and financial issues. Contrary to some of the ideas fashionable during the 1990s, which advocated changes in the terms of the traditional psychological contracts to a new, transactional employment contract based on employability and no long-term commitment to individual careers inside an organization (e.g. Cappelli, 1998), Pfeffer (2010) made it a central part of his argument that employment security provided the necessary 'table stakes' for sustainable organizations. He reviewed a number of studies that showed the negative consequences of downsizing, including important connections between downsizing and the adverse impact on organizational performance with its strong, negative correlations between employee turnover and positive assessments of customer service, a vital factor in establishing and maintaining strong brand identities. If downsizing had to be undertaken, Pfeffer argued that it could be accomplished sensitively and sensibly, in a way that retained the morale of those surviving and minimized the impact on the company's image in concurrent and future hiring campaigns. It should be noted, however, that some academics have criticized the notion of employer of choice as a recipe for breeding mediocrity in organizations, by sending untargeted signals to people that everyone is welcome and encouraging underperforming staff to remain. Thus, Becker *et al.* (2009) have argued for an 'employee of choice' approach, which signals that only highly qualified, motivated and performing people should apply and expect to be retained in the organization.

Employer branding

This final stream of work deals most obviously with issues of branding and attempts to use branding and marketing concepts to align employees behind strong corporate brands (Martin *et al.*, 2011). Our recent research into employer branding and organizational reputations (e.g. Martin and Hetrick, 2010; Martin *et al.*, 2011; Martin and Cerdin, 2014) has led us to define an employer brand as:

> 'a generalised recognition for being known among key stakeholders for providing a high quality employment experience, and a distinctive organizational identity which employees value, engage with and feel confident and happy to promote to others.'
>
> (Martin *et al.*, 2011)

The process by which branding, marketing, communications and HR concepts and techniques are applied externally and internally to attract, engage and retain potential and existing employees is known as employer branding. Prior to the Global Financial Crisis, most practitioner and consulting work focused on talent attraction because of longstanding labour market conditions in developed and developing countries. Thus employer branding became associated with the external application of marketing and communications tools. Since then, however, as we noted in Chapter 3, much of the focus of employer branding has been internal and aimed at establishing a sense of 'who are we'.

Employer branding is now big business, with a number of consulting firms specializing in helping firms to create distinctive identities. One good example is Universum, a British company who specialize in developing distinctive employer brands through the development of a unique employer value proposition (EVP). They claim that an EVP has to be an attractive, accurate (true), credible, distinctive and sustainable representation of an organization, which has its roots in the notion of 'strategy as a compelling narrative' approach (Barry and Elmes, 1997). The key questions to be addressed by firms (Martin *et al.*, 2011) are:

1   What is the compelling, novel and credible story that employees can tell about working here?
2   How can we convey that story to potential and existing employees and significant others (e.g. parents, suppliers, customers, universities, etc.) in a way that's compelling, credible and novel?

Universum's employer branding process involves establishing EVPs through internal and external research into four areas: (1) the current employer branding strategy, since all organizations have one – deliberate or accidental; (2) senior managers goals and visions for the organization – the story they want to tell to employees; (3) their corporate branding strategy, which is largely oriented to external stakeholders; and (4) how competitors position themselves in the labour market. Based on research into these four areas, they recommend developing EVPs for different employee segments/audiences, in much the same way that we discussed in the section of talent management in Chapter 3. Thus, for example, Universum claim that 'millennials', born between 1980 and the early 2000s, are interested in an EVP that stresses a sense of purpose and innovation. They seek to be inspired by an organization's values and wish to be given opportunities to develop and grow, which is why firms like Google and the large management consulting firms such as PwC and KPMG are attractive. They also claim that men and women differ in their motivations to join an employer. While both are looking for work–life balance, women place greater value than men on career security, international experience and ethical employment.

Once EVPs are established they have to be communicated to relevant audiences through appropriate channels. These channels are usually categorized as internal (e.g. leadership modelling, training, employer brand ambassadors), external offline (e.g. school lectures, job fairs) and external digital (campaigns, career websites, etc.). Social media are increasingly signaled as key channels for younger age groups, with firms making extensive use of social networking sites such as Facebook in sophisticated ways (Harquail and King, 2010; Martin and Hetrick, 2010).

The final stage of a typical consulting process is to evaluate the messaging, both prior to launch to test out the message and post-launch to evaluate if the employer branding signals are being interpreted as intended (Martin and Cerdin, 2014). This stage is critical because it completes the loop by telling an organization whether the signals align with the EVPs as intended, whether the signals are attractive to the target group and consistent with the corporate brand, and whether they help differentiate and legitimize the organization.

The corporate reputation approach

The corporate reputation literature itself has contributed directly to our understanding of how people, culture and organizational identity are linked to those corporate-level concepts discussed earlier (Harvey and Morris, 2012). Three contributions are of particular interest and are reflected in our model.

The first of these is the work by Davies *et al.* (2003) and Davies (2010), who have sought to develop a unified and objective way of measuring the gaps between external image and internal identity. The core argument is that reputation is 'the collective term referring to all stakeholders'

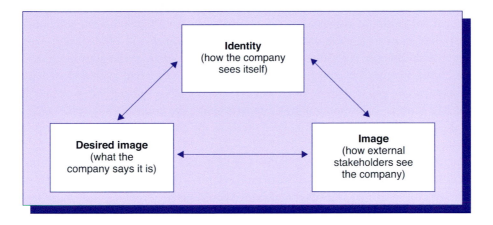

FIGURE 6.3 Gaps in reputation

(*Source*: based on Davies *et al.*, 2003, p. 62.)

views of corporate reputation' (Davies *et al.*, 2003, p. 62), including internal (organizational) identity and external image, which they define as the views of the company held by external stakeholders, especially customers. Their framework is set out in Figure 6.3, and highlights the potential for gaps between desired image, actual image and internal identity.

It is the way in which these gaps are measured, however, that is of most interest, because they use a single concept and set of measures to gauge differences, very unusual in this type of research. To get a 'clear line of sight' between internal and external perceptions of the organizations, they make use of the concept of stakeholder perceptions of the *organization's personality*, a construct borrowed from the psychology literature to describe generic organizational personality types. Organizational personality is defined in terms of agreeableness, trustworthiness, enterprise, chicness, competence, masculinity, ruthlessness and informality. Questions have been derived to assess these personality dimensions, and internal and external stakeholders are provided with the same questions. By doing so, the extent of the gaps can be measured and used to realign the three components of reputation. This work has been extensively used in research and consulting, and is useful in helping us understand the various views of the organization held by different stakeholders using the same set of measures.

The second is the work of Hatch and Schultz (2008) and Schultz *et al.* (2012), which we have already discussed. These researchers have developed a tripartite framework, based this time on corporate image, corporate vision and organizational culture. By image they mean the outside world's or stakeholders' impression of the company, including customers, shareholders, the media and general public. 'Vision refers to what senior managers aspire to for the company, and culture refers to the organization's key values, behaviours and attitudes' (Hatch and Schultz, 2008, p. 130). Hatch and Schultz have argued that, to build an effective corporate brand or corporate reputation, organizations must ensure that these three elements of an organization, which they call the *three strategic stars*, need to be aligned. According to these authors, misalignments occur when there are significant gaps in the following areas:

- The *vision–culture* gap results from senior managers moving the company in a direction that employees either do not understand or do not support. Sometimes this is a consequence of the pace of change, in which the vision is too stretching, whereas at other times it results from visions that sit uneasily with ethical or traditional values, such as the attempted rebranding of the UK Post Office as Consignia more than a decade ago, which had to be undone fairly quickly.
- The *image–culture* gap usually results from organizations not putting into practice their brand values, and leads to confusion among customers about the company's outside image. This gap is usually most apparent when employees' views of the company are quite different from those held by customers.
- The *image–vision* gap occurs when there is a mismatch between the external image of the organization and senior management's aspirations for it. The example used by Hatch and Schultz was an attempt by British Airways to globalize its image by removing the Union Jack from its tailfins. These actions led to a major public and press reaction, a cabin-crew strike, and key customers threatening to switch to different carriers.

Hatch and Schultz's framework (or 'toolkit') comprises a series of diagnostic questions to assess the extent of misalignment between these three strategic stars (see Figure 6.4). These questions do not break new ground in assessing culture, but they do point to the complex relationships between the external and internal aspects of managing effective corporate branding, placing equal weight on these dimensions.

Finally, Van Riel and Fombrun (2007) tackled the direct people management contribution to corporate reputation building by developing an *employee-expressiveness quotient* (EQ), which, in turn, is linked to strong identification with companies and to supportive employee behaviours (see Figure 6.5). They contended that companies have to express themselves to employees to build emotional appeal, comprising good feelings about the company, admiration, respect and trust in the company. Expression, in this context, referred to the corporate communications process in which companies are willing to 'put themselves out there, to convey who they are and what they stand for' (Fombrun and Van Riel, 2004, p. 95). Figure 6.5 shows the drivers of expression for employees and their relationship to the EQ. You can probably infer the implied proposition, which is: the greater the EQ, the greater the emotional appeal of the company to its workforce.

The EQ is close in tone and language to the notion of employer branding, both of which share an interest in telling credible, unique and compelling stories to employees as to why they should identify with the company. Van Riel and Fombrun (2007) also posited a two-way relationship between identification with the company and expressiveness: the greater the level of identification, the greater the expressiveness and resulting reputation. High levels of identification were likely to lead to employees engaging in supportive behaviours, such as managers 'walking the talk', senior executives constantly communicating results, and front-line, customer-facing staff communicating honestly with customers, behaviour that, in turn, will enhance the corporate reputation over time. Conversely, the better the reputation of the company, the more likely that employees would identify with the company and its mission, acting as 'ambassadors' for the company to potential recruits, to other less-committed employees and, of course, to customers.

This cause-and-effect model is set out more formally in Figure 6.6, which shows how reputation building, personalized communications, the quality of communications and the EQ (or emotional

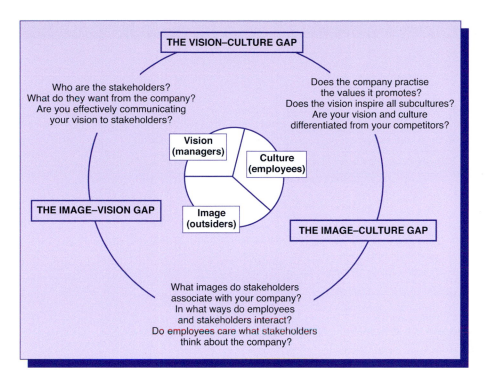

FIGURE 6.4 The corporate branding toolkit

(*Source*: adapted from Hatch and Schultz, 2008.)

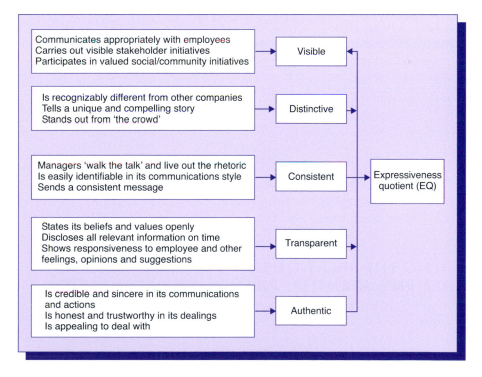

FIGURE 6.5 The expressiveness quotient

(*Source*: adapted from Fombrun and Van Riel, 2003, p. 96.)

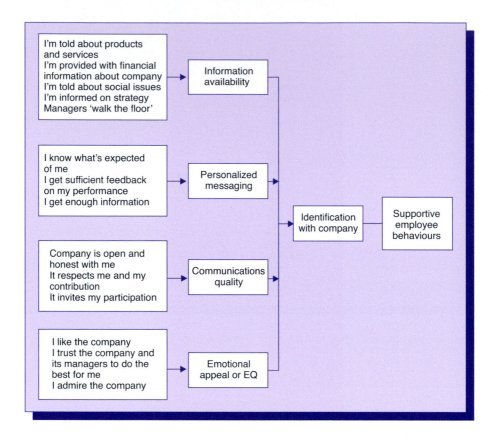

FIGURE 6.6 Measuring identification with the company and the links with employee behaviours
(*Source:* adapted from Fombrun and Van Riel, 2003, p. 100.)

appeal) are linked through increased levels of organizational identification with behaviours that are supportive of corporate reputation. The model also highlights the questions used to assess the levels of organizational identification. Interestingly, these mirror much of our discussion on psychological contracts and identification outlined in Chapter 3.

MODELLING THE RELATIONSHIP BETWEEN PEOPLE MANAGEMENT, IDENTITY, BRANDS AND REPUTATION

We are now almost in a position to develop our model, but first we have to decide on which of the corporate-level concepts discussed in this chapter are to be the *explained* variables and which are the most important *explainers*. As noted, a number of these compete for pre-eminence in corporate-level studies, and we need to be clear about our position on this issue.

Based on the evidence and arguments as they stand, we believe that corporate reputation and corporate brand are the two most important variables impacting directly on the market value of a firm and its capacity to compete in the future. As marketing academics and trust researchers have argued, however, these concepts are linked: brands follow from the trust key stakeholders have in an organization's reputation for competence, benevolence and integrity, and the continued support for its products and services. These concepts, then, need to be explained by a combination of other, important corporate-level concepts and people management variables. The case made by Balmer *et al.* (2006) for identity as the superior lens is a strong one, but it is still too closely aligned with the notion of corporate identity, logos, symbols, and the output of the communications and graphic design industries. Corporate branding is also a powerful and practical concept in describing corporateness, but cannot stand alone, because as pointed out earlier, it is not a state to which all organizations aspire. Corporate reputation also has detractors: as Balmer and Greyser (2003) pointed out, it is no guarantee of organizational success or longevity, and it is still redolent of public relations 'spin'. However, the arguments of Fombrun, his colleagues in the emerging corporate reputation field and researchers on organizational reputations (e.g. Barnett and Pollock, 2012; Deephouse and Suchman, 2008) make a compelling case for reputation being closely linked to business success and failure and its broader application to public sector and voluntary sector organizations, which make up large parts of the national economies.

So our model is based on explaining the interrelated concepts of corporate branding and corporate reputation and their links with people management explainers. In turn, these work through organizational identity and the process of identification (see Figure 6.7).

The core lessons of the model

The core lessons of the model for managers are threefold:

- Corporate reputation and evaluations of corporate brand strength (trust, confidence and support) are strongly influenced by a series of people management strategies, including the nature of HR strategies, formal and informal organizational communications, policies designed to influence psychological contracts, and the main processes connecting individuals to their organizations (the individual–organizational linkages). These processes focus on building identification, commitment and psychological ownership, as discussed in Chapter 3.
- These people management strategies and actions are, in turn, shaped by important corporate-level antecedents, including the corporate vision of leadership in the organization, the more analytical elements of corporate strategy and the expressed corporate identity.
- Finally, the people management strategies work through the reciprocal relationships between organizational identity and supportive employee behaviours to influence the corporate reputation and the corporate brand.

We believe that organizations can take a number of important steps in the area of people management to improve their corporate reputations and, if they so choose, their corporate brands. These are as follows.

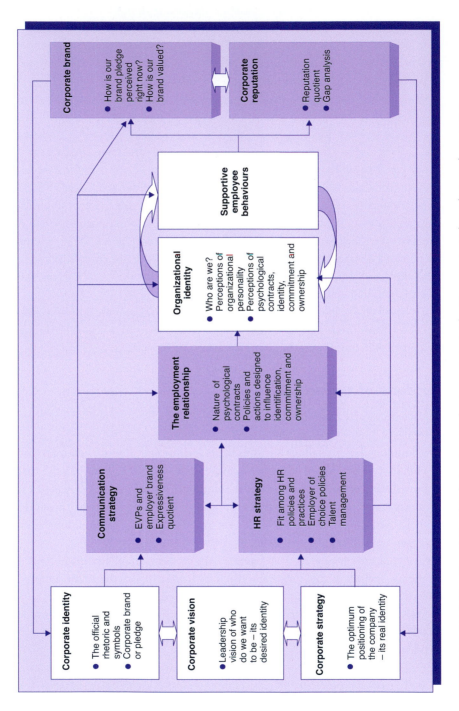

FIGURE 6.7 Modelling the relationship between people management, identity, corporate branding and reputation

Accurately measure what you are trying to achieve

- Organizations should design appropriate measures of corporate reputation and corporate brands, including quantitative measures and qualitative assessments of stakeholder perceptions of reputation and brands at regular intervals.
- Regular assessments should also be made of the organizational identity/identities and the kinds of behaviours associated with organizational identity. This process might include measures of the organization's personality or character, such as the one by Davies (2010) or the RepTrak® approach. It should also include assessments of psychological contracts and whether expectations are being met, and measures of identification with the organization, commitment to it and feelings of psychological ownership in the organization (see Chapter 3). Finally, the performance management literature suggests that regular assessments should be made of the behaviours displayed by employees, using individual and group-level appraisals, although recent claims by consulting companies have suggested this process may be too burdensome in terms of time in relation to the benefits gained.

Understand the nature of the employment relationship and its potential to influence organizational identity

- Managers should understand the various types of psychological contract that exist in their organizations, including the balance between transactional, relational and ideological contracts (see Chapter 3). They might consider segmenting their employees by psychological contract type and designing appropriate mixes of policies and communications to influence and meet employee expectations (see also Chapter 3), though remaining cognizant of the problems of doing so which we take up in the next section.

Use appropriate communications strategies to influence the psychological contracts, identity and supportive employee behaviours

- This should begin with the development of a relevant employee value proposition (EVP) for the company as a whole and a specific or tailored EVP for each of the different segments of employees identified by psychological contract type. These EVPs should contain a novel, compelling and credible story of why people should work for the organization.
- It might also include a tailored employer-branding 'toolkit', which sets out the EVPs, the appropriate behaviours, values and the ethical standards required by the organization.
- Personalized, face-to-face messaging that involves senior managers engaging all levels with employees throughout the process of establishing an identity is usually required, supported by online communications and appropriate written materials. Daniel Diermeier (2011) has gone a few steps further in arguing that reputation management is so important in a company that they should consider establishing a reputation council to act as stewards of the company's reputation, involving managers, employees and other key stakeholders. Their job would be to monitor all business decisions and their potential influence on reputation.

- The key messages should be expressed in such a way as to engage the emotions of employees, by having managers become visible and 'walking the talk', making distinctive promises, stating beliefs and problems openly, being willing to listen, being timely in communications, and being credible and honest. Managers should consistently measure their 'expressiveness quotient', as outlined earlier in the chapter.

Develop an appropriate mix of HR strategies that will facilitate segmentation of psychological contracts and influence organizational identification, commitment and psychological ownership

- Employ appropriate talent management strategies, as discussed in Chapter 3, but avoid the dark side of the 'star system'. This should include clear identification of different performance levels, written action plans for each group, making leaders responsible for developing their talent pool and thoughtful executive development. However, the focus on external recruitment should be viewed with caution, because there is strong evidence that the business of hiring 'stars' is very risky, often leads to companies underperforming and is detrimental to identification by existing employees (Groysberg, 2010).
- Consider developing an 'employer of choice' strategy, but remember that there is no 'one-size-fits-all' approach that will work in every situation. This is especially the case when employees are segmented by psychological contracts, when expectations and what is important are likely to vary by group and over time.

An integrative case study

To bring some of these ideas together, and to help you understand the value of the model in Figure 6.7, let's look at a case that we originally researched in 2002 and recently revisited to see what had become of the company. It's always interesting to write cases in this way because you get a better sense of how things have worked out over time, so telling you more about reputational success and failure than a snapshot view of contemporary cases for which we have no outcomes.

CASE 6.2 AGILENT TECHNOLOGIES IN SCOTLAND

Agilent Technologies is a major international company, formed as a spin-off from Hewlett-Packard (HP) in 1999. Its headquarters are at HP's original 'garage' site in Palo Alto. Agilent operates in 40 countries throughout the world, with more than half of its revenue generated from outside the USA. The company emerged from the original, non-computing product divisions of HP, and specializes in the design, development, production and marketing of communications and life sciences technology, which includes wireless communications, semiconductor products, test measurement and monitoring devices, and chemical analysis equipment. Agilent considers itself a knowledge-based enterprise, with high levels of skills required in research and development, production, marketing and management. It retains much of its HP heritage, and its corporate culture, values and ethics are strong features of the new company.

It is an organization which has attempted to live its global brand values of respect for individuals, even under very difficult market conditions. Following years of prosperity as a separate division of HP and early success as a new company, according to the HR staff the market for its products had 'virtually collapsed' after the downturn in the US economy in early 2001. This market downturn, the severity and length of which had never been experienced before when the company was part of HP, was 'uncharted territory' for all employees, and placed its employer of choice policy under considerable strain.

In March 2001 the company began a severe exercise in cost-cutting, which included a temporary 10 per cent salary cut. Then, in August 2001, Ned Barnholt, the CEO, announced the first redundancies in the history of the company, either as part of HP or as the newly formed Agilent. A second round of redundancies in November resulted in a total of 8,000 employees and 5,000 temporary staff worldwide being laid off. Yet despite these difficult times for the company, Agilent still ranked No. 39 in the 2002 *Sunday Times* annual list of Best Companies to Work for in the UK. This list ranked companies on employees' responses to a survey of their employers, conducted by a third party. Agilent was also ranked third for work–life balance, with 82.8 per cent of those surveyed saying they were encouraged to balance work with personal life. Finally, and perhaps most significantly, Agilent in the USA, where most of the cuts were felt, was also ranked 31st in *Fortune* magazine's Best Companies to Work For in 2002.

In the light of this downsizing, our research question back in 2002 was how had the company managed to retain its high rankings? To address this question, we undertook some case research for the Chartered Institute of Personnel and Development with the HR team in the major UK facility of Agilent Technologies' Test and Measurement Division, based in South Queensferry near Edinburgh, Scotland. Our findings showed that the UK HR staff believed these rankings were a product of consistency in the application of the company's values, and that they had reaped the rewards of a trust dividend created throughout its previous 60 years of operation. The first point made by the HR team was that making compulsory redundancies was the last option to be considered, with cost-cutting and voluntary pay reductions used to head off and curb the immediate need for downsizing. It was only when it became obvious that these other measures were not going to be sufficient that redundancies were considered, and these were handled with the utmost sensitivity. For example, 3,000 managers in the corporation were sent to outplacement consultants to help their staff cope with the problems of redundancy. As a further example of the company's sensitivity to its brand values, it has also remained true to its employer of choice policy. As one HR manager explained at the time:

'The company has stuck with its employer of choice policy. An example is graduate hiring. A year or so ago we were recruiting 100 graduates a year and competing for top talent, along with a number of major firms in Scotland. We were competing in a very competitive market for software engineers, electrical engineers, etc. Now there is no graduate hiring at all. As a consequence we were extremely worried that our reputation as a company may have suffered a little so we have still been active in graduate fairs and the like, explaining why we haven't been taking people on, because we see the need to demonstrate our commitment to the market and we expect things to change. You cannot turn off and on like a tap; you need to be visible.'

The employer of choice policy extended well beyond the hiring stage, as its rankings in *Fortune* and the *Sunday Times* implied, with employment conditions rated among the best in Scotland. These included performance-contingent pay, flexible working hours, group-wide bonuses, pensions and life assurance, employee assistance programmes to help with stressful personal and domestic issues, well-above-average holidays, subsidized high-quality cafeterias and excellent sports facilities. Agilent was also heavily committed to training and career development, with a well-funded employee educa-tion assistance programme providing support for training and education justified on the basis of business reasons. The HR managers also explained how HR had been involved in the corporate branding exercise, citing the tagline to the company name 'Agilent Technologies: Innovating in the HP way', which implied a major consideration of HR issues in the development of the brand name. They saw themselves as part of an integrated company, comprising a team of managers and employees living the Agilent brand values, which balanced business and employee needs. This was exemplified by the HR director, who saw no distinction between the external and internal role of branding:

'We are a values-driven company and cannot operate in any other way. The corporate values are extremely important to us, both inside and outside the company. For example, we have a Standards of Business Conduct Policy, in which we do business in a very different way from many other companies . . . We are a 60-year-old company with a history, the HP heritage, with policies that have stood us in good stead over that period. So we have a very high expectation of how people will behave externally and internally.'

When asked whether employees in the UK were 'living the brand' in 2002, they explained how recent employee survey results had surprised them:

'Given all that has happened – 10 per cent and then 5 per cent pay cuts, bonuses not paid, redundancies for the first time ever – the (survey) results hardly changed. We were still good against our internal and external benchmarks. There has been a falloff, but not nearly as much as we expected. What has happened recently has been a shock to the organization and a radical shift for many people but the value proposition has still been compelling to most of them.'

They also pointed out how 98 per cent of people in the UK company had volunteered for the first round of pay cuts as a way of lessening the impact of redundancies. This figure, however, was slightly less for the second round of pay cuts, indicating that this strategy was not seen as a sustainable solution by employees or the company.

Policy within the company was to continue to benchmark against the best companies to work for, wherever it operates. The HR managers reported that Agilent aimed to be in the top 20 *Fortune* and *Sunday Times* best companies, and to retain its excellent rankings in listings in countries such as India and Australia, where it ranked very highly.

By the summer of 2003, however, the market situation of Agilent in Scotland had deteriorated even more, and all of its business units were required to make further cuts and redundancies. In a presentation made by the Scottish general manager of Agilent to a group of executives, he rather despondently recognized that Agilent had breached the traditional psychological contract with the UK employees, especially over the issue of the traditional 'guarantees' of job security. In addition, he saw no benefit in continuing with the benchmarking exercises and objectives of being among the best companies to work for. He intimated that his major task, and that of his HR team, was to realign the psychological contracts of employees with the 'new realities', but wasn't at all sure how this was going to be achieved.

Revisiting this case in 2015, we find that Agilent is still a global brand but it sold its Test and Measurement Division in 2010, closing down the South Queensferry facility near Edinburgh at approximately the same time, with the loss of many jobs in Scotland. This outcome is a salutary lesson for those who believe in the lessons of the so-called culture excellence literature we briefly reviewed in this chapter. Even the best managed and most reputable companies fail to survive in difficult market circumstances, as has been evidenced many times in case studies of so-called 'excellent' companies (Rosenzweig, 2007), a point worth reflecting on.

Source: adapted from Martin and Beaumont, 2003.

1   What factors may have led to Agilent creating a reputation as a good company to work for, and why do you think they pursued this strategy?
2   How would you account for the positive rankings of Agilent as a good company to work for, even during the difficult circumstances of 2001–2?
3   Why do 'excellent' companies fail, despite have strong reputations internally and externally?

LEARNING SUMMARY

In this chapter we have discussed the importance of corporateness as a new lens through which to view organizations. Many organizations in all sectors of the economy view corporate reputation and a strong corporate brand as an essential component of their corporate strategy, and have invested heavily in image and brand building. This is especially true of international companies that seek to operate in global markets, and *leverage the benefits of trust and confidence in their products and services* worldwide. However, it is not only large organizations that need to secure trust and confidence; small companies, public sector organizations and not-for-profit organizations are especially vulnerable to problems connected with trust and confidence. Investment in strong trust relations has been associated with superior organization performance in the long term, because trust and confidence in an organization and its corporate brand result in customers, employees and other stakeholders continuing *to support the company* by purchasing existing products and services, buying new ones (brand extension) and recommending other people to do the same. Perhaps of equal importance, especially in modern knowledge- and service-based economies, trust and confidence in the organization result in existing and potential employees providing essential support through increased motivation, commitment, identification and psychological ownership. Indeed, as some writers have argued, and which is a central theme of this chapter, creating employee trust and confidence in organization is the most *important, necessary prior condition* for building, maintaining and defending *reputations and brands*.

One of the key problems bedevilling development of this field is the proliferation and confusion of terms: to follow the old management adage, if you can't define something accurately, you can't measure and manage it. As a result, we have spent some time defining the concepts associated with corporateness, including corporate identity, organizational identity, corporate image, corporate strategy, corporate vision, corporate communications, and the key outcomes of strong corporate reputations and brands. The AC²ID framework was used to illustrate these ideas and show you how it might be applied to the analysis of organizational problems.

Returning to the importance of people management in creating, sustaining and defending corporate reputations and brands, we have created a model to show how the complex relationships between HR strategies, communications strategy and the nature of employment relationships can impact on organizational identity and employee behaviours that, in turn, shape corporate brands and corporate reputations. This model has been built from extensive research in the field, and has been used by HR and marketing practitioners to analyse the process of building reputations and brands and to design appropriate people management policies. From the model we also drew some practical lessons concerning the measurement of reputations and brands, understanding the nature of the employment relationship, the use of appropriate communications strategies to influence employment relationships, and the use of different HR strategies to facilitate more refined segmentation of psychological contracts. We concluded the chapter by asking you to apply the model to a case study to illustrate its practical relevance.

REVIEW QUESTIONS

1 What strategies are most likely to create long-term *reputational* capital?
2 The HR department in a company has been given the task of developing a compelling employer brand to help develop employee attraction and engagement. How might they go about doing this?

REFERENCES

Albert, S. and Whetten, D. (1985) Organizational identity. In: L. L. Cummings and B. M. Staw (eds), *Research in Organizational Behaviour*, Vol. 7, pp. 263–295. Greenwich, CT: JAI Press.

Balmer, J. M. T. and Greyser, S. A. (2003) *Revealing the Corporation: Perspectives on identity, image, reputation, corporate branding and corporate-level marketing.* London: Routledge.

Balmer, J. M. T., Mukherjee, A. and Greyser, S. A. (2006) Corporate marketing: integrating corporate identity, corporate branding, corporate communications, corporate image and corporate reputation. *European Journal of Marketing*, 40 (7/8), 730–741.

Barnett, M. L. and Pollock, T. G. (eds) (2012) *The Oxford Handbook of Corporate Reputation*. Oxford: Oxford University Press.

Barney, J. (2002) Strategic management: from informed conversation to academic discipline. *Academy of Management Executive*, 16 (2), 53–58.

Barry, D. and Elmes, M. (1997) Strategy retold: toward a narrative view of strategic discourse. *Academy of Management Review*, 22 (2), 429–452.

Becker, B. E., Huselid, M. A. and Beatty, R. W. (2009) *The Differentiated Workforce: Transforming talent into strategic impact*. Cambridge, MA: Harvard Business School Press.

Boselie, P. (2013) Human resource management and performance. In: S. Bach and M. R. Edwards (eds), *Managing Human Resources*, 5th edn. Chichester, Sussex: Wiley, pp. 18–36.

Boselie, P. (2014) *Strategic Human Resource Management: A balanced approach*, 2nd edn. London: McGraw-Hill.

Boxall, P. and Purcell, J. (2011) *Strategy and Human Resource Management*, 3rd edn. Basingstoke, UK: Palgrave Macmillan.

Cappelli, P. (1998) *The New Deal at Work: Managing the market-driven workforce*. Cambridge, MA: Harvard University School Press.

Davies, G. (2010) The meaning and measurement of corporate reputation. In: R. J. Burke, G. Martin and C. L. Cooper (eds), *Corporate Reputation: Managing opportunities and threats*. Farnham, Surrey: Gower, pp. 45–60.

Davies, G. with Chun, R., Da Silva, R. V. and Roper, S. (2003) *Corporate Reputation and Competitiveness*. London: Routledge.

Deephouse, D. L. and Suchman, M. (2008) Legitimacy in organizational institutionalism. In: R. Greenwood, C. Oliver, R. Suddaby and K. Sahlin-Andersson, *The Sage Handbook of Organizational Institutionalism*. London: Sage, 49–77.

Diermeier, D. (2011) *Reputation Rules: Strategies for building your company's most valuable asset*. New York: McGraw-Hill.

Easterby-Smith, M. and Lyles, M. A. (2011) The evolving field of organizational learning and knowledge management. In: M. Easterby-Smith and M. A. Lyles (eds), *Handbook of Organizational Learning and Knowledge Management*. London: Wiley, pp.1–21.

The Economist (2004) Selling the flag. 26 February.

Elsbach, K. D. (2012) A framework for reputation management over the course of evolving controversies. In: M. L. Barnett and T. G. Pollock (eds), *The Oxford Handbook of Corporate Reputation*. Oxford: Oxford University Press, pp. 466–486.

Fombrun, C. J. (1996) *Reputation*. Cambridge, MA: Harvard Business School Press.

Fombrun, C. J. (2012) The building blocks of corporate reputation: definitions, antecedents, consequences. In: M. L. Barnett and T. G. Pollock (eds), *The Oxford Handbook of Corporate Reputation* (pp. 94–113). Oxford: Oxford University Press.

Fombrun, C. J. and Van Riel, C. B. M. (2003) *How Successful Companies Build Winning Reputations*. Upper Saddle River, NJ: Pearson Education.

Fombrun, C. J. and Van Riel, C. B. M. (2004) *Fame and Fortune: How successful companies build winning reputations*. Upper Saddle River, NJ: Financial Times/Prentice-Hall.

Fombrun, C. J., Ponzi, L. J. and Newbury, W. (2015) Stakeholder tracking and analysis: the RepTrak® system for measuring corporate reputation. *Corporate Reputation Review*, 18, 3–24.

Gioia, D. A., Patvardhan, S. D., Hamilton, A. L. and Corley, K. (2013) Organizational identity formation and change. *The Academy of Management Annals*, 7 (1), 123–193.

Giorgi, S., Lockwood, C. and Glynn, M. A. (2015) The many faces of culture: making sense of 30 years of research on culture. *The Academy of Management Annals*, 9 (1), 1–54.

Godard, J. (2014) The psychologisation of employment relations? *Human Resource Management Journal*, 24 (1), 1–18.

Groysberg, B. (2010) *Chasing Stars: The myth of talent and the portability of performance*. Princeton, NJ: Princeton University Press.

Hamel, G. (2007) *Leading the Revolution*. Cambridge, MA: Harvard Business School Press.

Harquail, C. V. and King, A. W. (2010) Construing organizational identity: the role of embodied cognition. *Organization Studies*, doi: 10.1177/0170840610376143.

Harvey, W. S. and Morris, T. (2012) A labor of love? Understanding the influence of corporate reputation in the labor market. In: M. L. Barnett and T. G. Pollock (eds), *The Oxford Handbook of Corporate Reputation*. Oxford: Oxford University Press, pp. 341–360.

Hatch, M. J. and Schultz, M. (2008) *Taking Brand Initiative: How the company can align strategy, culture and identity through corporate branding*. San Francisco, CA: Wiley.

Hatch, M. J. and Schultz, M. (2013) The dynamics of corporate brand charisma: routinization and activation at Carlsberg IT. *Scandinavian Journal of Management*, 29 (2),147–162.

Hatch, M. J. with Cunliffe, A. L. (2013) *Organization Theory: Modern, symbolic and postmodern perspectives*, 3rd edn. Oxford: Oxford University Press.

Joyce, W., Nohria, N. and Robertson, B. (2003) *What Really Works: The 4+2 formula for sustained business success*. New York: HarperCollins.

Kaplan, R. S. (2008) Conceptual foundations of the balanced scorecard. In: C. Chapman, A. Hopwood and M. Shields (eds), *Handbook of Management Accounting Research*, Vol. 3, 1253–1269. Oxford: Elsevier.

Kaplan, R. S. and Norton, D. (2001) *The Strategy-Focused Organization*. Cambridge, MA: Harvard Business School Press.

Kirn, S. P., Rucci, A. J., Huselid, M. and Becker, B. (1999) Strategic human resource management at Sears. *Human Resource Management*, 38 (4), 329–335.

Leary-Joyce, J. (2004) *Becoming an Employer of Choice: Making your own organization a place where people want to do great work*. London: Chartered Institute of Personnel and Development.

Martin, G. and Beaumont, P. B. (2003) *Branding and People Management: What's in a name?* London: Chartered Institute of Personnel and Development.

Martin, G. and Cerdin, J.-L. (2014) Employer branding and career theory: new directions for research. In: P. R. Sparrow, H. Scullion and I. Tarique (eds), *Strategic Talent Management: Contemporary issues in international context*. Cambridge: Cambridge University Press, pp. 151–176.

Martin, G. and Hetrick, S. (2006) *Corporate Reputations, Branding and HRM*. Oxford: Butterworth-Heinemann.

Martin, G. and Hetrick, S. (2010) Employer branding and corporate reputations in an international context. In: P. S. Sparrow (ed.), *Handbook on International Human Resource Management*. Sussex: John Wiley & Sons, pp. 293–321.

Martin, G., Gollan, P. J. and Grigg, K. (2011) Is there a bigger and better future for employer branding? Facing up to innovation, corporate reputations and wicked problems in SHRM. *International Journal of Human Resource Management*, 22 (17), 3618–3637.

Martin, G., Beech, N., MacIntosh, R. and Bushfield, S. (2015) Potential challenges facing distributed leadership in healthcare: evidence from the UK national health service. *Sociology of Health & Illness*. 37 (1), 14–29.

Martineau, P. (1958) The personality of the retail store. *Harvard Business Review*, January/February, 47.

Melewar, T. C., Sarstedt, M. and Hallier, C. (2012) Corporate identity, image and reputation management: a further analysis. *Corporate Communications: An international journal*, 17 (1), 1–5.

Michaels, E., Handfield-Jones, H. and Alexrod, B. (2001) *The War for Talent*. Cambridge, MA: Harvard Business School Press.

Miller, D. and Merrilees, B. (2013) Rebuilding community corporate brands: a total stakeholder approach. *Journal of Business Research*, 66 (2),172–179.

Peters, T. J. and Waterman, R. H., Jr (1982) *In Search of Excellence*. New York: Harper & Row.

Pew Research Center (2014) Which countries don't like America and which do? Available online at www.pewresearch.org/fact-tank/2014/07/15/which-countries-dont-like-america-and-which-do/.

Pfeffer, J. (1998) *The Human Equation: Building profits by putting people first*. Cambridge, MA: Harvard Business School Press.

Pfeffer, J. (2010) Building sustainable organizations: the human factor. *Academy of Management Perspectives*, 24 (1), 34–45.

Porter, M. P. (1996) What is strategy? *Harvard Business Review*, November/December, 61–71.

Porter, M. P. (2008) The five competitive forces that shape strategy. *Harvard Business Review*, January, 79–93.

Reay, T. and Hinings, C. R. (2009) Managing the rivalry of competing institutional logics. *Organization Studies*, 30 (6), 629–652.

Reputation Institute (2015) Global RepTrak 100-2105. Available online at www.reputationinstitute/com/Resources/Registered/PDF-Resources/Global-RepTrak-100-2105.aspx.

Rosenzweig, P. (2007) *The Halo Effect . . . and the Eight Other Business Delusions That Deceive Managers*. New York: Free Press.

Schein, E. (1992) *Organizational Culture and Leadership*. San Francisco, CA: Jossey-Bass.

Schultz, M., Hatch, M. J. and Adams, N. (2012) Managing corporate reputation through corporate branding. In: M. L. Barnett and T. G. Pollock (eds), *The Oxford Handbook of Corporate Reputation*. Oxford: Oxford University Press, pp. 420–445.

Sjovall, A. M. and Talk, A. (2004) From actions to impressions: cognitive attribution theory and the formation of corporate reputation. *Corporate Reputation Review*, 7, 269–281.

Van Riel, C. B. M. and Fombrun, C. J. (2007) *Essentials of Corporate Communication: Implementing effective reputation management*. Oxford: Routledge.

Chapter 7

The knowledge context, organizational learning and managing people

LEARNING OBJECTIVES

By the end of this chapter you should be able to:

- understand the nature of knowledge in society, its role in creating strategic advantage in knowledge-based enterprises and the role of people management;

- understand what knowledge is and its relationship to learning;

- describe the processes of knowledge management in organizations and use them to analyse an organization;

- understand how organizations create and share knowledge and learning;

- understand the relationship between knowledge and learning, especially the importance of tacit knowledge;

- apply a knowledge management perspective to an organization;

- understand the notion of intellectual capital, and advise on how it might be measured in different types of organization;

- use measures of intellectual capital to evaluate an organization;

- understand how different forms of knowledge relate to organizations and processes and the issue of managing people;

- advise managers on the nature of 'knowledge workers' and the issues connected with managing knowledge workers;

- advise on an appropriate performance management system for knowledge workers.

UNDERSTANDING THE NATURE OF KNOWLEDGE MANAGEMENT AND ORGANIZATIONAL LEARNING, AND IMPACT ON ORGANIZATIONS AND PEOPLE

Introduction

One of the received wisdoms in the strategic management literature is that organizations that are able to integrate disparate sources of *knowledge* across their boundaries will be those that survive and prosper. These disparate sources include not only formal, written or coded forms of knowledge but also the possession of some advantageous, intangible, knowledge-based assets (Easterby-Smith and Lyles, 2011). Indeed, as we have seen in Chapter 4, some writers on innovation go further to claim that the primary reason for an organization's existence is its ability to transfer knowledge and learning more effectively and efficiently than through external market mechanisms (Gupta and Govindarajan, 2004). This is especially true of international organizations, many of which have previously relied on establishing subcontracting relationships, based purely on market relations and the price mechanism, to extend their operations beyond their domestic boundaries. Nowadays, they are more likely to engage in networks or strategic alliances, as we discussed in Chapter 4. However, these arguments may also be applied to smaller- and medium-sized organizations that operate in mainly domestic markets in the developed world, as they increasingly find themselves in a knowledge-based economy, with intellectual rather than physical or financial capital being the source of their competitive advantage. Consider the following illustration of a Scottish financial services company in the case below.

CASE 7.1 STANDARD LIFE INVESTMENTS, KNOWLEDGE TRANSFER AND BUSINESS DEVELOPMENT OVERSEAS

Standard Life Investments (SLI) is a global investment company, which focuses on managing institutional investments for clients in a range of countries. It was formed as a separate division of its parent company, the Standard Life Assurance Company, which was founded in 1825, floated on the London Stock Exchange in 2006 and is a FTSE 100 company. SLI has offices in Boston, Hong Kong, Paris, Beijing, Sydney, London, Dublin and Seoul, and has established joint ventures in India and Japan. The company is headquartered in Edinburgh, Scotland, employs 1,100 people and manages assets worth £246 billion on behalf of clients through the world. This represents a three fold increase in the number of employees and a five fold growth in managed assets since 1998. The company has consistently won awards for its fund performance and levels of service to clients.

The company provides skilled investment experts to manage the assets that many organizations, including its own parent company, have entrusted to SLI. These investment experts are of two kinds. First, client fund managers are responsible for the full range of their clients' performance and servicing needs: in effect, they are customer relationship managers who provide a tailored portfolio-management service to key customers. Second, asset class managers focus on identifying investment opportunities and generate performance. These scarce, highly talented and experienced people, much of whose work is both esoteric and skilled, are attracted, motivated and rewarded by exceptional remuneration packages. The fund and asset managers are supported by a large 'back-office' team of marketing, information systems and HR professionals.

The company employs an investment philosophy and process that involves asset allocation, stock selection, portfolio development, risk management and dealing. It is research intensive and is built on a 'Focus on Change' philosophy, which provides early and detailed information on key drivers that affect markets and on the dynamics likely to influence the investment environment, particularly the pricing of stock. The webpage of the SLI explicitly states:

> 'we believe in a collaborative approach to business where knowledge and expertise are shared openly. When we work together, we work more effectively as a team. Our team-based approach encourages us to share ideas across asset classes, business areas and worldwide locations. We do this on a daily basis through cross-team communication and webcasts with our global offices.'
>
> *Source*: www.standardlifeinvestments.com/about_us/
> investment_approach/index.html

Investment decisions are based on five guiding questions:

- What are the key market drivers?
- What's changing?
- What expectations are priced in?
- Why will the market change its mind about these expectations?
- What will trigger these changes?

These questions represent a common 'language' that is used to guide all decision-making in all regional offices and on all asset classes. The 'Focus on Change' philosophy also recognizes that different factors drive markets at different times, and that prices are not inherently responsive to internal growth or momentum. Consequently, fund managers have an opportunity to outperform others during a cycle, but only if they are able to understand it better than fund managers in other companies. So, for example, through having deep knowledge of a macroeconomic analysis of China or of key competitors in the USA, they are better able to predict the price of stock in the UK. As one of their internal company documentation stated: 'The more pieces of corroborating evidence we can amass, the greater the conviction we can take behind these investment positions' (internal company documents).

Investment knowledge is gained from top-down and bottom-up information and is expressed in a house view by the chief investment officer and his team of analysts, who provide strategic direction for Standard Life Investments. As stated above, the success of the company also depends on its ability to learn from its offices in other parts of the world; in turn, they require having high-quality sources of knowledge on which to make their decisions. The company prides itself on global team-working and on its people management philosophies and practices, for which they have won awards. Standard Life has established a culture based on team autonomy and trust, and a strong employer brand that is used to attract and retain top talent (see Chapters 3 and 6).

SLI has grown rapidly through acquisitions, including a major one in 2014 with the UK company Ignis and joint ventures. However, it only does so with business partners that can exhibit similar business cultures and sound business processes, or at least ones that are complementary. When first researching this case, senior managers explained that India was a natural and desirable target for expansion because of a common language, laws and business practices. Conversely, however, their efforts to expand into the fast-growing Chinese market left managers challenged by the slow pace and rather 'exotic nature of the negotiation process', learning the language, ambiguities in the regulatory environment and simply finding a partner willing to accept Standard Life Investments' business model. However, that problem seems to have been solved.

SLI's origins and culture lay in the mutualized heritage of its parent company, which changed in 2006. Prior to demutualization, the parent company was a type of partnership of members (policyholders) in which the company reinvested all profits for the benefit of the members. Standard Life fought a long battle to resist demutualization but, given the pressures placed on it by some members and trends among most large insurance businesses in Europe, demutualization became inevitable. In addition to internal pressures and industry trends, the arguments for demutualization included increasing efficiency, gaining access to capital for expansion, increasing commercial flexibility, unlocking the value of ownership rights and benefits for staff, customers and future shareholders. Demutualization involved floating the company on the stock market and, second, changing the mindsets of managers to act in the interests of its new shareholders as well as its other stakeholders. It also brought with it the potential for takeover or merger, especially if it under-performed. Such a changed environment from 2006 onwards led the company to think very seriously about its knowledge management and human resource policies.

1 In what ways does Standard Life Investments rely on knowledge to operate its business? Are knowledge and learning core activities in its present and future success?
2 What problems do you foresee for Standard Life Investments in managing its current and future activities?

One very useful way of thinking about this case and, indeed, the whole subject area of the knowledge context is to draw on a framework we have adapted from an earlier model of strategic knowledge management by Choo and Bontis (2002) (see Figure 7.1). We continue to use this framework because it raises six sets of questions that organizations such as SLI need to address. Like many other companies, SLI compete with others on their ability to manage the *knowledge assets* they hold and the *processes they use to learn* from each other (Easterby-Smith and Lyles, 2011):

1   Why is knowledge seen as a strategic asset in modern societies, and why should organizations become more interested in managing knowledge and their intellectual assets? In the late 1990s there was much talk of a 'new economy' and the role of knowledge and technology in promoting changes in society. Given recent trends, was this new economy discourse justified?
2   What does a knowledge-intensive enterprise (KIE), such as SLI, look like? What are the essential features of such organizations? And can we learn about them from studying traditional

knowledge-based organizations, such as the universities and consulting firms? The terms 'knowledge-based economies' (KBEs) and 'knowledge-intensive enterprises' (KIEs) have entered the lexicon of management studies. What makes them different?

3   What are the processes by which KIEs *create, transfer* and *utilize knowledge* within and beyond their boundaries, and how effective are they? Organizations, such as those represented in the above cases, generate value from what they know, which can be defined as their stock of *intellectual capital* at a point in time. This intellectual capital, however, depends on an organization's ability to manage the processes of knowledge creation, dissemination and exploitation. The key questions connected with these processes are: What are the best means for such organizations to convert *tacit knowledge* (which resides in employees' heads and organizational processes) into *explicit knowledge* (which is formal, usually written, codified knowledge)? How can they share

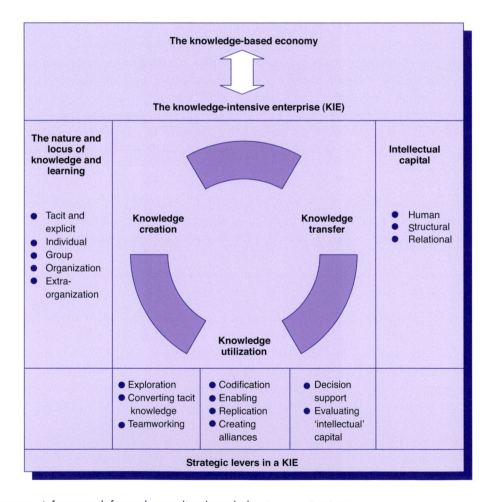

FIGURE 7.1 A framework for understanding knowledge in organizations

(*Source*: based on Choo and Bontis, 2002; Easterby-Smith and Lyles, 2011.)

such knowledge among their subunits and partners across national and international boundaries and time periods? How can they integrate and coordinate knowledge to develop goods and services?

4   How does a KIE facilitate and help *feed-forward* and *feed-back* knowledge creation and learning *between the different levels* in an organization – individual, group, organization and extra-organizational networks? Arguably, only individuals can learn about work, but how they learn, and from whom and where they learn, are matters of some debate. Is learning for work best undertaken by individuals in a 'schooled' environment away from work, or is learning essentially a group process that is most effective when it is carried out in the context of work? Equally important is to ensure that the learning that takes place in individuals and small groups becomes part of the wider processes of organizational learning, and in certain cases, extra-organizational learning (e.g. suppliers, customers, government and other key stakeholders).

5   What is the *nature of the intellectual capital* generated by the processes of knowledge creation, transfer and utilization, and how can it be exploited? Intellectual capital is often described as comprising *human capital* (the learning, knowledge and skills residing in people, groups and in an organization's unique culture, which cannot be owned by the company in any strict sense), *structural capital* (the hardware, software, organizational structure, databases, trademarks and brands that support employees, and which are owned by the company) and *relational or social capital*, the bonds, bridges and trust developed with customers, employees, suppliers and other key stakeholders.

6   What *strategic levers* can be 'pulled' to improve the processes described above? These levers include: methods of promoting knowledge creation through groups, etc.; forming cross-functional work teams; establishing enabling conditions for knowledge creation through appropriate human resource management practices; replicating organizational routines across different parts of an organization, e.g. building in automatic environmental scanning; methods of codifying knowledge to make it explicit and capable of being stored; designing decision support systems; and measuring and evaluating an organization's intellectual assets.

We shall use this framework to organize our discussion of knowledge management and organizational learning by examining in turn the nature of the 'knowledge-based economy' KIEs, the nature of knowledge and learning, the processes of knowledge creation, transfer and utilization, the strategic levers that can be pulled to enhance knowledge management and the outcomes of KIEs, and the creation of intellectual capital.

THE KNOWLEDGE-BASED ECONOMY

The idea of a knowledge-based economy (KBE), which advances the notion that knowledge industries, knowledge workers and knowledge assets are the most important sources of economic growth, has been around since the 1980s (Brinkley, 2008). Nevertheless, it remains a contested concept (James *et al.*, 2011). Following the problems associated with the de-industrialization of many Western economies, in which the traditional mass-production industries of America and Europe declined in importance, there was the search for a new, more optimistic theory of economic development. As Western economies moved from being powerhouses of manufacturing to becoming largely service-driven economies, a major, and seemingly intractable, problem presented itself: how to increase productivity in an economy based largely on services so that living standards could continue to rise. Because living standards are highly sensitive to productivity increases, economists were quick to point out that productivity in services industries was notoriously difficult to increase, because there are natural limits to the levels (quantity and quality) of service that customers desire – for example, in eating out at restaurants, attending concert halls, undergoing education, having new tyres put on their cars, having their investments managed and in taking holidays. Increasing inputs in customer care, it was argued, would yield rapidly diminishing returns (and eventually negative ones, as people came to resent the intrusive, 'have-a-nice-day' syndrome). Thus, economies such as those in the West, which were rapidly changing to include high proportions of such workers in their employment structure, would eventually move towards a position of zero productivity growth, and thus zero rises in standards of living. Such a view is consistent with the evidence on low productivity in developed economies such as the UK, which has relied heavily on services for economic growth.

Following the emergence of the new computer-based and digital technologies in the USA in the 1980s, the entrepreneurial spirit to which these gave rise, and the resurgence of the American economy in the 1990s, a set of new theories of economic growth began to emerge (Evans and Wurster, 2000; see also Chapter 8 on the technological context for more details). For example, an influential OECD report published in 2001, entitled *The New Economy: Beyond the Hype*, identified information and communication techniques (ICT), education levels and the proportion of knowledge-intensive employment as key factors in explaining differential growth rates among advanced industrialized countries. The core of these theories was that sustained economic wealth was most effectively created by focusing on knowledge and knowledge-based products – in effect in moving from a *hardware world* of bricks and mortar and manufactured goods to a *software-dominated world* of computer code, DNA-based biotechnology, educational and consulting services, and e-trading, all of which were reliant on new ICT and social media for their 'transport infrastructure' (Alavi and Denford, 2011). This knowledge-based version of economic growth was inherently optimistic, because it was not associated with a future based on diminishing returns or deteriorating productivity growth. Knowledge, it was argued, could be applied an infinite number of times with no decline in value, was relatively durable through time and space, and could be stored at very little cost using digital media. The uses to which knowledge could be put were also thought to be infinite, as innovation promised new ranges of products and services to new markets. Thus, for example, although people in the West might have natural limits to the levels of services they required, the emerging markets in Asia and Eastern Europe were thought to be infinitely susceptible to McDonald's franchises, digitized recordings of concert hall (or popular) music, online degrees and low-cost air travel, all of which are forms of knowledge-based products and services.

Thus, the new economics of knowledge focus on knowledge as a key factor in economic and technological growth (see the World Economic Forum, 2015). And, rather obviously, since knowledge is essentially a human construction, the new economics of knowledge and the new knowledge economies were seen to be largely dependent on the *quality and management of people* (Teece and Al-Aali, 2011). There are at least five strands to this argument:

1   Knowledge is seen as an important economic factor input, in the same way as the traditional economic factors of production – land, labour and capital. Like capital, knowledge can accumulate over time and is seen to be an important engine of economic growth. For example, as we have seen, the growth rates of economies are often linked to spending by organizations and government on research and development (R&D), and world competitiveness is linked to technological growth, so the proportion of knowledge workers in an economy and their levels of knowledge are thought to be critical (World Economic Forum, 2015).

2   Knowledge, however, is a rather different type of concept from the term 'information', widely used in ICT. Information is defined in terms of the codifiable 'know why' and 'know what'. As we have seen, however, much knowledge is tacit and is embedded in people and contexts – so-called 'know-how' – so the economic returns to knowledge workers tend to be high because of their relative scarcity value. This is most obviously reflected in the net worth of senior business figures and of certain engineers and scientists. Twenty-two per cent of the world's wealthiest people in 2015 had an engineering degree, while a further 20 per cent held degrees in maths or science, showing the value of the so-called STEM (Science, technology engineering and maths) subjects. Such people are said to earn *economic rent* – payment for relatively scarce knowledge and skills that are inelastic in supply. The same argument is also used to explain the high earnings of sport stars, investment managers and pop musicians.

3   Most knowledge is not of the pure, 'research and development' type, associated with scientific breakthroughs, but is embodied in products such as software, digital media, databases, financial bonds, video games and online courses. Organizations in knowledge-based industries, such as those offering these products, have been traditionally characterized by high fixed development costs but low marginal production costs, and have had major problems in recovering these costs in price-sensitive markets. Consequently, there have been great pressures on these organizations to protect their intellectual property rights and to reduce their fixed costs by 'off-shoring' some of the knowledge work to the newly emerging economies such as India in the fields of software writing and call centres.

4   Knowledge is thought to *spill over* and to be *localized*. Thus, breakthrough ideas created by one firm are thought to spill over to other firms and industries in a local region more quickly than between regions. Consequently, we often witness clustering of firms in knowledge-intensive sectors such as financial services, software, mobile telephones, e-learning and biotechnology, where face-to-face interaction and the rapid transfer of employees between firms in a region are thought to be important in knowledge transfer. These locally clustered labour market factors are extremely important in developing career opportunities and in establishing attitudes to work.

5   Enormous emphasis has been placed on the emergence of *knowledge networks* that facilitate the kinds of interactions between people and ideas central to the previous point concerning clustering. The diffusion of tacit knowledge, in particular, is facilitated by such networks, so access to such networks becoming critical for knowledge workers and knowledge transfer. However, these networks are heavily dependent on integrating increasing numbers of members for their added value, within and between organizations, as they seek to learn from each other and share out the costs of innovation. To succeed, these networks have had to develop a new form of integration, based more on trust and less on market/price coordination or hierarchical/

authority coordination (Van Wijk *et al.*, 2011a). This renewed emphasis on trust has enormous implications for the management of employment relations, and in recruiting, developing, motivating and retaining talented, trustworthy people (Siebert *et al.*, 2015). At the same time, such networks are thought to create lock-in effects, which mean that past decisions shape collective choices about new technologies and other forms of knowledge. Thus, being part of a network provides access to new ideas, but it can also create a form of 'psychic prison' that limits innovation and creativity.

Taiwan is an excellent example of an economy that is linking its desire to develop a national economic development strategy based on the growth of KIEs. An article in *The Economist* (15 January 2005) pointed out that three-quarters of the world's notebook computers, two-thirds of LCD panels and 80 per cent of personal digital assistants were made in Taiwan in 2000, but few people had heard of a Taiwanese brand. By 2005, Taiwanese manufacturers had transferred nearly all production to China. Companies such as BenQ and Acer design and manufacture many ICT products for other companies. These companies began as original equipment manufacturers (OEMs), producing to the designs of other companies, but gradually took over substantial parts of the design processes themselves to become original design manufacturers (ODMs). However, BenQ was the first company to try to build a world-class brand in its own right when it was spun off from Acer; it had 40 per cent of its business as 'own brand' by 2005. Since then, Acer has also established a brand name and is one of the largest computer brands in the world, especially for monitors and laptops in which it was in second position in 2011.

KNOWLEDGE-INTENSIVE ENTERPRISES

A definition and example

At the core of the arguments for the new, knowledge-based economy were so-called *knowledge-intensive enterprises* (KIEs). This notion of knowledge intensity indicated the relative nature of the reliance on knowledge in organizations. KIEs have been differentiated from other forms of organization because of their ability to bring together the knowledge of specialists more effectively than through contractual relations, the spot market and price mechanisms (Foss and Mahnke, 2011). In other words, they were seen as 'knowledge-integrating institutions'. Although some writers claim that the concept has gone out of fashion since its heyday in the early 2000s, it has been seen as a bridging concept that explains how firms based on knowledge assets and knowledge workers are different from traditional organizations (Makini and Marche, 2010). To explore the nature of KIEs and what makes them different, it is worth examining one of the oldest forms of knowledge-intensive institutions, with which all of you are familiar. Here, we are referring to universities, and we need look no further than university business schools, which are among the newest (and often most resented) departments in higher education, to reveal some of the problems and tensions that KIEs face (Pettigrew *et al.*, 2014).

BOX 7.1 **Universities as the archetypical KIE: the case of the business schools**

Contrary to the normal professional bureaucracy (see Chapter 4 on the organizational context) found in most universities, it would certainly be possible to operate a 'virtual' business school with a very small core staff of administrators and rely on entering into market-based, pay-for-performance, contract relations with academics from around the world to write and teach students. Such virtual schools can be more effective and efficient in operating a 'delivery model of education' and more flexible in responding to signals from the educational markets they serve. However, most university business schools have not followed that route, preferring to retain the 'brick' schools that reflect the traditional university model, staffed by traditionally employed experts on full-time contracts. This traditional brick or campus-based form of organization has remained the dominant one, despite the fashion for retrenching to core competences.

Arguably, this apparent conservatism is because university business schools see their core competences as more than delivering teaching, which, in its most basic form, can be seen as an individual relationship between teacher and student. There are major threats to the traditional business schools, however, from the new 'corporate universities' and consulting companies on the one hand and, on the other hand, from the university–corporate collaborations, which are moving rapidly into developing sophisticated business models for delivering high-quality online learning through so-called MOOCs (Massive Online Open Courses) on a global basis.

This example also illustrates the following three key features of KIEs:

- their needs to access core, advanced and innovative knowledge;
- their needs to build communities of knowledge workers;
- their needs and capacity to absorb new knowledge and transform it into useful products and services.

Core, advanced and innovative knowledge

It is often argued that all organizations need core knowledge merely to compete in an industry (on the basis of the existing 'rules of the game'). So, for example, all university business schools need to have access to certain core knowledge to teach MBA courses. However, certain schools invest heavily in advanced knowledge, often through unique, research-based content over which they have established some intellectual property rights, or through improved methods of learning. They do so to differentiate themselves from other schools (by attempting to change the existing rules of the game). However, business schools seeking to dominate the industry on a regional or global basis will need to draw on truly innovative knowledge to change the basis of competition (continuing with the games metaphor, to change the game itself). It is this innovative aspect of KIEs that makes them important to modern economies and provides them with a potentially powerful source of long-term strategic advantage. Much of the recent focus on innovation has been on the evolving power of ICT and social media in KIEs. In the context of university business schools, ICT and social media are seen as critical to extend their outreach into other countries, through for example, online learning, MOOCs, blogs and social networking, but to do so in such a way that those on the periphery of a business school's main campus are socially connected to each other and to the centre.

The communal nature of KIEs

The second way of looking at a KIE, also illustrated by the example of a business school, is to emphasize its needs for community and a sense of shared identity. It is argued that KIEs tend to rely on a strong sense of shared identity to reduce communication costs and minimize the degree of bureaucracy required for regulation purposes, an argument that reflects the importance of trust as a coordinating mechanism in the previous section on knowledge-based economies. However, the shared identity of KIEs also contributes to the propensity for organizations to learn by creating communities of practice that support individual learning and knowledge sharing (Wenger, 1998). We shall define and discuss such communities of practice later in this chapter, but the essential points are that communities are forms of social networks that create the social capital of an organization, and that they do so more effectively than through a purely market relationship. Such social capital, in the form of a set of unique relations between people (sometimes called its *cultural capital*), is leveraged to produce an organization's intellectual capital, and it is this aspect of organizations that provides them with a distinct and non-reproducible source of differentiated, competitive advantage. Thus, university business schools have traditionally seen themselves in the roles of facilitating and building knowledge production in research communities, in encouraging learners to participate in learning communities and in developing long-standing social networks that, by definition, require academics, students, practitioners and alumni to work together and to share their ideas (Pettigrew *et al.*, 2014).

The absorptive capacity of KIEs

A KIE both uses knowledge as a key input to its core business and produces knowledge as a key output for customers. Returning to our example of the business school, competitive advantage is more likely to accrue to those schools that have a well-developed capacity for absorbing leading-edge knowledge from industry and from other academic networks, such as alumni. Such a capacity is known as *absorptive capacity*. This refers to an organization's ability to *acquire, assimilate, transform* and *exploit* new knowledge (Van Wijk *et al.*, 2011b; Martin and Reddington, 2009) (see Figure 7.2). Thus, any KIE, including our business school exemplar, seeking to create new knowledge and create innovative products, services or processes needs a high *potential* for:

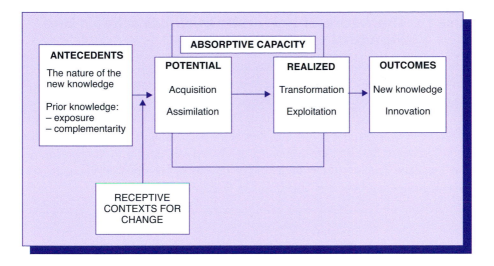

FIGURE 7.2 A KIE's absorptive capacity for new knowledge

(*Source:* based on Zahra and George, 2002; Martin and Reddington, 2009.)

- identifying and acquiring new knowledge with greater speed, intensity and focus than others;
- assimilating this new knowledge into the KIE's current routines and processes more effectively than others.

They also have to realize their potential by:

- transforming this knowledge by developing it and fusing it with existing knowledge to provide some novel ideas, products or processes;
- exploiting this newly transformed knowledge by leveraging existing learning competencies or developing completely new competencies.

The extent to which a KIE has the potential absorptive capacity for new knowledge is, however, dependent on key *antecedents*, including: (1) the nature of the knowledge it possesses; (2) whether it has had any previous exposure or past experience with related knowledge; and (3) whether this new knowledge complements its existing body of knowledge. It is also likely to be influenced by the existence of receptive contexts for change, such as a crisis in the organization, new legislation that supports the need for new knowledge, or new leadership and/or a new strategic direction.

EXERCISE 7.1 **The future of university business schools and Standard Life Investments**

1 Continuing with our example of university business schools, what practical measures could an established school implement to increase its absorptive capacity? What constraints can you envisage in increasing absorptive capacity in this context?

2 In the case of Standard Life Investments at the beginning of the chapter, to what extent is its absorptive capacity one of the key factors for success in its business? What problems do you foresee in the company exploiting its absorptive capacity in its overseas ventures?

3 What receptive contexts for change might influence the absorptive capacities of the university business school and Standard Life Investments?

KNOWLEDGE CREATION, TRANSFER AND UTILIZATION

Knowledge creation and learning

To deepen our understanding of the knowledge context, we need to address the nature of knowledge and learning, namely what knowledge is (and is not), what the different forms of knowledge are, how knowledge relates to learning, and the relationships between different forms of knowledge and organizational structures. Usually, the first distinction made in texts on the subject is between information and knowledge, in which information is treated as the organization of basic 'factual' data. Information becomes knowledge only when people apply their minds to change it in some way. In effect, knowledge is a human creation and is inherently subjective, whereas data and information are seen in a more objective and basic sense. It is this human and subjective quality of knowledge that makes it different from other factor inputs into organizations and, as we have seen, makes it a unique source of competitive advantage. There are at least three perspectives we can take on the nature of knowledge creation and learning:

1 To see knowledge as the *outcome of learning*. As individuals (and groups), we learn to acquire knowledge and also use knowledge to learn about something important to us. For example, in learning about the nature of knowledge in this book, hopefully you gain new knowledge to use in your workplaces.

2 To view knowledge as something *conscious and actionable* – people need to know what they know, know why they need to know and act upon it, for, as some commentators believe, it is only through conscious reflection and action that we truly understand. This perspective on knowledge and learning has become important in the field of training and development, and is embodied in the principles of action learning, which are based on the idea that you only really know about something – for example, the organization in which you work – when you have to change it. So, some learning theorists argue that understanding of theory and concepts to analyse

a situation only takes us so far in learning; the real problems and deep learning come at the implementation stage, and then only if we consciously reflect on what worked (or didn't work) and why.

3 To see knowledge as a *dynamic, social construction* – that is, knowledge is continuously created, sustained and changed by people, usually working in conjunction with others. This dynamic characteristic of knowledge places more importance on knowing than on knowledge itself. For example, it is often argued that knowing and teaching facts is less important than learning how to learn, as the useful lifespan of knowledge in modern societies is often short; therefore, we need to learn the skills of knowing to be able to operate in an increasingly unknowable world and in learning 'how to be' (Brandi and Elkjaer, 2011).

Explicit and tacit knowledge and learning

Another major issue that taxes most people in the field of knowledge management and learning is how you convert tacit knowledge into explicit knowledge. For example, in the case of Standard Life Investments, one of its biggest problems is converting the largely tacit knowledge of its 'star' fund managers into explicit knowledge. It needs to do this so that it can transfer its expertise to its overseas offices and joint ventures, and retain these fund managers so that their expertise doesn't 'walk out of the door'. Let's look at a classic illustration of tacit knowledge by John Seely Brown, one of the key thinkers in knowledge management and organizational learning over the last few decades, to help understand its nature and shed light on the problems involved in managing it.

CASE 7.2 JOHN SEELY BROWN ON LEARNING AND BRICOLAGE

This material is quoted verbatim from a presentation made by John Seely Brown in 2004, who was talking about his work as Chief Scientist at Xerox before he became an academic and consultant.

'There was also a second defining moment, a kind of event for me. I was initially trained in theoretical mathematics and hard-core computer science. The event that actually transformed me was something that showed me that there was a lot that a theoretical mathematician understood about how the world really works.

This had happened before, before I was working in Xerox. It's actually ironic that we are in this particular building. I had been doing a lot of work on troubleshooting for the Navy, and also how to build really hard-core computer science systems, these job-performance aids, for actually figuring how to really get people to be much more effective at troubleshooting. So I joined Xerox some time ago, and after a while, Xerox discovered my background in having worked for the Department of Defense (DoD), and the Navy in particular, and really rethinking troubleshooting.

So they said, "John, you really have to, kind of, help us." Most days, those machines broke down. No comment. (Laughter.)

So I said, "You know, it would be really helpful if I could actually meet some expert troubleshooters."

They said, "Fine, we've got a great expert troubleshooter, actually in Leesburg, Virginia, about 20 miles from here. Why don't you go meet him?"

So I said, "Well, great, I'll go and meet him." And they called in advance, and said that this guy is coming.

Well the first mistake that happened, I walked into the office, wearing a suit. This was not good.

He was a real kind of guy who fixes real machines. So he was not happy. He was saying to himself, "Now here's a suit, and it's going to be a total loss. And he's an academic, even more of a loss. Clearly, he has his head up in the sky somewhere. How can I get rid of him?"

And he kind of looks at me, and he says, "John, this letter says that you are an expert troubleshooter. I'm going to give you a little problem. Here is the problem. This is a relatively high speed copier. And this copier has an intermittent copy quality fault. Now those of you who have done any troubleshooting know that an intermittent fault is nasty. You know, if it's always broken, it doesn't take too much to figure it out. But if it's intermittent, it's tough."

So he says, "This is The Official Xerox Procedure for fixing an intermittent quality problem. It has five steps. So you take this brilliantly conceived computer-generated test pattern. And you put it on the platen. That's where you put the normal paper. We have a fancy term for everything. You dial in, '5000 copies'. And you push the START button." And then he said, "What do you do next?"

I said, "You get some coffee." So I scored one point. I can compute 50 pages into 5000. You know, a total loss.

He said, "Yes, that's what you do. You go get some coffee. A few minutes. Maybe half an hour. Then you come back and the next step is that you take this pile of 5000 copies, ten reams of paper by the way, and you kind of plough through this pile until you find an example of something bad, and then you save that. And you plough through the pile some more until you get something and then you save that. And that's how you do this."

And then he said, "You, John, would surely have a better idea than that, how to fix this machine, right? So why don't you tell me how you would go about doing this. Because clearly you are cleverer than this rote procedure."

And I hummed and hawed and I tried to put off answering, and was trying to get him to say something, an old trick in the Navy. (Laughter.) So for about ten minutes, I danced around, and then he got really impatient, and he said, "Blah, blah, dammit, tell me how you do it?"

And I said, "I can't. I mean, I would use something similar."

And he said, "I thought so!"

So I said, "Paul, how would you do it?"

And he looks at me and he says, "It is obvious what you do!" Probably some of you have already figured it out. He said as he walked across the room and he found the waste basket next to the copier. He takes the waste basket, picks it up and walks over to a table like this, dumps it on the table, quickly files through the paper, and about 30 seconds later, comes up with brilliant sets of copy quality problems.

And he said, "You know, John, what do you do if you discover a copy quality problem? You know, you don't classify it as a copy quality problem. You classify it as a damn bad copy and you throw it away. So why don't you let the world do a little bit of the work for you. Why don't you work with the world, and see that there's a natural way to have the world collect this information for you. Just step back and read the world a little bit."

Now maybe you can see where I'm heading with you. "Read the world a little bit" is almost a kind of judo, or a better term from the French, *bricolage*. And so he said, "This waste basket was ready at hand. It was already there. It was already full of this stuff. Learn to work with the world, and you're going to find your life a lot simpler."

And I walked out and I thought to myself, "This guy is a genius." I also realized that it was very hard to build computer systems that could do this.'

1   Would it be possible to take the knowledge of the expert troubleshooter in this illustration and turn it into explicit knowledge?

Explicit knowledge is what most of us in education have long since regarded as the most important form of knowledge and, in Western societies at least, it has been credited with material and scientific progress. Explicit knowledge can be formally stated and is relatively easy to codify, document, transfer, share and communicate. Typically, the learning of explicit knowledge is undertaken through books, manuals, computer-coded content and through educational or training institutions – so-called 'schooled' or 'delivery-based' learning. Precisely because explicit knowledge is accessible, KIEs have focused on this form of knowledge to develop their core competences. For example, until relatively recently, most university business schools in most countries, focused on developing content in the form of teaching 'packages' rather than research (Pettigrew *et al.*, 2014). Accessibility has also underlain the growth of the knowledge-management industry, which has sought to develop a wide range of technology-based knowledge management tools to make use of the explicit properties of knowledge, and to sell these onto KIEs. These software tools include coordinated databases, groupware systems, intranets and internets. However, codified explicit knowledge is synonymous with information and has to rely on people to understand and apply it subjectively. Thus, according to Polanyi (1966), who is credited with inventing the distinction between the two forms of knowledge, a wholly explicit knowledge is unthinkable.

So, in an important sense, all knowledge is either tacit or rooted in tacit knowledge. By tacit, we mean the often subconsciously understood or applied ideas and skills that we have but that are difficult to articulate in any formal sense. Tacit knowledge is learned from direct action and experience and shared through informal means such as conversations and storytelling. Polanyi argued that tacit knowledge was personal, context specific and therefore difficult to put into words. It could also be compared with acquiring skills such as riding a bike or playing soccer. Though we can read manuals to perform such activities, these do not explain the reality of performing such skills in context. For example, riding a bike on the roads is very different from riding a bike off-road. Similarly, playing five-a-side soccer in a gym with friends is a very different game from playing professionally in front of thousands of people. Thus, tacit knowledge is not generally revealed to us through texts, but is based on intangible thoughts and therefore comprises assets embedded in personal beliefs, experiences and values.

The idea that all knowledge is more or less tacit implies that we can distinguish between different types of tacit knowledge, perhaps in the form of a spectrum (see Figure 7.3). At one end, we can have semi-conscious and unconscious knowledge held in people's heads and bodies, that is unlikely to be codified; at the other end, we can have a pure form of explicit knowledge that can be codified and made available to anyone. For example, experienced selection interviewers often talk about 'gut instincts' when making decisions, rather than relying on objective information about candidates. However, ask an interviewer who relies on instinct or intuition to articulate why they know that this candidate is right for the job and it is very unlikely they will be able to explain fully. Indeed, as some studies have shown, forcing people (such as interviewers) to explain what they thought they knew about the process of learning (in this case learning about a candidate) may lead to a deterioration in performance (in this case in making wise decisions about candidates) (Leonard, 2011).

Tacit knowledge is also a property of groups as well as individuals. For example, some writers analyse organizational structure and stability through the notion of organizational routines, collective ways of working or embedded forms of tacit knowledge that no one person could articulate. However, these routines more or less 'automatically' nudge people into behaving in certain ways. This idea is very similar to the concept of culture, which we shall study in Chapter 10.

In discussing the process of innovation, one of the key outcomes of KBEs, Leonard and Sensiper (2002) outlined three types of group-level, tacit knowledge that need to be managed. These types form a hierarchy of abstraction, as represented in Figure 7.4.

- *Overlapping specific tacit knowledge* refers to the build-up of shared knowledge at the interfaces between specific domains. For example, in a case we researched on NCR, the world's largest producer of automatic teller machines for the financial services industry, a multifunctional design team working on a new form of automatic teller machine for a major UK bank spent time with its clients and customers trying to understand from first-hand observation what their problems were. On returning to work, the different functions represented in the design team had different tacit understandings of the bank and its customers' problems and issues, but the visit provided enough overlapping, common knowledge to create a shared understanding of the issues involved.

  Quite often 'apprenticeships' are used, especially in industries where the technologies are new, to build shared specific tacit knowledge, because the sciences involved are immature and

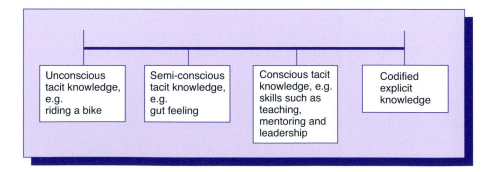

FIGURE 7.3 A spectrum of tacit knowledge

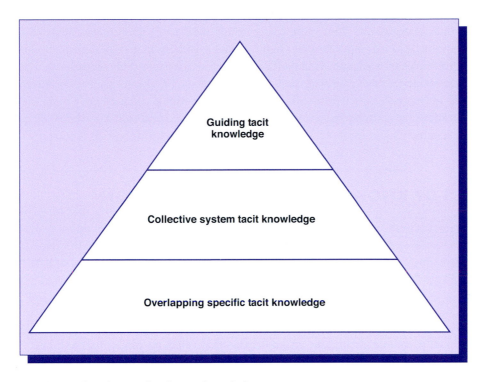

FIGURE 7.4 A hierarchy of group-level, tacit knowledge

(*Source*: based on Leonard and Sensiper, 2002.)

rarely completely codified. In this context, apprenticeship means working directly with people who are highly experienced so that the 'apprentices' can learn from them.

- *Collective system tacit knowledge* is community-based, tacit knowledge developed through the interactions between members of groups as they attempt to address common problems. Such knowledge resides largely in people's heads and is transmitted through stories and tales. We shall discuss this very powerful source of tacit knowledge when examining communities of practice. A good example, however, might be the shared understandings and ways of working of a top-class sports team. Even though their on-field and even training performances may be made public to anyone who wants to take the time to watch, it is almost impossible to imitate, because the knowledge and skills are largely tacit and diffused throughout the team. A similar argument is often used in the context of top business teams that are often only too ready to invite others to watch and learn from them, knowing full well that deep learning is available only to those people willing to engage in a significant period of apprenticeship in the organization and actively participate in the team.

- *Guiding tacit knowledge* is the tacit knowledge about the overall direction of the organization that goes beyond the explicit value statements frequently adopted by organizations. As innovations of products, processes or organizations break new ground, there is often little guidance for exercising judgement available to groups in the form of explicitly stated rules, or even mission and values frameworks. Thus, innovative groups need to develop tacit visions of the organization's unstated mission, often in a highly abstract way, so that they can function effectively. Good examples of guiding tacit knowledge are likely to be found in industries in which ethical decision-making is mission critical, such as biotechnology, or when organizations internationalize to parts of the world with quite different standards of ethical conduct. At a more prosaic level, organizations have attempted to manage this process of guiding tacit knowledge by introducing vision statements and logos. One good example is Nike, with its 'swish' logo and its strap line referring to speed and to 'innovate and inspire'.

IMAGES OF KNOWLEDGE AND ORGANIZATION

With our greater understanding of tacit and explicit knowledge, we can progress towards a more refined set of perspectives on knowledge, knowledge work and organizations. In this regard, Blackler's (2002) classic images of knowledge and learning help increase our understanding of KIEs. These are embrained, embodied, encultured, embedded and encoded images, all of which connote properties of people or of a system; the sixth image is 'knowing'. It is worth spending a little time discussing this, frequently cited, work.

- *Embrained knowledge* is the kind of knowledge that relies on conceptual and cognitive skills, often referred to as knowing about something. This kind of knowledge is usually abstract and involves higher levels of reasoning and understanding to make connections and explain what is going on around us. It is often the kind of knowledge associated with the world of theory and of 'schooled learning'.
- *Embodied knowledge* is knowledge usually acquired in action, e.g. by undertaking a project or apprenticeship, and is partly explicit and partly tacit. Sometimes it is described as 'know-how' and is contrasted with embrained knowledge. Embodied knowledge is not just gained through working on something, but depends on face-to-face interaction and discussion, emotional and sensory information, physical cues, etc. It is also knowledge rooted in specific contexts, such as when a mechanic learns how to repair specific makes of automobile but using only particular kinds of tool. As such, it is often not readily transferable to other situations, e.g. other types of automobile.
- *Encultured knowledge* refers to the process by which we arrive at shared understandings of our group, organizational, or even national, cultures. Learning about cultures is usually linked to the socialization (or indoctrination) processes and to acculturation, i.e. how we come to adapt and take on cultural norms, or the 'way we do things around here'. Learning about cultures is heavily dependent on sharing a common language and on negotiated meanings – for example, people coming to accept common metaphors about what an organization means to them. Thus, some people find it easy to work with the idea that their organization is like a soccer team, characterized by team players of different abilities playing on the same side to score into the opponent's goal. Other groups may use another kind of sporting metaphor to describe their version of teamworking, such as the relay race, or even American football, which differs from soccer in its approach to organization and winning.

- *Embedded knowledge* is knowledge located in organizational routines or capabilities or, at the societal level, in the social and institutional arrangements of a particular country or region. It has strong connections with our previous discussions in Chapters 1 and 2 on managerial work and the international context of people management in Chapter 5. Embedded knowledge can be found in systems of relations between, for example, technologies, the roles people perform, the formal procedures of the organization and the emergent routines. Thus, an organization's distinctive capabilities (or competences) are deeply embedded in how these factors come together or are consciously and unconsciously coordinated to produce skilled performance. Think about the example of what makes a great orchestra or soccer team. The distinction is often made between the expert knowledge or skills of the players and coaches or conductors and the 'architectural' or relational knowledge they require (or the coaches and conductors require) to work together to produce first-class performances. This refers not only to the way they work together (e.g. teamworking), but also to the tools they use (quality of equipment, arenas, etc.), the explicit codes of conduct (e.g. whether certain behaviours are demanded or prohibited), and the habits and ways of working (e.g. practising and dietary regimes, who works best with whom, etc.). Thus, embedded knowledge is systemic and requires an understanding of how all these factors interact to produce skilled performance. This notion may help explain why the talent transfer system doesn't always lead to immediate results for football teams or organizations that seek to buy in talent. It also helps explain why you cannot uproot the best players or the best practices from one context and transplant them into another context with the immediate expectation that they will take root and flourish in the expected or predicted fashion. Our example of the problems of talent management in financial services in Chapter 3 illustrates this point well.

- *Encoded knowledge* is close to what we have previously defined as information, which is more easily transmitted by signs and symbols. Written texts, drawing on abstract forms of language or pictorial language, have been the usual repositories of encoded knowledge, but it is increasingly to computer code and digital signals that we look for transmitting such knowledge, hence the coining of the term 'information and communications technologies'. However, we should not assume that such knowledge is neutral, because it has to be abstracted from the context in which it was produced, and can be highly selective in the impression it conveys. So-called 'factual reporting' on newscasts during wars, in which the horrors of wars are told from the perspective of one side or against a particular backdrop, illustrate this feature of the context-boundedness of information. Nor can we assume that encoded knowledge will be equally acceptable to people in different cultures. For example, when online learning first began to emerge in Europe during the early 2000s, we undertook research into the adoption and diffusion of so-called e-learning in Europe. Our data showed that people in different countries found the method of delivery to be more or less culturally alien to them. Thus, the acceptability of e-learning was quite different between Germany and the UK, found to be an important factor in influencing the absorptive capacity for e-learning in German educational and corporate organizations (Martin *et al.*, 2003). We have also found the same problems occurring in the roll-out of e-HR programmes in major multinational companies in later research (Martin *et al.*, 2008).

- *Knowing.* Blackler (2002) argued that it may be more important to concentrate on the verb 'knowing' than on the subject/object of knowledge, because organizations are always in the process of becoming something other than they are. Another way of saying the same thing is that the process of change in organizations is normal, whereas equilibrium is temporary. We shall consider this view of organizations in more detail later on in the book when we look at change and learning organizations. At this point, however, it is necessary to explore the image of knowing in more detail, because it has been an extremely influential perspective in the knowledge management literature and in practice.

Knowing as an image of organization

There are at least two sets of ideas built on theories of knowing and learning which help us shed light on how organizations innovate and change, discussed further in Chapter 10. The first focuses on the relationship between tacit and explicit knowledge discussed earlier, and is based on a set of ideas concerning knowledge conversion in innovative Japanese organizations. The second has its roots in encultured knowledge, and refers to the notion of communities of practice.

Knowledge conversion and learning

One of the landmark and most frequently cited studies in knowledge management (Curado and Bontis, 2010) came about as a result of the participation of Ikujiro Nonaka, with his colleagues Hirotaka Takeuchi and Kenichi Imai, at a Harvard Business School colloquium (Nonaka and Takeuchi, 1995). Following this colloquium, they agreed to do a joint project to study the innovation processes at several Japanese companies. Drawing especially on Polanyi's work, they conceptualized knowledge in terms of tacit and explicit knowledge, and argued that the dynamic interaction between the two led to organizational knowledge creation and innovation. This interaction between the two types of knowledge leads to four modes of *knowledge conversion*, which they labelled (1) socialization, (2) externalization, (3) combination and (4) internalization (see Table 7.1).

Socialization, involving tacit to tacit conversion, is conducted by individuals, sometimes without language. For example, apprentices often learn from their masters in this way. The key is learning from experience and from experienced people by sharing such knowledge. Combination, which involves learning through combining different bodies of explicit knowledge, can be found in meetings, telephone conversations and computer program exchanges. These media create new knowledge by sorting, re-categorizing or re-analysing these different bodies of knowledge. Internalization, which involves learning from explicit knowledge to create tacit knowledge in individuals, is similar to traditional notions of learning. Externalization, which involves learning from tacit knowledge to

TABLE 7.1 Four modes of knowledge conversion

	To tacit knowledge	To explicit knowledge
From tacit knowledge	Socialization	Externalization
From explicit knowledge	Internalization	Combination

Source: based on Nonaka and Takeuchi, 1995.

create explicit knowledge, is much less well understood and, as we have pointed out, is much more difficult to achieve.

Nonaka (2002) described the process of knowledge creation as a double spiral movement between (a) tacit and explicit knowledge and (b) individual, group, divisional and corporate levels in organizations (see Figure 7.5). Thus, although each of these four modes of knowledge conversion can create new knowledge in its own right, it requires the dynamic interaction of all four to produce real innovation over sustained periods of time. It also requires organizations to manage the process in the form of a continuous cycle. These management activities include (1) team-building to facilitate sharing of tacit experiences, (2) meaningful dialogue to allow members to externalize their tacit knowledge in the form of metaphors and concepts, (3) coordination and integration of teams into the wider organization and (4) the documentation of the knowledge that is produced.

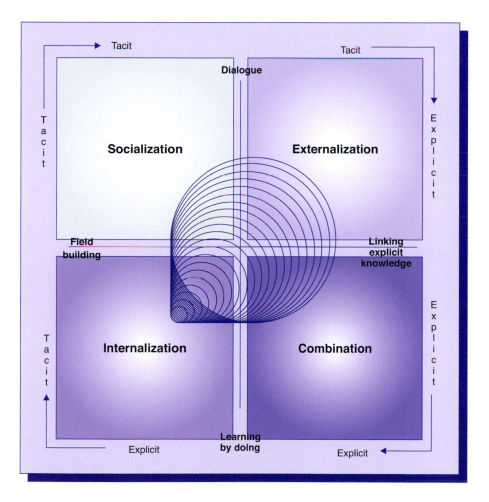

FIGURE 7.5 The spiral of organizational knowledge creation
(*Source:* based on Nonaka and Takeuchi, 1995.)

According to Nonaka, the basis for all organizational knowledge is an individual's tacit knowledge, built up through experience. Experience, however, can be a poor teacher unless it is of a particular quality. There are two factors that influence the overall quality of a person's experience. The first of these is the *variety of experiences* an individual has, especially of the non-routine type. We have all heard the criticism that many older people may have many years of experience, but it is often the same, routine experience repeated year after year. The second factor is the *knowledge of experience*. Because he came from an Asian culture, Nonaka drew on the Asian notion of the 'oneness of body and mind', in which people learn not only with the brain but through bodily recognition or realization. Though difficult to translate into Western terms, this seems to mean that deep learning can take place only through lived experience and not merely through concepts. He illustrated this idea by explaining how Japanese managers learn on the job through interactions with customers, shopfloor employees and reflective action rather than through courses. Such learning, however, is counterbalanced with combination methods of knowledge conversion in which people share their different bodies of explicit knowledge in meetings and seminars.

To create organizational knowledge, however, the process has to move beyond individual learning, which remains personal unless it is amplified through interacting with the group and the organization levels. Nonaka used the concept of a *field* (of play) where people can come together as a self-organizing team to work out their conflicts and collaborate in the knowledge creation process. He further argued that, to be effective, a team needed to be self-organizing, which connotes ideas of mutual self-interest, voluntarism and lack of hierarchy. Such teams also needed to be diverse in background to bring to the 'party' the basic ideas from the different functions and specialists who have something to add, sufficient variety to ensure that no function dominates, and just enough redundancy of information so that more than the basic ideas are brought to bear on the problems at hand.

Communities of practice

The term *communities of practice* is associated with the work of Lave and Wenger (1991), Wenger (1998; 2000), and Seely Brown and Duguid (2000). Like Nonaka, these writers saw learning as an act of membership of a group, but in this case they used the term 'community' rather than 'team'. Most of the writing on communities of practice seeks to understand the structure of naturally occurring, work-based communities, how learning occurs in them and how to put that learning into practice. In our own research, we have also applied the idea of communities of practice to three different eras of the training and development of doctors, during which inexperienced medical practitioners acquired the necessary tacit knowledge and skills to become accepted as full-fledged practitioners by working alongside more experienced doctors in clinical communal settings (Spilg *et al.*, 2012).

Etienne Wenger (2000), one of the main proponents of communities of practice, put the case for community-based learning as follows:

'Communities of practice are everywhere. We all belong to a number of them – at work, at school, at home, in our hobbies. Some have a name, some don't. We are core members

of some and we belong to others more peripherally. You may be a member of a band, or you may just come to rehearsals to hang around with the group. You may lead a group of consultants who specialize in telecommunication strategies, or you may just stay in touch to keep informed about developments in the field. Or you may have just joined a community and are still trying to find your place in it. Whatever form our participation takes, most of us are familiar with the experience of belonging to a community of practice.'
(p. 207)

Members of a community are informally bound by what they *do* together, whether this is engaging in discussions around the water cooler or lunch tables, or solving important problems through informal professional networks. In other words, action and experience are central to such communities. They are also bound by what they have *learned* together through their shared engagement in these activities. In these two senses, a community of practice is different from an interest group or from a geographical community, as neither implies shared learning by doing.

A community of practice can be defined in terms of three dimensions (Wenger, 1998):

- what it is about – the continuously evolving and negotiated understanding of the joint aims of the community;
- its mode of operation – how members mutually engage with each other to form a distinctive social entity;
- what it produces – the *shared repertoire* of resources, which include routines, group attitudes, artifacts, language and styles of operating, about which, as members develop over time, they learn.

To expand on these ideas, communities of practice are based on the following assumptions:

1 *Learning is a social, rather than individual, process.* The argument is that people organize their learning around the communities to which they belong. Thus, for example, business schools are at their most powerful as learning environments for students whose outside social communities connect with the school in some important ways.

2 *Knowledge and learning are integrated in the life of communities that share values, beliefs, languages and community routines.* Thus, real knowledge is integrated in doing or action in the social relations and networks, and in the expertise of these communities.

3 *The processes of learning and membership in a community of practice are intertwined.* Since learning is bound up with membership of the community, as we learn more, our identity and our relationship to the community change through continued participation. Thus, we go from being a peripheral 'apprentice' knowing very little to a fully engaged and committed master or mistress of practice, able to teach and mentor others.

4 *Knowledge is inseparable from practice.* It is argued that it is not possible to know without doing. Through action, we learn new skills and we change our ideas by reflecting on our practice.

5 *Empowering people to contribute to a community creates the greatest potential for learning.* By creating a set of circumstances that allows people to engage in meaningful action with real consequences

for both participants and the community, one can create the most powerful learning environment. Again, this is an argument for action learning in which participants work on 'live' problems with real consequences and are allowed to make and learn from mistakes. Such an idea is associated with the notion of a 'no-blame' culture where organizations are encouraged to let employees learn from mistakes and 'false starts'.

Drawing on the concept of communities of practice, Seely Brown and Duguid (1991), who worked at the Institute for Research on Learning at the Xerox Corporation, saw learning as the bridge between working and innovating. They led a cross-disciplinary approach to learning research, involving cognitive scientists, organizational anthropologists and traditional educators, and have become leading figures in organizational learning. They have argued that communities of practice, through their constant adaptation to changes in membership and changing environmental circumstances, are significant sources of innovation and learning in organizations. They proposed that, to foster working, learning and innovating, organizations needed to re-conceive themselves as *communities of communities*. By building on and legitimizing the naturally occurring communities at work, which often cut across the officially sanctioned work teams and formal practices in the organization, organizations could derive lasting benefits. They continued with the construction metaphor in suggesting ways in which such independent communities could be linked together to form an organizational architecture that preserved the autonomy of these communities but built interconnections and bridges between them. More recently, Seely Brown (2012) has seen technology, the Internet and social media as a way of creating such an architecture because many organizations operate without the physical proximity and stable relationship needed for more traditional communities of practice.

Let's look at a famous example of learning at work that illustrates different kinds of knowledge and learning, including the idea of communities of practice.

CASE 7.3 **MENDING PHOTOCOPIERS**

In what is regarded as a classic piece of research, Orr, an early anthropological collaborator of Seely Brown, provided various examples of how photocopier technicians diverged from established practice. For example, on one service call a 'rep' (technician) confronted a machine that produced copious raw information in the form of error codes and obligingly crashed when tested. But the error codes and the nature of the crashes did not tally. Such a case immediately fell outside the official instructional training and documentation provided by the organization, which ties errors to error codes. Unfortunately, the problem also fell outside the rep's experience. He called his technical specialist, whose job combined 'troubleshooting consultant, supervisor and occasional instructor'. The specialist was equally baffled. Yet, though the canonical approach (the officially sanctioned procedures of the organization) to repair was exhausted, with their combined range of unofficial practices the rep and technical specialist still had options to pursue.

One option – indeed, the only option left by official practice now that its strategies for repair had been quickly exhausted – was to abandon the repair and to replace the machine. This was deemed to be a loss of face and not good for the reputation of the company or for themselves. Such loss of face or faith was not just about embarrassment. The rep's ability to engage the future support of customers and colleagues would be jeopardized, because there was strong social pressure from a variety of sources to solve problems without exchanging machines. In addition to maintaining machines, the job of the rep was to enhance the social standing of the company. As Orr suggested, 'A large part of service work might better be described as repair and maintenance of the social setting.'

Solving the problem without removing the machine required constructing a coherent account of the malfunction out of the incoherence of the data and documentation. To do this, the rep and the specialist embarked on a long storytelling procedure. The machine, with its erratic behaviour, mixed with information from the user and memories from the technicians, provided essential ingredients that the two aimed to account for in a composite story. The process of forming a story was, centrally, one of diagnosis. This process, it should be noted, began as well as ended in a common understanding of the machine, one that was unavailable from the official sources.

While they explored the machine or waited for it to crash, the rep and specialist (with contributions from Orr himself) recalled and discussed other occasions on which they had encountered some of the present symptoms. Each story presented an exchangeable account, which could be examined and reflected upon to provoke old memories and new insights. Yet more tests and more stories were thus generated.

Orr continued his account. The rep and his boss were faced with a failing machine displaying diagnostic information that had previously proved worthless and in which no one had any particular confidence. They did not know where they were going to find the information they needed to understand and solve this problem. In their search for inspiration, they told stories. The storytelling process continued throughout the morning, over lunch and, back in front of the machine, throughout the afternoon, forming a long but purposeful progression towards a finally coherent account. The process lasted five hours, during which a dozen anecdotes were told during the troubleshooting, taking a variety of forms and serving a variety of purposes.

Ultimately, these stories generated sufficient interplay among memories, tests, the machine's responses and the ensuing insights to lead to diagnosis and repair. The final diagnosis developed from what Orr described as two different versions of the same story, in which the two characters talked about personal encounters with the same problem, but their two versions were significantly different. Through storytelling, these separate experiences converged, leading to a shared diagnosis of certain previously encountered but unresolved symptoms. The two characters had constructed a common interpretation of until now uninterpretable data and individual experience. The rep and specialist were now in a position to modify previous stories and build a more insightful one. They both increased their own understanding and added to their community's collective knowledge. Such stories were passed around and became part of the repertoire available to all reps. Orr reported hearing a concise, assimilated version of this particular false error code passed among reps over a game of cribbage in the lunch room three months later. Thus, the story, once in the possession of the community, was used – and further modified – in similar diagnostic sessions.

Source: adapted from Seely Brown and Duguid, 1991.

1 What kind of knowledge does the rep and his boss draw upon to mend the photocopier and how much does it depend on a community of practice?

The relationship between different images of knowledge, organizational structures and managing people

Knowledge and organizations

How do these different versions of knowledge and learning relate to organizational structures and people-management problems? Blackler's (2002) now classic work drew on two dimensions central to the production of knowledge to produce a typology of organizations based on knowledge and learning. As Crane (2013) argues, his work is among the most insightful in the field because he emphasized the role of social learning and language, and in taking a constructivist approach to understanding learning in organizations (see Figure 7.6). The first dimension Blacker used was whether knowledge is seen as the product of individuals or of groups, which reflects the debate over communities of practice. The second is whether the organization deals with essentially familiar or routine problems (manufacturing repeatable solutions to known problems), or is tasked with providing innovative solutions to new problems. This dimension reflects the often-used distinction between wicked and tame problems (Rittel and Webber, 1984). A wicked problem is difficult to solve because of incomplete, contradictory and changing requirements that reflect complex inter-dependencies in organizations, whereas tame problems may be complex but have known or routine solutions.

Many organizations in industrialized countries are moving away (or being exhorted to move away) from organizing and strategizing on the basis of routine knowledge, given the opportunities provided by access to information and communications technologies and social media to enhance communications and performance support. However, Blackler also pointed that these four boxes are bi-polar typologies, thus it would be a mistake to think of these different types of knowledge as independent of one another. Many organizations reveal aspects of all four images, sometimes simultaneously. For example, different departments or divisions in the same company may see their knowledge management and HR problems through one of these images and use this dominant image to frame solutions to their perceived problems. Alternatively, organizations may strive to move between these images over time, using them as a form of blueprint and as a set of organizational development techniques.

EXERCISE 7.2 **Standard Life Investments**

Re-read the case of Standard Life Investments and its progress to demutualization. Which of these four images of organization does Standard Life Investments most resemble and what problems does this imply for the future of the company?

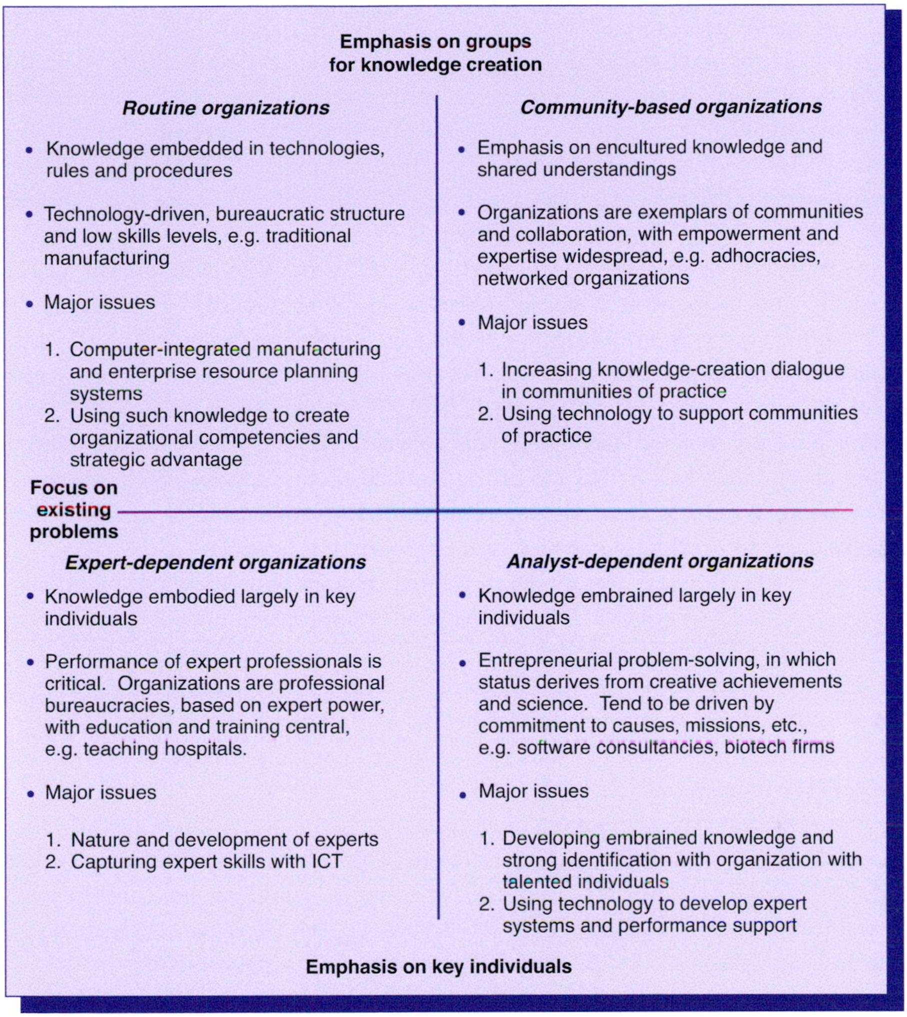

**Emphasis on groups
for knowledge creation**

Routine organizations	*Community-based organizations*

Routine organizations

- Knowledge embedded in technologies, rules and procedures

- Technology-driven, bureaucratic structure and low skills levels, e.g. traditional manufacturing

- Major issues

  1. Computer-integrated manufacturing and enterprise resource planning systems
  2. Using such knowledge to create organizational competencies and strategic advantage

Community-based organizations

- Emphasis on encultured knowledge and shared understandings

- Organizations are exemplars of communities and collaboration, with empowerment and expertise widespread, e.g. adhocracies, networked organizations

- Major issues

  1. Increasing knowledge-creation dialogue in communities of practice
  2. Using technology to support communities of practice

**Focus on
existing
problems**

Expert-dependent organizations

- Knowledge embodied largely in key individuals

- Performance of expert professionals is critical. Organizations are professional bureaucracies, based on expert power, with education and training central, e.g. teaching hospitals.

- Major issues

  1. Nature and development of experts
  2. Capturing expert skills with ICT

Analyst-dependent organizations

- Knowledge embrained largely in key individuals

- Entrepreneurial problem-solving, in which status derives from creative achievements and science. Tend to be driven by commitment to causes, missions, etc., e.g. software consultancies, biotech firms

- Major issues

  1. Developing embrained knowledge and strong identification with organization with talented individuals
  2. Using technology to develop expert systems and performance support

Emphasis on key individuals

FIGURE 7.6 A typology of organizations based on knowledge

(*Source*: based on Blackler, 2002.)

Managing knowledge workers

These different types of organization raise a number of issues concerning the management of knowledge workers, including the management of expertise, developing expertise, and encouraging and facilitating knowledge workers to share their expertise with others (Child and Rodrigues, 2011). As we have already suggested, knowledge work and knowledge workers are nothing new, a notion reflected in the image of the *routine organization* in Figure 7.6. What has become the focus of much attention in HR, however, is the role knowledge workers are seen to play in value creation, which we have already discussed in relation to talent management in Chapter 3 and shall touch on in the next section on intellectual capital.

Traditional economic approaches to management in these organizations are based on the so-called *agency model*, consisting of a 'principal' employer, an 'agent' employee and the relationship between them. The motivations of these actors can be stated quite simply in economic terms: an agent (e.g. a senior manager) is not motivated to expend effort but is motivated by getting paid; the principal (investors and owners) dislikes paying the agent, but likes the valuable work that the agent does. In this scenario, the objectives of principal and agent are set in opposition to one another. The agent wants as much pay as possible for as little work or effort as possible, whereas the principal wants to get as much work as possible from the agent while paying as little as possible. Devising an appropriate contract for wages in return for work – the employment contract – is complicated by the fact that the principal is rarely around to see how much effort the agent is expending but can only observe the result or output of the agent's work. This wage–work bargain and output control is also subject to a set of more or less random factors over which the principal has little or no control, including the agent's tacit knowledge and skills, and factors connected with clients and customers, which also depend on random factors. However, the primary conclusion of agency theory is to link pay to performance, to provide employees with appropriate incentives.

As we have already discussed, this model runs into problems with knowledge workers, especially expert professionals such as doctors, lawyers and academics, for a number of reasons:

1   There are the problems of observing knowledge work and even understanding what is going on. For example, hospital managers, unless they have medical training, have major problems in making reasoned judgements on what goes on in an operating theatre or on the results of the operation (Martin *et al.*, 2015).

2   Agency models that focus on output incentives may be inappropriate for knowledge workers, who are likely to be driven by the nature of the work itself and a desire to be known as an expert. Many workers in the public services, for example, would fall into this category, including many academics, doctors and social workers (Brinkley, 2008). Agency models are not particularly helpful in leveraging such desires, and may even be counter-productive.

3   Agency models are frequently uni-dimensional in their measures of productivity. Usually, this is seen as a simple relationship between inputs, such as how hard someone works, and, often crude, measures of outputs such as sales or customer satisfaction ratings. However, knowledge work is much less capable of being measured by single, short-term criteria; it is often related less to how hard someone works and more to how smart someone works. As a consequence, agency-based incentive schemes can sometimes distort effort allocations of knowledge workers by forcing them to apply effort in measurable, but not necessarily meaningful, directions. Again, this is evident in recent research we have undertaken on doctors who are measured against targets set to reduce waiting lists, regardless of the severity of the clinical need to see patients (Martin *et al.*, 2015).

4   Work in routine organizations, which is often characterized by production environments, usually requires major initial investments in technologies and processes, such as when designing and building a new automobile. As a consequence, planning and linear thinking tend to dom- inate, because getting something right first the time will avoid the problems of retooling and

scrap. However, in organizations that focus on tackling novel problems, linear planning and making 'big decisions' can be counter-productive by locking organizations into a set strategy. This approach to strategy through planning is often inconsistent with innovation and change, which require knowledge workers to 'act their way into thinking' and to evolve emergent strategies for change. Thus, forcing knowledge workers into a planning and measurement straitjacket can be extremely counter-productive in innovative environments.

The images of organization depicted in Figure 7.6 pose a range of different problems for KIEs, especially in the management of knowledge workers. The growing literature in this area, however, suggests two main principles for the future of management in a knowledge context (Austin, 2002; Wang and Noe, 2010):

- The first suggests a move away from traditional incentives and an emphasis on developing collaboration, trust and professionalism, based on employer of choice policies, developing strong internal employer brands and changed psychological contracts (see Chapter 6 on the corporate context). As we saw in Chapters 3 and 6, the management of employee engagement and the management of external and internal corporate reputations or brands to attract, retain and motivate knowledge workers is likely to become an even more important issue than it currently is.
- The second emphasizes emergent strategizing and planning and iterative work structures, rather than linear planning and structured forms of organization. Knowledge creation and diffusion often iterate daily, and are based on alternative periods of unstructured work in communities of practice or small groups and in situations where managers have to exercise more strict control.

THE NATURE OF INTELLECTUAL CAPITAL

In the introduction to this chapter and in Figure 7.1, we referred to the nature of intellectual capital as an outcome of the knowledge management process in organizations. The term is increasingly being used to refer to the knowledge assets of organizations (Serenko and Bontis, 2013). In this section we explore what is meant by intellectual capital in more detail, the components of intellectual capital, some of the problems involved in measuring intangible assets, and the methods currently used to value intellectual capital. This is an important discussion, because there is pressure on organizations to value human capital and to include it on the balance sheet.

Approaches to intellectual capital management

The term 'intellectual capital' began to enter the field of management in the late 1960s and has become part of the standard terminology of knowledge management, with endorsement by highly respected scholars, consulting organizations and companies. Like many academic disciplines, it now has a journal devoted to research in the field. There have been several generic attempts to show how knowledge assets and intellectual capital relate to each other and to business performance (Hsu and Sabherwal, 2012). Perhaps the best known of these is the well-known *balanced scorecard*, which we examined in Chapter 6. This approach set out cause-and-effect relationships between strategic success and four areas of measurement that relate directly to knowledge management: financial measures; customer measures; internal process measures (e.g. cycle times, levels of waste); and learning and growth measures. A second generic approach is the *knowledge assets map*, which was designed to help companies identify and measure their knowledge-based assets and their contribution to the firm (CIMA/Cranfield, 2004). This approach identifies a hierarchy of knowledge assets (see Figure 7.7).

The nature and examples of these assets to which this hierarchy refers are illustrated in Table 7.2. It should be noted that these measures are illustrative and have to be related to the context of the organization.

Defining and measuring intellectual capital

Edvinsson, the architect of the well-known Skandia framework, has suggested that intellectual capital comprises the hidden factors of human and structural capital (Edvinsson and Malone, 1997). *Human capital* is the combined current stock of knowledge, skills, innovativeness and abilities of an organization's individual employees. The distinguishing feature of human capital is that it cannot be owned by the company, and 'walks out of the door' most evenings. *Social capital* (Adler and Kwon, 2002), which refers to bonds (in the form of shared culture and values), bridges (the strength of networks) and trust within and between organizations, is another key form of capital. *Structural capital* is the hardware, software, organizational structure, patents, databases of customers, logos, etc. that supports employees. These more tangible assets, which are left behind when employees leave or go home at night, are capable of being owned by the company and are tradable. Structural capital also generates a third form of capital, which Edvinsson originally described as *customer capital*. This class of asset has been widened to incorporate not just customers but all stakeholders and is increasingly

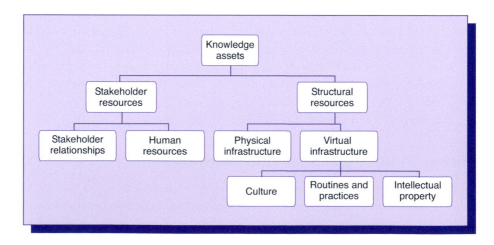

FIGURE 7.7 The hierarchy of knowledge assets

known as *relational capital*. Research by Subramaniam and Youndt (2005) found that social capital is often the most important in developing the intellectual capital of organizations. Without social capital, human capital does not come into play and investing only in human capital through the recruitment of stars can lead to a deterioration in intellectual capital, as we saw in Chapter 3.

> '. . . all the resources linked to the external relationships of the firm – with customers, suppliers or partners in research and development. It comprises that part of human and structural capital involved with the company's relations with stakeholders (investors, creditors, customers and suppliers), plus the perceptions that they hold about the company. Examples of this are image, customer loyalty, customer satisfaction, links with suppliers, commercial power, negotiating capacity . . . and environmental activities.'
>
> (CIMA/Cranfield, 2004)

TABLE 7.2 Knowledge asset indicators

Stakeholder relationships	All forms of relationship established by the company, including numbers of partnering agreements; number/quality of licensing agreements; market share; public opinion surveys, partnership satisfaction index, customer retention, brand loyalty, customer complaints
Human resources	All knowledge provided by employees in form of competencies, commitment, motivation and tacit knowledge. Measures include: • Demographic indicators: number of employees, ages, etc.; length of service, % full-time employees; diversity measures, including number of woman managers, ethnic minorities, foreign nationals • Competence indicators: employees with degree qualifications and above; average years service with company; competence levels • Attitude indicators: employee satisfaction; commitment or engagement levels, stress levels, new ideas generated by staff, etc. • HR practice indicators: training expenses per employee; time in training, recruitment indicators; rankings in best places to work for league tables
Physical infrastructure	All infrastructural assets, including structure and ICT assets, including scalability/capacity measures; number of computers per employee; server response times; use of knowledge-sharing facilities
Culture	Corporate culture/reputation/internal branding, e.g. number of internal disputes, engagement surveys, organizational personality surveys and strength of psychological commitment, external measures of best places to work for
Routines and practices	Covers internal practices and virtual networks, including process quality, number of codified processes, intranet use; usage of e-learning platforms
Intellectual property	Sum of patents, copyrights, brands and processes owned by the company, e.g. revenues from patents, number of patents, value of copyrights, brand recognition surveys

Source: adapted from CIMA/Cranfield, 2004; Marr, 2008.

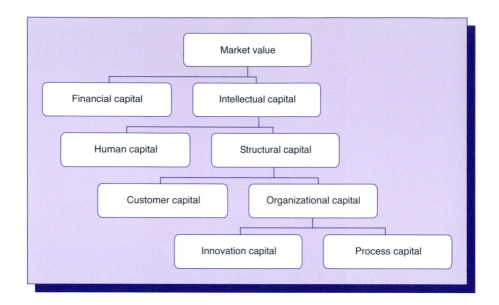

FIGURE 7.8 Skandia's value scheme

(*Source*: adapted from Bontis, 2001.)

Often, when an organization is being sold to a new owner, it is the relational capital that is being purchased, along with the human and structural capital. The key point about this framework is that intellectual capital is set alongside financial capital (see Figure 7.8), and can account for the difference between a company's traditional balance sheet assets and investors' valuations of companies.

LEARNING SUMMARY

In this chapter we have described and evaluated one of the major contexts of modern organizations and its implications for managing people. Knowledge and learning are important in all organizations, but are a major source of strategic advantage for many organizations in the so-called new economy. We began by raising six questions that all organizations need to address, based on the framework of knowledge management in Figure 7.1. The key 'takeaways' from these questions and framework are as follows:

- The knowledge-based economy and the new economics of knowledge are heavily dependent on the quality of so-called knowledge workers and on finding more appropriate ways of managing knowledge workers.

- Knowledge is seen as the key factor input into the generation of wealth and organizational success, is the source of high economic returns for people whose knowledge is scarce, is localized in certain regions, leading to an important local labour market for knowledge, and depends for its successful transfer on knowledge networks.

- Knowledge-intensive enterprises (KIEs) are knowledge-integrating organizations that rely on access to and the creation of advanced and innovative knowledge for sustained strategic success. They also tend to be based more on communal relations and trust than on markets and price mechanisms for their effective operation. Finally, they need to have high levels of absorptive capacity to create new knowledge.

- Knowledge is different from information because it is essentially a human creation, which makes it much more difficult to manage.

- Knowledge is usually depicted in terms of the split between its tacit and explicit forms; it is the tacit nature of knowledge that makes it difficult to manage. However, it is more useful to think of knowledge as a spectrum, ranging between unconscious tacit knowledge, through semi-conscious tacit knowledge to explicit knowledge, because all knowledge has tacit roots.

- Tacit knowledge is also to be found in groups as well as individuals, and learning is often undertaken in groups. Indeed, group-based learning is often seen as superior to individual learning in the field of innovation.

- We can think of different images of organizations, based on the type of knowledge they most use. Tacit and explicit knowledge can be related to individual and group-based knowledge to produce four different images of organization, raising different problems for managing people.

- Agency models of management, which rely heavily on traditional structures and financial incentives, are relevant mainly to organizations that use knowledge in a routine way. Other images of organizations require different solutions to managing knowledge workers. These solutions are to be found in new forms of trust, commitment and development models, and in more flexible and less directive forms of organization.

- Developing and converting tacit knowledge to explicit knowledge is *the* key managerial problem in KIEs. Developing tacit knowledge by increasing the variety and quality of experience among knowledge workers is critical in increasing the knowledge stock of a KIE.

- Creating and harnessing naturally occurring communities of practice are the principal means by which tacit knowledge can be increased and transferred in organizations. Communities of practice are based on community theories of learning and assume that learning and practice are intertwined. Empowering people to create such communities unleashes organizational potential for learning and knowledge creation.

- Intellectual capital has to be placed on the same level as financial capital in organizations, and has to be measured and managed. New methods of valuing intellectual capital may change the focus of many organizations and their reporting systems towards knowledge management.

REVIEW QUESTIONS

1 What distinguishes a knowledge-intensive enterprise from other forms of organizations?
2 How do communities of practice facilitate organizational learning and the creation of intellectual capital?

REFERENCES

Adler, P. S. and Kwon, S.-W. (2002) Social capital: prospect for a new concept. *Academy of Management Review*, 27, 17–40.

Alavi, M. and Denford, J. S. (2011) Knowledge management: process, practice and Web 2.0. In: M. Easterby-Smith and M. Lyles (eds), *Handbook of Organizational Learning and Knowledge Management*, 2nd edn. Chichester, Sussex: Wiley, pp. 105–124.

Austin, R. (2002) Managing knowledge workers: evolving practices and trends. *Next Wave*. http://sciencecareers. sciencemag.org/career_development/issue/articles/2380/managing_knowledge_workers_rules_for_absolute_ beginners.

Blackler, F. (2002) Knowledge, knowledge work and organizations: an overview and interpretation. In: Y. Choo and N. Bontis (eds), *The Strategic Management of Intellectual Capital and Organizational Knowledge*, pp. 47–64. New York: Oxford University Press.

Bontis, N. (2001) Assessing knowledge assets: a review of the models used to measure intellectual capital. *International Journal of Management Reviews*, 3 (1), 41–60.

Brandi, U. and Elkjaer, B. (2011) Organizational learning viewed from a social learning perspective. In: M. Easterby-Smith and M. Lyles (eds), *Handbook of Organizational Learning and Knowledge Management*, 2nd edn. Chichester, Sussex: Wiley, pp. 23–42.

Brinkley, I. (2008) *The Knowledge Economy: How knowledge is reshaping the economic life of nations*. London: The Work Foundation.

Child, J. and Rodrigues, S. (2011) Social identity and organizational learning. In: M. Easterby-Smith and M. Lyles (eds), *Handbook of Organizational Learning and Knowledge Management*, 2nd edn. Chichester, Sussex: Wiley, pp. 305–330.

Choo, C. W. and Bontis, N. (eds) (2002) *The Strategic Management of Intellectual Capital and Organizational Knowledge*. New York: Oxford University Press.

CIMA/Cranfield (2004) *Understanding Corporate Value: Managing and reporting intellectual capital*. Available online at www.cimaglobal.com/downloads/intellectualcapital.pdf.

Crane, L. (2013) A new taxonomy of knowledge management theory: the turn to knowledge as constituted in social action, *Journal of Knowledge Management Practice*, 14 (1). Available online at http://www.tlainc.com/ articl332.htm.

Curado, C. and Bontis, N. (2010) Parallels in knowledge cycles. *Computers in Human Behavior*, 27, 1438–1444.

Easterby-Smith, M. and Lyles, M. (2011) *Handbook of Organizational Learning and Knowledge Management*, 2nd edn. Chichester, Sussex: Wiley.

The Economist (2005) Moving on: manufacturing is out, knowledge-based industries are in. Dancing with the enemy: a survey of Taiwan. 15 January, pp. 9–11.

Edvinsson, L. and Malone, M. S. (1997) *Intellectual Capital: Realizing your company's true value by finding its hidden brainpower*. New York: HarperCollins.

Evans, P. and Wurster, T. (2000) *Blown to Bits: How the new economics of information transforms strategy*. Cambridge, MA: Harvard University Press.

Foss, N. and Mahnke, V. (2011) Knowledge creation in firms: an organizational economics perspective. In: M. Easterby-Smith and M. Lyles (eds), *Handbook of Organizational Learning and Knowledge Management*, 2nd edn. Chichester, Sussex: Wiley, pp. 125–153.

Gupta, A. K. and Govindarajan, V. (2004) *Global Strategy and the Organization*. New York: John Wiley.

Hsu, I. C. and Sabherwal, R. (2012) Relationship between intellectual capital and knowledge management: an empirical investigation. *Decision Sciences*, 43 (3), 489–524.

James, L., Guile, D. and Unwin, L. (2011) *From Learning for the Knowledge-based Economy to Learning for Growth: Re-examining clusters, innovation and qualifications*, published by the Centre for Learning and Life Chances in Knowledge Economies and Societies at: www.llakes.org.

Lave, J. and Wenger, E. (1991) *Situated Learning: Limited peripheral participation*. New York: Cambridge University Press.

Leonard, D. (2011) *Managing Knowledge Assets, Creativity and Innovation*. Danvers, MA: World Science Publishing.

Leonard, D. and Sensiper, S. (2002) The role of tacit knowledge in group innovation. In: C. W. Choo and N. Bontis (eds), *The Strategic Management of Intellectual Capital and Organizational Knowledge*, pp. 485–500. New York: Oxford University Press.

Makini, J. and Marche, S. (2010) Towards a typology of knowledge-intensive organizations: determinant factors. *Knowledge Management Research Practice*, 8, 265–277.

Marr, B. (2008) *Impacting Future Value: How to manage your intellectual capital*. Society of Management Accountants of Canada/Institute of Certified Public Accountants/The Chartered Institute of Management Accountants. Available online at www.cimaglobal.com/Documents/ImportedDocuments/tech_mag_impacting_future_value_may08.pdf.pdf.

Martin, G. and Reddington, M. (2009) Reconceptualising absorptive capacity to explain the e-enablement of the HR function (e-HR) in organizations. *Employee Relations*, 31 (5), 515–537.

Martin, G., Massy, J. and Clarke, T. (2003) When absorptive capacity meets institutions and (e)learners. *International Journal of Training and Development*, 7 (4), 222–244.

Martin, G., Reddington, M. and Alexander, H. (eds) (2008) *Technology, Outsourcing and Transforming HR*. Oxford: Butterworth Heinemann.

Martin, G., Parry, E. and Flowers, P. (2015) Social media and HRM: Insights from dialogue theory and a critical case study. *Human Resource Management Journal*. doi: 10.1111/748-8583.12081.

Nonaka, I. (2002) A dynamic theory of organizational knowledge creation. In: C. W. Choo and N. Bontis (eds), *The Strategic Management of Intellectual Capital and Knowledge Creation*. New York: Oxford University Press.

Nonaka, I. and Takeuchi, H. (1995) *The Knowledge-Creating Company*. Oxford: Oxford University Press.

Pettigrew, A. M., Cornuel, E. and Hommel, U. (eds) (2014) *The Institutional Development of Business Schools*. Oxford: Oxford University Press.

Polanyi, M. (1966) *The Tacit Dimension*. Garden City, NY: Doubleday.

Rittel, H. and Webber, M. (1984) Dilemmas in a general theory of planning. *Policy Sciences*, Vol. 4, pp. 155–169. Amsterdam: Elsevier Scientific Publishing Company, Inc., 1973. Reprinted in: N. Cross (ed.), *Developments in Design Methodology*. Chichester: Wiley & Sons, Chichester, pp. 135–144.

Seely Brown, J. (2012) Cultivating the entrepreneurial learner in the 21st century. Available at www.johnseelybrown.com/el.

Seely Brown, J. and Duguid, P. (1991) Organizational learning and communities-of-practice: toward a unified view of working, learning, and innovation. *Organization Science*, 2, 40–57.

Seely Brown, J. and Duguid, P. (2000) *The social life of information*. Cambridge, MA: Harvard University Press.

Serenko, A. and Bontis, N. (2013) Investigating the current state and impact of the intellectual capital academic discipline. *Journal of Intellectual Capital*, 14 (4), 476–500.

Siebert, S., Martin, G., Bozic, B. and Docherty, I. (2015) Looking beyond the factory gates: a critique and agenda for organizational trust research. *Organization Studies*, 36, 1033–1062.

Spilg, E., Siebert, S. and Martin, G. (2012) A social learning perspective on the development of doctors in the UK national health service. *Social Science and Medicine*, 75, 1617–1624.

Subramaniam, M. and Youndt, M. A. (2005) The influence of intellectual capital on the types of innovative capabilities. *Academy of Management Journal*, 48 (3), 450–463.

Teece, D. J. and Al-Aali, A. (2011) Knowledge assets, capabilities and the theory of the firm. In: M. Easterby-Smith and M. Lyles (eds), *Handbook of Organizational Learning and Knowledge Management*, 2nd edn. Chichester, Sussex: Wiley, pp. 505–534.

Van Wijk, R., Van Den Bosch, F. A. J. and Volberda, H. W. (2011a) Organizing knowledge in social, alliance and organizational networks. In: M. Easterby-Smith and M. Lyles (eds), *Handbook of Organizational Learning and Knowledge Management*, 2nd edn. Chichester, Sussex: Wiley, pp. 477–504.

Van Wijk, R., Van Den Bosch, F. A. J. and Volberda, H. W. (2011b) Absorptive capacity: taking stock of progress and prospects. In: M. Easterby-Smith and M. Lyles (eds), *Handbook of Organizational Learning and Knowledge Management*, 2nd edn. Chichester, Sussex: Wiley, pp. 273–304.

Wang, S. and Noe, R. A. (2010) Knowledge sharing: a review and directions for future research. *Human Resource Management Review*, 20 (2), 115–131.

Wenger, E. (1998) *Communities of Practice: Learning meaning and identity*. Cambridge, UK: Cambridge University Press.

Wenger, E. (2000) Communities of practice and learning systems. *Organization*, 7 (2), 225–246.

Wenger, E. (2000) Communities of practice: the structure of knowledge stewarding. In: C. Despres and D. Chauvel (eds), *Knowledge Horizons: The present and the promise of knowledge management*. London: Routledge.

World Economic Forum (2015) Global competitiveness report 2014–15. Available online at http://reports.weforum.org/global-competitiveness-report-2014–2015/.

Zahra, S. A. and George, G. (2002) Absorptive capacity: a review, reconceptualization and extension. *Academy of Management Review*, 27, 185–203.

Chapter 8

The technological context, organizations and managing people

LEARNING OBJECTIVES

By the end of this chapter you should be able to:

- understand the nature of technological change and its relationship to people management;
- understand the trends in technological developments and use these trends to analyse your strategic environment;
- apply the notion of a technological system to your own workplace or one with which you are familiar to analyse its essential components;
- distinguish between how technologies are used to empower people at work and to disempower them;
- apply the concepts from the chapter to design a system of work and work roles that minimize the negative influences of new technologies on people.

UNDERSTANDING THE NATURE OF TECHNOLOGICAL CHANGE AND ITS RELATIONSHIP WITH MANAGING PEOPLE

Introduction

In this chapter we synthesize a wide range of literature and research from different disciplines, including some of our own, to help you *understand* the importance of technological change to the management of people and be able to *use* these ideas to improve your thinking and performance as a manager. It is clear that the relationship between changing technologies, organizations and people is an extremely important one, as it has been at the heart of nearly all management thinking and a good deal of economic policy in various countries for many years. It is also clear that this is an ever-moving target because, in one key sense, there is nothing new about changing technologies; they are always with us and always presenting managers with new problems as well as new opportunities. These ever-present dynamics have never been more obvious than during recent times, following the advent of digital information and communications technologies (ICT). The rate of recent technological progress, the ubiquity of ICT at most workplaces and the emerging cluster of related technologies to which ICT has helped give birth – e.g. biotechnology, nanotechnology, new material science, robotics, mobile technologies, cloud computing and social media – has radically changed many businesses and economies. However, we need to be careful in getting carried away with some of the hype. For example, a few years ago much was made of how mobile telephones have transformed banking in sub-Saharan Africa, with people such as Bill Gates, founder of Microsoft, predicting cataclysmic change in the number of bank accounts held by people in that continent; however, the reality had not matched the hype, nor have mobile technologies acted as a 'silver bullet' for economic development (Aker and Mbiti, 2010) – at least at the time of writing (which should be a recurring disclaimer in this chapter).

If we focus on these new technologies, much of the recent work by academics and practitioners is on ICT as a *general-purpose technology* and its relationship with economic growth, productivity, and the future problems and opportunities at work created by new business models. In the past decade since writing the first edition of this book, much of this work has focused on mobile technologies and social media, research to which we have contributed (Martin *et al.*, 2009; Martin *et al.*, 2015). This interest was initially generated by comparisons in the early 2000s between the so-called 'new economy' and the old economy, as many countries sought to play 'catch-up' with the long-standing perceived American advantage in technologically led productivity, the African story being one such example (Obijiofor, 2015).

There has been a considerable debate, however, over the extent to which a new economy actually exists and whether it was fundamentally different from the old economy, even in the USA where the concept first saw daylight. This debate began following the bursting of the dot-com bubble in 2000, when the American securities market for technology stocks collapsed. It continued after the Global Financial Crisis in 2007–8, when the increasing 'financialization' of economies such as the USA and UK became a source of significant problems for most taxpayers, many of whom were forced to bail out financial services companies that used technology *in extremus* to develop new products and services that turned out to worthless (Thompson, 2011). But, if we accept the idea that there is something quite different about economies such as the USA and its recent productivity levels, can other countries hope to match it by creating an economic and industrial structure based on new types of business models to which new technologies have given rise? The evidence on this question is mixed. Certain countries in northern Europe, such as Finland and Sweden, and smaller countries such as Singapore have been successful in creating technologically advanced economies and organizations. Many companies in these countries have followed a *'high-road' competitive strategy* (see Box 8.1).

However, one of the key messages from research has shown that most companies still follow a *'low-road' strategy*, even in countries as technologically advanced as Britain (CIPD, 2014). The dominance of a low-road strategy amongst companies in a national economy is often used to explain why they lag behind the USA, with Britain being the example *par excellence* of technology-lag productivity. For example, the UK had the second highest level of demand (after Spain) for workers

---

BOX 8.1 High and low 'roads' to economic growth

A *high-road strategy* to economic growth is based on having a high proportion of either significant ICT-producing industries, such as chip manufacturers, or significant ICT using industries, such as financial services and education, to create high added-value products and services based on high levels of education and skills. Such a relationship between technology, products and services, and skills is thought to create a self-reinforcing equilibrium. Silicon Valley in America, Boston and North Carolina in the USA and Cambridge in the UK are good examples of such clusters of companies linked with world-class universities.

A *low-road strategy* is associated with minimal effective use of ICT in organizations, coupled with a self-reinforcing concentration on products with low skill requirements, and competition based on low costs and prices. Such a strategy is thought to produce a negative dynamic, because it generates a workforce unable to operate effectively in a high skills/advanced technology environment. Nor does the strategy provide any incentive for employees to acquire and be paid for advanced technology-based skills.

Sources: based on CIPD, 2014; Finegold and Soskice, 1988; Taylor, 2004.

---

with no education beyond basic schooling (OECD, 2014). If this is the case among developed European countries, what price the success of the developing world, particularly if they lose their current comparative advantages in low labour costs due to high growth rates? Thus, nearly every country in the world has a policy on how to take advantage of the new technologies to create successful firms and generate economic progress. India is a good example of such a country in the developing world, with its significant cluster of ICT-based companies in Bangalore; Taiwan and South Korea are other good examples, with their strategy of building branded goods on the back of high levels of research and development into new computing technologies. Finally China is investing hugely in its universities and science to generate economic development by following a high road to growth strategy, which has become evident through the inclusion of some Chinese universities in the elite reputation rankings since 2012.

It follows that taking advantage of technological change is usually seen as the *necessary* condition for economic and business success for all countries in the long run, but, as we shall see, technological investment in firms by itself is not the *sufficient* condition. Most researchers agree that it is the *interrelationships* among technology, institutions, organizations and people that seem to matter in delivering the promises made for new technologies. In this chapter we shall explore these interrelationships and the implications for managers by addressing three sets of related questions:

1   To what extent are organizations in the new economic environment different in their requirements for people and for the experience of people working within them? To what extent are they different in making use of technology, particularly investment in ICT, to produce innovations and productivity growth? And how can we best manage the relationship between investment in ICT and the exploitation of knowledge as discussed in the previous chapter?

2   To what extent do we have a choice in shaping such technological change to become a progressive and empowering force for the people working in the new economy? Can we design jobs and organizations so that adopting new technologies will lead to liberating employees from routine and boring jobs and enhance their ability to use knowledge for their own good and for the good of the firm? Or will the choices we make result in dominating employees, perhaps leading to a widespread deskilling for the majority of people?

3   What can managers do to prepare themselves to make appropriate choices in the technology–people management relationship?

DEFINING TECHNOLOGIES AND NEW TECHNOLOGIES: A COMBINATION OF 'HARDWARE AND SOFTWARE'

A technological system

Often, one of the most puzzling aspects for managers and management students, especially those coming from a non-technical background, is to understand what is meant by technology. Defining technology in a general sense helps us understand not only what we mean by new and old technologies, but also their distinctive nature.

However, a problem arises when different writers and traditions in the literature have different conceptions of where technology begins and ends, so to speak. This is especially so in relation to the 'hardware' of material objects, such as networked computers and computer code, and the software of organizations, including structures, systems and processes. In the field of business and management studies, technology is traditionally seen as the means by which a desirable outcome or goal is achieved, such as the development of a new product (e.g. automobiles) or service (e.g. online delivery of your course), or the development of a new process (the e-enablement of HR). From this perspective, technology can be defined by the three elements in Case 8.1.

CASE 8.1 DEFINING TECHNOLOGY

- The physical objects or artefacts – products, tools and equipment – that are used to create these outcomes (e.g. moving assembly lines to produce automobiles, networked computers to create an e-enabled solution to HR or virtual learning environments to facilitate e-learning).
- The activities or processes that constitute the method of production (e.g. the design of flowline production methods to produce automobiles, software programming to network computers for a talent management system, or online discussions and online assessments).
- The knowledge needed to develop and apply the physical objects and processes to produce a particular output (e.g. the know-how to design and assemble an automobile, the knowledge of HR activities in the workplace, or the knowledge of a field of study to be learned and knowledge of how people learn online).

Source: based on Hatch and Cunliffe, 2012.

1 Think about your own work organization or one with which you are familiar. Use the above definition and the three elements to define the technology of the organization or department.

This view of technology is based on an open-systems perspective, which sees the organization as a technological process converting inputs from the environment into outputs. It allows us to relate organizational technologies to resource requirements and to the objects of technology such as automobiles, improved communications through social media or elaborated knowledge structures in the heads of employees.

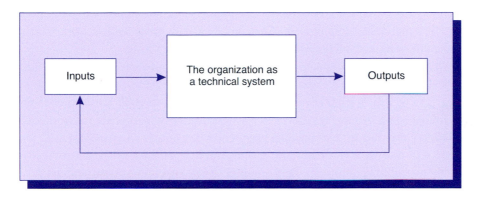

FIGURE 8.1 A basic open-systems model of organizations

We usually distinguish between an organization's core technology, which is the technology it uses to produce its key products or services (e.g. flowline technologies in manufacturing), and technologies that indirectly maintain the production process (such as the e-enablement of HR or some forms of online learning), or technologies used to adapt organizations to their environment (such as planning and market research). We shall use this broader definition of technology throughout this chapter, because it steers us away from a purely 'technicist' perspective, which has restricted discussions in this important field of study to discussions of ICT hardware and digital systems. It also helps explore the interfaces between the various components of a given technical system and its relationship with the management of people.

EXERCISE 8.1

Use Figure 8.1 to map out a basic systems view of your organization or department, or one with which you are familiar.

1 What are the key inputs and outputs?
2 What are the key features of the technical system? Here you may wish to refer to the review question in Case 8.1.

Stages in technological development and new technologies

One of the key questions raised earlier in this chapter was the distinction between old and new technologies and their different impact on organizations and people management. A conventional way of thinking about this is to refer to the stages of technological development described in Box 8.2. Stages 3 and 4 broadly correspond to what we mean by the new technologies, all of which, to a greater or lesser degree, are based on computers and computing power for their emergence and impact. Stage 3, which is based on computing and information systems, became important in the 1980s with the development of the microchip. However, it was not until the late 1990s and the widespread adoption of the Internet and ICT that we saw new business models emerging, in the form of e-commerce and m-businesses (businesses based on mobile telephone technologies). Well-known international examples are Amazon, Dell and eBay, which have transformed the bookselling, computing and auction industries respectively.

When writing this chapter originally in 2005, stage 4 was only beginning to emerge. Such has been the progress in technological development over the last decade that much of what was seen as new is now rather old hat, or is at an advanced stage. Robotics is one good illustration of the lowering costs of technology and its new applications. For example, co-bots (collaborative robots that work alongside people) have begun to change the way in which products are manufactured. *The Financial Times* in 2015 reported on how a Danish firm, Universal Robots, have developed a cheap new 'table-top' robot to assemble, polish, glue and screw a range of components, and pack eggs, while Volkswagen was using robots to cope with a shortage of workers in its German engine plants.

BOX 8.2 Stages in technological development (based on earlier work by Coyle and Quah, 2004, and Hatch and Cunliffe, 2012)

- Stage 1. Use of machines driven by steam power to replace labour in the transformation of raw materials into products.
- Stage 2. Use of electrically powered machines to move materials between machines and to power moving assembly lines and flow production.
- Stage 3. Use of electronics-based ICT to coordinate and control transfer of information and tasks.
- Stage 4. Use of several related technologies, all of which reinforce each other and are based on increasingly cheap computing power and the Internet. These include biotechnology to analyse and synthesize the genetic basis of plants, animals and humans, nanotechnology, robotics and advanced forms of materials to transform the production of goods and services, big data analytics to use large data sets to uncover hidden trends, unknown correlations, market, customer and employee attitudes, etc., cloud computing and social media to store digital information, enhance communications, learning, knowledge sharing, etc.

Clearly, as we highlighted in the introduction, different forms of technology and technological change have been at the heart of people management problems and the work of human resource professionals for many years. There is also a long and distinguished history of research and writing linking technology and technological change in the broadest sense of these terms to economics, organizational studies, psychology, and personnel and industrial relations management. For example, the work of notable figures in economics and management, such as Adam Smith, Karl Marx and Frederick Taylor, was concerned with the role of technology. In more recent times, however, the role of ICT in transforming societies, transforming economic progress and in how we work in such societies has resulted in a renewed interest in the relationship between these new technologies and the management of people.

As we also flagged in the introduction some academics are sceptical about the competitive advantages of investment in ICT for organizations, a point to which we shall return later in this chapter. Most informed opinion, however, points to at least the potential for ICT and other new technologies to have a major impact in transforming economies, organizations and the ways in which people work. Researchers typically point to at least five reasons that point to the transformative potential of ICT:

1   ICT has driven down the costs of information flows and speeded up the transmission of information, which, in an increasingly knowledge-based economy, is a critical success factor. In addition, low costs increase the adoption and diffusion of information. As technology gathers pace, advanced economies are combining technology with knowledge to create a new basis for competition and competitive advantage, drawing on knowledge management and social media.
2   The lowering of costs and ubiquity of information has assisted companies in developing new international markets and in internal coordination and learning in multinational companies.
3   ICT has led to new applications and business models. It is not just a technology but is also a marketplace, a method of manufacturing and a means of communication. We are also witnessing a new agenda made possible by these technologies in promising new ways of organizing work, including virtual working and e-lancing.
4   ICT has the potential to make all kinds of work more productive, because it increases access to information and makes markets more efficient. Good examples are the way in which Amazon has changed book publishing and firms such as Uber have changed personal transport services in many countries.
5   ICT speeds up the adoption of new techniques and innovation by connecting people and organizations, often across time zones and distance. For example, we have a developing concern in the notion of community and how Internet technologies may link up people across time and space in virtual communities of practice.

Other strategic management writers have pointed to how the new economics of information have transformed business strategy by changing the traditional trade-off in information between reach and richness (Hitt *et al.*, 2008). Reach is easily understood, being the number of people exchanging information; richness is more complicated, referring to bandwidth, the customization of information, connectivity, and the reliability, security and value of near-instant information. Their claim is that this traditional trade-off, a basic law of economics, has been disrupted, leading to simultaneous greater reach and richness, and thus the deconstruction of traditional industries such as retail banking and automobile retailing, and the creation of new ones in virtual entertainment (e.g. Netflix), gaming and music provision (e.g. Spotify and Apple Music).

In addition to these more general reasons, research into the concerns of senior HR managers in international companies has singled out technology as the most important transforming force, especially social media, and its impact on the creation and transfer of knowledge among firms (Martin *et al.*, 2009). As we have discussed in previous chapters, access to instant knowledge and learning from others is one of the key strategic drivers of global companies in industries as diverse as news media, investment banking and manufacturing. One good example from our research is IBM, who developed social media platforms for internal use before turning it into a source of revenue by selling its solutions to other organizations and supporting the solutions-based business of IBM more generally (Martin *et al.*, 2009). However, managing the volume of information or 'overflow' generated by these technologies is becoming as much a problem for firms as not having enough information (Czarniawska and Lofgren, 2012), which is a significant problem for academics and their students alike!

This brief discussion of the new technologies leads us to ask the following important set of questions: Are there common issues confronting old and new technologies and their relationship with work and people management? If so, what can we learn from the introduction about older technologies? Or are the new technologies, based on the Internet and perhaps even newer ones such as biological sciences, nanotechnology, robotics, materials sciences and social media, raising new questions? In the next part of this chapter we shall attempt to shed some light on these questions by a brief examination of two lines of enquiry concerning the relationship between technology and people management:

- the new economics of knowledge and technology, and the rise of knowledge-intensive enterprises, which we have already discussed in previous chapters;
- the organizationally based, micro-level research into technology, knowledge work and knowledge workers.

Following this examination, we developed a framework to help us understand the key issues concerning technology and the 'human condition'. This framework will then be used to organize and analyse the discussion and evidence concerning the new technologies and people management, and suggest some pointers for organizations that wish to improve their performance in the area of technology investment.

DEVELOPING A FRAMEWORK FOR EXPLORING THE RELATIONSHIP BETWEEN TECHNOLOGY AND HUMAN RESOURCE MANAGEMENT

The new economic environment: combining technology, knowledge and organizational change

We addressed the new economy literature in the last chapter on knowledge work in the shape of the relationship between the knowledge-based economy and knowledge-based enterprises (KBEs).

That discussion, however, did not really examine the critical role of technology, particularly ICT, which we shall now explore in a little more detail.

The story of the new economy began with the emergence of the new computer-based and digital technologies in the USA during the 1980s, the entrepreneurial spirit to which these gave rise and the resurgence of the American economy in the 1990s. Following these developments, a set of new theories of economic growth, which economists labelled the *new economy*, emerged in the USA during the late 1990s. However, just what the new economy looked like, and whether this model has been replaced by newer variants, is a matter of some debate.

On the one hand, some writers equated it with ICT and its sectoral consequences. For example, various OECD reports have examined the impact of ICT on the *ICT-producing industry* itself, including manufacturers of semiconductors, computer equipment and peripherals, telephony and software companies. They also examined the *ICT-using industries* – intensive ICT users such as retailing, financial services, news media, academia, healthcare and consulting. The general conclusions of the report were that the ICT-producing sector were characterized by very high rates of productivity growth and economic performance in the countries where significant clusters of such companies were found, such as Korea, Finland, Ireland, Sweden, Japan and the USA. With regard to the ICT-using sector, the picture was still positive because it was associated with productivity growth, particularly labour productivity, but it had a different international distribution. For example, the contribution of ICT-using industries in Sweden and Finland to economic growth was modest; in contrast, it was large for countries such as the UK, Australia, Canada and the USA. In part this was explained by the importance of intensive ICT-using industries to an economy, such as retailing and wholesaling, and financial services (e.g. securities). In contrast, Sweden and Finland have not been traditionally noted for having a high preponderance of these intensive ICT-using industries.

On the other hand, other writers took a broader perspective on the new economy, more akin to the knowledge-based economy discussed in the last chapter. Indeed, some commentators equated the new economy with a form of post-industrial society, in which not only knowledge work but also services have replaced manufacturing as the dominant sectors in the economy. Thus Diana Coyle (2007) used the metaphor of *weightlessness* to characterize an economy in which creating value relies less on physical mass and more on intangibles, such as building intellectual capital through knowledge and creativity, and performing 'emotional labour' (continuously being pleasant to unpleasant customers, smiling, etc.) in delivering high-quality customer services. This notion has recently been extended to include what has been termed the *sharing economy* (Sundararajan, 2013), which provides access to products, services and unique skills beyond single ownership. This new form of economic and organizational structure is based on the application of web-based technologies to work, resulting in people shifting from being employees working under a contract *of* services to becoming independent workers, freelancers and e-lancers, working under a contract *for* services. Good examples are the hundreds of thousands of part-time 'driver-partners' who are contracted to Uber, a firm that claims to provide taxi services cheaper and more convenient in major cities in many countries.

Support for these trends in advanced economies comes from evidence on the changing occupational structure in the UK: the number of people employed in traditional professional jobs (doctors, lawyers, accountants, etc.), managerial and intermediate professional (nurses) occupations grew by more than 50 per cent over the period 1981–2008, while the numbers employed in routine administration and manual categories (e.g. clerical jobs and process operators) declined by 36 per cent and 50 per cent respectively. Interestingly, the category with the fastest growth was non-routine services, which grew by 72 per cent between 1981–2008 (Holmes and Mayhew, 2012). These figures confirm a significant increase in these knowledge-intensive occupations, which require high levels of education and skills acquisition, and a significant increase in service occupations such as care assistants in homes for the elderly and hospitals, which are relatively low-skilled occupations and low users of ICT. Indeed, ICT may well replace many of the functions carried out by such occupations, with the advent of 'ubiquitous computing' and the 'internet of things' (see Box 8.3).

So, whether an economy can be described as new, weightless or sharing, all variations give a prominent role to ICT, especially to its contribution at the level of the firm. Studies on the economic impact of ICT (e.g. OECD, 2004; UNCTAD, 2011) have shown the following:

- Enterprise-level studies showed that ICT use typically had a positive but variable effect on company performance, demonstrating the fact that investment in ICT was not enough by itself to guarantee success.
- Some ICT technologies had a bigger impact than others on productivity and performance, with *communications networking* being especially important in industries such as financial services, and mobile phones in small businesses. This was especially the case when broadband was advanced in a particular country.
- They also showed that there were important sectoral differences in the impact of ICT on performance at the level of the enterprise, with firms in the service sectors of retailing and financial services making large gains from ICT investment, and larger firms benefitted from e-commerce and other e-business applications.
- Significantly, ICT effectiveness was found to be complementary to *human capital investment*, which helps explain the first set of findings. For example, studies in different countries showed that the use of ICT was linked to higher levels of skills, and that they became even more productive as they became more experienced in using these technologies. Yet others found that firms that adopted advanced technologies also increased their expenditure on education and training, while reducing their demand for less skilled people.
- Finally, ICT effectiveness was complemented by investment in successful *organizational change*, also helping to explain the first set of findings. For example, studies (Martin *et al.*, 2015) found close relationships between ICT investment and performance, but usually only when combined with complementary changes in new strategies, business processes, and/or new ways of organizing and working. These organizational changes included team-working, flattening out of hierarchies, employee involvement schemes and improved communications.

Thus, this new economics, based on the knowledge-based economy and on new knowledge-intensive enterprises (KIEs) (see Table 8.1), has two important implications for the relationship between technology, organizations and the management of people. The first of these implications focuses on knowledge, education and skills as one of the key factors in productivity and perform-ance, and a general-purpose *enabling technology* such as ICT as both the key *input* and key *output* of knowledge creation (Brynjolfsson and McAfee, 2011). For example, if we map out a basic, open-systems model, the development and diffusion of genetic profiling, a new form of knowledge, is

---

BOX 8.3 Ubiquitous computing and the Internet of things

An alternative vision of ICT promises to transform work, which is where computing is 'made to appear everywhere and anywhere', forcing computers to live out there in the world of people. The notion of ubiquitous or pervasive computing is based on cheap and low-powered computers with convenient displays embedded into our everyday environments, including homes, work, hospitals, offices and public places. These devices are wired or wireless networked and supported by applications software. The ubiquitous nature of computing will pervade common places and be embedded in clothing or the fabric of buildings. The computers can deal with many inputs, including voice data, acoustics, images, motion and gestures, light, heat, moisture and pressure.

Examples of the applications of ubiquitous computing have been demonstrated at the Xerox PARC laboratory. As soon as people enter the work environment, they are immediately authenticated, thereby triggering a range of resources available to them, including visual displays, computing devices and knowledge resources. These resources can be easily manipulated to create rapid analysis and synthesis of new knowledge in a range of visual and textual forms, much faster than using conventional means.

This notion of ubiquitous computing is also being used in environments such as care homes for the elderly in Wisconsin, USA, in which diagnostic computers are embedded into the clothing of old people to provide constant monitoring of the location and, in a limited sense, state of health. Residents carry dual-channel radio frequency locator tags, which serve as their apartment keys and emit periodic infrared pulses to the sensors in each room. Beds have embedded weight sensors. Each apartment has motion and health vital sensors plus a networked computer with touch interface screen, enabling communication through e-mail, video-conferencing and voice communication. These systems and sensors feed personalized databases to monitor personal health, activity levels, interactions with medical attention and status of medication. Managers use the information to monitor staff performance, and residents use the information to monitor themselves. Residents in such environments claim greater control and autonomy, feeling that if they become disoriented or wander, require help or medicine, assistance will be at hand immediately.

---

dependent on ICT, but also advanced biotechnological know-how and complementary organizational inputs are synonymous with a KIE. In turn, it is hoped that these inputs, transformed by the KIE, will lead to improvements in the quality and reductions in the costs of key healthcare technology such as cancer treatment and heart disease. These improvements arise not only from the development of new treatments, but also in improving the intangible aspects of existing treatments such as convenience, timeliness, quality and choice available to patients. In addition, increased productivity through improved quality and reduced costs also arises through the development of new forms of organization and know-how to be able to take advantage of these discoveries (see Figure 8.2).

TABLE 8.1 The old and new economies compared

Issues	Old economy	New economy
Economy-wide characteristics		
	Industrial	*Weightless, post-industrial*
Markets	Stable	Dynamic
Scope of competition	National	Global
Organizational form	Hierarchical, bureaucratic	Networked
Structure	Manufacturing core	Services core
Source of value	Raw materials, manufactured goods, financial capital	Knowledge and skills, human and social capital, emotional labour
Business		
	Fordist	*KBEs*
Organization of production Key drivers of growth	Mass production/Fordism	Flexible Innovation/knowledge and skills
Key technological driver	Mechanization and electrical power	Digitization and related technologies
Source of competitive advantage	Lowering costs through economies of scale	Innovation, quality and speed through whole supply chain
Importance of research/ innovation	Low–moderate	High
Relations with other firms	Go it alone, competitive	Alliances and collaboration, outsourcing
Workplace relations	Adversarial	Collaboration and partnership
Nature of employment	Stable	Marked by insecurity, risk and opportunity
Consumers		
Tastes	Stable	Rapidly changing
Skills	Job specific	Broad, transferable skills and adaptability
Educational needs	Craft skill or degree: one-off requirement	Lifelong learning
Government		
Business–government relations	Impose regulations	Encourage growth opportunities
Regulation	Command and control	Market tools, flexibility and devolved government
Government services	Nanny state	Enabling state

Source: adapted from Coyle and Quah, 2004.

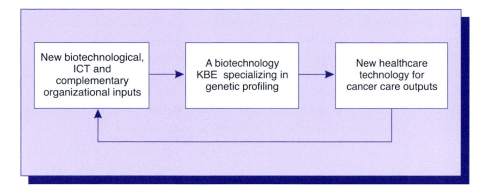

FIGURE 8.2 A basic open-systems model of knowledge-based enterprise in the biotech industry

The second implication, and perhaps more important from the perspective of human resource management practitioners, is that the new economics of knowledge and technology, both of which are essentially human constructions, depend to a large extent on the management of intangible assets. Most notably, these include the *quality and management of people and their tacit knowledge, and how they are organized*. This has been the explicit message of well-known researchers in the field such as Brynjolfsson and McAfee (2011), who have argued that a significant component of the value of ICT investment is its ability to enable complementary organizational investments, such as new business processes and new forms of working, to become effective (see the case of MacroMed below). These MIT-based researchers, who described themselves as 'digital optimists', argued that while the Global Financial Crisis, off-shoring of jobs, taxes and regulations all had an impact on jobs in the United States, technology was also a significant factor in shaping employment practices. Claiming that advanced economies such as the US were facing a 'Great Restructuring', they argued that ICT-based technologies were racing ahead but many skills and organizations were lagging behind. Thus it was necessary to understand these technologies, phenomena, discuss their implications and derive strategies that allowed people to 'race with machines instead of racing against them'.

CASE 8.2 **MACROMED**

MacroMed is a large, US-based medical products manufacturer, which was one of the world leaders in its field in 2015. In order to provide greater customization and variety two decades ago, it embarked on a major investment in computer-integrated manufacturing. This investment coincided with a number of other changes in people management, including eliminating payment by results, giving workers authority for scheduling machines, decentralizing decision-making, more frequent and richer interactions with customers and suppliers, increased communications and teamworking, and changes in skill levels and organizational culture.

However, the new system fell way below expectations for greater flexibility and responsiveness to customer demands. Investigations into the causes of the problem showed that employees still retained many old ways of doing things, not to be deliberately obstructive, but because that was the way they had always done their jobs. Somewhat ironically the new machines were so flexible that workers could operate them and work in the same old ways, but without securing the improvements promised by the new computer-controlled technology.

Management decided after some time to set up operations on a new, 'green-field' site, with a set of handpicked, younger employees who had not been part of the old culture of work practices. The improvements in productivity were sufficiently dramatic to make the management team paint the windows of the new factory black so that competitors could not look in.

Source: based on earlier work by Brynjolfsson and Hitt, 2000.

1 Can you explain the causes of the dramatic improvements in productivity?
2 Given its current position as a world-leader in its field, were management justified in worrying about competitors 'seeing into the new factory'? Or would they have done just as well had they allowed competitors to see in?

Despite the findings of these digital optimists and the hype generated by notions such as the new economy and sharing economy, events such as the 'dot-bomb' crisis in 2000 and the Global Financial Crisis in 2007–8 provoked a major backlash and widespread criticism among economists and business academics. These critics argued that the new economy was 'stillborn', especially in countries such as the UK and much of Europe where, according to some economists and politicians, these countries still follow a low road to growth. So, for example, the UK Commission for Employment and Skills (2015) pointed out that despite having a highly skilled workforce, UK productivity had 'tanked'.

Thus, a key question arises: Is there really anything new or special about new economy knowledge work and knowledge workers? To answer this, we need to examine some of the older work on the relationship between technological change, organizations and people management.

The old orthodoxy: technology, knowledge work and knowledge workers in the old economy

Is there anything new about new technologies? In one sense, the answer to the question is 'no': 'New' technologies and various forms of knowledge work have always combined to create a form of 'new economy', represented by stages 1 and 2 in Box 8.2. Indeed, the history of management studies can be portrayed in terms of the evolving relationship between technological change, knowledge work and the management of knowledge workers (see Chapter 7). This concern dates back to Taylor and his disciples, whose work was characterized by an attempt to relocate the knowledge of craft workers – skilled machine-tool men who fashioned the major parts of early motor cars by brain and by hand – into procedures manuals and machines, a subject discussed in Chapter 1 of this book. These developments culminated in the era of Fordism, often stylized as the application of technology to Taylorism to create the dominant mode of production in the last century. Another answer is to draw on the data we used earlier in this chapter to show how the occupational structure of the UK is changing. Thus, although the use of ICT in some occupations has advanced rapidly over the last two decades (e.g. medicine, accounting and even academia), it has not done so among large sections of the population of manual, unskilled and personal service workers.

Before embarking on a review of more contemporary work, it is necessary to revisit some of the earlier, 'classical' studies to see what we can learn and use in our understanding of new technologies and the kinds of problem managers are likely to confront. Four competing perspectives on the effects of technology on work help us here, each of which sees technology in a different light:

- technological determinism;
- labour process;
- strategic choice perspectives;
- new theories linking technology and the experience of work.

Technological determinism

In any history of management and organizational studies, the 1950s marked something of a watershed. From that time, technology became the favoured variable for explaining how people behaved at work (Child, 2015), rather than the nature of the human relations climate, which had characterized most of the writing between the 1920s and 1940s (Rose, 1975). This relationship between technology and people was sometimes treated as a direct one, in so far as the nature of the technology itself was thought to have an immediate effect on work behaviour. For example, producing motor vehicles using craft-based technology had a very different impact on skills and levels of job satisfaction from production methods associated with assembly line, mass production technology. More often than not, however, it was taken to mean the complementary relationships noted earlier between the technological 'hardware' – plant and machines – and a form of organizational 'software'. Such changes shaped work behaviour in particular ways:

- The first was the system of rules that governed management and employee relations in the industry or workplace where unions were recognized. For example, technology shaped the kinds of people who were employed, and collective bargaining agreements between managers and unions would often dictate which trades or occupations were allowed to use or supervise particular machines in industries such as engineering, construction, motor vehicle manufacture and printing.
- The second was the particular form of production systems and work processes, i.e. the methods of production and knowledge required to develop and use the technology determined the work behaviour.

Four such works serve as good illustrations of these links between technological hardware, organizational forms and human behaviour, which are still very relevant today. The first was Woodward's (1965) studies of the effects of organizational structure on the performance of 100 manufacturing firms operating in the south-east of the UK. Initially, she could make little sense of her findings, which seemed to show that the form of organization (as measured by factors such as spans of control, levels of management or centralization) had little relationship with performance. Only when these structural characteristics were related to the different types of technology she identified (unit and small batch production, mass production and the types of continuous production found in chemicals, etc.) did they make any sense. That is, the highest levels of performance found in her sample of firms were correlated with either mass production technologies being combined with mechanistic organizations, or unit/small batch technologies and continuous process technologies being combined with organic organizations.

The second piece of research was by Leonard Sayles (1958), who noted that particular types of workplace were marked by high rates of grievance activity that were wholly unrelated to variations in managerial policies or style. At that time, this was a counterintuitive finding, because the dominant explanation of industrial conflict focused on human relations and management style as key variables in explaining the quality of employee relations in organizations. His research showed that different types of groups, which he labelled apathetic, erratic, strategic and conservative, were products of different types of technological system found in the 30 companies in his study. In short, it was different types of technology and not managers that caused high and low levels of grievance.

The third was the well-known study by Robert Blauner (1964), who claimed that the most important single factor that determined an industry's character was its technology. Blauner attempted to show a direct relationship between worker *alienation*, which was made up of objective conditions and feeling states, and different forms of technology. He classified alienation in terms of powerlessness (the lack of control over conditions of work), meaningless (the work and its products have no meaning for employees), isolation (referring to the lack of community in certain types of plants) and self-estrangement (roughly comparable to current notions of employee identification with the work and organization). Blauner related scores on these different forms of alienation to four types of technological system, comprising craft production, machine tending, mass production and process production. We return to this issue of alienation in a later section of this chapter.

The fourth work was by Charles Perrow (1986), a well-known American organizational theorist. Perrow's major contributions were in recognizing that the same organization may have a number of different core technologies, and in producing a typology of the relationship between technology and organization that is still highly influential. He proposed that different units and subunits of an organization can be compared along two dimensions relating to its core tasks:

- *Task variability* was defined in terms of the number of exceptions from standardized procedures evident in the application of a given technology. For example, moving assembly lines are portrayed as dictating how workers perform their tasks, whereas design engineers have considerable latitude in how they arrive at solutions.
- *Task analysability* was defined in terms of the extent to which there were well-known analytical methods for dealing with any exceptions to standard procedures. For example, lower-level administrators are always able to refer problems to higher-level managers, a well-documented procedure for dealing with problems, whereas scientists in leading-edge computing or

biotechnological research often lack the procedures or training to deal with exceptions to the rule. In effect, they have to invent them.

Combining Perrow's two dimensions resulted in four different forms of organizational technology:

1   *Routine technologies* are characterized by low task variability and high task analysability, exemplified by assembly line work and lower-level clerical work. Many modern call or service centres fall into this category.
2   *Craft technology* is described by low scores on both dimensions. For example, workers on a building site face few exceptions to standard operating procedures laid out by architects' plans and building regulations, but when they do, they often have to invent ways of dealing with a lack of materials or mistakes made by the architect. In effect, they have to craft a solution based on their tacit knowledge and experience of such work.
3   *Engineering technologies* are characterized by high scores on both dimensions. For example, though software engineers are likely to face many exceptions to standard practices in creating new programs, the increasing body of knowledge in this field and their specialized education and training provide them with known and codified methods of solving such problems. The work of many human resource management departments falls into this category.
4   *Non-routine technologies* are high on task variability and low on task analysability. Such technologies of organization are to be found in advanced research work, high-level consultancy and managerial work, and in entrepreneurial science firms.

The critical point about Perrow's work, which has much modern-day application to new technologies and knowledge workers, is the distinction between *routine* technologies, which allow for few exceptions to known procedures and provide well-documented ways for dealing with any exceptions that arise, and *non-routine* technologies, which permit many exceptions and rely on high levels of worker discretion and levels of tacit knowledge to deal with these exceptions. This is a point that informed our discussion of knowledge management in the previous chapter, and to which we shall return later in this chapter.

Labour process theory

Much of the above work was prescriptive, and treated technology as a progressive and optimistic force in the economy, or at least neutral when applied to work and workers, i.e. in itself neither good nor bad. Accompanying these studies throughout the last century, however, were those of a more critical and pessimistic bent. From the perspective of the authors of these studies, technology was seen to have a 'dark side': it was rarely seen as neutral in its political impact on work and workers, nor was it viewed as a necessarily progressive force in society. In these senses, many of these critical studies were influenced by Marx's dialectical method of social theory, which turned on the idea that every theory of technological progress created its own antithesis. This dialectical theory of technological change has been illustrated by the widespread opposition in some countries to the recent introduction of biotechnology and genetics, particularly in relation to GM food technology and to genetic engineering.

They were also influenced by Marx's class conflict theory of societies and organizations. Nowhere was this more apparent than in the writings of the labour process school, whose inspiration was Harry Braverman's (1974) criticism of Taylorism and the organization of manual and knowledge work during the twentieth century. Braverman's deskilling thesis claimed that the development of capitalism as an economic system had given rise to a mode of production and work organization that was being systematically fragmented and deskilled in the pursuit of rational efficiency. The logic of deskilling was to replace expensive and powerful craft (and knowledge) workers with more easily trained and less expensive unskilled labour and, eventually, machines (read 'computers' in the modern parlance). Such deskilling led to a reduction in employee bargaining power, and thus to maximizing profits. It also had the effect, reflecting Blauner and others, of alienating employees from their work and from the products of their labour. For example, studies showed that workers on an assembly line rarely felt committed to their work or organization, nor did they feel that they had contributed to the overall product or feel any sense of ownership for mistakes or successes.

Such literature portrayed Taylor as the arch-enemy of workers and was heavily critical of Fordist systems of production. During the early 1980s, when the labour process school was probably most prominent in academic terms, it influenced the more practical concerns of trade unions in some countries. Many of these adopted a defensive posture in opposing the introductions of microprocessor-based technologies during the early 1980s, especially if it were to be used to deskill the labour process and lead to even greater unemployment than existed at the time. This resistance to technological change is an underlying cause of many industrial disputes, and can often help explain why some countries and some organizations are able to adapt to technological change more effectively, and why others are less able or willing to adapt.

In the 1990s the focus of this work turned to the effects of computing technology on work and work behaviour, with a series of articles and books produced by critical theorists writing from a labour process perspective and, increasingly, producing 'gloomy analyses of emerging factory regimes in which workers lose even the awareness of their own exploitation' (McKinlay and Taylor, 1998, p. 175). This kind of thinking has infused the HRM literature on call centres as the 'factories of the future' and studies that have criticized the low-road/low-skills equilibrium followed by many organizations. It has also been critical of the routinization of workers in information technology and software writing (Thompson and Smith, 2010). Thus, various reports on the 'information society' and the role of ICT have found that many employees are unwilling to give up knowledge, or have resented the introduction of ICT when used to blur the lines between work and leisure – for example, by being always 'on call'. However, most of the more sophisticated studies of deskilling have noted the limits to degradation of this type of knowledge work. For example, in a study of software firms, it was found that commercial pressures, which have been seen as the engine of deskilling in software production, can also lead to software developers using their own initiative to create viable software (often in conjunction with users with whom they were not supposed to have formal contact) (Beirne *et al.*, 1998). The central message of this literature, in contrast to the digital optimists, is not the limitations of technological forms of control, but that the logic of capitalism as an economic system ineluctably leads to a degraded form of knowledge work, regardless of how individual firms might behave. In that sense, managers have very little control over how they use technology, because it is the logic of profits that dictates how technology and work are related.

Strategic choice perspectives

If gloom was the flavour of much of the writing on technology during the twentieth century, the strategic choice perspective has represented something of a balance between the optimism and political neutrality of the technological determinist school and the 'dismal science' predictions of the labour process school. Strategic choice implied that introducing new technologies did not need to result in deskilling or in any form of predetermined work organization. Instead, different groups of employees and managers had different objectives for any form of technology, based on their values and perceptions of their power, and the eventual outcomes of any technological innovation depended on negotiations between these groups (Child, 2015). Perhaps the original inspiration for such work was the socio-technical systems approach of the Tavistock Institute of Human Relations in the UK (Trist *et al.*, 1963), which set out the choices of social organization available for any given form of technological system. This work focused on the importance of meshing technology with the needs, characteristics and attitudes of workers in order to optimize outcomes. People were organized into groups or autonomous work teams, completed whole tasks with minimal external supervision, and experienced variety, support and recognition in achieving the goals that were set. The work of the Tavistock group had a major influence on subsequent attempts to operationalize socio-technical systems during the 1980s in Sweden and Germany, most notably at Volvo and Saab. For example, during the 1980s both of these organizations undertook major experiments that eliminated assembly line technology and introduced autonomous, multi-skilled workgroups, which built the major parts of a motor vehicle. These experiments were seen as a partial return to the traditions of craft-based manufacture, enhanced by the use of modern manufacturing technologies.

Modern expressions of what might be called a socio-technical approach to organizational studies and HRM are to be found in the 'lean production' literature that had such a major impact on vehicle manufacture during the 1990s and on services in the decades following. This work was provoked by a major series of studies, culminating in the book *The Machine That Changed the World* (Womack *et al.*, 1990). The book set out the findings on world motor vehicle manufacture and the choices facing vehicle manufacturers in developing organizations and work teams. One of its key messages was that managers had a technological and organizational choice over how to produce motor vehicles, and that Japanese organizations seemed to have reached an optimal compromise between the tightly coupled design based on standardization and economies of scale of Fordism on the one hand, and the more loosely coupled design based on innovativeness and quality on the other, by using teams and employee involvement strategies (see also Chapter 4). These studies have had enormous influence on current ways of organizing work in many different industries, especially in the USA and Europe, and provide the stereotypical model of modern manufacturing. Nowadays lean production ideas are also being applied to the public sector in an administrative setting, because productivity improvements in services are required. However, bringing lean ideas into service industries have not been as easy as first thought (Staats and Upton, 2011). Not all of the ideas and principles of the Toyota system translate from the factory floor to the office.

CASE 8.3 LEAN PRODUCTION, THE TOYOTA SYSTEM AND ITS MODERN APPLICATION

Assembly line technology and social organization have dominated manufacturing methods for nearly all of the last century, especially in the motor vehicle industry and among component suppliers for motor vehicles. Such systems of manufacture have allowed companies to reap enormous benefits from economies of scale by producing vehicles and components for inventory. However, they have been associated with unwanted stocks, poor quality and high levels of employee dissatisfaction due to the mechanical pacing of jobs and lack of autonomy on behalf of workers. In the 1980s companies such as Volvo and Saab attempted to do away with assembly lines and introduced state-of-the-art factories built around the concept of autonomous workgroups of multi-skilled people who would build a major part of a car by themselves. These experiments generated a lot of interest, which has recently been rekindled in Sweden by Volvo.

Lean production as a method of manufacturing is an alternative to traditional mass production and the more craft-based, autonomous workgroups. It is an assembly line manufacturing methodology developed originally for Toyota and the manufacture of automobiles. It is also known as the Toyota Production System. The goal of lean production is described as 'to get the right things to the right place at the right time, the first time, while minimizing waste and being open to change'. Engineer Ohno, who is credited with developing the principles of lean production, discovered that, in addition to eliminating waste, his methodology led to improved product flow and better quality.

Instead of devoting resources to the planning required for future manufacturing under mass production, Toyota focused on reducing system response times so that the production system was capable of immediately changing and adapting to market demands. In effect, their automobiles became made-to-order. The principles of lean production enabled the company to deliver on demand, minimize inventory, maximize the use of multi-skilled employees, flatten the management structure and focus resources where they were needed.

During the 1980s the practices summarized in the ten rules of lean production were adopted by many manufacturing plants in the USA and Europe, and, more recently, they have been adopted in services. The management style was tried out with varying degrees of success by service organizations, logistics organizations and supply chains, and, more recently, in knowledge work (Staats and Upton, 2011). Since the mid-2000s, there has also been a renewed interest in the principles of lean production in manufacturing, particularly as the philosophy encourages the reduction of inventory and waste. Dell Computers and Boeing Aircraft have embraced the philosophy of lean production with great success. However, researchers have found that the implementation of lean production in manufacturing has been variable, especially over how it impacts on employee learning and job quality. For example, Sterling and Boxall (2013) found that only where line managers had given up some control and employees had the necessary levels of literacy did mutually beneficial learning tend to result. And even then, these positive outcomes were dependent on the level of production pressures and investments by firms in developing supervisors and workers literacy.

The 17 rules of lean production can be summarized as follows:

1 Set up cross-functional design and development teams.
2 Develop a *kaizen* philosophy of continuous improvement.

3 Flexible machines, low set-up costs.
4 Broad product lines.
5 Targeted markets.
6 Eliminate waste.
7 Minimize inventory.
8 Maximize flow.
9 Pull production from customer demand – make to order rather than for stock.
10 Meet customer requirements.
11 Do it right the first time.
12 Empower workers through quality circles and improvement groups.
13 Develop highly skilled and cross-trained workers.
14 Design for rapid changeover.
15 Partner with suppliers.
16 Create a culture of continuous improvement, involving workers on the shopfloor.
17 Build long-term, trusting relationships with key suppliers.

Note that these features are complementary to one another, and adopting only some of them will not produce the gains that Toyota experienced. This has been one of the reasons why many firms in the West have not been able to achieve Toyota's quality and productivity levels.

1 How do you think that workers in manufacturing would respond to lean production techniques?
2 Why might these rules be difficult to apply to the service sector, especially public services?

New theories linking technology and the experience of work

The above theories tended to separate out technology from work and to see technology in a deterministic way, as if it was something out there, independent of our own interpretations of what technology actually meant as how it influenced our work behaviour. So, by the 1990s researchers began to view technology as socially constructed by us in our everyday work experience, and to look into how the same technological hardware and software might generate quite different outcomes, for example as something which dominated us or something which liberated us, or both simultaneously. A number of theoretical perspectives have been influential in this respect. The first is *sociomateriality*, a deliberately fused term, signifying an approach to understanding how technologies are used by people in their day-to-day actions in a process that Orlikowski and Scott (2008) have described as 'constitutive entanglement'. In other words, they focused on how the social and the material entwine and mutually constitute each other. One good example of research in this tradition has been the examination, *in situ*, of how e-mail is used by different people, resulting in a change in its material nature and meaning to users. You might want to think about how you use e-mail and whether you see it as an invasive technology to be avoided outside of working hours, or as a liberating technology, allowing you to keep in touch and exercise influence over your work situation 24/7.

A second variation on this theme is Stephen Barley's (2015) *role theory*. This approach focuses on how the introduction of specific technologies changed the tasks that people did. As a consequence of these changes, people may begin to interact differently with co-workers in their 'role-set' and even begin to interact with new people outside of the traditional role-set. Barley argued that if these role relations change, then relations within the social network may also change, and thus the material nature of technology can be said to change a work system. In turn, however, the changed work system can also lead to changes in the technology and how it is used. For example, his early research examined how the introduction of ultrasound and CT scanners altered professional power between technologists who produced traditionally produced x-rays and radiologists who interpreted them. With the introduction of these new technologies, technologists who understood how computerized images were produced acquired greater power and autonomy, which in turn changed the nature of hierarchical relations in the hospital department. He also cited a study of the introduction of minimally invasive cardiac surgery in 16 hospitals in the USA. The introduction of this technology worked best when there was greater relational coordination, (see Chapter 3) collaboration and less hierarchy among surgeons, nurses, technicians and anesthesiologists in departments.

Is there something different about new technologies and their effect on the world of work?

Social scientists, Erik Brynjolfsson and Andrew McAfee are two of the most respected researchers in this field. In two books (Brynjolfsson and McAfee, 2011, 2014), they attempted to answer this question. Firstly, they saw the new digital technologies, the linked systems of computer hardware, software and networks referred to in this chapter, as driving forces in improving productivity and growth. Secondly, they saw these changes as largely beneficial because they are capable of increasing the variety and volume of consumption, including information, entertainment, and expertise from teachers and doctors. Such volume and variety, they claim, have altered the basis of traditional economic theory from resource scarcity to abundance. Thirdly, as we noted earlier in this chapter digitalization brings with it the problems they discussed in the 'Race Against the Machine' thesis: that these technologies are racing ahead of the capabilities of workers and managers to keep up with them. Like other researchers in the field, they see the divergence between highly skilled and lower skilled workers, between the highly scarce superstars and everyone else, and between capital and labour becoming much greater, trends borne out by economic data in the developed world. Their pessimism on this last front is tempered only by the extent that workers and managers learn to use new technologies as assets and allies rather than adversaries, destroying jobs and opportunities.

A framework for explaining the relationship between new technology and managing people

This review of some of the newer and older studies in which technology, organization and people management are linked raises two sets of important questions that has helped us develop a framework (see Figure 8.3) for thinking about newer technologies, including ICT and digital technologies, and managing people:

1   To what extent are the new *non-routine, knowledge-intensive organizations* different from old-style *knowledge-routinized organizations*? To what extent are the new non-routine, knowledge-intensive organizations different in making use of technology, particularly investment in ICT and digitalization, to produce innovations and productivity growth? And is there, as much of the literature suggests, a direct relationship between investment in these new technologies and the exploitation of knowledge in organizations?

2   To what extent is there a choice for managers between using ICT as a *dominating and centralizing force*, perhaps leading to a deskilling of employees, or as a potentially *liberating and empowering force*, enhancing the role of employees and HR managers and in re-skilling work? This dualism between control and freedom has been an important feature in the organizational writing on technology (e.g. Brynjolfsson and McAfee, 2011, 2014), and posits a role for managers as strategic enablers of business directions and visions rather than as passive recipients or 'handmaidens' of technological investment and general economic trends.

The answers to these sets of questions, we argue, lie along two continua, which, when related orthogonally, create four scenarios or images of organization. These images can then be used as prisms to view the relationship between newer technologies, organizations and people management. Each of these images reflects a dominant view of organization within a firm, or characterizes certain departments or divisions within a firm. The critical point is that, although one image may be a way of seeing technology and people management, it is also a way of not seeing.

One of the best uses to which these images can be put is to generate four sets of questions managers might ask of the relationship between new technologies and the management of people, the answers to which are of enormous practical value:

1   To what extent might these new technologies facilitate advances in intelligent relationships between organizations, groups and individuals that are based on increased employee voice dialogue and participation (Martin *et al.*, 2015) rather than through existing patterns of control and domination?

2   How might these new technologies allow organizations, groups and individuals to make things happen (i.e. create new business models to make and sell innovative products and services) rather than have things happen to them, in the context of organizational and societal goals (Brynjolfsson and McAfee, 2011, 2014)? How might these technologies facilitate employee productivity? How might organizations use technology to follow a high-road route to international competitiveness?

3   In what ways can these new technologies create new forms of community and new forms of organization, bringing together organizations, groups and individuals that up until now have been separated by time, space and culture? Or will they lead to new forms of social disintegration by alienating people who once worked together?

4   In what ways can new technology create new ways of limiting the damage caused by economic pressures on organizations, groups and individuals (i.e. deskilling and work intensification), or will these new technologies lead to even greater damage (e.g. stress and intrusion problems, health and safety problems, increased human vulnerability and the '24/7–always on' problems)?

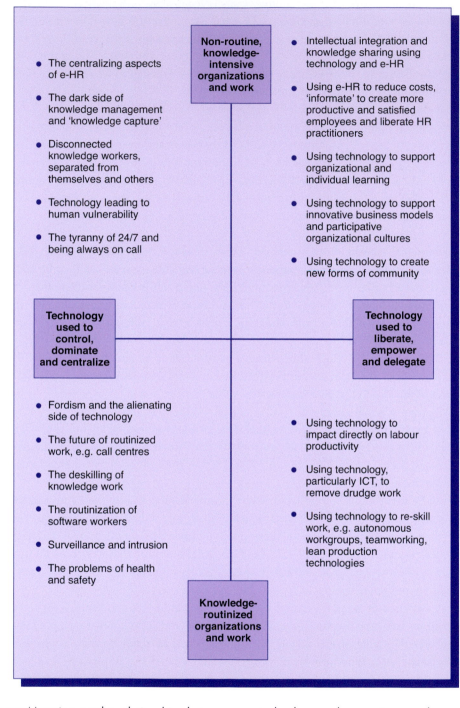

FIGURE 8.3 Mapping out the relationships between new technology and managing people

Inevitably, this framework and certain of these questions imply an ideal to be achieved of progress through technology, with a movement in the general direction of greater freedom for most employees in knowledge-based organizations. We need to suspend judgement, however, because much of the evidence is running behind the rhetoric. That said, as Malone (2004) argued some time ago, the new factors to be considered are the costs of communication and the value of remote information, both of which are being rapidly changed by new ICT. Perhaps it is these factors more than any others that provide the potential for new business models, new forms of organization and people management.

NEW TECHNOLOGIES AND MANAGING PEOPLE: THE ROLE OF SOCIAL MEDIA IN COLLABORATION, SHARING KNOWLEDGE, COMMUNICATING AND EXPRESSING VOICE

Since writing the first edition of this text, one of the most notable developments has been the introduction of social media into organizations and the world of work. By social media, we refer to the ICT tools that enable people to create, share and exchange digital information, ideas and pictures in virtual communities and networks, including blogs, wikis, media sharing sites, social networking and virtual reality worlds. In this final section of the chapter, we shall discuss the role of these social media and their relationship with work organization and people management, since these media have had a highly significant impact on employees' experience of work and the capacity of businesses to innovate because of accessibility and immediacy in cyberspace. As a McKinsey report stated in 2012, if Facebook were a country it would be the world's third most populous one, after China and India (Divol *et al.*, 2012). Maybe by the time you read this book, it will be the largest; on the other hand, maybe it will decline in numbers in much the same way that one of its predecessors, MySpace, did in the last decade. One method of answering this question is to explore the potential for social media by undertaking some scenario analysis.

Social media and engagement

As we noted earlier, a technological system comprises not only hardware and software but also embraces the knowledge needed to use the technologies and the work organization to implement it. As an example, mass production is a technology based on the hardware of a moving assembly line to produce, say, motor vehicles, software such as manufacturing resource planning (MRP) systems, work organization based on a detailed division of labour, and relatively low levels of employee knowledge and skills to work on an assembly line.

Thus, how we make choices on technological systems and the choices we make has a significant impact on work organization and people management. One of the most important influences on these choices has been the extent to which employees and managers are *engaged* by and with them. By engagement in this context we draw on our definition in Chapter 3 to mean whether employees:

- *identify* with a particular technology (does it help employees express their personal and organizational identity?)

- *internalize* the technology's built in values (does the technology embrace the values they hold?)
- feel a degree of *psychological ownership* over it (to what extent is the technology 'theirs'?)

So, in respect of social media technologies, the key question we have to answer is: how easy is it for employees to engage with specific media (or combination of media) to collaborate, share knowledge, communicate and express authentic voice in their organizations? By easy, we mean not just ease of use and access, but also these aspects of identification, internalization and psychological ownership. Indeed, identification with technological change by employees has been shown to be one of the key factors in its acceptance (Tripas, 2008). Moreover new generations of employees (the 'net generation') are much more likely to identify and engage with these social media technologies than previous generations.

Social media and control

Control is another widely discussed and contested idea in management and employee relations, especially in relation to the distribution of power between employers and employees. In the context of social media, control seems to be expressed in the answer to another important question: How easy or difficult is it for organizations to cope with the power employees enjoy from easy access to decentralized and open forms of communication and collaboration? Some of the earlier discussions on the introduction of social media into organizations seemed to suggest that many HR managers at least saw the answer to this question as a 'zero-sum' game – the more control and power employees had, typically to misuse these social media at work for personal reasons, the less control organizations and HR were able to exercise (Martin *et al.*, 2009). As we found, social networking and blogging were typically banned from organizations, resulting in a time-consuming battle of blocking and unblocking sites from view. This control focus was also evident in legal cases and advice by lawyers on the use by employees of social media technologies during the latter part of the last decade. As a result lawyers began to advise employees not to post any comments online that could remotely be connected with their employer's business.

However, we also found that the introduction of social media into organizations was not always seen as a win–lose scenario: employees and employers were able to gain if they agreed to a 'win–win' solution (Martin *et al.*, 2009). Participants in a number of cases we researched spoke of a 'positive-sum' game, in which organizations and employees both gained from 'better morale', not being seen to ban 'freedom of speech' and in encouraging experimentation with these media technologies that resulted in significant innovation.

Four scenarios for the future of social media in organizations

Combining engagement and control, we propose four scenarios that describe modes of communication, knowledge sharing, collaboration and voice in organizations (see Figure 8.4). These scenarios help us think about the challenges that HRM faces and possible strategic choices organizations can make with respect to using social media.

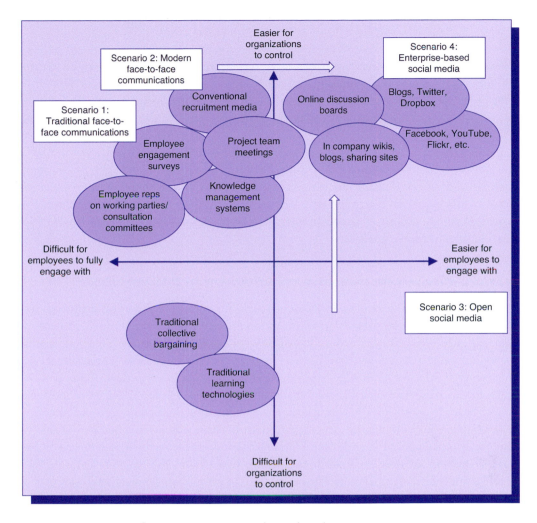

FIGURE 8.4 Four scenarios for communications and social media

Scenario 1–Traditional face-to-face communication and collaboration

This scenario represents the typical, existing face-to-face system of collaboration and communication, the latter of which is typically conducted through the formal collective bargaining system. Union representation provides the main medium for employee voice, and knowledge management and collaboration continues to be viewed as a 'contested terrain'. Knowledge and skills are seen as issues to be bargained over since knowledge is power and not something to be readily given up by employees, who seek to capitalize on their tacit knowledge and skills.

In this scenario, the challenges to both managers and union representatives are that:

- new generations of employees begin to use social media as a means of expressing their own, often negative, voice, as unions are seen by an increasing number of workers to be less relevant in expressing their interests (Martin *et al.*, 2015);
- employees don't engage in much formal or informal collaboration and knowledge-sharing with one another since their tacit knowledge and skills are their main source of power to enhance their careers at work.

Managers view employees' use of these technologies in a largely negative light, often attempting to proscribe their use at work, or else ignore them as a means of finding out what employees think and want to discuss. Such a scenario may be typical of many organizations in traditional manufacturing and service industries, and in certain parts of public services with high levels of routine manual and administrative grades.

Scenario 2–Modern face-to-face communication and collaboration

This represents a modern, consultative system in which communication takes place through working parties, joint consultation and regular attempts to tap into employee voice through attitude surveys and focus group. Collaboration and knowledge management are typically based on face-to-face teamworking, project teams and traditional employer-centred knowledge management systems, which attempt to capture knowledge, store it and disseminate it in a top–down fashion.

Again, in this scenario the challenge to managers and representatives is that new generations of employees begin to adopt social media as a means of expressing their own voice and to collaborate in naturally occurring communities of practice. Both of these employee initiatives remain largely untapped and unmanaged as in scenario 1. HR continues to rely (a) on top–down means of assessing what really matters to employees, such as attitude surveys and (b) on representative forms of workplace democracy/participation to allow employees to express concerns and take part in decision-making. Knowledge management continues to be formal, drawing on traditional non-participative software systems that are relatively inaccessible to employees.

Such a scenario is probably typical of most organizations in many of the knowledge-intensive and creative sectors of the economy, including 'professional bureaucracies' such as healthcare, education and professional services, defence, the prison and police services, and in industries such as financial services and others (Birkinshaw and Pass, 2008). Data protection in these organizations is a sensitive issue, as are concerns over protecting brand identities and the desire to exercise a duty of care to employees. HR's role in this scenario remains focused on policing, rather than encouraging, the innovative and experimental use of social media.

Scenario 3–Open social media

This scenario, drawing on open social media such as Facebook, Twitter and other blogs, represents a relatively anarchic situation in which some organizations may find themselves in the not-too-distant future. Organizations may begin in scenarios 1 and 2 but come to resemble a more decentralized system of informal bottom–up communications and knowledge-sharing as more and more people, especially members of the net generation, become employees. Much communication becomes virtual, in which knowledge-sharing and employees voicing their concerns take place *outside of formal employer-controlled media*, especially in locations geographically and functionally distant from head office among remote workers (CIPD, 2008) and among higher educated and paid networked workers (Li and Bernoff, 2008). It is this scenario that seems to worry a number of HR professionals. As we have noted, it is the lack of organizational control over social media and the ease with which employees can engage with various applications that causes many organizations and HR professionals to worry about these media, with some organizations placing outright bans on their use at work or substantially restricting the ability of employees to access them at work. Time-wasting at work and the potential for organizational misbehaviour by disenchanted employees has dominated the HR agenda with firms ready to discipline employees for using social networking sites during working time, and banning the use of such sites at work. Thus, for example, a UK Government review of social media found a number of barriers to its more widespread adoption in various departments, despite the official line that encouraged the use of these media to communicate and engage users in dialogue. These barriers were:

- a lack of understanding and expertise among civil servants, especially higher-level ones;
- following on from this lack of understanding, a lack of high-level support for wider use;
- lack of data and uncertainties about the costs and benefits of various media;
- the risk of public exposure, damage to customer and employer brands, and general loss of control;
- the limitations placed on social media by IT departments that didn't want to damage the integrity of their systems.

Underlying such concerns were the very features that make social media attractive to organizations and employees. These were its openness, the ease of use for employees and users to engage with these media (spontaneity, conversational and democratic), its new rules of engagement and the different behaviours required by civil servants, and its newness and experimental nature.

Scenario 4–Enterprise-based social media

This scenario is the one that represented the best solution for many of the case study companies in our research (Martin *et al.*, 2009, 2015) and seems to be the route larger organizations seek to follow (Bondarouk and Olivas-Lujan, 2013). Advocates of enterprise-based social media recognize that social media are fast becoming a fact of life among the more educated and more highly paid networked workers and new generations of employees. This scenario is based on one in which organizations are driven by the net generation or by the need to secure collaboration and voice of increasingly geographically dispersed workers, often in other countries, working from home or who rarely visit head office locations. Organizations attempt to regain control by developing social media applications inside of firewalls and by encouraging or facilitating employees to make use of these technologies (see Box 8.4 and the case of KPMG).

According to Andrew McAfee, who is usually credited with coining the term 'Enterprise 2.0', this route is probably the most promising way forward for organizations seeking the benefits of social media but wishing to minimize the downside (see Figure 8.3). He defined Enterprise 2.0 (his term) 'as the use of emergent social software platforms *within* companies and their partners or customers'. He used the term 'social software' to describe how 'people meet, connect and collaborate through computer mediated communication and form online communities'. Platforms are defined as 'digital environments in which contributions and interactions are widely visible and persistent over time'. Emergent means the software is freeform, in the sense that people can choose to use it or not, is egalitarian and can accept different forms of data. He ruled out (a) open web-based platforms, such as Wikipedia, YouTube, Flickr and Facebook, because they were widely available to individuals, (b) corporate internets because they are not emergent and (c) traditional e-mail and messaging services because they weren't persistent.

Figure 8.4 shows a potential trend away from the very open social media towards Enterprise 2.0. The diagram also hints at the potential trend away from traditional media used to give employees a say in decisions, such as face-to-face representation in consultative committees, focus groups and online surveys, towards Enterprise 2.0 read-write media. Just as the web has allowed the so-called power law to operate in firms such as Amazon by allowing them to cater for the long tail of profitable customers comprising only 20 per cent of its total sales, so organizations can now reach out to the 'long tail' of employees. These comprise previously marginalized or disengaged groups who weren't economically possible to reach or who rejected the normal consultation process through union representation and organizationally determined (and often meaningless to them) questionnaires.

BOX 8.4 **KPMG and enterprise-based social media**

KPMG is a UK limited liability partnership and a subsidiary of KPMG Europe LLP. It is a leading provider of audit, tax and advisory services. KPMG in the UK has over 10,000 partners and staff in over 22 office locations, having merged with the German, Spanish and Swiss member firms.

Due to the scale, complexity and geographical spread of KPMG's business operations, collaboration and knowledge-sharing among KPMG's primary asset – its people – is vital to its success. Underpinning the drive to constantly improve this aspect of its business, Enterprise 2.0 applications, such as wikis, blogs and data aggregation, are being adopted with the key aim of delivering better services to the firms' clients.

The benefits that KPMG's senior managers saw in introducing an enterprise-based social media strategy were as follows:

- It facilitated a convenient but secure method of stimulating and maintaining knowledge-sharing of sensitive information and group-working among teams separated by geography, time zones and office locations.
- Simple and intuitive tools that people used in their non-work lives were developed in-house in a single point of access, secure KPMG portal behind their firewalls.

- They helped KPMG's network of knowledge managers, who became confident in using the different tools and understanding their most appropriate application. These knowledge managers supported the client-facing teams by raising awareness of the tools and providing direct support if required.
- They supplemented the knowledge managers' work with a variety of online support, such as short video clips of relevant case studies, and encouraged teams to use the tools.
- The tools appealed to new generations of staff, thus were seen to enhance KPMG's employer value proposition to this audience.

However, managers also saw some challenges lying ahead, the principal one being to encourage sceptical individuals and groups to use the new tools.

Question

Why might some individuals or groups be sceptical about using social media for collaboration and knowledge sharing?

LEARNING SUMMARY

In this chapter we have attempted to show how new technologies and the changing technological context can impact on organizations, groups and individuals. New technologies, especially ICT, have had an enormous impact on the work of many individuals in a variety of industries. From the perspective of managers, investment in new technologies often delivers less than it promised, because it is poorly implemented or misaligned with the necessary organizational and human factor changes. From the perspective of ordinary employees, sometimes the introduction of new technologies has been perceived as positive by empowering or liberating these people; sometimes it has been perceived as negative, by increasing perceptions of lack of control, and removing decisions and tasks that once were an essential and desired part of jobs. Managers need to understand the complexities associated with the introduction of new technologies, especially the impact on productivity and people, before embarking on major programmes of technical change. Understanding the concepts, examples and cases in this chapter should help them do so.

REVIEW QUESTIONS

1 What do you understand by: *A high-road to growth strategy*?
2 You have been asked to evaluate the strengths and weaknesses of using social media to encourage collaboration and knowledge sharing in your organization. What would you advise and why?

REFERENCES

Aker, J. C. and Mbiti, I. M. (2010) Mobile phones and economic development in Africa. *Journal of Economic Perspectives*, 24 (3), 207–232.

Barley, S. (2015) Why the internet makes buying a car less loathsome: how technologies change role relations. *Academy of Management Discoveries*, 1 (1), 5–35.

Beirne, M., Ramsay, H. and Panteli, A. (1998) Developments in computing work: control and contradiction. In: P. Thompson and C. Warhurst (eds), *Workplaces of the Future*, pp. 195–209. Basingstoke: Macmillan.

Birkinshaw, J. and Pass, S. (2008) *Innovation in the Workplace: How are organisations responding to generation Y employees and Web 2.0 technologies?* London: Chartered Institute of Personnel and Development. Available online at www.cipd.co.uk/subjects/maneco/general/_inwrkplgny.htm.

Blauner, R. (1964) *Alienation and Freedom: The factory worker and his industry.* Chicago: Chicago University Press.

Bondarouk, T. and Olivas-Lujan, M. R. (2013) *Social Media in Human Resources Management.* Advances Series in Management, Vol. 12. London: Emerald.

Braverman, H. (1974) *Labor and Monopoly Capital: The degradation of work in the twentieth century.* New York: Monthly Review Press.

Brynjolfsson, E. and Hitt, L. (2000) Beyond computation: information technology, organizational transformation and business performance. *Journal of Economic Perspectives*, 14 (4), 23–48.

Brynjolfsson, E. and McAfee, A. (2011) *Race Against the Machine: How the digital revolution is accelerating innovation, driving productivity, and irreversibly transforming employment and the economy.* Lexington, MA: Digital Frontier Press.

Brynjolfsson, E. and McAfee, A. (2014) *The Second Machine Age: Work, progress and prosperity in a time of brilliant technologies.* New York: Norton.

Child, J. (2015) *Organization: Contemporary principles and practice*, 2nd edn. Chichester, Sussex: Wiley.

CIPD (2008) Smart working: the impact of work organization and job design. Available online at www.cipd.co.uk/nr/rdonlyres/64a02358-8993-4185-beeb-981299175383/0/smartworking.pdf.

CIPD (2014, February) *Industrial Strategy and Future Skills Policy.* Research Insight, London: Chartered Institute of Personnel and Development. Available online at www.cipd.co.uk/binaries/industrial-strategy-and-the-future-of-skills-policy_2014.pdf.

Coyle, D. (2007) Sex, drugs and economics (revised edition). Published under creative commons. Available online at www.enlightenmenteconomics.com/about-diane/assets/sderevisecc.pdf.

Coyle, D. and Quah, D. (2004) *Getting the Measure of the New Economy.* London: The Work Foundation. Available online at www.theworkfoundation.com/research/isociety/new_economy.jsp.

Czarniawska, B. and Lofgren, O. (eds) (2012) *Managing Overflow in Affluent Societies.* New York: Routledge.

Divol, R., Edelman, D. and Sarrazin, H. (2012) Demystifying Social Media. *McKinsey Quarterly*, April. Available online at www.mckinsey.com/insights/marketing_sales/demystifying_social_media.

Financial Times (2015) Robots rub shoulders with human buddies, March 19. Available online at www.ft.com/cms/s/0/ed7be188-cd50-11e4-a15a-00144fe-ab7de.html#axzz3vtRu411d.

Finegold, D. and Soskice, D. (1988) The failure of training in Britain: analysis and prescription. *Oxford Review of Economic Policy*, 4, 21–53.

Hatch, M. J. and Cunliffe, A. (2012) *Organization Theory: Modern, symbolic and postmodern perspectives*, 3rd edn. Oxford: Oxford University Press.

Hitt, M. A., Duane Ireland, R. and Hoskisson, R. E. (2008) *Strategic Management:Competitiveness and globalization, concepts*, 8th edn. Mason, OH: South Western Cengage Learning.

Holmes, C. and Mayhew, K. (2012) *Resolution Foundation Report on the Changing Shape of the UK Job Market.* London: Resolution Foundation.

Li, C. and Bernoff, J. (2008) *Groundswell: Winning in a world transformed by social technologies.* Cambridge, MA: Harvard Business School Press.

Malone, T. W. (2004) *The Future of Work: How the new order of business will shape your organization, your management style, and your life.* Cambridge, MA: Harvard Business School Press.

Martin, G., Reddington, M. and Kneafsey, M. B. (2009) *Web 2.0 and Human Resource Management: 'Groundswell' or hype?* London: Chartered Institute of Personnel and Development.

Martin, G., Parry, E. and Flowers, P. (2015) Do social media enhance constructive employee voice all of the time or just some of the time? *Human Resource Management Journal.* doi: 10.1111/748-8583.12081.

McKinlay, A. and Taylor, P. (1998) Through the Looking Glass. In: A. McKinlay and K. Starkey (eds), *Foucault, Management and Organization Theory*, pp. 173–190. London: Sage.

Obijiofor, L. (2015) *New Technologies in Developing Societies: From theories to practice.* London: Palgrave MacMillan.

OECD (2004) *The Economic Impact of ICT: Measurement, evidence and implications.* Paris: Organization for Economic Development.

OECD (2014) OECD skills outlook 2013 – first results from the survey of adult skills. Paris: OECD. Available online at http://dx.doi.org/10.1787/9789264204256-en.

Orlikowski, W. J. and Scott, S. V. (2008) Sociomateriality: challenging the separation of technology, work and organization. *Annals of the Academy of Management*, 2 (1), 433–474.

Perrow, C. (1986) *Complex Organizations: A critical essay*, 3rd edn. New York: Random House.

Rose, M. (1975) *Industrial Behaviour: Theoretical developments since Taylor.* London: Allen Lane.

Sayles, L. R. (1958) *The Behavior of Industrial Workgroups: Prediction and control.* New York: John Wiley.

Staats, B. and Upton, D. M. (2011) Lean knowledge work. *Harvard Business Review*, October, 97–106.

Sterling, A. and Boxall, P. (2013) Lean production, employee learning and workplace outcomes: a case analysis through the ability-motivation-opportunity framework. *Human Resource Management Journal*, 23 (3), 227–240.

Sundararajan, A. (2013) From Zipcar to the sharing economy. *Harvard Business Review*, 3 January.

Taylor, R. (2004) *Skills and Innovation in Modern Britain.* ESRC future of work programme seminar series. Available at www.leeds.ac.uk/esrcfutureofwork/downloads/fow_publication_6.pdf.

Thompson, P. (2011) The trouble with HRM. *Human Resource Management Journal*, 21 (4), 355–367.

Thompson, P. and Smith, C. (eds) (2010) *Working Life: Renewing labour process analysis.* Critical perspectives on work and employment. Houndmills, Basingstoke: Palgrave Macmillan.

Tripas, M. (2008) *Technology, Identity, and Inertia through the Lens of 'the Digital Photography Company'.* Harvard Business School Working Paper, 9–42. Available online at www.hbs.edu/faculty/Publication%20Flles/09-042.pdf.

Trist, E. L., Higgin, G. W., Murray, H., and Pollock, A. B. (1963) *Organizational Choice.* London: Tavistock Institute of Human Relations.

United Kingdom Commission for Employment and Skills (2015) Working futures, 2012–2022. Available online at www.gov.uk/government/publications/working-futures-2012-to-2022.

United Nations Conference on Trade and Development (2011) *Measuring the Impacts of Information and Communications Technology for Development.* Available online at http://unctad.org/en/docs/dtlstict2011d1_en.pdf.

Womack, J. P., Jones, D. T. and Roos, D. (1990) *The Machine That Changed the World.* New York: Ranson.

Woodward, J. (1965) *Industrial Organizations: Theory and practice.* Oxford: Oxford University Press.

Chapter 9

Managing creativity and innovation

LEARNING OBJECTIVES

By the end of this chapter you should be able to:

- understand the difference between creativity and innovation;
- understand the shift away from the individualistic approaches to creativity towards systems perspectives;
- evaluate the ways in which creativity can be managed;
- analyse the relationship between networks and creativity.

INTRODUCTION

Before we move on to discussing the process of organizational change in the next chapter, we are going to explore two organizational processes which are closely related to change – creativity and innovation in organizations. Why are creativity and innovation important? In the times of fierce business competition, shorter product life cycles and more demanding customers, organizations' success depends on being able to create competitive advantage by offering new products and services, and constantly adapting to the changing environment. Encouraging the generation of new ideas is key to securing competitive advantage, hence creativity and innovation are central to business development, and are crucial in repositioning of organizations. New ideas also present managers with unique problems in creating a context for creativity and innovation.

According to the most frequently cited definitions, for example by Jane Henry (2006), creativity is the thinking process that drives employees to generate new and useful ideas, which usually challenge others' preconceptions. Innovation, on the other hand, is about successful exploitation or *implementation* of these ideas usually through commercial application. OECD (2005) define innovation as 'the implementation of a new or significantly improved product (good or service), or process, new marketing method, or a new organizational method in business practices, workplace organization or external relations'. Not all creative ideas lead to innovation, and there are some ideas that are never commercialized. So while organizational creativity refers to the generation of novel and useful ideas, organizational innovation is used to describe the realization of those ideas, e.g. new product development, a new process or a new service. In other words, creativity is the starting point of innovation, or as Amabile (1996) argued it is a necessary but not sufficient condition for the process of innovation.

REFLECTION

The majority of innovative ideas never get a chance to be implemented. When employees hear dismissive comments from their managers, they become increasingly frustrated and either give up trying to be innovative, or move to a different organization. Why are some managers reluctant to support innovation? What are other possible reasons why some ideas are dropped, whereas others are picked up and lead to the development of innovative products, processes or services?

The exercise above suggests that although creativity and innovation are crucial to the survival of organizations, some organizations stifle new ideas. Kanter (2013) claims that many leaders operate hidden principles that are aimed at preventing innovation. Her list of anti-rules includes being suspicious of new ideas, invoking past experiences, over-burdening people with work, confining strategic plans to a small group of people and punishing failure. Innovative ideas are usually risky and uncertain, and many leaders will see them as threats to stability and profitability, and react against them by shelving them. Why is it the case? The answer to this question probably lies in the notion of a political organization, which we examined in Chapter 4. McCalman *et al.* (2015) define organizational politics as 'the use of power through influencing techniques and tactics (sanctioned or unsanctioned) aimed at accomplishing personal and/or organizational goals'. The presence of politics in organizations cannot be denied, and it often affects all aspects of management. According to Buchanan and Badham (1999) managers engage in 'turf game tactics' to further their own agendas, even if it sometimes means destroying the enterprise of others, and these include people's creativity and innovative initiatives.

CHANGING APPROACHES TO CREATIVITY

There have been numerous attempts to develop theories of creativity. One of the most influential theories was proposed by Teresa Amabile (1996). She developed the five-stage componential model of creativity, which identified three key components: task motivation (intrinsic and extrinsic motivation which trigger the creative process); domain relevant skills (skills that determine the approach); and creativity relevant skills (variables of personality and individual differences). Amabile's stages of the creative process were:

1   *Task representation* – the creative process is triggered by extrinsic and/or intrinsic motivation;
2   *Preparation* – this is when individuals gather information before generating responses;
3   *Response generation* happens when individuals search through different solutions to come up with a response;
4   *Response validation* – individuals draw on their domain relevant skills to validate the value of the product/response;
5   *Outcome evaluation* – outcomes are evaluated based on evaluation in stage 4.

If, in the final stage of this process, the outcomes are successful or unsuccessful, the process ends. If the outcomes are partially achieved, the process then returns to stage 1.

Our understanding of creativity has been changing over the years. In the past creativity was often associated with an ability granted only to a few very talented people, usually working in isolation, and relied on a set of cognitive factors such as mental flexibility, ability to 'think out of the box', originality of thinking and ability to link remote associations (Andripoulos and Dawson, 2010). Creativity was also associated with some personality traits such as risk taking, self-confidence, tolerance of ambiguity, non-conformity and a motivation to achieve. However, examinations of biographies of great artists and inventors from the past proved largely inconclusive in finding the magic ingredient of a genius. Very little evidence of creative competences was found, as many brilliant inventors did not appear to share similar personality traits. This growing scepticism of individual, trait-based approaches in recent years resulted in a noticeable shift towards the approaches based on groups of individuals working together. Researchers have also begun to question the cause-and-effect relationship – whether certain traits result in creativity, or do the pressures of creative work result in certain psychological consequences (Bilton and Cummings, 2010).

Today there is a wider recognition that creativity exists in communities, and that the creativity of a group or a team is greater than the sum of creative traits of individuals within them (Henry, 2001, 2006). There is also a more marked recognition of the context for creativity, i.e. external conditions that either hinder creative thinking, or facilitate it. Mihaly Csikszentmihalyi (1999) argued that creativity is as much a cultural and social as it is a psychological event which takes place within a certain environment. For him there are two aspects of the creative environment: the domain (for example Florence in the fifteenth century, or Silicon Valley since the 1970s), and the field, i.e. the social context within which creativity takes place. Creativity understood in this way is a process that can be observed at the intersection of individuals, domains and fields. Csikszentmihalyi's argument led him to develop the system's theory of creativity whereby the creative individuals are embedded in informal networks of collaboration, which extend horizontally – through peer-to-peer relationships – and vertically – through supply chain relationships in the process of cultural production. This means that creativity requires the act of creation, but also a system of relationships underpinning this act of creation. What it means in practice is that to be successful it is not enough for an individual to have a good idea, but to also to have a network of contacts which will facilitate the development of the idea. Bilton (2010) summed it up: 'the bright sparks of illumination only catch fire when the right combination of elements is assembled'.

READER ACTIVITY

Csikszentmihalyi (1999) suggested that some conditions in the external environment are more conducive to creativity than others. Think about different contexts and consider these questions:

- Are big cities more conducive to creativity than small villages?
- Are some cities more creative than others?
- Are rich people more creative than people who are less well-off?
- Does external threat mobilize creativity?
- Are egalitarian societies more likely to support the creative process than societies with aristocracies and oligarchies?
- Do young people tend to be more creative than older people?
- Is necessity the mother of invention?

To understand better how the environment may influence creativity, let's look at the case study of the city of Dundee where one of us is based.

CASE 9.1 DUNDEE AS THE CREATIVE INDUSTRIES HUB

Csikszentmihalyi (1999) argued that the domain is very important for creativity. You will recall the example of Florence in the fifteenth century as a place particularly conducive to creativity. A question arises whether the domain itself can be created? *The Guardian* in an article entitled 'Dundee: From black sheep of Scottish cities to "living cultural experiment"' throws some light on this question.

Dundee used to be perceived as one of the most deprived places in Scotland. Heavy industry began to disappear from the 1970s onwards, leaving behind a scarred industrial landscape. Although Dundee has population of only 150,000 (down from 180,000 a century earlier), its post-industrial problems are often overshadowed by those encountered in other bigger Scottish cities, such as Glasgow.

But despite pockets of severe deprivation still visible to visitors, Dundee's image is changing and the city is reinventing itself as a creative hub. Now over 3,000 people work in Dundee's creative industries, which generate turnover of £200 million. DC Thomson, the famous publishing house, is one of the major employers in producing comics and newspapers in the UK. In 2014 Dundee received the UK's first UNESCO City of Design award for its contributions to the world.

Dundee is known for its video games. Chris Van Der Kuyl set up his first video game company in Dundee in the mid-1990s, which then helped develop Minecraft. Dundee is the heart of Scotland's gaming industry with around 40 gaming firms based there. There are also long established links between Dundee's universities and the creative industries in gaming. For example, in 1997, Abertay University designed and delivered the world's first degree in computer games technology, and in ethical hacking.

But Dundee is known not only for its games development, but also its cultural offering. The Dundee Contemporary Arts Centre (DCA) was opened in 1999, and it now contains a print studio, cinema, a gallery and a cafe. Thousands of children every year attend screenings at the two-week Children's Film festival there. There are some exciting developments on the banks of the River Tay.

- The Victoria and Albert Museum, the only branch of the V&A museum outside London, is scheduled to be open in 2018.
- Plans to open a new digital headquarters on the city's docks.
- Plans to implement a £120 million project to bring a film studio to Dundee.
- Plans for a hotel, retail units and apartments, as part of an ambitious regeneration project to connect Dundee city centre to the water.

In 2015 *The Guardian* observed: 'Dundee was known as the city of "jute, jam and journalism". Now, with the mills gone and the printing presses quieter, [Dundee] has a rather different claim to global fame: not just Minecraft but Grand Theft Auto and other classic video game titles were born or raised on the banks of the River Tay.'

The change of Dundee's image not only involved investment, it also required a change in the attitudes of the citizens of Dundee. Dundee still has its economic and social problems. Even when the cultural offering in Dundee is better, there are still going to be barriers for some people to access it. A lot needs to be done to avoid polarization where the new creative sector is separated from the citizens of Dundee. The change in attitude is being achieved by collaboration between schools, universities and businesses in order to mentor young people to show them how culture can change their lives. A lot is being done to attract people to come and live in Dundee and also encourage those who left to return.

Some argue that Dundee has shaped its own future, and has become an example of culture-led regeneration 'partly by accident, partly by design, building on what was already' (*The Guardian*, 2015).

Source: www.theguardian.com/cities/2015/jun/22/dundee-scotland-design-v-and-a-culture-regeneration-minecraft-grand-theft-auto.

1 Does the case of Dundee provide convincing evidence for creating environment for creativity?
2 What role do universities play in promoting creativity and innovation?
3 As the case study demonstrates, investment was crucial in the city reinventing itself. But investment is not enough. What can be done to promote the culture of creativity among people who traditionally worked in heavy industries?

So while creativity is a solitary act of a talented individual, it is also a social experience, and today's theories of creativity overlap with management theories of teamwork, the study of networks, knowledge management and organizational learning. In the following sections of this chapter we will consider creativity and innovation through the lens of some of these theories.

TEAMS

We start our discussion of teams with a short discussion exercise about your own experiences of working in teams.

REFLECTION

Drawing on your experience of working in teams in the past – at work, at school or university and in other contexts – what were the advantages and disadvantages of working in teams? Why do teams sometimes fail?

Katzenbach and Smith (1993, p. 113) defined the team as 'a small number of people with complementary skills who are committed to a common purpose, set of performance goals, and approach for which they hold themselves mutually accountable'.

Teamworking was introduced as an alternative to repetitive work routines because it allowed for rotation of tasks within a team, and was said to enhance employee commitment. There is also some evidence to suggest that teamworking improves organizational performance, (Delarue *et al.*, 2008) mainly because it constitutes a move away from control towards more participative forms of management. Teamworking was advocated by management 'gurus' such as Drucker (1988) and Peters (1989), and was an integral part of the Japanese models of management, the socio-technical systems, the quality of working life movement in the 1980s, Japanese Total Quality Management and Business Process Re-Engineering. In their seminal book, Katzenbach and Smith (1993) argued that teams will become the primary unit of performance because they are based on mutual accountability, and allow team members to take responsibility for their own contribution to the achievement of the common goals.

Management scholars have studied teams extensively and produced various classifications of team roles. In his study of teams Belbin focused on the roles people assume when they work in teams. For him team role is 'a pattern of behaviour that characterises one person's behaviour in relation to another in relation to the progress of the team' (Belbin, 2000, p. 15). Team roles are different from functional roles (such as an engineer, a marketing expert or an accountant); they are the ways in which team members contribute to the working of the team. Thus Belbin argued that people can contribute to team effort in the following nine ways: coordinating the teams efforts, imparting drive, creating ideas, exploring resources, evaluating options, organizing the work, following up on details, supporting others and providing expertise.

Based on these ways of contributing he proposed a classification (Belbin, 2015):

- *Plant* – creative and generates new ideas, but does not always communicate effectively.
- *Resource investigator* – outgoing and communicative, but tends to lose interest when enthusiasm has passed.

- *Co-ordinator* – mature and confident, identifies talent, but can be seen as manipulative.
- *Shaper* – thrives on pressure, has determination to overcome obstacles, but is prone to provocation and sometimes offends people.
- *Monitor-evaluator* – sober and strategic, sees all options and judges them accurately, but lacks drive and ability to inspire others.
- *Teamworker* – cooperative, perceptive and listens to others, but indecisive and avoids confrontation.
- *Implementer* – practical, reliable and efficient, turns ideas into action but sometimes inflexible.
- *Completer finisher* – conscientious, polishes and perfects, but reluctant to delegate, and inclined to worry.
- *Specialist* – single-minded and dedicated, provides knowledge and skills, but tends to dwell on practicalities.

The diagnostic tool for identifying the primary and secondary team roles is Belbin's self-perception inventory (SPI), which sometimes is accompanied by an observer checklist. According to Belbin, an individual can function well both in a primary and secondary team role, and can contribute to more than one team at the same time. The key idea behind Belbin's classification is the notion of a 'balanced team', i.e. it is crucial who works with whom in a team. Belbin found that complementary combinations of people tend to be far more effective, and making up a team of people who tend to contribute in very similar ways might be counter-productive.

Belbin's classification of team roles has not been without critics. For example Senior (1997) argued that the meaning of team performance is usually far more complex, and Belbin's perspective fails to capture this complexity. In her view, teamwork is not always about winning or losing, different people may define team success differently, and team members' contributions may be different depending on the subjective goals. From the methodological point of view, Belbin's inventory was criticized for two reasons. Firstly, its weakness is in over-reliance on self-perceptions; secondly not enough research has been done on the psychometric properties of the inventory and its validity (Wilson, 2014).

Problems with teams

The benefits of teamworking outlined above are not uncontroversial either, and researchers over the years have discussed numerous problems with the effectiveness of teams, or their appropriateness for dealing with the issues of management control.

One of the problems raised by Wilson (2014) is possible inequality in teams. Although teams are meant to be largely more democratic, the team members often bring in their status from outside the team, and consciously or subconsciously try to reconstruct it in the team. Team members who are normally in lower rank positions, very often assume a background role in the team. Wilson (2014) refers to this phenomenon as the 'seduction of hierarchy'. Different position of individuals in a team can also be determined by the unequal distribution of resources, different educational backgrounds and simply different levels of self-confidence.

One of the problems related to teams often raised in the literature is the phenomenon of conformity. Conformity occurs when people change behaviour/attitudes to match those of a group, as a result of real or imagined group pressure. In his seminal study, Asch (1956) tried to answer the question: What happens when an established norm is wrong? In his experiment he found that when faced with peer pressure his experimental subjects made significantly more errors than his control group subjects. Asch found that conformity to the group pressure resulted in distortion of perception, distortion of judgement and distortion of action, in other words, when subject to group pressure individuals were more likely to give wrong answers to the questions asked. Conformity to the group results in what in the literature on teams referred to as groupthink.

Teams in the creative industries have their problems, too. Bilton (2010) warns that counter-intuitively the team-based organization can sometimes appear no less constraining than the traditional corporations. This is because the horizontal lines of communication within project-based teams cross with vertical lines of functionally-based hierarchies. Also the focus on the task on hand, and the planned outcomes of the project may hinder an ability of the team to see the big picture. A lack of continuation of project work sometimes negatively affects learning (Grugulis and Stoyanova, 2011). Again the focus on the task may reduce opportunities for self-fulfilment of individuals.

Creativity and teams

One of the earlier attempts to understand creativity in teams is Michael Kirton's (1976) theory of complementary opposites, i.e. adaptation-innovation theory (A-I Theory). Kirton argued that creativity requires a connection between opposite thinking styles, and developed his Kirton Adaptation-Innovation Inventory (known as KAI, www.kaicentre.com) to explore individuals' thinking styles to indicate what roles they might play in creative teams. He researched teams of engineers and found that everyone could be located on a continuum ranging from highly adaptive to highly innovative.

Adaptors are individuals who produce ideas based closely on, but stretching, existing definitions of the problem and likely solutions. They usually proceed within the established theories, policies and practices of organizations, and their effort is directed at improving things. Innovators on the other hand are more likely to reconstruct the problem, separate it from the accepted paradigms and produce much less expected solutions. In other words, innovators are interested in doing things differently. Kirton did not argue that one type is in any way more superior than the other, and successful teams and organizations need a mixture of both. Innovators usually come up with new concepts, but they need adaptors who are able to develop these concepts into practical solutions. Kirton argued that balanced teams are most effective, while teams consisting of one type were less successful. For example teams consisting of innovators only were unable to progress their idea, whereas teams with the majority of adaptors lacked the initial impetus to initiate new ventures.

Organizations differ in what thinking styles they favour, and the mean KAI score will reflect an organization's ethos. For example banks, certain types of hospitals and government organizations tend to employ adaptors. Similarly bureaucratic organizations want to minimize risk and they tend to encourage adaptation, i.e. precision, reliability and efficiency that come with it. On the other hand, adaptors are usually in short supply in the creative industries. Kirton noted that adaptors are found in departments where solutions to problems come from within the unit, whereas innovators are found in departments that act as interfaces (i.e. cross-disciplinary boundaries).

Kirton's idea was extremely influential on theories of innovation because it drew managers' attention to the fact that creativity and innovation in organizations can be *managed* through recruitment and selection. Selecting candidates for jobs cannot involve only choosing the most qualified or experienced candidate, but should also involve candidates' creativity, the roles they assume in teams and how they collaborate with others. Taking into consideration these other characteristics, and designating candidates as psychological types, led to a more widespread use of psychometric tests in talent management (see Chapter 3).

MANAGING CREATIVITY

Before discussing the role of managers in managing creativity and innovation, we start by discussing a broader question whether change can be managed. Change management textbooks often raise a question – can change be managed, or should it be 'left alone'? Different organizational scholars answer this question differently – some believe that organizations need to manage change in line with the organizational strategy, business environment and available resources. Others, for example advocate 'letting things happen', for example Robert Chia (2014) is highly sceptical of the leader-centric theories of heroic action which see change as highly visible, dramatic and rapid interventions, often associated with top-down, system-wide management initiatives (Peters, 1989; Kanter, 1983). Chia calls such interventions 'owned' processes as they privilege management agency and play down the role of serendipitous chance. On the opposite end of the spectrum there are 'unowned' change processes that take into account the complexity of context within which organizations operate. Change, seen from this perspective is a naturally occurring phenomenon, and managing change simply means relaxing organizational orders, and letting change happen.

The team based approaches to creativity and innovation resulted from the systems theories of creativity as well as from the observable shift away from economy based on material production to creative economy based on ideas and knowledge. In manufacturing product development, teams draw on the expertise from across the organization, and utilize the insights of engineers, programmers, designers and artists.

Creative teams in the creative industries also rely on networks. Creative individuals rarely operate on their own and are often are embedded in systems and networks (Florida, 2002; Torr, 2008). And although individual talent still needs to be valued and celebrated, this embeddedness must not be ignored as the creative processes in the creative industries are essentially collective. Bilton (2010) also noted that individualization and specialization of creative work results in high levels of mutual dependency. This mutual dependency is largely determined by the structural characteristics of the sector, for example the predominance of project work, which requires access to networks of self-employed specialists. Such work is often conducted on a temporary contract basis.

Mutual dependency is also a feature of creative organizations. Such organizations are often small, and individuals working in them have to be able to step into different roles when needed. This tendency towards multi-tasking facilitates creativity, because swapping roles allows for changes in perspective, and promotes a holistic understanding of the business. On the other hand, however, Bilton observes, people in a small organization face the danger of over-familiarization. When they become too familiar with each other, they no longer question each other, resulting in like-mindedness and groupthink, which in turn negatively affects creativity. As the organization grows, multi-tasking gives way to specialization, and individuals begin to assume more clearly defined roles. They specialize in selected areas of the business – design, marketing, operations, finances, etc. The danger of this tendency is over-specialization where individuals are not able to step into the roles of other team members. This may result in alienation where individuals retreat into pre-defined roles.

So can a creative team be managed?

Before we attempt to answer the question whether creative teams can be managed, it is important to look at the role of a manager (see also Chapter 2). Mayle (2006) argued that close control and supervision on the part of the manager is often seen as detrimental to creativity. Creative teams however require managerial involvement not through command and control but through monitoring and modifying the relationships that underpin this process. The advice often given to managers and leaders of creative teams is 'don't try to be a boss, act like a coach instead'. Micro-managing the creative process may be detrimental, and too much intervention might lead to unnecessary confrontation. Excessive focus on one talented individual might be damaging for the team spirit, and other members' motivation.

There are some areas where a manager has an important role to play. One of those areas is recruitment and managing the allocation of roles in a creative team. Bilton (2010) suggests a powerful theatrical metaphor of managing teams being like casting actors in a play. Recruiting team members is not about who is the best for this job, but what kind of character a certain team or an organization needs. This is where understanding team roles discussed previously is important. By bringing new people into the team managers can disrupt consensus, avoid development of groupthink and create an opportunity to realign the existing roles. Each new individual provides an opportunity to recast the others, and this is when the manager can have a role in managing creativity by brokering relationships within a team and by connecting people with different talents. By being outside of the teams, managers often see 'the big picture' which team members miss. They should also build an internal culture of communication and collective ownership of the task. Related to culture is trust, and to achieve creative collaboration between individuals, team members need to develop mutual trust and respect, again a topic we have previously discussed.

Related to the composition of a team is a manager's role in encouraging team diversity. The link between diversity of a team and a team's creativity has been explored extensively by researchers in recent years. What most studies suggest is that diversity positively impacts on creativity. Diverse teams may include people from different cultural and national backgrounds, at different ages, and having different specializations. Such diversity allows for the interplay of different perspectives and experiences, which in turn disrupts consensus, and as Bilton notes, disrupts the drift towards like-mindedness.

CASE 9.2 *LINKLATERS* BY TONY NWACHUKWU AND MARK ROBINSON

(used with kind permission of the Arts Council England)

Linklaters is one of the five largest global law firms in London. It has 26 offices in 19 countries, almost 5,000 staff and revenue in 2009/2010 of £1.2bn. It works only on the most complex deals and cases, with 70 per cent of its work being on multi-country or multi-practice issues.

It has very strategically and consciously embraced diversity. The Global Diversity Manager puts this very simply, and in words which certainly find an echo in arts rhetoric: 'As a talent-driven organization, Linklaters needs to attract the most talented people it can, to attract the kind of customers it wants to serve to meet its business goals.'

A strong business case for diversity has been developed and accepted within the organization. This responds to three external pressures as well as the case for talent. Firstly, there is increased regulation of diversity and equality issues. Secondly, the media increasingly scrutinises the age, ethnicity and gender of lawyers, especially in high-profile cases, and looks for diversity. Thirdly, and perhaps most crucially, clients increasingly ask for diversity information – driven by their own shareholders or by regulatory contexts. Clients increasingly expect to see diverse teams working on projects, rather than all-male, all-white teams, for instance – an obvious parallel with the arts sector.

Linklaters describes itself as essentially a people business, based on relationships as well as legal expertise. Its corporate responsibility strategy is built around three pillars: colleagues, clients and community, with diversity sitting across all three strands.

One rationale for this derives from key demographics for Linklaters. More than 40 per cent of law graduates in London are non-white, and there is now a 50–50 gender split. The workforce, especially at 'partner' level, understandably lags behind this, but it is crucial to recruitment for the firm to demonstrate that it is taking positive steps. There are parallels with the steps taken in the cultural sector to change the face of organizations in order to attract those who might not have previously recognized themselves in the image of certain institutions.

Culture can only change over time. Elements of working practice remain challenging to diversity, especially for the fee-earning lawyers who may find it very difficult to work flexible hours to allow for caring and child-care responsibilities, for instance. It is a highly competitive culture, with a 24/7 service to clients leading to elements of unpredictable and long-hours working, with a heavy emphasis on intellectual prowess and influence rather than clear, structured hierarchy.

Linklaters has developed a number of affinity groups, including groups based on faith and gender and a lesbian, gay, bisexual and transgender network. The latter has moved over time from being invitation only, and run off-site, to being open, internal and running client-focused events, sharing the development of a more diverse culture with clients and stakeholders. The faith groups now work together to run 'Faith in the City' events and collaborate with clients. Work is client or colleague facing rather than 'issue awareness' building: there is always a strong business rationale for activity.

Linklaters is cautious regarding the effectiveness of specific diversity training and coaching, preferring to build understanding and skills into its general approach to professional development. They network with other firms including competitors and clients to draw on others' expertise.

The global nature and size of Linklaters are key to its approach to diversity – the diversity feeds into marketing to graduates and to clients. This may suggest that within the arts sector, a collaborative approach, based on either locality (e.g. city-based groups of organizations) or artform, may be more able to develop a strong strategic approach to embracing diversity.

Source: www.creativecase.org.uk/creativecase-linklaters.

1 How does Linklaters attempt to achieve greater diversity of the workforce?
2 What are the benefits of workforce diversity for Linklaters?
3 How can Linklaters use its workforce diversity to gain competitive advantage?

THE IMPORTANCE OF NETWORKS

Another important concept in understanding creativity is networks (Townley and Beech, 2010; Hesmondhalgh and Baker, 2010). Networks are said to foster collaboration, trust and cooperation, but in recent years researchers have also noted that networks are also important for creativity. This is because creativity lies in organizing a system of relationships, and the act of creation depends on the system of relationships. According to the systems theory, creativity is dependent on the relationships between individuals in organizations and between organizations. This suggests mutual dependence in a network where individuals' expertise can be utilized when needed.

Networks of individuals and organizations also underpin creative, project-based work (Banks, 2007; Flew, 2012). Creative industries are often fragmented, and consist of small creative organizations that cannot sustain permanent employment of specialists. When faced with such fragmentation, the industry often counteracts the fragmented organizational structures by fostering cooperation between organizations and individuals. Seen in this way networks are not only used as an informal recruitment method (Antcliff, 2005; Van Hoye *et al.*, 2009), but also as a way of sourcing expertise and creative input from others.

Networks in the creative industries

Creativity and innovation are crucial to all organizations, however, the sector where they are particularly important is in the creative and cultural industries. For example, the UK government Department for Culture, Media and Sport defined creative industries as those industries which 'have their origin in individual creativity, skill and talent and which have a potential for wealth and job creation through the generation and exploitation of intellectual property' (DCMS, 2001). The creative sectors include arts, design, film, advertising, music, publishing, computer games, interactive media, TV and radio, but they overlap with cultural industries which also include cultural tourism, heritage, museums, libraries and cultural events. Although classified as separate by the DCMS, creative and cultural industries sectors are similar in the type of work and the patterns of work that individuals undertake.

The nature of work in the creative and cultural industries is primarily based on post-industrial, employment relationship (Antcliff *et al.*, 2007), which includes portfolio careers with workers being in multiple jobs including self-employment, working freelance or running a business. This non-linear career progression pattern does not appear to change over time and remains the same some years into individuals' careers. Because of the uncertainty, work in this sector is becoming increasingly precarious, i.e. uncertain and volatile and competitive (Hesmondhalgh, 2007). In order to engage in the creative work, individuals rely on networks as a source of economic and social benefits. Networks are said to foster collaboration, trust and cooperation, and they lead to personal economic advantage in the labour market. Forming and maintaining social and professional contacts has been found to be crucial in securing employment in the creative and cultural industries, but it is also important in fostering creativity and sharing knowledge.

Various studies into creativity in the creative and cultural industries draw on a seminal study by Granovetter on weak and strong ties. Granovetter (1973) highlighted the importance of inter-connectedness among members of a social network and emphasized the role of weak ties in gaining personal advantage. 'Weak ties' are loose links which are 'indispensable to individuals' opportunities and their integration into communities. In contrast to weak ties, strong ties are links with close family and friends, and they breed social cohesion, and lead to overall fragmentation (1973, p. 1378). What follows is that the multitude of weak ties offers individuals a number of advantages, for example in finding employment opportunities. Granovetter's study also suggests that informal 'weak' ties might lead to innovation more than strong family ties. This is because strong ties are developed between people who are similar, hence they produce 'more of the same', whereas weak ties may lead to the development of wider networks and promote creative thinking.

MANAGING INNOVATION

'Innovate . . . or die' is a mantra of many of the executives of contemporary organizations. To avoid bankruptcy or oblivion, companies have to constantly come up with novel ideas for products and services (Tidd and Bessant, 2009). By pursuing innovation, companies stay ahead of competition. Kanter (2009) refers to the need to stay ahead as the 15-minute competitive advantage, i.e. 'changing in short fast bursts rather than waiting for the breakthrough that transforms everything'. To illustrate her point, Kanter evokes a Woody Allen comedy routine about humans' first contacts with UFOs on Earth. Instead of worrying about alien civilizations which are light years away in technological advancement, humans should worry about civilizations which are just 15 minutes ahead of us – 'That way they'd always be first in line for the movies, they'd never miss a meeting with the boss . . . and they'd always be first in every race'.

The case study of Deutsche Bank demonstrates how the need to fend off the threats from competitors leads to companies engaging in new ways of doing business.

CASE 9.3 DIGITAL INNOVATION IN DEUTSCHE BANK

Banks are under constant pressure from other businesses that take over the functions traditionally performed by banks. The main driver for innovative change have been the rapid advances in technology, especially digital and mobile solutions. These advances force the banks to rethink the traditional model of working with clients, which mainly involve branch banking. The launch of Apple Pay allowing iPhone users in the US to pay with their mobile phones was one of the initiatives seen as a potential threat to the traditional banking model. Because of the competition from innovative solutions such as Apple Pay, and in an attempt to improve the use of digital technology, most banks round the world have recently been trying to make links with financial technology groups. *The Financial Times* reported that Spain's BBVA has been one of the most high-profile investors in technology start-ups that has backed a dozen groups including Coinbase and Simple, the US digital bank. 'Others have followed suit, such as HSBC, which last year established a $200m fund to invest in start-ups' (*The Financial Times*, 2015).

In an attempt to improve the use of digital technology, Deutsche Bank, Germany's largest bank, decided in 2015 that it is going to open innovation hubs in London, Berlin and Silicon Valley. The Bank's collaborators in this initiative are IBM in Silicon Valley, Microsoft in Berlin and HCL in London. In these hubs Deutsche Bank plans to work with start-up companies and researchers from universities to develop ideas that can improve internal processes as well as can be applied to the products the bank offers to their customers, initially planning to evaluate more than 500 start-up ideas every year. This change will signify a shift away from the reliance on 'bricks-and-mortar branches' (*Financial Times*, 2015), towards capitalizing on the novel IT systems and utilizing digital capabilities. As part of this change the Bank intends to close about 200 of its 700 retail branches in Germany, and instead invest up to €1bn into digital initiatives.

Henry Ritchotte, Deutsche's chief operating officer, has been given responsibility for the bank's digital transformation. This change is part of a wider programme of changes involving a management reshuffle, a recent deal with Hewlett-Packard and other attempts to reduce the bank's cost base.

Source: The Financial Times (2015) Deutsche Bank to create innovations hubs to boost technology, www.ft.com/cms/s/0/402ced62–09d0–11e5-a6a8–00144feabdc0.html#axzz3dyhLXrnl.

1 How can the move away from the 'bricks-and-mortar' branches towards digital solutions help Deutsche Bank fend off competition?
2 Are there any disadvantages to this approach? Can you think of the arguments for banks to sustain the traditional branch-based ways of providing banking services?

Smith (2015) distinguishes between three types of innovation: product, service and process innovation. *Product innovation* is about the development of a new/novel product, for example Dyson's 'dual cyclone vacuum, or Apple's iPhone. This is done by using new technology, re-configuring old technology or meeting new consumer needs. *Service innovation* is about offering a new/different service to consumers, for example new ways of selling things on the Internet by Amazon.com, introduction of low-cost airlines such EasyJet or the development of social media. *Process innovation* is about developing new ways of making things or delivering services, such as Taylor's scientific management, or the Toyota just in time production process.

READER ACTIVITY

Think of one of the acknowledged innovations, and try to answer these questions:

- What was so innovative about this product or service?
- Did it solve an existing problem?
- Who came up with an idea and when?
- What were the potential difficulties in the process of innovation?

Problems with innovation

As mentioned earlier in the chapter, innovation is not always an uncontested territory. Organizational change often triggers resistance on the part of employees, and so does innovation, which is sometimes seen as a threat to the established order. Resistance often comes from those who have done well under the old system, and are fearful of the future, so innovative solutions to running a business may bring about risks of losing position, control and reputation (McCalman *et al.*, 2015).

It is also worth remembering that innovation is not always for the better. The Global Financial Crisis of 2007–8 is a good example of how innovative banking practices beyond the understanding of senior management led to the collapse of many banks. The RBS case in Chapter 2 is a good example here.

The case study of Google illustrates that the perceptions of organizational initiatives aimed at innovation may be evaluated differently by different stakeholders. As the pluralist perspective of organization (Fox, 1966) tells us, the organization is made of related but separate interests, and managers have to accept that conflict is not always unavoidable.

CASE 9.4 **INNOVATION IN GOOGLE**

Google is a company that cultivates the culture of innovation in order to stay at the forefront of innovation. One of the initiatives aimed at promoting innovation in Google is the 80/20 Innovation Time Off (ITO) model.

The 80/20 ITO model, which dates back to 2007, allows Google employees to spend 80 per cent of their time on their substantive projects, and 20 per cent (which usually amounts to around one day per week) on innovation activities which are of interest to them. These activities are believed to keep employees engaged in their work, empowered and constantly challenged to come up with new ideas. When freed from the pressures of deadlines and targets, employees are said to be more creative. As part of the programme, employees form 'Google grouplets' comprised of engineers who share an interest in a novel idea, and aim to work on it to bring this idea into fruition. These grouplets do not have budgets, or any decision-making powers, but are aimed at attracting individuals who are keen on pursuing innovation together.

The 80/20 ITO model is said to have built foundations for many successful business ideas. Google claims that many of its new products including Gmail, Google News and AdSense came into existence because of the employees' involvement in the ITO program.

Perceived as a good idea, the ITO programme was emulated in other companies, for example HootSuite. However, the 80/20 ITO model has its problems and was discontinued.

One of the issues was employee scepticism of Google acting in good faith. The 80/20 rule is said to violate the 'normal expectations of corporate life' (*Wired*), and is seen as ineffective when the organizational culture in general does not support innovation. An article in *Wired* states: 'Innovation never happens in a vacuum. Which is why the focus on the 80/20 rule is a red herring. It's merely the iceberg-tip of a much larger, and more fundamental, set of issues plaguing modern corporations.' Over time the programme narrowed in scope, and employees who wanted to take advantage of the 20 per cent time off for innovation had to seek approval from their managers, who for the sake of efficiency and productivity were not always willing to support it.

The scepticism of the 80/20 ITO model comes from the idea that innovation cannot be achieved by giving employees time to engage in innovation activities, innovation also needs proper investment (staff and funding), and management endorsement.

Sources: www.cloverleafinnovation.com/blog/secrets-innovative-companies-innovation/,
www.wired.com/2013/08/innovate-or-die-why-googles-8020-rule-is-a-red-herring/,
www.fastcompany.com/3015877/fast-feed/why-google-axed-its-20-policy.

1 Are you convinced by Google's 80/20 Innovation Time Off model as a way to achieve organizational innovation?
2 The 80/20 ITO model resonates with the idea of employee empowerment – employees are given more discretion in deciding how to spend the 20 per cent of their time as long as the activities are company-related. Can empowerment enhance innovation?

LEARNING SUMMARY

In this chapter we focused on two concepts which are important for understanding of the management of organizations – creativity and innovation. We defined the concepts, explained the differences between them and discussed a shift away from creativity as a feature of an individual towards more distributed conceptions of creativity as a feature of a system. While creativity is a solitary act of a talented individual, it is also a social experience, and today's theories of creativity overlap with management theories of teamwork, the study of networks, knowledge management and organizational learning. We considered creativity and innovation through the lens of these theories. The central question raised in this chapter is whether creativity and innovation can be managed, and if so what are the possible ways of doing it.

REVIEW QUESTIONS

1 Based on the reading of this chapter and your own observations do you agree that creativity in organizations can be managed? If so what are the ways in which managers can manage creativity?

2 Not all ideas are implemented and lead to innovation. What are the factors which enable or hinder innovation in organizations?

REFERENCES

Amabile, T. M. (1996) *Creativity in Context*. Oxford: Westview Press.

Andripoulos, C. and Dawson, P. (2010) *Managing Change, Innovation and Creativity*. London: Sage.

Antcliff, V. (2005) Broadcasting in the nineties: competition, choice and inequality. *Media Culture & Society*, 2005, 27 (6), 841–859.

Antcliff, V., Saundry, R. and Stuart, M. (2007) Networks and social capital in the UK television industry: the weakness of weak ties. *Human Relations*, 60 (2), 371–93.

Asch, S. E. (1956) Studies of independence and conformity: I. A minority of one against a unanimous majority. *Psychological Monographs: General and applied*, 70 (9), 1–70.

Banks, M. (2007) *The Politics of Cultural Work*. Basingstoke, UK: Palgrave Macmillan.

Belbin, R. M. (2000) *Beyond the Team*. Oxford: Butterworth-Heinemann.

Belbin, R. M. (2015) Belbin Team Roles. www.belbin.com/rte.asp?id=8.

Bilton, C. (2010) *Management and Creativity: From creative industries to creative management*. Oxford: Blackwell Publishing.

Bilton, C. and Cummings, S. (2010) *Creative Strategy: Reconnecting business and innovation*. Chichester: Wiley.

Buchanan, D. A. and Badham, R. (1999) Politics and organizational change: the lived experience. *Human Relations*, 52 (5), 609–622.

Chia, R. (2014) Reflections in praise of silent transformation – allowing change through 'letting happen'. *Journal of Change Management*, 14 (1), 8–27.

Csikszentmihalyi, M. (1999) A Systems Perspective on Creativity. In: R. J. Sternberg (ed), *Handbook of Creativity*. Cambridge: Cambridge University Press, pp. 313–335.

Delarue, A., Van Hootegem, G. V., Proctor, S. and Burridge, M. (2008) Teamworking and organizational performance: a review of survey-based research. *International Journal of Management Reviews*, 10 (2), 127–48.

DCMS (Department for Culture, Media and Sport) (2001) Creative industries mapping documents 2001. www.gov.uk/government/publications/creative-industries-mapping- documents-2001.

Drucker, P. (1988) The coming of the new organization. *Harvard Business Review*, January–February, 45–53.

The Financial Times (2015) Deutsche Bank to create innovations hubs to boost technology. www.ft.com/cms/s/0/402ced62-09d0-11e5-a6a8-00144feabdc0.html#axzz3dyhLXrnl.

Flew, T. (2012) *The Creative Industries: Culture and policy*. London: Sage.

Florida, R. (2002) *The Rise of the Creative Class: And how it's transforming work, leisure, community and everyday life*. New York: Basic Books.

Fox, A. (1966) *Research Papers 3: Industrial sociology and industrial relations*. London: Her Majesty's Stationery Office.

Granovetter, M. S. (1973) The strength of weak ties. *The American Journal of Sociology*, 78 (6), 1360–1380.

Grugulis, I. and Stoyanova, D. (2011) The missing middle: communities of practice in a freelance labour market. *Work, Employment and Society*, 25 (2), 342–51.

The Guardian (2015) Dundee: from black sheep of Scottish cities to 'living cultural experiment'. www.theguardian.com/cities/2015/jun/22/dundee-scotland-design-v-and-a-culture-regeneration-minecraft-grand-theft-auto.

Henry, J. (2001) *Creativity and Perception in Management*. London: Sage.

Henry, J. (2006) *Creativity, Cognition and Development*. London: Open University Press.

Hesmondhalgh, D. (2007) *The Cultural Industries*, 2nd edn. London: Sage.

Hesmondhalgh, D. and Baker, S. (2010) *Creative Labour: Media work in three cultural industries*. London: Routledge.

Kanter, R. M. (1983) *The Change Masters*. New York: Simon and Schuster.

Kanter, R. M. (2009) Find the 15-minute competitive advantage. *Harvard Business Review*, 9 November, https://hbr.org/2009/11/find-the-15minute-competitive/.

Kanter, R. M. (2013) Nine rules for stifling innovation. *Harvard Business Review*, January, https://hbr.org/2013/01/nine-rules-for-stifling-innova.html.

Katzenbach, J. R. and Smith, D. K. (1993) *The Wisdom of Teams: Creating the high performance organization*. Cambridge, MA: Harvard Business School Press.

Kirton, M. (1976) Adaptors and innovators: a description and measure. *Journal of Applied Psychology*, 61 (5), 622–629.

Mayle, D. (2006) *Managing Innovation and Change*, 3rd edn. London: Sage.

McCalman, J., Paton, R. and Siebert, S. (2015) *Change Management: A guide to effective implementation*, 4th edn. London: Sage.

OECD (Organization for Economic Cooperation and Development) (2005) *Oslo Manual: Guidelines for collecting and interpreting innovation data*, 3rd edn. Paris. www.oecd.org/sti/inno/oslomanualguidelinesforcollectingand interpretinginnovationdata3rdedition.htm.

Peters, T. (1989) *Thriving on Chaos*. London: Pan Books.

Senior, B. (1997) Team roles and team performance: is there really a link? *Journal of Occupational and Organizational Psychology*, 70, 241–58.

Smith, D. (2015) *Exploring Innovation*, 3rd edn. London: McGraw Hill.

Tidd, J. and Bessant, J. (2009) *Managing Innovation: Integrating technological, market and organizational change*, 4th edn. Chichester: Wiley.

Torr, G. (2008) *Managing Creative People: Lessons in leadership for the ideas economy*. Chichester: Wiley.

Townley, B. and Beech, N. (2010) *Managing Creativity? Exploring the paradox.* Cambridge: Cambridge University Press.

Van Hoye, G., van Hooft, E. A. J. and Lievens, F. (2009) Networking as a job search behaviour: a social network perspective. *Journal of Occupational and Organizational Psychology,* 82, 661–682.

Wilson, F. (2014) *Organizational Behaviour and Work: A Critical Introduction,* 4th edn. Oxford: Oxford University Press.

Chapter 10

Managing organizational change

LEARNING OBJECTIVES

By the end of this chapter you should be able to:

- understand the issues facing managers in attempting wholesale organizational change;
- apply the ISM model to an organizational change situation;
- apply the strategic change process model to the process of managing organizational change;
- understand the different views on organizational culture change;
- apply the Goffee and Jones culture change framework to organizational culture change problems;
- suggest recommendations on workable principles of organizational change, and on how they might evaluate the success of change initiatives.

INTRODUCTION

We began this book by examining the nature of management and managers and their roles in a changing world. Following this, we looked at the key contexts of change in contemporary business: the individual–organizational context, the organizational context, the international context, the global branding and corporate reputation context, the knowledge context, the technological context and the innovation context. In our model of management we identified three levels at which managers operate: the individual level, the team level and the organizational level. We examined the issues of managing at these different levels in some detail. It just remains, as the title of the book suggests, to examine the change process itself in more detail because it is often in this implementation phase that many good ideas fall down, or remain only good ideas. So, what can managers do to ensure that the changes they introduce, whether they are changes in strategies, systems, products or processes, become effectively embedded in their organizations?

To begin a discussion on this question, let's look at a research project that one of us was involved in during the late 1990s. This project is relevant as it is set in some of the contexts discussed in the book – technology, corporate reputation, internationalization and knowledge management. It also highlights some of the problems of managing individual–organizational linkages. We were able to research the case in depth over a long period of time and know the outcomes of the change initiatives; its findings may help you understand how the processes and outcomes of change initiatives are embedded in particular contexts and time frames. This message will be an important one in this chapter because, as we have already argued, there is no one best way, only a series of promising practices that have always to be related to contexts. We shall look at this idea in more depth at the end of the chapter. After reading the case, we would like you to work through the three change frameworks discussed in the two subsequent sections. These will provide a set of practical tools with which to understand this and other major change problems you may meet in your working lives.

CASE 10.1 AT&T AND NCR – A CLASSIC CASE OF ATTEMPTING TO DEVELOP A GLOBAL BRAND THROUGH CULTURE CHANGE

The history and context of the change programme

The following case is a classic and somewhat typical example of culture change attempted by the headquarters of a US-based multinational enterprise (MNE), which we researched in the early 2000s. We can learn a lot about studying such a case because the outcome is well known. For those of you who are interested in finding out what actually happened to the company later, you might want to refer to the company's website.

The case study plant began life as a subsidiary of NCR, a mid-western-based US multinational enterprise (MNE) that underwent significant changed fortunes during the period 1945–1979. During this period, when the UK plant was used largely as a second-source manufacturing facility to US plants, employment rose dramatically to 6,300 employees in 1970 and fell to 820 people in 1980 following a decline in traditional markets. At that time, there were strong rumours that the plant was scheduled for closure.

However, by the time of the launch of the cultural change programme in the mid 1990s, the fortunes of the Scottish subsidiary had turned around dramatically, associated with what came to be known locally as the 'Fortress Dundee' policy, in which local management sought and fought for 'independence through local success'. By 1985, it had acquired a significant design and development facility and had become NCR's headquarters for the newly created Self-Service and Financial Systems Division, which designed and developed automatic teller machines (ATMs) for the banking industry. In short, it had turned the tables on its US sister plants and had become something of a star in the US parent company's portfolio of assets. The Scottish subsidiary consistently outperformed sister NCR plants in the USA and Canada as measured by rate of return on assets, which grew from 54 per cent in 1984 to a yearly average of over 100 per cent from 1987 to 1992. In 2004 it was still the world's leading designer and producer of ATMs, employing some 1,700 assembly workers, managers, design and development engineers (including the largest private sector development community in Scotland), and has won the 'Best Factory in Britain' award on two occasions.

This brief history of the changing fortunes of the Scottish subsidiary shows how it has become increasingly independent of NCR corporate headquarters for resources. Furthermore, there was a history of opposition or reluctant compliance by the Scottish subsidiary to previous headquarters' initiatives on HRM practices. Much of this reluctance stemmed from headquarters' unsympathetic attitudes towards trade unions, which frequently posed problems for the local management of the highly unionized Scottish plant. This uneasy relationship between corporate and local subsidiary management has played itself out in various ways over time. In particular, there was local subsidiary criticism and reluctance to adopt certain heavily American HRM practices (e.g. the content and terminology of employee attitude questionnaires), and there was corporate-level coolness towards certain home-grown initiatives in the Scottish subsidiary intended to forge a closer working relationship with its union representatives.

AT&T's takeover and its culture change programme

Events in the marketplace in the early 1990s had a major impact on the Dundee company's fortunes. AT&T acquired the NCR Corporation in 1991 following a hostile takeover bid. Initially, the headquarters management of AT&T followed a strategy of controlling only the financial direction of NCR and not its product–market strategy, allowing the Scottish plant to function as a semi-independent unit, largely because its product range fell outside top management's main interests. However, after an agreed period of two years of little or no strategic intervention, AT&T's corporate management team sought to engineer a radical change throughout the corporation using a global branding strategy in which the name of NCR would be exorcized from its history and replaced by AT&T – Global Information Solutions (AT&T (GIS)). This radical change was also viewed to be necessary by headquarters because of the large financial losses incurred by virtually every business unit in NCR – that is, apart from the Scottish subsidiary, its only profitable arm.

AT&T's president brought in Jerre Stead, a new US-based president for AT&T (GIS), largely because of his high-profile track record in turning around an ailing electrical contracting company and another AT&T unit. Strongly influenced by some US academic-consultant 'gurus', the new president sought to re-engineer AT&T (GIS) through a major attempt at 'rebranding', organizational identity/culture change programme. This rebranding process was marked by: (1) disposing of many of the NCR management team in the USA; (2) developing a much more strategic and 'hands-on' approach to strategy and tactics, rather than the purely financial control focus of the previous NCR management team in Dayton; and (3) introducing a cultural change programme that placed employees and customers at the heart of the new corporation's policies. The programme involved two central elements. The first was christened the 'Common Bond': this included a best practice, ethical mission statement, a new values framework and a set of working principles designed to 'empower employees and customers'. The ethical and empowering features of this programme are worth emphasizing at this stage, because it has been argued that the 'mutuality model' of HRM (based on treating people with respect) was more likely to lead employees to view the effort positively and to accept company actions that might have negative consequences for a minority of employees. Second, the programme involved a further flattening of organizational structures and an attempt to empower the local managers and workforce by, among other techniques, relabelling managers and supervisors as 'coaches' and workers as 'associates'. The list below provides further details of the cultural change programme.

Key elements of the cultural change programme

'Opportunities, vision and values'

1 'Common Bond' values:

- respect for individuals;
- dedication to helping customers;
- highest standards of integrity;
- innovation;
- teamwork.

2 Accompanying education/communication sessions:

- opportunity and change: create an awareness of the forces of change and how each associate, by understanding the dynamics of change, could take advantage of the opportunities that arose;
- vision and direction forum: to ensure that all associates would understand, through interactive discussions, the major issues affecting the company.

3 Supporting actions:

- further attempts to flatten the organizational hierarchy;
- coach and associate labels assigned;
- casual dress policy introduced;
- introduction of diversity and harassment policies;
- employee feedback sessions implemented based on repeated surveys;
- establishment of a 24 hours a day hotline to the US president and Common Bond champion;
- introduction of a new company magazine.

It is important to emphasize five key characteristics of the rebranding and culture change programme:

1 The programme was very much a personalized one that was driven by the new US president of AT&T (GIS) Jerre Stead – and the external US academic consultant who worked closely with him. Although a small number of UK managers were incorporated into the design of the programme, none of these was from the Scottish subsidiary.

2 The programme was viewed by local management in the Scottish subsidiary as a US-originated and oriented programme. This was because: (a) it was driven by the two US nationals from headquarters; (b) the language and content of the programme were very American in nature; and (c) its track record of success was based on two US organizations formerly managed by the new appointee.

3 This sense of US parentage was markedly enhanced by an absence of prior consultation and discussion with local management in the Scottish subsidiary, apart from some HRM staff. Quite simply, the views of the prominent and well-respected local CEO, Jim Adamson, and many of his staff had not been sought on the appropriateness of the change initiative in the Scottish context.

4 The president and lead consultant had set themselves very ambitious deadlines for launching the change programme. The stipulated timetable was couched in months rather than years.

5 The president of AT&T (GIS), Jerre Stead, who championed the cultural change programme, remained with the organization for only 18 months. Following his departure, his successor failed to continue to endorse the programme.

1 How do you think the Scottish management team and the workforce would have reacted to the programme?

MODELS OF ORGANIZATIONAL CHANGE

To help you understand the problems raised by this attempt at a wholesale, organization-wide rebranding and identity reconstruction, and to predict the response of employees, you will need a more in-depth understanding of the organizational and cultural change processes. In these next two sections we have brought together two generic models used to analyse and guide the process of strategic change in complex organizations, followed by one that deals specifically with culture change. First, let's look at the two change models:

- the intervention strategy model (ISM);
- the strategic change process model.

The intervention strategy model

The intervention strategy model (ISM), developed originally by Paton and McCalman (2006), and recently discussed in McCalman *et al.* (2015) is based on the idea of an open systems approach, which we have met earlier in this course when discussing technology and people management. Open systems approaches view organizations as a series of interlinked and interdependent elements and components of systems and subsystems. However, in defining a system, we have to be aware of the motives and values of those providing the definition and their purposes in providing it, for what might be defined as a system in one case may be little more than a component of a much wider system. An example that McCalman *et al.* (2015) use is a motor vehicle, which is made up from a series of elements, such as a gearshift to facilitate driver/gearbox interaction; components, such as a fuel pump, the job of which is to provide petrol to the combustion chamber; subsystems, such as the gearbox, which is there to engage and influence the driving force of the vehicle; or the engine, which is designed to provide the driving force. Then there is the driver, who manages and controls the technical system. Note that, from the perspective of a car designer, the vehicle itself can be viewed as the complete system to transport people and their luggage/goods. However, from the perspective of transport engineers, the car is only a small part of a wider transport system, comprising roads, rail, waterways, air routes, etc. From the perspective of the car designer, this wider transport system is its external environment. Note also that this kind of system is a socio-technical system, comprising a technological subsystem and a human subsystem, the two having to be designed to operate in balance.

Open systems have certain key properties that it is important to understand in an organizational context. The first of these is *system autonomy*, which refers to the process of mapping out the boundaries of the system and its environment (see the comments on 'problem definition' later in this section). As suggested in the previous paragraph, these boundaries depend on the purposes of the exercise and the person or persons conducting it. The main point when mapping out organizational systems is to ensure that all non-essential relationships are excluded and all essential ones are included. As McCalman *et al.* (2015) point out, a *change environment* has to include all of the systems and subsystems directly and indirectly affected.

The second key property is *system behaviour*, which refers to three factors:

- the physical processes of the system itself;
- the communication processes used to handle and transfer information within and between systems;
- the monitoring processes that maintain the system's stability.

For example, in a manufacturing plant, we can identify: (a) the physical processes, e.g. the speed and nature of a moving assembly line in motor vehicle manufacture; (b) the communications systems, which plan and provide the assembly line manufacturing system with the correct materials and amount of labour; and (c) the monitoring systems of production control and quality control, which ensure that what is being produced is on time, at the right cost and of the right quality.

By examining these linkages, one can determine the extent to which the systems are interdependent and likely to behave in relation to one another. A systems analysis of any change programme then should begin with a detailed understanding of these linkages and the change environment or context in which they operate.

The ISM itself is a set of basic investigative techniques built around the notion of open systems and their key properties. It is linked to three stages of system intervention:

Stage 1: Problem definition

1   Clarifying the objectives of the change
2   Capturing data and performance indicators
3   Diagnosing the systems' properties

Stage 2: The evaluation and design phase

4   Analysing the system
5   Determining options or solutions
6   Evaluating options or solutions

Stage 3: The implementation phase

7   Implementing the chosen option or solution
8   Appraisal and monitoring.

Problem definition

In stage 1, the objectives of the change and the general problem environment have to be made clear. This is followed by a thorough analysis and evaluation of the system and its environment. One major problem sometimes encountered at this stage concerns our ability to map out the environment in relation to the organizational systems (Hatch and Cunliffe, 2012). Many senior organizational analysts and managers, when asked to discuss their environment, tend to place themselves at the centre of their world and construct (or literally enact) a picture of their environment as revolving around them or radiating from their system. For example, if we asked you to draw a picture of your organization and its environment, it is likely that you would construct something like Figure 10.1. However, the danger of thinking in this way is that the system and its managers become self-referential and egocentric: all analysis and action is made and taken in relation to the organizational system itself, without stepping outside the 'centre circle'.

Unless your organization or system is literally in the centre circle, say the dominant market player or the headquarters of a highly centralized company, perhaps a more accurate construction of the environment for most organizations would be to place themselves more towards the periphery, while major new competitors, suppliers, customers or even overseas subsidiaries are at the centre, and the organization and/or its senior managers are at the periphery (see Figure 10.2).

Perhaps the main player in the industry, B, might be a close competitor, while C might be head office or a key subsidiary division.

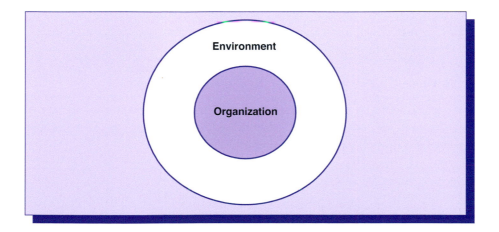

FIGURE 10.1 The egocentric perspective on organizational–environmental relations

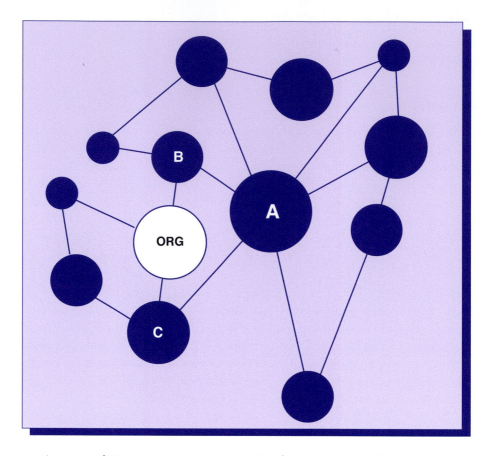

FIGURE 10.2 A more realistic perspective on organizational–environmental relations

(*Source*: adapted from Hatch, 1997.)

EXERCISE 10.1

Could Jerre Stead and his advisers have interpreted the organization–environment relationship in a different way, one that might have helped them avoid some of the problems they encountered? If so, what might this interpretation look like?

The evaluation and design phase

During the evaluation and design phase, organizational change specialists have to use the data they collect to analyse the problems in context and to arrive at a set of possible solutions. These solutions should then be evaluated. One of the most useful techniques for undertaking evaluation is scenario writing or planning. Although forecasting the future has a notoriously poor reputation (Graham, 1999), organizational change specialists can and need to ask sensible questions about their possible future(s) so that they can anticipate problems and produce possible solutions. Creating strategic scenarios or scenario planning has become an accepted method of engaging with the future by asking such questions and using a more discursive approach than traditional forecasting techniques. Scenario planning has been used effectively in diverse situations, such as Shell Oil's attempt to deal with oil price rises during the 1990s, to stimulate debate on the future of South Africa and, more recently, to identify potential 'white spaces' between the old and new economies and old and new industries. For example, we have been involved in a large-scale scenario planning exercise for the Scottish e-learning industry that has helped local companies develop more adaptive and relevant strategies (Bell *et al.*, 2004).

Most of the expertise in this field lies not so much in the academic domain as in the large consulting companies. Thus, it is worth quoting Global Business Network (GBN) at length on strategic scenarios, because they are acknowledged to be one of the leading consultancy organizations in this field. This consulting company grew out of the well-known Royal Dutch/Shell scenario planning group, whose work in the 1990s promoted the use of this approach.

> 'Scenarios are tools for ordering one's perceptions about alternative future environments in which today's decisions might be played out. In practice, scenarios resemble a set of stories, written or spoken, built around carefully constructed plots. Stories are an old way of organizing knowledge; when used as strategic tools, they confront denial by encouraging, in fact requiring, the willing suspension of disbelief. Stories can express multiple perspectives on complex events; scenarios give meaning to these events.
>
> Scenarios are powerful planning tools precisely because the future is unpredictable. Unlike traditional forecasting or market research, scenarios present alternative images instead of extrapolating current trends from the present. Scenarios also embrace qualitative perspectives and the potential for sharp discontinuities that econometric models exclude. Consequently, creating scenarios requires decision-makers to question their broadest assumptions about the way the world works so they can foresee decisions that might be missed or denied.
>
> Within an organization, scenarios provide a common vocabulary and an effective basis for communicating complex – sometimes paradoxical – conditions and options. Good scenarios are plausible and surprising, they have the power to break old stereotypes, and their creators assume ownership and put them to work. Using scenarios is rehearsing the future. By recognizing the warning signs and the drama that is unfolding, one can avoid surprises, adapt and act effectively. Decisions which have been pre-tested against a range of what fate may offer are more likely to stand the test of time, produce robust and resilient strategies, and create distinct competitive advantage. Ultimately, the result of scenario planning is not a more accurate picture of tomorrow but better thinking and an ongoing strategic conversation about the future.'
>
> (www.gbn.org/AboutScenariosDisplayServlet.srv)

EXERCISE 10.2

1 The so-called 'law of the instrument' states that if you 'give a small boy a hammer, every problem becomes a nail'. Does this comment seem to apply to Jerre Stead and his advisers?

2 Apart from the change strategy they chose, what alternative scenarios could Stead and his team have envisaged at the time of the design of the programme?

The implementation phase

Assuming that you have followed the advice provided in the two previous phases and you have arrived at a sensible change strategy, this is still no guarantee of success. In fact, many writers in the field of strategy suggest that it is during this third, implementation phase that most trouble occurs and most change programmes fail (Whittington and Mayer, 2002; Clarke *et al.*, 2007). Getting the balance right between *thinking* and *doing* (or strategy and action) is a very difficult problem in itself, often with too much emphasis given to the former and not enough to the latter.

Let's go back to the idea, introduced in the previous pages, concerning organizations enacting their environments through their definitions of the situation and through their behaviour. Enactment refers to how organizations make decisions about what features of their world to focus on, how they collectively define these features, and how they account for and shape these features. For example, we might ask: What aspects of the external change environment did Jerre Stead and his advisers choose to focus on? Could they have defined the external environment in a different way, perhaps using scenario planning techniques discussed above, which would have allowed them to construct other, more realistic scenarios? By way of illustration, had they been less US- and head office-centric, could they have created a more accurate picture of the organization and its problems, one that would have allowed them to see the potential for the problems they would create in Scotland, their key subsidiary location? The central point of this message is that managers are active agents, not merely passive recipients of abstract and external market forces. Good managers understand how to enact their environment in order to control it through more intuitive and creative interpretations, re-definitions and action (Weick, 2001).

Weick argues that managers are often better advised to 'act their way into thinking', by taking smaller, incremental steps and learning from them, rather than 'think their way into acting' through top-down, transformational planning strategies such as those depicted in the AT&T case. The dangers of a top-down, planning-then-action approach are twofold. The first danger is that by making big changes there is little chance for learning to occur because you don't really know which of the many components of the change had the most effect. The second danger, and more likely consequence, is that by constructing a complex plan you are likely to fall into the trap of 'paralysis by analysis'. Many organizations that spend most of their time analysing and planning often end up like 'rabbits caught in the lights of a car', taking no action at all, either because they don't leave enough time or because they can't decide what to do. In this scenario, planning and strategy-making become the 'endgame', not the means to achieve success.

Think about this example, which is a story told by Karl Weick to illustrate this point and a further, important one. A group of Italian soldiers are out on a winter exercise in the Alps and get lost. They are on the verge of dying in extreme weather conditions when one of them finds a map that points to a direction to go in. They end up safe, but when they get back home they find that the map was of the Dolomites, a completely different mountain range, and not the Alps. The moral of this tale is twofold. First, a map is not the territory; it is extremely important to understand that planning is no substitute for doing, and no representation can capture the nuances of life on the ground. Second, it may be that the real function of the map is to get you moving or acting your way into thinking: 'fire, ready, aim' as Tom Peters, the management guru, has put it. Perhaps too much of a belief in the strategic planning model of management, and all students and managers should take note, is a dangerous thing because you can confuse simple theories (or maps), such as the ubiquitous two by two models found in strategy, with reality itself (the territory). Or even worse, as some generals in battle have found out from spectacular and costly failures, their plans may even become objectified as the territory, sometimes labelled the 'fallacy of misplaced concreteness' – in which they fight out their battles from headquarters without ever setting foot on the ground. This 'arm's length, officer class' managerialism is one of the dangers associated with having business analyst/planners remote from the day-to-day operations of a business.

The strategic change process model

The second model, the strategic change process model, which was developed by Martin and Beaumont (Martin and Beaumont, 2001; Martin *et al.*, 2003), is based on extensive research into the problems of change and change agents at different levels in a range of multinational organizations. The model (see Figure 10.3) complements the ISM framework in explaining the implementation stage in more detail. It focuses on the complex set of events, activities, language practices, emotions and reactions that help explain:

- what would be needed for successful change to occur in organizations;
- why most change initiatives are rarely successful in embedding change in organizations.

Much of the value of this model lies in seeing strategy as a convincing narrative or storyline that managers and employees construct, 'buy into' and use to give a sense of mission and purpose to their organizational lives. The notion of discourse and change conversations plays a major part in this model.

Although the model was originally developed to explain the process of strategic change in multinational organizations, such as the one in our AT&T and NCR case study, it can easily be adapted to analyse all forms of complex organization such as those discussed in Chapter 4. To incorporate the particular problems of managing across international boundaries (see Chapter 5), we have included the social context. This refers to the differences in cultures and institutions between a parent company's home country and those of the countries of subsidiary units, such as the Scottish plant in our case study.

BOX 10.1 Definition – the view of strategy as narrative

Rather than seeing strategy as a set of plans with an objective reality, strategy is sometimes better conceived as a story that managers tell to provide guidance and purpose to their organizations. The best strategic stories or strategic discourses are *novel*, *credible* and *compelling* for others to follow. By discourse, we mean a set of communicative practices that are closely linked to specific purposes of powerful groups. Discursive practices in management include strategic conversations that managers use to promote change. Four types of strategic conversation have been identified that good managers use in promoting their change initiatives:

- Initiating conversations that are used to get the change process under way, which include assertions, directives, promises, etc. that engage employees and outline what is needed.
- Understanding conversations to test the reality of the change propositions and to generate involvement. These conversations focus on claims, evidence, theories of cause and effect (if we do this, we shall achieve . . .) to help employees understand what is needed and what will result for the organization and for them.
- Performance conversations to generate action, which focus on conversations, promises and directives that are intended to produce results.
- Closure conversations, which are assertions and declarations used to signify the successful (or unsuccessful) completion and 'celebration' of the change process.

Source: Ford and Ford, 1995.

The key features and stages of the model are as follows:

1   *Receptive contexts for change.* These contexts are especially important for successful change to become embedded in complex organizations. We can identify five such levels of context: the societal, the industry, organizational context, the inner organizational context and the relational context. The societal context we have already described as having an important influence on the process of strategic change. However, the nature of the industry in a particular locality or country and its environment is also potentially important, as we saw in Chapter 4 in the case of Innovative Petroleum Engineering with the different market circumstances between the US parent and the European subsidiary. The inner organizational context, which in a multinational environment refers to the differences in organizational cultures, attitudes to learning and compatibility of practices between the parent and subsidiaries, can have a great bearing on the effectiveness of change initiatives. These intra-organizational differences are potentially relevant in explaining the success or failure of corporate-wide initiatives such as branding. Finally, the attitudes of local managers and their relative power in relation to the parent company or head office will shape the reception of change programmes, again as we also saw in the case of Innovative in Chapter 4.

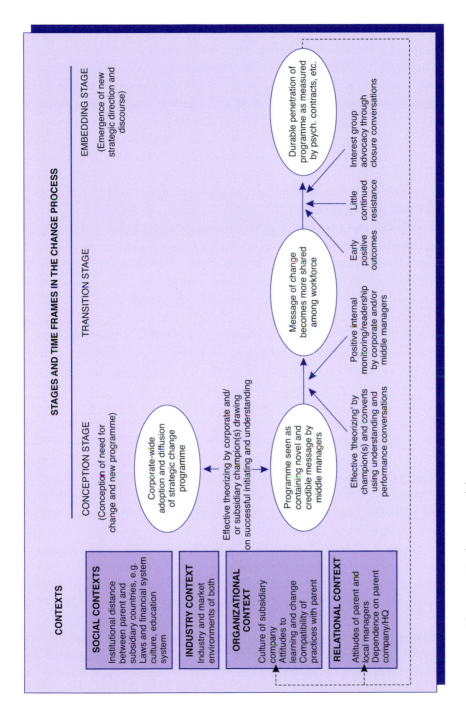

FIGURE 10.3 The strategic change model

(Source: based on Martin and Beaumont, 2001.)

It is also important to note that the process aspects of the model (the various stages, patterns of events and language practices) are embedded in these changing contexts over time. This is particularly true of major culture and HR changes, such as the study we undertook in the UK North Sea oil industry (discussed in Chapter 3), in which legislative change in the UK during 1999 left the subsidiaries of multinational drilling companies operating in the UK open to claims for union recognition for the first time since the 1970s. Despite strong initial resistance from the US headquarters of a number of the firms in the industry, a successful and arguably more sophisticated and stable form of employee relations has evolved, based on union recognition and collective bargaining. In that study we argued that the positive early engagement and experience with the union had created the receptive context for further changes towards union recognition and in dissipating the anti-union stance and policies of these US-based headquarters of the drilling companies. Without this positive atmosphere created by the unions, further progress would have been impossible.

2   *The conception stage.* This is the stage during which new strategies and new strategic discourses are developed. Note that the process model allows for two-way development of the strategic changes, in which the ideas are just as likely to come from middle managers, HR specialists and internal/external change consultants. High-level corporate support, adoption and sponsorship of the change discourse and programmes are a necessary, but not sufficient, condition for further progress towards successful change.

3   *The transition stage.* For the key messages of change to progress to the transition stage, credible and novel culture changes and HRM strategies (occurring in, and through, effective communications) have to be read positively by all levels of management, including main board, subsidiary and middle-level operational managers. In a study we conducted on ABB, it was evident that the managers in certain subsidiaries of one of the company's major divisions became highly skilled at denying the need for change, using many examples of why such changes in culture were unnecessary and difficult to implement in their specific circumstances (Martin and Beaumont, 1998). Chris Argyris (1993) has labelled this process of using skilled communication to deny problems as *skilled incompetence*. This is one of the principal reasons for organizational resistance to change, because managers, often for the first time in years, are asked to question the very assumptions on which they have always operated. One of the main reasons for the failure of many programmes of change is because employees are subject to a constant stream of unfinished managerial fads and fashions. These employees become adept at ignoring these programmes of change, most of which have little impact and regularly fail to become embedded in the organization. However, these incomplete programmes, based on fads and fashions in management, result in increased levels of cynicism towards future change initiatives (Pate *et al.*, 2000).

4   *The embedding stage.* For the message of change to continue to progress towards the embedding stage, where a new strategic discourse of change has taken root, the communication of early positive outcomes, supported by evidence of its benefits, is necessary to overcome continued resistance or, often more likely, the kind of benign neglect by employees that often accompanies change programmes. The notion of 'early wins' is one of the most important and enduring in the change literature; it suggests that small-scale experiments and initiatives rather than

wholesale, top-down programmes are the best way forward. One of the few near-certainties in business is that 'big change invokes big opposition', so it is critical to identify the groups that you 'trial out'. We also refer to measures of the extent to which the messages of change are embedded in an organization. Excellent examples of such measures are the state of psychological contracts and the extent of commitment, identification and psychological ownership of the changes (see Chapters 3 and 6).

5   *The feedback stage.* This stage is critical for continuous change in the organization, during which the outcomes of strategic innovations are fed back into the organizational contexts – particularly new employee attitudes and behaviours, the capacity of employees to unlearn, change and innovate, and positive attitudes towards the ways in which changes were implemented. This positive feedback loop is likely to set the tone for the reception of future change initiatives. In a study we conducted of a Scottish-based textile company (Martin *et al.*, 1998a), we noted how previously negative experiences with change programmes had led employees to develop strong feelings of cynicism towards senior managers and their efforts to introduce continuous changes in work practices. Such cynicism made future change initiatives almost impossible to implement.

The strategic change process model and eight guidelines for evaluating and managing strategic change in organizations

We have developed eight guidelines for evaluating and managing successful strategic change, which correspond to the four stages discussed above.

The conception stage

1   Without a convincing discourse (or language) of change, effectively conceived and put into practice by corporate or mid-level management champions, corporate-wide adoption and the diffusion of major change initiatives are unlikely to progress beyond the conception stage. A novel, credible and compelling story has to be told and 'fleshed out' with some detail. However, the senior managers don't always need to do the fleshing out; much of the advice in this area suggests that broad guidelines, missions and values are set out but there has to be something left for middle managers and employees to contribute to, especially at the level of operational detail.

2   The strategic discourse and stories generated by the leaders of change should draw on the strategic change conversations in Box 10.1, including:

-   realistic *initiating conversations*, which set out the reasons for the change;
-   *understanding conversations*, including those that are directed at enhancing the credibility and novelty of the assertions, the declarations and promises made at the early stages, the rationale and evidence used to support these assertions;
-   the *likely actions and benefits* that will result from the proposed changes, especially those that address the 'what's in it for me' question.

3   The messages of change, as set out by the leaders of change, have to be perceived and read positively by lower-level managers as containing a credible, compelling and novel message to secure their acceptance of the change programme. This means that listening and seeking active feedback at an early stage of any proposed changes should be sought by senior managers.

The transition stage

4   In the absence of a credible and novel message, other corporate and middle managers not yet involved in the change process are unlikely to have the incentive to read the story in a positive light, and may look for reasons for the changes to be discontinued, resisted or ignored. Often, middle managers and employees become skilled in denying the needs for change, such as the veracity of benchmarks or best practices drawn from other companies against which their performance is measured.

5   For the new language of change and its manifestations to become more widely shared by employees at all levels in the organization, the champions of change, aided by their middle management converts, have to continue to draw on new understanding conversations and promises or directives that will engage or compel the majority of employees to accept strategic change. Many change programmes are aimed at securing the cooperation of a limited number of managers or groups in the organization, a strategy that only serves to reduce its impact in the future.

6   For change to progress towards the embedding stage there has to be evidence of, and publicity for, early victories for managers, and evidence and publicity for positive outcomes for the majority of employees.

7   The champions or leaders of change have to continue to embed change in the organization by drawing on *closure conversations* intended to signify the success of these intermediate positive outcomes. US texts and consultants tend to talk about celebrating success, and frequently have institutionalized events to demonstrate success, e.g. through passing-out or awards ceremonies or 'employee of the month' schemes.

The embedding stage and the emergence of a new discourse

8   The extent to which strategic change is embedded in the organization can be measured by the degree of *penetration* and *durability* of changes in the outcomes of employee psychological contracts, including the effects on employee attitudes, commitment and satisfaction, and their levels of identification with the organization's goals. This work lies at the heart of the new language of employer branding and corporate reputation management that we met earlier and which seeks to align external image with internal employee identity.

EXERCISE 10.3

Using the ideas from the strategic change process model, particularly the guidelines for evaluating and managing strategic change in organizations, how would you analyse the problems in the AT&T case?

CHANGING ORGANIZATIONAL CULTURES

You should have sensed by now that much of organizational change and people management is concerned, one way or another, with the subject of culture. We have met the notion of culture in previous chapters on the international context, the corporate context and managing organizations. Although we have preferred to use more precise terms such as organizational identity and engagement in our examination of individual–organizational linkages and corporate reputation management, culture and culture change is a topic that has remained 'centre stage' in business and management studies (Hatch *et al.*, 2015). Indeed, according to some authors, creating and sustaining strong corporate cultures has been seen as the single most important factor in designing and managing successful organizations (Balogun and Hope-Hailey, 2004). Although this faith in culture as the key to unlocking organizational success may have been misplaced, the interest in culture management shows no real signs of abating. In this section of the chapter we want to examine the notion of culture to determine whether it has any useful and practical value to managers. In other words, can we talk sensibly about organizational culture and can we manage organizational cultures?

Organizational culture: different meanings and key questions

There has been a massive growth of the literature on organizational culture since the 1970s. The most prominent contributions include Van Maanen and Barley (1984), Schein (1985), Barley (1983), Hatch (1993), Pettigrew (2012) and Hatch *et al.* (2015). Before we discuss some of the ways in which researchers theorize culture, let's look at what culture means, and how it can be 'observed'. If you wish to change something, you need to be able to access it. In other words, you have to define it and understand what you are trying to change. Organizational culture has caused some controversy among academics and consultants because it can be defined and understood in quite different ways, all of which have distinctive, practical implications. There are at least four such views:

- the unitary view and mono-cultures;
- the anthropological view and subcultures;
- the conflict view and 'brandwashing';
- the fragmented view and paradoxes.

The unitary view

The unitary view of organizations rests on the assumption that companies are, under normal circumstances, best characterized by common interests and consensus between different stakeholders. For example, it is assumed that employees and managers are broadly in agreement about the aims of the business and the rights of managers to be able to set the direction of the organization and the work of employees, usually without interference from bodies such as trade unions. When conflict does arise, it is seen as a consequence of poor management or disruptive employees who don't fully understand the nature of the business. From this perspective, an organization is assumed to have a single, dominant culture that can be measured and controlled in the same way as you would measure and control employee performance or other key variables. For example, in our discussion on corporate reputation, we used the term 'organizational personality' to describe something that an organization possesses, just like people possess individual personalities. And, as we discussed in Chapter 5 on the international context, culture as a variable is seen as a set of shared meanings, embracing both the formal and informal aspects of organizations. The key point is that culture, once understood, is treated as a highly manageable feature of organizations. This seemed to be the perspective of Jerre Stead, the CEO of AT&T (GIS) in the case study. Such unitary assumptions and analysis may have a degree of validity in certain contexts, but in others they are likely to be misplaced and misleading. Ask yourself the questions in the AT&T case: (1) How realistic were the assumptions made by Stead regarding the potential to create a unified culture in the company? (2) Were leadership and communications all that was necessary to overcome barriers to change? Perhaps he could have taken a different view, distinguishing between:

- the *corporate culture*, which is essentially what managers want the organization to be like, similar to the concept of corporate identity in Chapter 6 and more amenable to control; and
- the *organizational culture and subcultures*, which are more akin to the notions of organizational identity in Chapter 6, and which are less amenable to control, for a variety of reasons.

We examine this distinction in the next few paragraphs.

The anthropological view

This is a quite different perspective on culture; it has much less to do with managerial control than with understanding organizations. Culture, rather than being treated as something an organization possesses, is seen as the very *essence* of the organization. In other words, culture is something an organization *is* rather than *has*. This view of organizational culture has some fundamental implications, the most important of which is that an organizational culture cannot be owned and managed in the strict sense of these terms. For an organizational culture to develop and evolve, it has to be created, shared and 'lived' by the majority of employees, not just managers. Often, however, we find that organizations are better characterized as loose groupings of subcultures, perhaps overlaid with a managerial culture. Therefore, we can talk about the cultures of different professional and occupational groups in an organization, such as those in sales, production, and research and development laboratories. We also talk of the culture of white-collar and blue-collar employees. Thus, it is argued, managers have no greater access to the culture of organizations than other employees, and although they can shape culture over time through branding and vision and values programmes, they cannot alter it radically, especially in a short time frame. Perhaps these were points of which Jerre Stead should have been more aware.

Moreover, it is difficult for people who are part of the culture, including managers, who create and recreate it every day through their enactment of reality, to step outside themselves and then change it. One of the most important features of culture is that often we cannot see it, especially if we are steeped in an organization's history and way of thinking. In this situation, we require outsiders (researchers or consultants), literally, to 'help us see ourselves as others see us'.

The conflict view

A third view, widely held among critical organizational theorists and many union officials, sees culture management as a form of organizational domination and social engineering, in which managers attempt to manipulate organizations for their own aims through the selection and development process. This approach questions the ethics of culture change programmes and rebranding exercises, seeing them as little more than exercises in brainwashing or 'brandwashing'. Naomi Klein's (2001) book *No Logo* and the book by Joel Balkin (2004), *The Corporation*, are good examples of this conflict view on large corporations, arguing that their attempts to brandwash people into accepting the views of business are detrimental to their long-term interests and the interests of society as a whole. The case study on AT&T raises some of the issues connected with ethics and the domination perspective, which we shall look at in the review questions at the end of this section. This conflict view is one that is held by the labour process school, which we discussed in Chapter 8 on technology, and provides one of the intellectual justifications for global opposition groups such as international trades unions.

The fragmented view

A final view is associated with the school of thinking called postmodernism. It is not necessary to go into the ideas of postmodernism in any depth for our purposes, but one of its key contributions to management thinking is to question the notion of a single and permanent reality. For example, Joanna Martin's (2002) account of culture highlights the fragmentary, contradictory and paradoxical aspects of organizational culture, especially the gaps that exist between official managerial rhetoric and the behaviour of the self-same managers who devised the rhetoric. Thus, we often find organizations espousing an official discourse of 'resourceful humans', while treating them as 'human resources' to be cut and controlled like any other resource. We can also observe people at all levels in an organization making contradictory comments and taking contradictory actions. One famous example of this was a study in the 1960s, when workers at a car plant in the south-east of England were asked to state their degree of agreement with the statement: 'A firm is like a football team with workers and managers on the same side and kicking into the same goal for most of the time.' Seventy-five per cent of the workers agreed with the statement, but three months later they were seen to be marching through the factory, singing the well-known communist anthem, 'The Red Flag', and threatening to hang the industrial relations manager (Goldthorpe *et al.*, 1968).

Therefore, we have to ask ourselves: Do most employees hold a coherent worldview of their organizations as a unified culture? Obviously, as managers we need to look for generalizations about organizational life, especially about cultures, otherwise we couldn't manage effectively. However, this should not blind us to the potential for differences of interests and values among groups in organizations, sometimes quite fundamental ones. To return to a point made in earlier chapters, what we see depends on where we stand (the position we view from).

The fragmented view sees organization cultures as consistent and inconsistent, contradictory and confused, all at the same time. Managers, consultants and academics of this persuasion argue that there is no such thing as strong and endurable corporate or subgroup culture, and that culture is better described as a jungle, in a permanent state of flux and transformation. Understanding this view of organizations prevents us from placing too much faith in culture management techniques and programmes of culture change: as organizations are always in a state of becoming something else, 'the only constant is change'.

So the answers to the questions posed at the beginning of this section about organizational cultures, and whether or not they can be managed, depend very much on your definition and perspective of culture. Mintzberg *et al.* (1998) have synthesized a number of these views by linking organizational culture to the strategy-making, organizational design and change processes in organizations. They argue that strategy can be seen as a perspective, rather than as a planning process.

1   Strategy formation and organizational design form a cultural *process of social interaction*, based on beliefs and shared understandings of members.
2   Individuals acquire these beliefs through acculturation or socialization, which is largely tacit and non-verbal, but this sometimes involves a degree of indoctrination through training and induction programmes.
3   Thus, the members of an organization can only partly describe the beliefs that underpin their culture.
4   As a result, strategy takes the form of a *perspective* or a world-view, rooted in collective intentions and reflected in patterns of activity embedded in resources or capabilities.
5   Culture does not encourage change, but allows shifts in position.

They further argue that the linkages between culture and strategic and organizational change are as follows:

- Culture influences decision-making style by influencing the style of analysis and what gets analysed, because we all have different *perceptual filters*.
- Culture can act as a restraint on strategic change because of shared commitments to consistent action and deep-seated beliefs and tacit assumptions.
- Paradoxically, *culture can promote change* by emphasizing innovation, education and flexibility.
- So, culturally dominant values can be a key *source of competitive advantage*.
- However, cultures can clash and be the *source of failure* in alliances, mergers, supply chain relationships, etc.

EXERCISE 10.4

Of the four perspectives outlined in the previous section, which one helps you best understand the AT&T case? Explain your reasoning.

MORE WAYS OF THEORIZING CULTURE

In their 2015 article Giorgi, Lockwood and Glynn identified further ways in which culture can be conceptualized. These include culture as values, culture as stories, culture as frames, culture as toolkits and, finally, culture as categories which flesh out the previous analysis.

1   *Culture as values* – is 'what we prefer, hold dear, or desire' (Giorgi *et al.*, 2015, p. 4). Values are the drivers of social structure and action, they are perpetuated through socialization, leadership and rituals. Examples of culture as values can be found in banks in the US and in the UK before the Global Financial Crisis of 2007–08, where some practices normally frowned upon were seen as legitimate and widely used implemented by the bankers.
2   *Culture as stories* – culture consists of stories that convey ideas and meanings, they are 'narratives with causally linked sequences of events that have a beginning, a middle and an end' (Giorgi *et al.*, 2015, p. 9). One good example is the study by Linde (2001) of an insurance company in which values are conveyed through repeated stories of its history, and the life and character of its charismatic founder and leader. The story of the company's commercial and ethical success is about development from selling solely car insurance to offering a full service while following the idea that farmers of good moral character should be charged lower rates for car insurance, because they run lower risks than drivers in the city.
3   *Culture as frames* – this perspective builds on the social constructionist perspective (Berger and Luckmann, 1967) and states that we cannot objectively assess reality, because our attention is delimited by 'filters' or 'brackets'. Giorgi *et al.* (2015) argue that frames can be formed within an institutional field where multiple actors negotiate the norms within broader ideological traditions.
4   *Culture as toolkits* – these are 'grab bags' of stories, frames, categories, rituals and practices that actors draw on to make meaning or take action. The metaphor of the toolkit shifts the emphasis away from values towards 'bits and pieces of culture that can be differently assembled' (Giorgi *et al.*, 2015, p. 13). Goffee and Jones' (1988) framework discussed in detail below is an example of a culture management toolkit.
5   *Culture as categories* – 'social constructions or classifications that define and structure the conceptual distinctions between objects, people and practices'. This is about delineating both sameness and distinctiveness with other categories. Organizational actors engage in sensemaking and sensegiving as mechanisms for category construction. For example the famous study by Rao *et al.* (2005) analyses the erosion of categorical boundaries in opposing category pairs: traditional cuisine and nouvelle cuisine. Elite French chefs, as high status actors, blended elements from these two rival cuisines creating new styles of dishes positively evaluated by the critics. By doing that the chefs redrew the boundaries of culinary categories.

Arguably, there is some overlap in these categories, and some studies span their boundaries, however the above classification of the ways in which culture is theorized suggests that the study of culture is a very rich field, in which researchers draw on a wide range of disciplines – psychology, sociology and anthropology.

The culture matrix toolkit

One of the best researched and most useful of a culture management toolkit approach is the typology developed by Rob Goffee and Gareth Jones (1998), who have written about the *character of the corporation* and the *double S* model (see Figure 10.4). Drawing on a wide range of previous research into leadership and organizational behaviour, they identified two dimensions along which organizations can be plotted. These dimensions may be familiar to you.

1   *Sociability* refers to the degree of 'friendliness' among members of a community. Sociability comes from mutual esteem and concern for one's colleagues, and is reflected in the quality of interpersonal relations among them. High levels of sociability are found in organizations where people take an interest in the well-being and work of colleagues. Low levels of sociability are found in organizations where the main focus is on the task or work to be done.
2   *Solidarity* refers to relationships based on mutual (self) interest and thinking alike, regardless of the degree of sociability in the organization. High levels of solidarity are found in organizations in which people are bound together by common goals, such as trades unions, voluntary organizations and armies, regardless of whether or not employees like each other. Low levels of solidarity are found in organizations in which employees pursue their own interests first and foremost.

Unlike other work in this field, Goffee and Jones suggested that these two dimensions have their negative as well as their positive sides. So, for example, high levels of sociability can have a 'negative

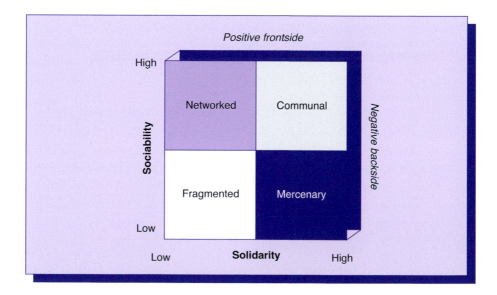

FIGURE 10.4 The culture matrix

(*Source:* based on Goffee and Jones, 1998.)

backside' in situations where people cover up for each other to hide poor performance. Similarly, low levels of solidarity can have their positive 'frontside', in so far as pursuing one's self-interest can be the best way to benefit an organization. To an extent, paying people on the basis of their individual performance is based on this feature of organizational life and nature of motivation among certain occupations.

Combining these two dimensions, they identify and describe four cultural types, each with a positive frontside and a negative backside. Although none of these cultural types, in and of themselves, is bad, all of them can be damaging if not managed properly.

1   The *networked culture* or *'between friends'*. An organization high on sociability but low on solidarity is referred to as a networked culture. Especially as organizations grow, smaller but more tightly knit organizational entities with a high level of sociability may develop, sometimes at the expense of solidarity. For knowledge-intensive companies with long development cycles and with a strong need for knowledge sharing, a networked culture can be a major asset. The same holds true for many companies in marketplaces in which relationships with customers and service are more important than offering them the lowest prices. A typical characteristic of networked companies is great pride in their products and services. Sometimes, however, the focus on the well-being of the organization and its employees has a negative side to it, such as carrying poor performers and 'face-saving' behaviour. Networked cultures have the following characteristics:

    •   open physical spaces, including social areas;
    •   decorations, such as photos and other group symbols;
    •   separated marked spaces to show territory (especially in negative forms);
    •   much talk, including informal meetings round the 'water cooler';
    •   lots of intensive conversations, use of e-mail, phones, etc.;
    •   attention to communicating in the 'right' way;
    •   socializing during work hours, which can be long;
    •   people identifying with one another.

2   The *mercenary culture*, or *'getting to work on Sunday'*. Where sociability is low but solidarity is high, Goffee and Jones have labelled this the 'mercenary' culture. In this culture, focus is ruthlessly targeted on key performance metrics and the 'bottom line'. The organization's products and services may be reduced to simple means for realizing the company's financial targets. From the employees' perspective, achieving personal rewards, usually financial ones, sometimes overrides pride in products or services. There are no family like ties protecting poor-performing colleagues. Although this culture in its extreme form may seem unattractive, arguably it could be seen as a necessary antidote to a networked company, that has not experienced the kind of market dynamics in which the lowest prices rule. Employees of well-run mercenary companies know their competitors, are eager to beat them and are energized by the mission statement of their company. Mercenary cultures have the following characteristics:

    •   functional office spaces, which provide basic accommodation and little more;
    •   displays of awards and recognitions for achievement;

- communications and talk short and to-the-point;
- meetings frequently confrontational;
- long and unsocial hours when needed, which is often;
- people identify with competing and winning.

3   The *fragmented culture*, or '*all together alone*'. In situations where both sociability and solidarity are low, we find fragmented cultures. Typical examples are research organizations such as universities and some consulting firms, especially law, accounting and consulting engineering firms. We might also find some examples in departments of larger companies that employ highly paid specialists, such as investment analysts or economists in the financial services industry. In these cultures the individuals often see themselves as more important than the groups they are part of and the company they work for, and have an outward orientation to their professional standing and professional careers. Fragmented cultures are characterized by:

- private offices, or people who work mainly from home;
- little talk or communications (with little opportunity for casual chat either);
- communication and talk focused on specific topics and kept brief;
- most communication directed to people outside the organization;
- people identify with individualism and value their autonomy.

4   The *communal culture*, or '*we are family*'. Goffee and Jones label the culture in the top right-hand quadrant as 'communal'. A typical example of a company high on solidarity as well as sociability is a business start-up. The founders are often very focused on their mission and employees are hand-picked for the organization, creating a family like atmosphere. Such an organizational culture can be extremely powerful, but it can also have a dark side if the organization becomes self-sufficient and too demanding of its members, like some religious sects. Being high on both solidarity and sociability has an inherent tension built into it, and as communal organizations grow they are likely to drop on one, or perhaps even both, dimensions. Communal cultures are characterized by:

- open-plan spaces to facilitate the family atmosphere;
- highly visible corporate symbols and logos;
- focus on face-to-face communications;
- moral persuasion, rather than direction, which often leads to guilt or shame being a motivating force;
- people living to work and working to live, with work–life balance as irrelevant;
- high levels of identification with organizational values.

Features of the different cultural types

We have already mentioned that none of these cultures is inherently good or bad. They can all have their functional and dysfunctional sides. A further key finding of Goffee and Jones' work is that organizations may have a dominant culture but most companies exhibit several subcultures at the same time. For example, many universities, especially in the USA and UK, which have a strong element of performance measurement, are characterized by dominant fragmented culture. Yet some departments may reflect a communal culture, a networked culture or even, in the case of some business schools, a mercenary culture, which mirrors the culture of their key clients.

Their research also pointed to the potential for a form of 'life cycle' that resembles an S-shaped transition through the four cultures. For example, a company may be formed as entrepreneurial and prospecting (communal). As it gains success and grows, it may become too 'fat' and too comfortable (networked). This may lead to a lowering of performance, necessitating a turn-around to get the company back in shape (mercenary). However, in the process of changing the culture from high–low to low–high on sociability and solidarity respectively, the management loses out on both counts and the organization ends up fragmented, with all employees working as independent contractors. This life cycle is not necessarily typical, but it illustrates some of the negative sides to the different cultures and the challenges in managing them. Indeed, this is one of the key strengths in the Goffee and Jones model in assessing how best to deal with organizational change. It is also useful to have an understanding of what needs to be compensated for, as each of the cultures has its drawbacks. Furthermore, if a culture is not sustainable, e.g. in a growing communal company or in a networked company that is hemorrhaging cash, it can be helpful to know some of the pitfalls to avoid.

LESSONS FOR SUCCESSFUL ORGANIZATIONAL CHANGE

We have reviewed some of the key ideas on organizational change and, especially, culture change. We hope by now that you are aware of the difficulties involved, but have a better understanding of how to go about implementing change in organizations, and how not to do it! As we have discussed, some writers and managers believe that organizations and their cultures can be socially engineered using a set of tools and techniques drawn from organizational development research; indeed, they place great faith in their ability to bring about major changes in performance from such programmes of change. Others, however, are more sceptical and believe that cultures cannot be managed in the sense that they can be controlled through managerial actions alone. Nor can they be easily changed from the outside, especially by using consultants who can rarely hope to gain the in-depth understanding necessary to help shape cultural change.

Our position on this issue is somewhere between the two: that organizational cultures can be shaped by managers and by consultants, but usually only with a sensitive and in-depth, 'insider' understanding of the issues involved, with the commitment of the majority of employees to change, and through sustained and sensitive effort by managers and change agents over many years.

Factors facilitating change

In a study of a Scottish city government organization (Martin *et al.*, 1998b), we provided a list of useful ideas (but not principles) about change. These ideas seem to resonate with our experience of research and consulting in this field over a long period of time. To these we have added some ideas or 'tips' from the work of writers/researchers whose ideas seem to make most sense to us. These are set out in Table 10.1.

Evaluating culture change

One final point that we have skirted over, but which is crucial to organizational change, is the question: How do you know when the hoped-for changes and/or new culture have taken root in an organization?

We have dealt with this briefly in our strategic change model, but Paul Bate (1996) has addressed this issue in depth and has identified five criteria for evaluating change. These are worth thinking about when considering the extent to which changes have penetrated the organization. They are

TABLE 10.1 Factors facilitating successful organizational change

1   Know where you are starting from. Usually, a receptive context for culture change together with the managerial ability to create a positive climate for culture change is necessary. One useful maxim that seems to apply is that 'often big change produces big opposition' in threatening the social identities of key players and their investment in the status quo.

2   Establish a sense of urgency by creating the necessary levels of tension (or mechanisms of discomfort) in the organization for culture change, and by assembling and facilitating a powerful group of people who act as champions to lead the change.

3   Create a vision (though it may, and perhaps should, be imprecise) and/or values framework which should help direct the culture change effort.

4   Use all possible means to communicate the vision/values deep into the organization (see the use of discourse and strategy as convincing stories) and ensure that managers 'walk the talk' to demonstrate the importance of the new culture and the kinds of behaviour associated with it.

5   Empower others to act by removing structural blockages to the new culture (e.g. organizational and architectural), and encourage innovation and group learning activities.

6   Encourage and use 'deviants' and 'heretics' to critically evaluate existing practices by 'speaking up to power' and to bring in fresh ideas.

7   Plan for and create short-term wins to encourage long-term persistence with the culture change initiatives.

8   Reinforce changes in culture with changes in structure and in the reward systems to reflect the kinds of behaviour that are appropriate.

9   Be aware of the ethical issues, personal choices and questions that most people have to face when being asked to commit themselves to culture change. These include: what can people reasonably be expected to do in the name of the organization, what kind of vision and values are people likely to buy into (how do they define the key stakeholders), how closely should the organization touch on peoples' private lives, and what values do they place on different kinds of justice?

10 Finally, be patient and persistent, as major changes in culture and structure may take many years to bring about.

Sources: Pettigrew, 1990; Schoenberger, 1997; Goffee and Jones, 2006; Hatch, 1997; Kotter and Schlesinger, 2008; McCalman *et al.*, 2015.

also useful in showing just how difficult and long term a task changing a company's culture might be. He suggests that, for a change programme to be successful, it must be able to:

- express a core idea that engages people's feelings by creating a credible, novel and compelling message;
- create a universal set of shared values that employees at all levels can buy into;
- penetrate deep into the organization, beyond the corporate, managerial culture and into the 'bowels of the organization';
- adjust to changing circumstances over time by being sufficiently flexible to cope with unforeseen challenges and opportunities;
- endure the test of time and the almost natural tendency of managers to introduce further changes.

Jerre Stead and those of a similar persuasion, please take note.

CASE 10.2 **LIVING WITH A PURIST**

The Kirk Russell Studio was a highly successful private architectural and interior design practice based in continental Europe, owned by its American founder, Kirk Russell. Its company logo, which dominates all company collateral, is 'Obsession with world-class design is our credo'.

The company was started in 1987 by Russell, who stated that he wasn't interested in beginning a run-of-the-mill architectural practice, tendering for basic contracts. Instead, he sought to develop a 'School of Excellence' for innovative young architects and interior designers, where they could hone and practise their talents on high-profile design work. He made the comment that he wasn't interested in offering these people jobs, but 'a unique experience' that they would always carry with them. And because Russell had a good reputation in the industry in Europe, his purist claims were taken seriously in most quarters.

Russell's approach to potential staff members was a little unorthodox. Instead of offering high salaries and bonuses, he stressed the difficulties of working in a 'School of Excellence'. 'You won't make as much money as you could do elsewhere, and you won't get a high-class office overlooking the Lido,' he used to state in his opening interviews with recruits, 'but you will get the most satisfying and high-profile experience around. However, the quid pro quo is that I demand a purist obsession with design quality and I know, because you are good, that you will produce it.'

Using this approach to talent management, Russell was able to put together a first-class team of architects, designers and technicians in a short space of time. This image of the School of Excellence was one he also used as a sales pitch to potential clients. 'If you want architects who are merely cost engineers, go elsewhere; if you want the best quality and buildings that will be monuments to their owners, you have come to the best practice in the country.'

By 1990 the company had carved itself out a highly profitable and high-profile niche in the European market and had won a number of major contracts in Italy, Spain and the UK. The staff became captivated by Russell's vision of the School of Excellence as time passed, many of them working very long hours way beyond contract. Most of them knew they weren't making the kind of money they might make in London, New York or other big-city practices, but valued the intangible rewards more. They were working on some of the most high-profile projects in Italy and Spain, which provided them with the kinds of satisfaction and career development that couldn't be gained elsewhere – at least, that was what they told colleagues in other practices when they were out socializing with them or met them on the conference circuit. Some of their colleagues resented having their work degraded during these conversations, and did not take kindly to their work and careers being called into question; the implication was always that they were 'in it for the money and not the higher-order values of architectural work'. There was also the issue of taste and judging quality. 'Who says your work is so great? Is designing a school that has to meet cost and quality standards not just as valuable as designing a high-profile office or government building?' became a common question and source of increasing friction between members of the 'Russell School' and outsiders during heated arguments in the bars.

By the mid 1990s, the Russell School of Excellence, as it was now known informally, had become one of the most respected practices in Europe, and was often invited to submit projects in design competitions for major building projects throughout the continent. Employees became even more committed to the cause, with almost no one leaving and many more joining as the practice expanded. From the perspective of those working in the practice, leisure time and work time became indistinguishable, and they boasted about the family type culture. Russell himself led by example and was seen as an inspirational leader, with frequent motivational talks around the theme of 'no compromise with quality' and 'designing buildings or great architectural significance'. He was also a man who 'walked the talk', always in the practice, reviewing the work of others and coaching the newer and often the even more experienced members of the teams. Long hours for everyone were the natural consequence, with excellence and the search for more high-profile projects the bywords.

In 1998 a defining moment occurred, however, when one of the, by now, senior and most respected architects was forced to make a choice between family and career. He decided to leave, not feeling able to give the commitment necessary to the company, and his departure was handled smoothly, with a party thrown in. However, in trying to replace this key member of staff, real difficulties were encountered. Russell had decided that every staff member should have a say in who was to be recruited into the 'family', rationalizing his decision on the basis of team-fit and the fact that staff would spend more time with the company's family than with their natural ones. Naturally, staff were enthusiastic that they were involved and that the new person should embrace the School's mission. However, all interviewees fell short in one way or another. One could not commit the time, another wasn't seen as a team player and yet another was rejected because she didn't have the right 'attitude'. After several months the key position remained unfilled.

During this time, Russell had to concentrate on running the business side of the School, and began to neglect his coaching and development functions. Everyone saw this happening, but thought it was only temporary until the new person was recruited. However, Russell himself began wondering in his private moments if they would ever be able to recapture the spirit of the School of Excellence, especially as the practice was doing well financially, with healthy profits and new projects coming in.

In 1999 another key member left the practice to set up on his own. On returning a few months later, he found Russell on the drawing board filling in for him. While staff still talked about the concern for obsessive quality, and felt that it was only a short time before the Academy got back on track, the visitor detected a degree of doubt about the statements made. Employees seemed much less confident than before, but weren't going to make it obvious to someone who was now an outsider.

The vacancy for the senior position was never re-advertised. In 2002, while most of the original staff were still with the organization and it was still turning in respectable profits, it wasn't appearing in the trade press quite so much, nor securing such high-profile projects.

Source: this material is based on two real-life cases, including 'Perfection or bust', by Gareth Morgan (1989).

1 How would you describe the culture of the Kirk Russell Studio?
2 What advice could be given to Russell to help make his company more effective?

COMPETING PERSPECTIVES ON ORGANIZATIONAL CHANGE

Organizational change is a contested terrain. In their book on managing change McCalman *et al.* (2015) emphasize the point that there are multiple ways in which managers can approach change, and managers often face what can be referred to as 'competing narratives'. Rather than ignoring these competing narratives, managers should recognize and see them as a legitimate source of alternative views. One source of difference in the way individuals perceive change is related to their position in the organization. Managers may see change differently from the way their employees do. Also a top-down change initiated by managers may not be seen in a positive light by the employees, while bottom-up change might unsettle managers who may fear of losing control by giving too much power to their employees (Dawson and Buchanan, 2012).

Bearing in mind the preceding 'health warnings', and the concerns expressed about the concept of unitary cultures, managers need to have a set of sophisticated techniques to identify and manage their organizational cultures. For example, in the AT&T case, Jerre Stead and his colleagues might have benefited from constructing alternative scenarios of what the organization might have looked like. More importantly, they would clearly have benefited from an understanding of the nature of the different subcultures in the various subsidiaries of AT&T (GIS).

One way in which these competing perspectives on change might be conceptualized is the notion of pluralism introduced in the 1970s by an industrial sociologist Alan Fox. In his writing (Fox, 1966; Fox and Flanders, 1969) Fox argued that a pluralist frame of reference was a more realistic analysis of industrial relations, and a more relevant model of industrial organization, which was made up of divergent interests and sectional groups. The pluralist view of organizations perceives a multitude of related but separate interests and objectives as the norm. Recognition of divergent interests held by managers and employees also involves an acceptance that there was only a limited degree of common purpose. Understanding the spirit of pluralism with its emphasis on conflicting interests is crucial to managing change. In any change initiative there are winners and losers, and managing change often involves managing competing interests.

Some, more recent, studies of change conducted through the lens of institutional theory capture the conflicting interests of organizational stakeholders. These conflicting interests are often closely linked to the differences in power that organizational actors have. Maguire *et al.* (2004) noted that dominant actors in an organization may have the power to pursue change, but they often do not have the motivation to change the organization for the simple reason that they benefit from the existing institutional arrangements. On the other hand the peripheral actors may have the incentive to promote change, but they may lack the power to change institutions. One way out of implementing change is allowing individuals to break with existing rules and practices associated with the dominant practice, and create alternative rules and practices (Battilana, 2006; Garud and Karnøe, 2003; Mutch, 2007). This process is referred to as institutional entrepreneurship (Maguire et *al.*, 2004). But it has to be remembered that, above all, we regard organizational change as a political process. The best advice we can give you is to develop political skills and build your internal and external networks. However, remember the lessons of the too-much-of-a-good-thing-effect: one of which should read that political managers create political organizations, so, as with most things in life, balance and restraint is probably the best way forward.

LEARNING SUMMARY

In this chapter we have looked at the process of changing organizations in the light of the different contexts of change. We addressed the key questions of what makes for successful change in an organization, and the practical steps that managers can take. The following points should be noted:

- The ISM model is a series of interlinked and interdependent elements of systems and subsystems which depends on the perspective of the developer. The model asks: What are you doing? How could you do it better? How do you effectively implement changes?
- Evaluation and design involve analysing the system, devising and evaluating viable solutions, and scenario planning.
- The implementation phase requires a balance between thinking and doing. Change agents must provide a convincing narrative for change through discourse and language – the *why* factor. Good narratives must be novel, credible and compelling.
- Organizational culture is one of the defining factors in understanding change. Strategy can be seen as a perspective, requiring social interaction.
- Organization culture can be analysed according to the extent to which it exhibits sociability and solidarity. Too much or too little of either can be a problem and can mean a shift to the other extreme.
- Cultures can be shaped, not controlled, by managers, but they need an in-depth understanding of the organization's specific needs and context.

REFERENCES

Argyris, C. (1993) *Knowledge for Action*. San Francisco, CA: Jossey-Bass.

Balkin, J. (2004) *The Corporation: The pathological pursuit of profit and power*. New York: Free Press.

Balogun, J. and Hope-Hailey, V. (2004) *Exploring Strategic Change*, 2nd edn. London: Prentice Hall.

Barley, S. R. (1983) Semiotics and the study of occupational and organizational cultures. *Administrative Science Quarterly*, 28 (3), 393–413.

Bate, P. (1996) Towards a strategic framework for changing corporate culture. *Journal of Strategic Change*, 5, 27–42.

Battilana, J. A (2006) Agency and institutions: the enabling role of individual's social position'. *Organization*, 13 (5), 653–676.

Bell, M., Martin, G. and Clarke, T. (2004) Engaging in the future of e-Learning: a scenarios-based approach. *Education and Training*, 46 (6/7), 296–307.

Berger, P. L. and Luckmann, T. (1967) *The Social Construction of Reality: A treatise in the sociology of knowledge*. New York: Anchor Books.

Clarke, C., Hope-Hailey, V. and Kelliher, C. (2007) Being real or being someone else? Change, managers and emotion work. *European Management Journal*, 25 (2), 92–103.

Dawson, P. and Buchanan, D. A. (2012) The way it really happened: competing narratives in the political process of technological change. In: S. Clegg and M. Haugaard (eds), *Power and Organizations*, pp. 845–864. London: Sage.

Ford, J. D. and Ford, L. W. (1995) The role of conversations in producing intentional organizational change. *Academy of Management Review*, 20, 541–570.

Fox, A. (1966) *Research Papers 3: Industrial sociology and industrial relations*. London: Her Majesty's Stationery Office.

Fox, A. and Flanders, A. (1969) The reform of collective bargaining: from Donovan to Durkheim. *British Journal of Industrial Relations*, 7 (2), 151–180.

Garud, R. and Karnøe, P. (2003) Bricolage versus breakthrough: distributed and embedded agency in technology entrepreneurship. *Research Policy*, 32 (2), 277–300.

Giorgi, S., Lockwood, C. and Glynn, M. A. (2015) The many faces of culture: making sense of 30 years of research on culture in organization studies. *The Academy of Management Annals*, 9 (1), 1–54. DOI: 10.1080/19416 520.2015.1007645.

Goffee, R. and Jones, G. (1998) *The Character of the Corporation*. New York: Harper Business.

Goffee, R. and Jones, G. (2006) *Why should anyone be led by you?* Cambridge: Harvard Business School Publishing.

Goldthorpe, J., Lockwood, D., Bechhofer, F. and Platt, J. (1968) *The Affluent Worker: Industrial attitudes and behaviour*. Cambridge: Cambridge University Press.

Graham, G. (1999) *The Internet: A philosophical inquiry*. London: Routledge.

Hatch, M. J. (1993) The dynamics of organizational culture. *Academy of Management Review*, 18 (4), 657–693.

Hatch, M. J. (1997) *Organizational Theory: Modern, symbolic and postmodern perspectives*. Oxford: Oxford University Press.

Hatch, M. J. and Cunliffe, A. (2012) *Organizational Theory: Modern, symbolic and postmodern perspectives*. Oxford: Oxford University Press.

Hatch, M. J., Schultz, M. and Skov, A. M. (2015) Organizational identity and culture in the context of managed change: transformation in the Carlsberg Group, 2009–2013. *Academy of Management Discoveries*, 1 (1), 58–90.

Klein, N. (2001) *No Logo*. London: Flamingo.

Kotter, J. P. and Schlesinger, L. A. (2008) Choosing strategies for change. *Harvard Business Review*, July/August.

Linde, C. (2001) Narrative and social tacit knowledge. *Journal of Knowledge Management*, 5 (2), 160–170.

McCalman, J., Paton, R. A. and Siebert, S. (2015) *Change Management: A guide to effective implementation*. London: Sage.

Maguire, S., Hardy, C. and Lawrence, T. B. (2004) Institutional entrepreneurship in emerging fields: HIV/AIDS treatment advocacy in Canada. *Academy of Management Journal*, 47 (5), 657–679.

Martin, G. and Beaumont, P. B. (1998) Diffusing 'best practice' in multinational firms: prospects, practice and contestation. *International Journal of Human Resource Management*, 9 (4), 671–695.

Martin, G. and Beaumont, P. B. (2001) Transforming multinational enterprises: towards a process model of strategic HRM change in MNEs. *International Journal of Human Resource Management*, 10 (6), 34–55.

Martin, G., Staines, H. and Pate, J. (1998a) The new psychological contract: exploring the relationship between job security and career development. *Human Resource Management Journal*, 6 (3), 20–40.

Martin, G., Beaumont, P. B. and Staines, H. J. (1998b) Managing organizational culture. In: C. Mabey, T. Clark and D. Skinner (eds), *Experiencing Human Resource Management*. London: Sage.

Martin, G., Beaumont, P. B. and Pate, J. (2003) A process model of strategic change and some case study evidence. In: W. Cooke (ed.), *Multinational Companies and Transnational Workplace Issues*, pp. 101–122. Westport, CT: Quorom Press.

Martin, J. (2002) *Organizational Culture: Mapping the terrain*. Foundations for Organizational Science Series. Newsbury Park, CA: Sage.

Mintzberg, H., Ahlstrand, B. and Lampel, J. (1998) *Strategic Safari: A guided tour through the wilds of strategic management*. New York: Free Press.

Morgan, G. (1989) *Creative Organizational Theory*. London: Sage.

Mutch, A. (2007) Reflexivity and the institutional entrepreneur: a historical exploration. *Organization Studies*, 28 (7), 1123–1140.

Pate, J. M., Martin, G. and Staines, H. (2000) Mapping the relationship between psychological contracts and organizational change: a process model and some case study evidence. *Journal of Strategic Change*, 9, 481–493.

Paton, R. A. and McCalman, J. (2006) *Change Management: A guide to effective implementation*, 3rd edn. London: Sage.

Pettigrew, A. M. (1990) Is corporate culture manageable? In: D. C. Wilson and R. H. Rosenfeld (eds), *Managing Organizations: Text, readings and cases*. London: McGraw-Hill.

Pettigrew, A. M. (2012) Context and action in the transformation of the firm: a reprise. *Journal of Management Studies*, 49 (7), 1304–1328.

Rao, H., Monin, P. and Durand, R. (2005) Border crossing: bricolage and the erosion of categorical boundaries in French Gastronomy. *American Sociological Review*, 70, 968–991.

Schein, E. H. (1985) *Organizational culture and leadership*. San Francisco, CA: Jossey-Bass.

Schoenberger, E. (1997) *The Cultural Crises of the Firm*. Oxford: Oxford University Press.

Van Maanen, J. and Barley, S. R. (1984) Occupational communities: culture and control in organizations. In: B. M. Staw and L. L. Cummings (eds), *Research in Organizational Behavior*, 6, 287–365. Greenwich, CT: JAI Press.

Weick, K. E. (2001) *Making Sense of the Organization*. Oxford: Blackwell.

Whittington, R. and Mayer, M. (2002) *Organising for Success in the Twenty-First Century: A starting point for change*. London: Chartered Institute of Personnel and Development.

Chapter 11

Corporate governance and corporate (social) responsibility

LEARNING OBJECTIVES

By the end of this chapter, you should be able to:

- Define what is meant by good corporate governance;
- Describe and critically evaluate the main theories of corporate governance;
- Critically assess the application of corporate governance theories to cases of poor governance;
- Define what is meant by corporate social responsibility;
- Critically evaluate the business case for corporate social responsibility;
- Critically evaluate measures of the outcomes of corporate social responsibility;
- Apply a model of inputs, mediators, moderators and outcomes of corporate social responsibility to cases and practical decisions facing managers.

INTRODUCTION

In this final chapter we examine two, increasingly prominent, corporate-level concerns, which have a major impact on how people are managed in organizations. These are the linked fields of corporate governance and corporate social responsibility (CSR), or corporate responsibility as it is increasingly coming to be known. Let's begin with short case study from Japan to illustrate the kinds of problems that these bodies of literature attempt to address. Following some reflection on the case, we will present some of the key arguments in these rapidly expanding bodies of literature, including some research of our own on corporate governance models and governance problems.

BOX 11.1 **Toshiba's fall from grace in 2015**

Toshiba is one of Japan's best-known companies, producing consumer electronics on an international scale. As a *Financial Times* article stated in July 2015, it has been a model of corporate governance in Japan and its corporate leaders have frequently been hailed as exemplary in their approach to running a successful multinational company with a strong sense of purpose and corporate culture. Following government reforms to corporate governance legislation in 2001, Japanese firms were required to appoint at least three external directors, which was at odds with conventional practice in Japan. Toshiba embraced the concept wholeheartedly, and in 2013 was ranked very highly among Japanese companies for its corporate governance approach and compliance practices with respect to financial reporting.

However, external auditors uncovered a corporate-wide attempt to inflate profits in July 2015, which caused severe reputational damage to the firm and led directly to the resignation of its CEO and other board members. The report produced by its external auditors showed that the board and internal auditing committee were aware of irregularities in accounting practices since 2008, but took no action because of the overarching requirements set out by its senior leaders to pursue profits and meet earnings targets. This requirement for profits became exceptionally strong following events in 2011/12, when many Japanese companies were recovering from the tsunami disaster, the Fukushima nuclear accident and a strong Japanese yen. As the auditors' report noted, the pressure to improve profit margins and generate new sources of business to make the company less reliant on chip-making led to pressure on managers to inflate profit figures.

The report also found that underpinning this drive for profitability in Toshiba was a corporate culture reminiscent of many large Japanese corporations that privileged hierarchy and obedience to senior leaders, with a concomitant failure on the part of divisional level managers to speak up to power and challenge decisions. Senior leaders in the company 'challenged' managers to continuously improve profit performance and to be intolerant of failure, sometimes threatening them that their divisions would be closed down if they failed to achieve targets. This led managers to engage in misreporting figures and other forms of deceit that would make them look good, rather than question the wisdom and authority of the board.

One further factor not noted by the auditors but which appeared to influence corporate governance and the culture of Toshiba was the failure of previous leaders to give up their positions and hold on company culture on retirement, which led to factional rivalries and unhealthy competition among divisions and managers. The influence of previous genera- tions of leaders on corporate culture and governance in Japanese corporations is especially strong where the corporation is dominated by family shareholdings. One consequence of this traditional hegemony is that women held only 3 per cent of seats on company boards in large Japanese firms in 2015, despite the Japanese government setting out guidelines for 30 per cent of board positions to be held by females to increase diversity and improve innovation.

Corporate governance

The Toshiba case deals directly with the problems of internal and external governance (Aguilera *et al.*, 2015). Internal governance raises questions concerned with how boards of directors are constituted and act, who owns/should own the corporation, and how do we ensure that managers act in the interests of owners. External governance, on the other hand, looks at how these internal questions are shaped by (a) the legal system, (b) the market for corporate control (i.e. the existence of an active takeover market if a firm is underperforming), (c) the role and power assigned to external auditors, (d) stakeholder activists (e.g. celebrity shareholders, socially aware investors, etc.), (e) rating organizations and business/financial analysts and (f) the business press. Both internal and external governance mechanisms work to create good corporate governance, which Aguilera *et al.* (2015, p. 485) define by referring to four principles:

1 'Good governance should protect the rights of stakeholders and provide the means to enforce those rights by monitoring executives and holding them accountable',
2 'Good governance is supposed to help mediate between the different interests and demands of various stakeholders',
3 'Good governance provides transparent information disclosure',
4 'Good governance involves the provision of strategic and ethical guidance for the firm'.

Questions

1 To what extent does the Toshiba case violate all four principles?
2 Why do you think any violation of these principles has occurred?

Various theories help explain effective corporate governance. However, since corporate governance is a socially constructed concept, what is meant by effective is in the eye of the beholder. So depending on one's theoretical stance, what is meant by good governance principles may vary. To help us understand some of these debates we need to examine these theories.

The first point to note is that the issue of corporate governance has a long history, first coming to prominence with advances in industrial capitalism during the early part of the twentieth century with the rise of the joint stock company, large-scale enterprises and the separation of ownership by shareholders from control by professional managers. The classic works on these developments pointed to a managerial 'revolution' and the beginnings of an early stakeholder theory of the firm, in which managers held effective control over the different interests represented within it (Berle and Means, 1967). Managers were thought to act in such a way as to 'hold the ring' between the competing claims of shareholders, customers, employees, government and the general public in a pluralist theory of industrial government.

Since then, there have been a number of interesting developments, all of which have tried to answer the question: What is the best means of controlling the supposed controllers (i.e. managers) to protect shareholders and other stakeholders? From our research, four such theories stand out (Martin and Gollan, 2012):

- Agency theory and shareholder value;
- Stakeholder theory;
- Stewardship theory;
- Enlightened shareholder value.

DEFINITION Agency theory

Agency theory was the response of neo-classical economists to the agency question in positing a contractual view of the firm. Basically they argued that there was a legal and metaphorical contract between owners (the financiers of the business and thus the principals) and managers (their agents). Managers raised funds from financiers to operate the business; financiers, in turn, needed managers to generate returns on their investments. In essence, the contract that ensued specified what managers would do with the funds and what the division of returns would be between the principals and agents. The main problem resided in the unforeseeable future contingencies, leaving open the question of residual control rights – the rights to make decisions not foreseen by the contract. In reality, managers retained substantial control over these residual rights and could exercise great discretion over how to allocate funds. So, agency theory concerned itself with the central problem of how to constrain managers from misallocating funds and acting in their own interests rather than those of the principals.

For neo-classical economists, it is shareholders whose interests should dominate the corporate agenda and for whom the corporation should be run; it is they that bear the residual risk whereas managers effectively get paid whether or not the firm makes a profit or loss and are simply a charge on the business in the same way as other preferred creditors. Investors, however, only get paid if the firm makes a profit and do not get paid if the firm makes a loss. Consequently, investors have the greatest inherent interest in ensuring that the firm makes the greatest amount of profit and are the party in whose interests the firm should be run. According to agency theorists, maximizing shareholder value leads to superior, overall economic performance for the firm and for the economy at large because short-run interests in securing adequate earnings and long-run interests in increasing the capital value of the firm converge (Roberts, 2004).

Agency theory assumes efficient markets, including markets for corporate control, for managerial labour and for corporate information. Efficiency results from many buyers and sellers, all of whom have perfect information on which to base their interactions. To the extent that efficient markets in these areas exist, managers will bear the costs of any misconduct and, therefore, are much more likely to exercise self-control in awarding themselves excessive pay increases and in conducting business affairs. In essence, a firm is depicted as a market made up of many contractors – owners and managers – negotiating and re-negotiating their interests. In case the assumptions underlying perfect markets are absent for a short while, checks and balances have to be built into the system, including an effectively structured board of directors, compensation for managers tied to shareholder interests and a fully functioning external market for corporate control to discipline managers and incumbent boards. This situation could occur when, for example, there is a temporary shortage of managerial talent or when there is a potential for serious market failure under monopoly conditions.

Newer versions of agency theory complicate the argument by positing a permanent hierarchy of managerial control within organizations, rather than the market metaphor (Aguilera *et al.*, 2015). According to these new institutional economists, firms arise because of the nature of market imperfections and the need to keep down transaction costs among contractors. Nevertheless, attention still remains focused on the relationships between shareholders and managers, but this time shareholders are deemed to be facing a diffuse but significant risk of self-interested opportunism by managers because the assets of the firm are too numerous and too ill-defined to fully describe in contractual agreements (Lan and Heracleous, 2010).

Whether in its neo-classical or institutional variants, however, agency theory relies on a mixture of converging economic incentives – pay tied to shareholder value – and power-sharing through bargaining and coalition-building to bring about cooperative behaviour between the two principal parties in governance – shareholders and managers. No other parties are really considered as having long-term and significant interests in the firm. Good examples of firms run according to these principles are firms bought over by new financial intermediaries, such as hedge funds, private equity or sovereign wealth funds, which are often claimed to be interested only in short term returns (Appelbaum *et al.*, 2014). However, as both Appelbaum *et al.* and other researchers in this tradition (e.g. Bacon *et al.*, 2013) argue, there are different types of private equity buyouts and not all such acquisitions are focused on the short term. Instead, both sets of authors conclude that some private equity backed buyouts do look to the long term and growth, and in doing so, can enhance employees' interests and improve human resource management.

This theory fits in well with the assumptions of the corporate reputation approach we examined in Chapter 6, which recognizes the importance of constituencies including customers, suppliers, employees, business partners, government, the press, investors and, increasingly, society at large. Stakeholder theory is closer to the models of governance found in continental Europe and in some countries in the Asia–Pacific region than the Anglo-Saxon external focus on shareholder value model assumed by agency theory. See the example of Volkswagen, a multinational German vehicle manufacturer, in Box 11.2.

DEFINITION **Stakeholder theory**

Stakeholder theory adopts a different line of argument. For the proponents of this view, firms are not bundles of assets that belong to shareholders, nor can they be in a modern world when the key assets are largely intangible and under the control of employees. Instead, governance structures and the work of senior managers are aimed at maximizing the total wealth of the organization for the benefits of those *inside* it that contribute firm-specific assets, i.e. their knowledge and skills, as well as those outside it (Freeman *et al.*, 2007).

BOX 11.2 Stakeholder theory in operation at Volkswagen

Volkswagen, the German automobile manufacturer, is part owned by the Government of Lower Saxony, which retains 20 per cent of voting rights. In line with many large German companies, it also has a Supervisory Board, which is responsible for:

> 'monitoring the Management and approving important corporate decisions. Moreover, it appoints the Members of the Board of Management. The Supervisory Board of Volkswagen AG comprises twenty members and conforms to the German Co-determination Act. Half of the overall twenty members of the Supervisory Board are shareholder representatives. In accordance with Article 11(1) of the Articles of Association, the State of Lower Saxony is entitled to appoint two of these shareholder representatives for as long as it directly or indirectly holds at least fifteen per cent of the Company's ordinary shares. The remaining shareholder representatives on the Supervisory Board are elected by the Annual General Meeting. The other half of the Supervisory Board consists of employee representatives elected by the employees in accordance with the Mitbestimmungsgesetz (German Codetermination Act). A total of seven of these employee representatives are Company employees elected by the workforce; the other three employee representatives are representatives of the trade unions elected by the workforce.'

Source: Volkswagen website (available at www.volkswagenag.com/content/vwcorp/content/en/investor_relations/corporate_governance/supervisory_board.html.

Question

1 To what extent does this model of governance ensure that the Government of Lower Saxony and employees' interests are taken into account?

Is there a possibility of *convergence*? The success of the USA and its new economy during the 1990s, coupled with problems in Asia and continental Europe during the same period, provided a great fillip for outsiders, Anglo-Saxon market-based shareholder value models of governance, and the assumptions underpinning them. In countries such as Germany, Sweden and France, there were enthusiastic calls by certain sections of the business and financial community and supporting political parties to embrace shareholder value principles and to rid themselves of stakeholder constraints. However, as we are all aware, the problems of Enron and others in the early 2000s resulted in a re-think of models of governance among American and British companies, which led to passing of US legislation, including Sarbanes–Oxley in 2002 and attempts by the OECD to set world standards on corporate disclosure and governance. The fall-out from the Global Financial Crisis in 2007–8 and the passing of the Dodd–Frank Wall Street Reform and Consumer Protection Act in 2010 has only served to accentuate and accelerate this search for new models of governance, which has led to an enlightened shareholder value model.

DEFINITION **Stewardship theory**

Stewardship theory is a more recent perspective on governance, which seeks to explain how governance works in practice and how it should work in the future. As we have seen, agency theory proposes a self-interested model of management and in-built conflict with shareholders. Stewardship theory argues that such conflict of interests should not exist because good managers, who have the skill and will, are naturally inclined to act in the interests of shareholders because their interests, and those of other stakeholders in the firm, are broadly similar and contingent on the long-term wealth creation of the organization. Essentially, this is a unitary ('we are all in it together with the same aims') and benign view of organizations, which also posits a strong degree of managerial choice based on their motivations to act as stewards on behalf of everyone in the business and its long-term survival. Although it recognizes that there are situations when managers may not always exercise good or well-meaning judgements, stewardship theories are not hung up on the downside risk of managerial misbehaviour that dominates agency theory. Instead, stewardship theorists, such as Colin Mayer (2014) and John Kay (2015) focus on the importance of building trust relationships and social networks to coordinate actors in and across organizations. Building trust between these principal actors, they argue, is characteristic of institutional and funding arrangements more likely to be found in Europe and Asia, e.g. networks of banks, privately owned and family owned firms, and the new forms of organizations we have discussed in the previous chapters.

DEFINITION **Enlightened shareholder value**

Enlightened shareholder value has been proposed by those financial economists and lawyers who remain wedded to the core principles and benefits of agency theory. They seek to balance the interests of investors with those of other stakeholders to ensure that the long-term interests of shareholders are achieved. Such an Anglo-Saxon model is in line with global trends in the internationalization of finance, equity markets and various financial instruments, which is forcing organizations from all parts of the world that wish to borrow to conform to certain governance conditions, e.g. the OECD's principles of Organization and Governance. This convergence, inevitably, is on the Anglo-Saxon model, though critics argue there are limits to such convergence.

However, as Clarke (2007) and others point out, the 'sharpest skirmish' has been over the idea of shareholder value in any form following the scandals of Enron and the other examples of corporate malfeasance associated with the Global Financial Crisis (Martin and Gollan, 2012). Nevertheless, there are many Americans and British lawyers, financiers and business people who stick to the dictums proposed by the neo-classical economist Milton Friedman in the 1970s 'that the social responsibility of business is to increase profits', so serving the interests of us all in the long run (Mayer, 2014).

Enron and more recent cases such as RBS in the UK (see Chapter 2), and Toshiba in this chapter have caused economists and moralists to argue that even an enlightened shareholder value model is inappropriate in a modern world (Davis, 2009; Stout, 2012). Critics believe the ability of directors to monitor executive behaviour and the temptations of making enormous gains by cashing in the huge stock options that form the basis of many executive pay packets have created an unworkable system (Bebchuk and Fried, 2010). Enron was the classic example of how self-interested and financially motivated senior leaders could not only poorly serve shareholders, but also its customers and employees in bringing companies down. Agency theory has been proven right by Enron in that such managers were all-powerful in governance and shareholders needed protection through governance mechanisms and the introduction of legislation such as Sarbanes–Oxley. However, according to critics, one of agency theory's most sacrosanct principles of tying pay to shareholder value was its undoing. Perhaps as important, the pursuit of shareholder value has disconnected corporations from their moral purposes, according to stakeholder theorists, which is to serve the wider interests represented within firms and changing values in society. Trustee theorists, such as Mayer, also argue that the job of governance is to 'sustain the corporation's assets', not merely its financial assets. He has proposed the 'trust firm' as a solution that aligns the needs for corporations to be efficient with the need for corporations to uphold the values of sustainability.

'The trust firm defines the period and the scope of the corporation's credible commitment. It delineates for how long and over what activities the corporation can credibly commit and the boundaries beyond which it cannot do so. It does this through committing its controlling shareholders to retain their share ownership for pre-determined periods of time and by conferring powers on a board of trustees to prevent the corporation from abusing parties who would otherwise be exposed to its activities.'

(Mayer, 2014, pp. 15–16)

It is in the above sense in which the calls for a new, more socially responsible and sustainable theory of governance have been framed, which lead us into a more in-depth discussion of the corporate (social) responsibility (CSR).

CORPORATE SOCIAL RESPONSIBILITY

CSR, or CR as it is increasingly known, has been touched on in most chapters in this book, since it is one of the most rapid growth areas of interest for modern businesses and is the basis on which a corporate identity can be built. But what exactly do we mean by CSR, why should it be of interest, especially given the dominance of the shareholder value model of governance among so many companies throughout the world, and how effective is it in changing the nature of business? To answer these questions, we will outline the case for CSR/CR and then examine some of the criticisms of this contested concept from the right, the left and from within.

Drawing on these ideas, CSR advocates contend there is a more or less fundamental tension between the pursuit of private profit and public good, usually because a pursuit of profit at the expense of society is unsustainable in the long run. The basic argument underlying the business case

DEFINITION The case for CSR

The case that is usually made for CSR is a business case for pursuing socially and environmentally friendly policies, rooted in a stakeholder theory of governance and Rawlsian theory of social justice. Rawlsian ethics are associated with a 'theory of good', which focuses on defining the characteristics of a just society. Imagine a society in which there were no laws, social conventions or political state. Then ask yourself the question: What principles might reasonable people agree on to guarantee order while placing few constraints on individual freedoms? When applied to organizations, a theory of good states that these principles and the outcomes that result from these principles must be distributed with full consultation and so that no organizational stakeholders are losers while others are clear winners. Responsible leaders should place organizational survival and the long-term interests of its stakeholders over any single interest (Mayer, 2014).

DEFINITION The business case for CSR

Given the problems that big business has experienced in reputational terms over the last decade or more, especially since the Global Financial Crisis, CSR has itself become big business. Many governments, business organizations and professional bodies now promulgate the CSR agenda. Prominent among them is the British government. The UK government sees CSR as good for society and good for business. They argue that a better understanding of the potential benefits of CSR for the competitiveness of individual companies and for national economies can help encourage the spread of CSR practice. The Department for Business Innovation and Skills has therefore supported work exploring the 'business case' for CSR in a range of publications, available on its website (www.gov.uk/government/consultations/corporate-responsibility-call-for-views).

for CSR is twofold. First, profit in its own right is not pursued by companies for the public good but for private gain, which has little or nothing to do with the public good. If the pursuit of profit is to advance social welfare, it cannot be left to the hidden hand of the market and powerful business leaders, a form of very rough justice. Instead, it often requires active regulation from outside bodies, such as the Financial Conduct Authority in the UK and the 'FED' (Federal Reserve System or central bank) in the USA. Second, in the pursuit of private gain, companies are driven by their internal business logic of maximizing revenues and minimizing costs to place enormous burdens on society and on the environment. Economists call this process one of placing *externalities* on society, defined as companies taking action that affects others' welfare without having the incentive to recognize this impact in their decision-making, nor fully accounting for it in their evaluation of the costs and benefits of particular decisions. The consequences are that these externalities lead to inefficiencies for society if businesses do not pay their fair share of costs (Roberts, 2004). For example, there is a concern over the true costs of encouraging people to fly on low-cost airlines more than they need to or buy more cars because of the contribution of frequent flying and petrol consumption to global warming. Thus for many governments, NGOs (non-government organizations) and critics of the Anglo-Saxon shareholder value model, the untrammelled pursuit of profit yields little or nothing for many ordinary citizens, but costs them plenty. Unless it is checked either by CSR or by government regulation, private enterprise is bound to make losers of everyone apart from private business and its owners.

There are several international networks promoting CSR and its more modern focus on sustainable development, including the World Business Council for Sustainable Development (available online at www.wbcsd.org/home.aspx). Its membership is made up of 180 multinational enterprises including the European-based Shell, BP, Nokia, Michelin, SKF, Novartis, ABB, Volkswagen and Daimler-Chrysler, and major US-based Dow Chemicals, Ford, General Motors, Procter & Gamble, Time Warner, GE and HP. The Council invites 'companies committed to sustainable development and to promoting the role of Eco-Efficiency, Innovation and Corporate Social Responsibility'. One of the Council's publications acknowledges the legal requirement to promote 'acceptable returns for its shareholders and investors' but argues that 'business and business leaders have . . . made significant contributions to the societies of which they form part' and that responsible leadership is necessary for business and societal progress.

The Chartered Institute of Personnel and Development in the UK have also been vigorous in pursuing the CSR agenda and in promoting the need for HR specialists to champion CSR. Their position is informed by a stakeholder view of ethics in business, in which employees are one of the principal stakeholders, and a view that employees' beliefs and actions are also the main vehicle for putting CR into action. They see CR as continuing to move up the business and HR agenda, which can become an important instrument of change. To do so, they argue, HR specialists need to broaden their own understanding and skills and take an active role in what they regard as a new form of strategic management (www.cipd.co.uk/hr-resources/factsheets/corporate-responsibility.aspx#link_cipd_view).

In effect, 3BL has been proposed as a planning and reporting mechanism, and a decision-making framework used to achieve sustainable development. It has been adopted by organizations as diverse as local government in Australia, major corporations such as Monsanto, the BBC and British Petroleum, and a range of small firms (see for example the cases available online at the Business and Sustainable Development Global website at www.bsdglobal.com/tools/principles_triple.asp). The financial community is also paying attention in the form of a new Dow Jones Sustainability Index tracking the economic, environmental and social performance of more than 300 global companies, such as Siemens, Citigroup and Volkswagen, all industry leaders (see www.sustainability-indices.com/images/130912-djsi-review-2013-en-vdef.pdf). Not surprisingly, consultants have been at the forefront of CSR. For example, PWC have argued that firms 'need to be a part of a global conversation and movement towards creating responsible business practices that change the world' (www.pwc.com/gx/en/corporate-responsibility/strategy.jhtml), by measuring how firms build responsible business, improve diversity and inclusion, create community engagement and develop environmental stewardship.

So what evidence do we have on the motives of firms to engage in CSR? To answer this question, we might want to reflect on some research conducted into CSR in the pharmaceuticals industry by Hayley Droppert and Sara Bennett (2015).

BOX 11.3 **A case illustration of corporate social responsibility: Fujitsu (UK)**

Fujitsu won an award in 2015 from the UK Business in the Community organization for being the most 'Responsible Business of the Year'. The company's entry proclaimed it was 'committed to integrating responsible business issues into core strategy and day-to-day operations. It is passionate about responding to the unprecedented social and business risks caused by resource scarcity, population growth, an aging society and mass urbanisation by pioneering ICT solutions to create a fairer society'.

The company has led the industry in making datacentres, which consume up to 2 per cent of electricity globally, and 27 per cent of Fujitsu's energy, more sustainable. Fujitsu's UK datacentres use 100 per cent renewable energy, and the company operates the first European datacentre to be certified as Operational Sustainability Gold. It has also worked with suppliers to reduce CO_2 emissions in its supply chain, achieving a 32 per cent decrease.

Fujitsu has commissioned its own 'Collaboration Nation' research on working with SMEs and responded to it by changing its approach, resulting in 23 per cent more contracts being awarded to SMEs year on year.

The company collaborates to innovate and strategically help others. Projects include developing a supercomputing infrastructure which makes High Performance Computing capabilities available to SMEs, Kiduku, a research project pioneering sensor technology to help the elderly live well for longer in their own homes, and BITC Connect, which captures the impacts of BITC's Business Connector programme.

Fujitsu is also working to redress the gender imbalance in its sector. Despite males making up over 80 per cent of undergraduates in Engineering, Technology and Computer Science, Fujitsu's graduate female intake has averaged 40 per cent since 2010. Senior leaders across Fujitsu are engaged with and advocate its responsible business agenda, including Duncan Tait, Head of EMEIA, who is a member of BITC's board. The company produces an independently verified annual report against GRI standards including detailed data on non-financial capital, and an independently assured CSR report containing material issues, objectives, targets and policies' (See more at: www.bitc.org.uk/our-resources/case-studies/fujitsu-responsible-business-year-award#sthash.Z3sgcgNt.dpuf).

Criticisms from the right

We have already discussed the shareholder value credo of many businesses – 'the business of business is business' – which was given moral support by neo-classical economists such as Friedman during the 1970s. Currently, there is a battle being waged by economists, corporate lawyers and business ethics writers who argue there are two reasons for sticking with the shareholder value/agency theory model. The first is the agency theory position that managers of public companies are not owners but are employed by the firms' owners to maximize the long-term value of the owners' assets, within a framework of law that sets out rights and wrongs, the responsibilities and accountabilities of

DEFINITION Measuring CSR

Inevitably, when making a business case for any investment, this turns on the issue of measurement – how do we know there is a payoff for stakeholders? Numbers are language that business people understand and need to use to convince the financial community that pursuing goals other than shareholder value are likely to pay off for all in the long run. Managers also need measurement for performance management reasons and to keep them focused. As a result, many of the companies mentioned in this section have adopted the 'triple bottom line' (3BL) as a performance measure. The idea was first proposed by John Elkington (1997), when he described a framework for measuring and reporting corporate performance against economic, social and environmental parameters. However, he also made a more far-reaching claim:

'At its broadest, the term is used to capture the whole set of values, issues and processes that companies must address in order to minimize any harm resulting from their activities and to create economic, social and environmental value. This involves being clear about the company's purpose and taking into consideration the needs of all the company's stakeholders.'

managers and corporate leaders. Some business ethics advocates believe that putting those assets to any other use, such as CSR, is effectively robbing the owners of their just (and ethical) rewards (Sternberg, 2000, 2004, 2009). The ethical decision for a manager who believes that the business s/he is working for is causing harm to society at large is either not to work for that business in the first place or to leave it. Elaine Sternberg, a UK academic and former corporate executive, believes in two principles of business ethics that underlie a shareholder value model. These are *ordinary decency* and *distributive justice*, without which the conduct of business would not be possible. These principles are based on a theory of rights. Paramount among these rights are those of property owners, which must be respected; these, however, do not extend to 'lying, cheating, stealing, killing, coercion, physical violence and most forms of illegality'. Instead, managers should pursue 'honesty and fairness', reflecting the demands of 'ordinary decency'. Her second component of business ethics, distributive justice, refers to the alignment of organizational rewards and managers' contributions towards achieving shareholder value. Two canons of modern-day HR, performance-linked pay and merit-based promotion, are manifestations of distributive justice within the company. So, for Sternberg and others, promoting people on the basis of anything other than merit or to reward a manager for anything other than pursuing shareholder value is bad for business and bad ethics. Her arguments were summed up in her 2009 paper, which concluded that organizational missions statements containing a conventional business ethics discourse on corporate responsibility, was confused and dangerous. This was because CSR threatened the very basis of business, which was based on private property and individual liberty. Sternberg believes that organizations need to 'maximize long term owner value while respecting distributive justice and ordinary decency' (Sternberg, 2009, p. 48).

Criticisms from the left

As is often the case in social debate, the right and left of the political spectrum often agree on the analysis, but come to entirely different conclusions on the prescriptions. Such is the case over CSR. The left criticism, which has been acknowledged by some business leaders as a legitimate one, was forcibly put by Joel Bakan (2004, 2011), a North American law professor, who wrote two very powerful books about the impact of modern corporations in society.

From his examination of legal documents, Bakan (2004) argued that corporations are bound by mandate to pursue relentlessly and without exception self-interested shareholder value, regardless of the harmful consequences it might cause to others. This is an extreme version of agency theory, which few corporate leaders would openly subscribe to; nevertheless, he claimed, they had very little choice because of the legal, political and economic logics and structures of capitalist societies. His view was that such mandated corporations have come to dominate our lives in the developed and developing world, determining our lifestyles, culture, employment, economic and political choices. Moreover, they were having an enormous negative effect on the lives of children, the subject of a later book in 2011, by targeting the growing 'kid market', creating child health problems and commoditizing learning. Aside from the iconography and ideology of modern business, which is all around us, corporations go further in dictating the decisions of national governments and controlling societal decisions that were once part of the public domain and subject to genuine political decisions by ordinary people. So, according to Bakan, it is corporations that govern society, not governments. Yet, he argued that every thesis brings about its own antithesis: it was the very power of modern, global corporations that left them open to reputational risk in the form of public mistrust, fear and demands for social and environmental accountability from society. The response has been an acknowledgement by corporate leaders to understand and address the costs of poor reputations, and work hard to regain and maintain the trust of 'stakeholders', including an increasingly vociferous investor community and financial press. The vehicle for this identity and image change had been CSR, which is nothing but a means of persuading a sceptical public of the virtues of capitalism.

Like many critics from the left, Bakan's view of CSR is that it is largely fraudulent because corporations, in the final analysis, cannot do anything other than engage in the 'pathological pursuit of profit and power', his 2004 book's subtitle. He cited the case of Sir John Browne, former BP CEO and once an icon of the CSR movement, and BP's pursuance of a green agenda as a mask behind which to 'maintain consumer demand for petrochemicals':

'The days when our business had a captive market for oil are probably ending . . . So we have to compete to ensure that oil remains the fuel of choice (quote from Sir John Browne)' (Bakan, 2004, p. 46).

On the potential for CSR, Bakan concluded:

'More generally, for Browne and all other business leaders, social and environmental goals are, and must be, strategies to advance the interests of their companies and shareholders; they can never legitimately be pursued as ends in themselves . . .' (p. 46).

Criticisms from within

Bakan's thesis is predicated on CSR being an important movement in society, yet even its adherents remain unconvinced of some of the arguments and evidence used to support it. First, the business case for CSR has often rested on the assumption that 'doing good leads to doing well'; that creating product or service differentiation through CSR is a way of satisfying the firm's needs for superior profits and serving societal goals. Aguinis and Glavas (2012) in an extensive review of the literature concluded that there was wide variation in results supporting this claim. For example, they cited a meta-analysis conducted by Peloza (2009), who found that only 59 per cent of the 128 studies reviewed showed a positive relationship between CSR and financial performance, with 27 per cent showing a mixed/neutral response, and 14 per cent a negative outcome, while a large study of 599 companies in 28 countries by Surroca *et al.* (2010) found no direct relationship between CSR and financial performance. Thus, according to Aguinis and Glavas, although firms undertook CSR to benefit materially, there was only a small positive financial gain at best. However, they also concluded that there were a number of non-financial outcomes that resulted from CSR, including 'better management practices, product quality, operational efficiencies, attractiveness to investors and enhanced demographic diversity (e.g. women and ethnic minorities)' (Aguinis and Glavas, 2012, p. 943).

Daniel Diermeier (2007, 2011), a long time CSR supporter from the University of Chicago, has provided an alternative argument for firms to engage in such behaviour. His view is that long-run cost reduction that is the best justification for CSR, because it is concerned with managing the downside of reputation risk rather than the upside of differentiation. Note the similarity between this argument and Bakan's, but for very different reasons.

Diermeier (2006, 2011) makes a value case for CSR, claiming that values matter and that the values of the newer generations in advanced industrial societies were more inclined to be post-materialist, with a concern for the environment, tolerance and social issues that are different from the materialist values of earlier generations that were influenced by hardship. Moreover, he argued that these values would remain relatively permanent throughout the lifetime of this new generation, precisely because their formative years were shaped by times of plenty rather than hardship. The consequences, according to Diermeier, were that the shift to CSR is real and permanent. As a result, companies would be increasingly pressurized into responding to these value-changes, especially when competing in the global market for talent. In other words, there was a 'market for virtue' – but only under certain conditions.

First, CSR issues are likely to vary in the same way that cultural values vary; some emerging economies not only cannot afford CSR but do not value it so highly because the values of their nationals have been formed under conditions of relative hardship, exacerbated by the growing gaps between rich and poor and by the impact of modern communications in highlighting that gap to the poor.

Second, the consequences of these value-changes for competitive positioning were that businesses must be able to adapt their strategies to different segments of product markets (and employment markets), as we have consistently argued throughout this book. As Diermeier argued, for a product differentiation strategy to work by creating and capturing value from customers for socially responsible brands (e.g. Fair Trade, the Body Shop or Patagonia), three factors have to be present:

BOX 11.4 **Corporate social responsibility in global health (based on Droppert and Bennett, 2015)**

These authors undertook an exploratory study into six highest earning pharmaceuticals companies, using publically available data and interviews with key representatives. They found that the meaning, motivation and approach to CSR differed in each of the firms. Four out of the six had clearly defined CSR, with only two setting out clear criteria for what they meant by CSR and three having specific policies. Three had a CSR department but all had a CSR committee or steering group. The most common CSR activities were: differential pricing for resource poor countries, donations of drugs to poor countries, developing mobile or m-health (e.g. by providing text message reminders on when to take drugs), improving product distribution activities in developing countries, and targeting research and development to diseases that disproportionately affected developing countries.

The motivations for undertaking CSR were also varied. However, five or the six reported entering new markets as a key motivation, with four anticipating long-term financial gain. Reputational benefits also figured strongly, particularly in influencing the perception of the firm by consumers and improving employee recruitment and engagement. Finally, all six stressed philanthropic and health benefits, especially improving population health and increasing patient access to necessary medications/health services.

One of their conclusions was that 'pharmaceuticals companies struggle with how other actors perceive and define CSR and that CSR is not even understood in the same way across the pharmaceuticals industry'. However, they did conclude that CSR was playing an increasingly major role in the industry, and that it offered real opportunities for developing countries to take advantage of this trend.

Questions

1 To what extent does this study confirm the 'view from the left', and does it matter anyway, especially if it is doing good in developing countries?
2 Do the problems of definition cause problems for measuring the impact of CSR?

- Customers must be willing to pay more for socially responsible goods and services to cover the fixed and variable costs of providing them, implying that customers must be willing to pay sufficiently high marginal prices and the market segment must be large enough to cover the fixed costs.
- Socially responsible brands must be difficult to imitate to allow for both socially responsible and non-socially responsible brands to coexist.
- The claims for social responsibility must be credible and customers must be able to verify these claims in some way.

Thus, in sufficiently large markets, it is possible for firms to earn superior profits from socially responsible brands by charging a premium price for them if these three conditions hold. And there are examples of markets in which socially responsible brands do earn superior profits through charging more for their goods and services, such as the food market in which organic and 'fair play' producers are carving out a niche.

However, the case for CSR does not really rest on this 'doing business by doing good' argument, but in lowering long-run costs and reducing reputational risk. This, Diermeier argued, were the main arguments for CSR: it does not rest on offering higher consumption value to willing consumers, which is difficult for them to verify anyway, but in delivering goods and services at lower costs to the environment, which is simply a principle of good management and is independent of offering higher value. To prove his point he used the example of the contrast between BP and Shell in the 1990s, when BP attempted to market 'cleaner fuel'. Clearly, there was only a small segment willing to pay higher prices for a commodity product such as petrol for their cars, but, he claimed, BP's strategy was not driven by a need to differentiate themselves in small segment markets; it was driven by its reputation for CSR and in protecting it. Shell, on the other hand, had a number of problems with its reputation, resulting from its confrontation with Greenpeace, its proposed disposal of rigs in deep water and in its operations in Nigeria where human rights were an issue. As a result, Shell had to invest heavily in CSR to lower its costs arising from reputational risk in the long run and has had to work very hard to catch up with BP in particular markets. However, this would only be worthwhile if the expected savings from avoiding reputational damage were greater than the costs of complying with CSR practices. So in essence these are cost-driven strategies, arising from the nature of the markets they operate in, not from price differentiation.

This argument can also be extended to the market for talent. While there may be niche markets for talented people who are attracted by working for companies that offer socially responsible goods and services, more people are likely to be attracted to and remain with organizations with a history of avoiding damage to their reputations, since the individual reputations of talented individuals are likely to suffer from association with firms that have not invested in avoiding reputational damage.

To date, there are no known, universally accepted standards for measuring an aggregated bottom line, and given different versions of ethics in business, it is probably not theoretically possible. The social and ethical accounting, auditing and reporting movement (Gray and Laughlin, 2012) has influenced a number of standard-setting bodies in the past few years, including the Global Reporting Initiative, SA 8000 Workplace/employee relations, AccountAbility 1000 Stakeholders, ISO 9000 Organization and Governance standards, but would not claim to have provided an aggregate measure of 3BL. Their job has been to identify performance indicators of the social and ethical behaviour of companies and to find ways of auditing it. However, this is some way short of providing valid and reliable aggregate measures of CSR, which was and is the novel claim of 3BL. Indeed, to be plausible, the concept needs to remain vague, qualitative and generalized; the closer one gets to specifying a measure of 3BL, the less plausible it becomes. Part of the reasoning for this is the 'apples and oranges' argument; there is simply no universal, common currency for equating financial performance with all aspects of social and environmental impact, or even one unit of social good with another, e.g. donating money to charity for food aid or donating money to education. So, is this situation simply a case of what is measurable isn't always meaningful, and what is meaningful isn't always measurable? Another part of the reasoning is a more fundamental one and

DEFINITION Criticisms of measurement

While the idea of a triple bottom line has appeal to a number of firms and government departments that have used it in their public relations, including BT, AT&T, Shell and Dow Chemicals, the UK government and state governments in Australia, critics point out some fundamental problems with it, even as a metaphor. These are based on the contention that what is sound about 3BL isn't novel and what is novel isn't measurable (Norman and MacDonald, 2004; MacDonald and Norman, 2007), or in creating compliance (Sridhar and Jones, 2012). The claims of its proponents, in line with stakeholder theories of governance, are that firms should assess their overall long-term contribution to society as well as to shareholders, that the social and environmental impact of firms can be measured in much the same way as the financial impact and that these individual measures can be aggregated to provide something akin to a societal profit or loss. While those adhering to the strict shareholder value version of corporate governance, such Elaine Sternberg, may take issue with the first of these claims, in no way could they be regarded as novel, according to Norman and MacDonald, since they have been at the heart of the CSR agenda since the 1980s. The more important criticism, however, lies in the measurement aspects of 3BL.

relates to our debate over different versions of governance and their moral stance. CSR and stakeholder theory, according to Norman and MacDonald, are largely premised on a theory of good: How does a business add value to the world? However, this is sometimes at odds with a theory of rights, which underpins the case for shareholder value. This concerns itself, as we noted, with whether individual rights are respected and societal obligations exercised in relation to these individuals. Thus, fulfilling obligations to shareholders may not always have a net positive impact on society but it does respect their rights and discharge society's obligations to them. From a rights perspective, it is not possible to say that maximizing three lines of promises to shareholders, employees and the public at large, as required by 3BL, is better than fulfilling one obligation to shareholders.

PREDICTING THE OUTCOMES OF CSR

So while there are major issues surrounding the value and measurement of CSR as a way of doing business, is there a way to predicting outcomes so that managers have a better understanding of what they are likely to gain, what is necessary in terms of inputs and what factors may shape this relationship between CSR inputs and outputs? One answer to this question is to return to the work of Aguinis and Glavas (2012), who provided a model of CSR predictors and outcomes for researchers. We believe that an adapted form of this model can be useful for managers in showing how complex the process is, especially in showing the factors that might 'moderate' and 'mediate' the relationship between inputs and outputs. By moderate, we mean the variables that are likely to affect the strength and direction of the relationship between inputs and outputs, e.g. gender differences, nationalities of employees, levels of salary, etc.; by mediate, we mean a variable that explains the relationship between inputs and outputs, e.g. perceptions of staff of leadership, values of employees, etc.

The Aguinis and Glavas model also makes an important distinction between the levels of analysis (as we did in our change framework in the previous chapter) between the institutional, organizational and individual levels. So for example, institutional predictors of CSR outcomes might be the nature of regulation in a society concerning corporate governance – does legislation recognize stakeholders other than investors? Organizational predictors could refer to a corporation's motives for engaging in CSR as illustrated by the case of the pharmaceuticals industry in Box 11.4. Individual predictors might refer to the values of key players in the organization, such as the CEO or Chairman.

Figure 11.1 is our adaption of their model, which shows some of the key relationships and variables that managers might need to consider when introducing any CSR system and what kinds of outcomes they may need to measure to evaluate its success and their motivations for engaging in these kinds of activities.

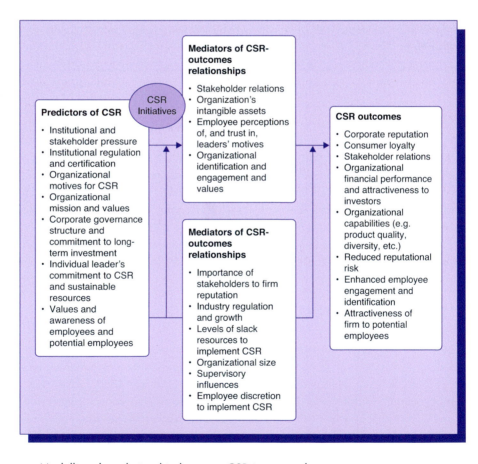

FIGURE 11.1 Modelling the relationship between CSR inputs and outputs

(*Source:* based on Aguinis and Glavas, 2012, p. 952.)

LEARNING SUMMARY

The key learning points from this chapter are:

- Corporate governance is recognized to be one of the most important influences on how firms are organized and managed, especially following corporate governance scandals in the early part of the previous decade and the events surrounding the Global Financial Crisis.
- Different models of corporate governance have been devised to deal with the problem of providing fair rewards to investors and to other key stakeholders. Agency theory and shareholder value are the dominant theories underlying corporate governance practice in Anglo-Saxon economies, but these have been criticized for their lack of fairness and short-term time horizon. Stakeholder theory, stewardship theory and enlightened shareholder value have been implemented to deal with the problems of shareholder value thinking, but all have models create problems in balancing out the competing claims on firms to create wealth, protect wealth and distribute wealth on a sustainable basis.
- Corporate social responsibility (or corporate responsibility) has arisen as a means of dealing with problems of good governance, especially in addressing the needs and demands of key stakeholders who are not investors in firms.
- The argument for private sector organizations to engage in socially responsible behaviour is usually made by managers through reference to a 'business case' and future financial outcomes. However, the evidence on the links between CSR and financial outcomes is not strong, and other outcomes need to be taken in to account to justify CSR initiatives.
- Being socially responsible depends on where you stand. Proponents of the business case for CSR, critics of CSR from the left and right, and advocates of CSR who believe in firms doing well by doing good all see things differently and use different measures of CSR effectiveness.
- Our model of the inputs, mediators, moderators and outcomes of CSR shows how complex the process of implementing successful initiatives are likely to be. Managers need to take into account a complex range of factors at the institutional, organizational and individual levels of analysis if they want to create sustainable organizations.

REFERENCES

Aguilera, R. V., Desender, K., Bednar, M. K. and Lee, J. H. (2015) Connecting the dots: bringing external corporate governance into the corporate governance puzzle. *The Academy of Management Annals*, 9 (1), 483–573.

Aguinis, H. and Glavas, A. (2012) What we know and don't know about corporate social responsibility: a review and research agenda. *Journal of Management*, 38 (4), 932–968.

Appelbaum, E., Batt, R. and Lee, J. E. (2014) Financial intermediaries in the United States: development and impact on firms and employment relations. In: H. Gospel, A. Pendleton and S. Vitols (eds), *Financialization, New Investment Funds, and Labour: An international comparison*. New York: Oxford University Press.

Bacon, N., Wright, M. and Ball, R. (2013) Private equity, HRM and employment. *Academy of Management Perspectives*, 27 (1), 7–21.

Bakan, J. (2004) *The Corporation: The pathological pursuit of power*. New York: Free Press.

Bakan, J. (2011) *Childhood Under Siege: How big business targets your children*. New York: Simon & Schuster.

Bebchuk, L. A. and Fried, J. M. (2010) Paying for long-term performance. *University of Pennsylvania Law Review*, 158, 1915–1959.

Berle, A. A. and Means, G. C. (1967) *The Modern Corporation and Private Property*, 2nd edn. New York: Harcourt Brace.

Clarke, T. (ed.) (2007) *International Corporate Governance: A comparative approach*. New York: Routledge.

Davis, G. F. (2009) The rise and fall of finance and the end of the society of organizations. *Academy of Management Perspectives*, 29 (3), 27–44.

Diermeier, D. (2007) Introduction: from corporate social responsibility to values-based management. In: A. Dayal-Gulati and M. Finn (eds), *Global corporate citizenship*. Chicago: North Western University Press, pp. 1–23.

Diermeier, D. (2011) *Reputation Rules: Strategies for building your company's most valuable asset*. New York: McGraw-Hill.

Droppert, H. and Bennett, S. (2015) Corporate social responsibility in global health: an exploratory study of multinational pharmaceutical firms. *Globalization and Health*. Available online at www.globalizationandhealth.com/content/11/1/15.

Elkington, J. (1997) *Cannibals with Forks: The triple bottom line of 21st century business*. Oxford: Capstone.

Freeman, R. E., Harrison, J. S. and Wicks, A. C. (2007) *Managing for Stakeholders: Survival, reputation, and success*. New Haven, CT: Yale University Press.

Gray, R. and Laughlin, R. (2012) It was 20 years ago today: Sgt. Pepper, accounting, auditing and accountability journal, green accounting and the blue meanies. *Accounting, Auditing and Accountability Journal*, 25 (2), 228–225.

Kay, J. (2015) *Other People's Money: Masters of the universe or servants of the people?* London: Perseus Academic.

Lan, L. L. and Heracleous, L. (2010) Rethinking agency theory: the view from law. *Academy of Management Review*, 35 (2), 294–314.

MacDonald, C. and Norman, W. (2007) Rescuing the baby from the Triple Bottom Line bathwater: a reply to Pava. *Business Ethics Quarterly*, 17 (1), 111–114.

Martin, G. and Gollan, P. J. (2012) Corporate governance and strategic human resources management in the UK financial services sector: the case of the RBS. *International Journal of Human Resource Management*, 23 (16), 3295–3314.

Mayer, C. (2014) *Firm Commitment: Why the corporation is failing*. Oxford: Oxford University Press.

Norman, W. and MacDonald, C. (2004) Getting to the bottom of the 'Triple Bottom Line'. *Business Ethics Quarterly*, 14 (2), 243–262.

Peloza, N. (2009) The challenge of measuring financial impacts from investments in corporate social performance. *Journal of Management*, 35, 1518–1541.

Roberts, J. (2004) *The Modern Firm: Organizational design for performance and growth*. Oxford: Oxford University Press.

Sridhar, K. and Jones, G. (2012) The three fundamental criticisms of the Triple Bottom Line approach: an empirical study to link sustainability reports in companies based on the Asia-Pacific region and TBL shortcomings. *Asian Journal of Business Ethics*, 2 (1), 91–111.

Sternberg, E. (2000) *Just Business: Business ethics in action*. Oxford: Oxford University Press.

Sternberg, E. (2004) *Corporate Governance: Accountability in the marketplace.* London: Institute of Economic Affairs.

Sternberg, E. (2009) The need for realism in business ethics. *Reason Papers: A journal of interdisciplinary normative studies*, 31, 33–48.

Stout, L. A. (2012) *The Shareholder Value Myth: How putting shareholders first harms investors, corporations and the public.* San Francisco, CA: Berrett-Koehler.

Surroca, J., Tribo, J. A. and Waddock, S. (2010) Corporate responsibility and financial performance: the role of intangible resources. *Strategic Management Journal*, 31, 463–490.

Index

Nottingham College
Library